Sticky Power

Sticky Power

*Global Financial Networks
in the World Economy*

DANIEL HABERLY
DARIUSZ WÓJCIK

OXFORD
UNIVERSITY PRESS

OXFORD
UNIVERSITY PRESS

Great Clarendon Street, Oxford, OX2 6DP,
United Kingdom

Oxford University Press is a department of the University of Oxford.
It furthers the University's objective of excellence in research, scholarship,
and education by publishing worldwide. Oxford is a registered trade mark of
Oxford University Press in the UK and in certain other countries

Published in the United States of America by Oxford University Press
198 Madison Avenue, New York, NY 10016, United States of America

British Library Cataloguing in Publication Data
Data available

Library of Congress Control Number: 2021946292

ISBN 978–0–19–887098–2

DOI: 10.1093/oso/9780198870982.001.0001

Printed and bound in
Great Britain by Clays Ltd, Elcograf S.p.A.

Cover image: Daniel Haberly

Links to third party websites are provided by Oxford in good faith and
for information only. Oxford disclaims any responsibility for the materials
contained in any third-party website referenced in this work.

To Ania, Qingling, and Lucas

Contents

Preface

In 1922 William T. Foster published a paper in the *American Economic Review* on the circuit flow of money. He wanted to draw attention to the nature of these flows and their potential significance to understanding business fluctuations. He defined money as currency and checking deposits moving in the opposite direction to the flow of goods. In contrast to goods, which disappear from circulation when a good is consumed or disposed of (environmental and energy considerations notwithstanding), money keeps circulating endlessly. Hence the notion of the circuit flow, which Foster illustrated with a diagram made of reservoirs and pipelines (Figure 0.1).

By Foster's own admission the drawing was influenced by Malcolm C. Rorty, who studied engineering at Cornell University, cofounded the National Bureau of Economic Research, and was the president of the American Statistical Association. Data to quantify financial flows were starting to become available in the USA, and with his paper Foster was clearly encouraging his fellow economists and statisticians to use such data, and his engineering-inspired circuit model, to better understand money. The most important application for him was to study the effects of the circuit flow on the business cycle, as well as multiple potential factors that can slow down the flow, from lower wages, to higher taxes and lower expected inflation (or expected deflation), to higher rate of savings and retained earnings.

The paper was part of the book co-authored by Foster with his Harvard classmate Waddill Catchings, which was published in 1923 under the simplest possible title, "Money." Catchings at that time was making a fortune on Wall Street, becoming the first senior partner at Goldman Sachs from outside of the Goldman or Sachs families. His financial engineering nearly bankrupted Goldman Sachs through the creation of a highly leveraged investment trust called Goldman Sachs Trading Corporation, which pooled investors' money to invest in stock, and unraveled in the wake of the 1929 great crash, to which it in fact directly contributed.

Also in 1929, on the banks of the river Euphrates in erstwhile Mesopotamia (today's southern Iraq), German archaeologist Julius Jordan unearthed a vast cache of clay tablets from Uruk, one of the world's first large cities. The tablets, written in an abstract script known as cuneiform, are the oldest form of writing yet discovered, dating from around 3100 BCE. It was not until the 1970s that the French archaeologist Denise Schmandt-Besserat began to figure out what the tablets were for. As it turns out, they were not poetry, but rather records of transactions and obligations; records of what has been paid and what is owed and should be paid in the

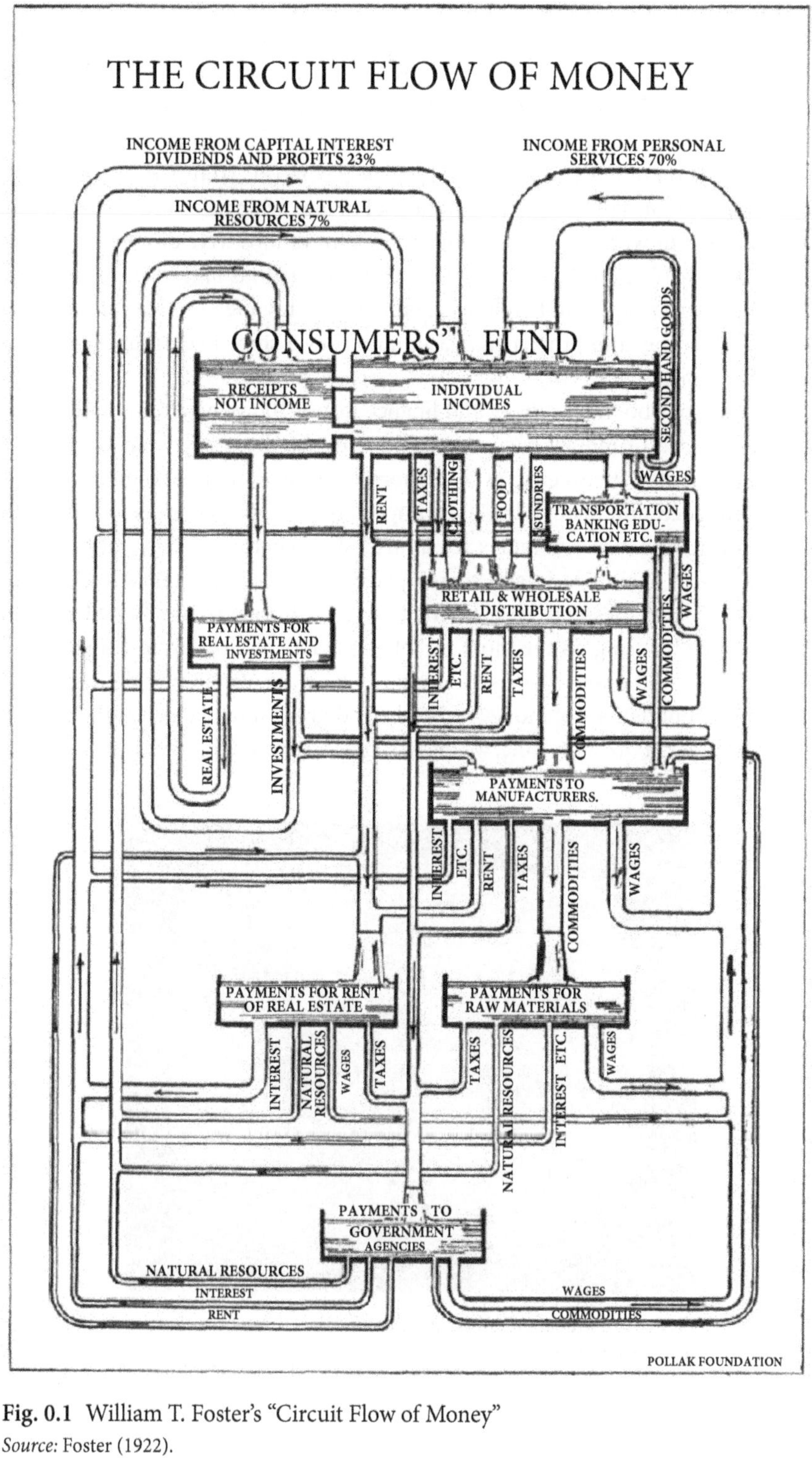

Fig. 0.1 William T. Foster's "Circuit Flow of Money"
Source: Foster (1922).

future. As such, these tablets simultaneously represent the world's first known ac-counts and legal contracts. The practice of accounting for transactions, payments and claims, also involved the first known use of abstract symbols for numbers, in-cluding stunningly large figures. One demand for war reparations, for example, was for 4.5 trillion liters of barley grain, more than fifteen times the global an-nual production of barley today. As such, the clay tablets from Uruk represent a financial, accounting, and legal innovation all in one, which also brought with it a breakthrough in writing and counting. These innovations were developed, in the words of Tim Hartford "to deal with a web of obligations and long-range plans between people who did not know each other well, who might perhaps never even meet" (2017). The same problem has faced society ever since, in ever more complex forms (Figure 0.2).

Finishing our book on money and finance nearly 100 years after Foster's 1922 article, our idea of money has more to do with the discovery from Uruk than Foster's circuit flow. Between us as co-authors, we have training in accounting, eco-nomics, finance, and history, but most importantly we are geographers. As such, we approach money as a complex social institution central to civilization, that is simultaneously grounded in and shapes place and space. Like Julius Jordan and Denise Schmandt-Besserat we have tried to unearth the geography and history of money, by focusing on the more recent successors of Uruk from Amsterdam, through London to New York and Hong Kong, while also taking the legal and accounting foundations of money seriously by digging into places like the British Virgin Islands. At the same time, we understand the spirit of Foster's work, and the

Fig. 0.2 Clay tablet from late Uruk period, between 3100 BCE and 3000 BCE
Source: © The British Museum.

need to systematically capture flows and stocks of money and to visualize them boldly. As such, our method mixes quantitative and qualitative data collection, and makes liberal use of tables, diagrams, and maps. Our understanding of finance is also enriched by hundreds of interviews with professionals in finance, law, accounting, and government, conducted over the last decade mostly in skyscrapers, the 20th-century successors of Mesopotamian ziggurats.

Unlike the Foster–Catchings duo, neither of us has made a fortune in finance or otherwise. However, we had the great fortune to meet at the Summer Institute in Economic Geography organized by Christian Berndt and Jamie Peck in Zurich and the nearby mountains in 2012. It was in the "land of milk and money" that we first had a chance to discuss ideas on financial networks, the entanglements between and histories of finance, law and accounting, and financial flows and stocks recorded in the latest economic data. This stimulated a series of papers published over the following years, some of which have been updated and revised for the purposes of inclusion in this book. Another big push in the development of ideas was provided by linking financial networks to global production networks, in a collaboration with Neil Coe and Karen Lai in 2012/2013, which led to the launch of the concept of global financial networks.

Many people and organizations have helped us along the way. Dariusz Wójcik has drawn on funding from the Leverhulme Trust (RPG359), the Research Grants Council Hong Kong (T31-717/12/R), the Australian Research Council (DP160103855), and most recently and importantly the Cities in Global Financial Networks: Financial and Business Services in the 21st Century (CityNet) project funded by the European Research Council under the European Union's Horizon 2020 research and innovation program (681337). In his research for the book, he has built on advice and comments from Gordon L. Clark, his life-long mentor, and has benefited enormously from collaboration with James Camilleri, Stefanos Ioannou, Duncan McDonald-Korth, Vladimír Pažitka, and Michael Urban, and exchanges within the thriving community of the Global Network on Financial Geography and beyond. Wei Wu has dedicated long working days to help us compile the bibliography.

Daniel Haberly has drawn on funding from the UK Foreign, Commonwealth and Development Office (FCDO), via a Global Integrity Anti-Corruption Evidence (GI-ACE) grant (PF8874), to support his research on the architecture and impacts of global offshore networks. In this FCDO-funded research he has benefited immensely from collaboration with and input from Valentina Gullo, Alex Cobham, Mick Moore, and others at the Tax Justice Network, International Centre for Tax and Development, and Global Integrity. In addition, he has been inspired by the ongoing work of his doctoral students Dulcelino Vicente-Ferreira and Nathanathon Sawangnetr—who have sought to understand how their own home countries are impacted by, even while also exercising their own agency to shape, the global financial networks and power structures examined in this book. He has also benefited from an ongoing collaboration with Adam Dixon problematizing the diverse financial institutional landscape of the United States, which has directly informed some of the analyses in this book, and broader discussions and collaborations with Ronen Palan, Jason Sharman, Petr Janský, Javier Garcia-Bernardo, Miroslav Palanský, Valeria Secchini, Delphine Nougayrède, Léonce Ndikumana, and many others. In addition, several of the chapters in this book have previously been presented at various conferences and workshops, and appeared as working papers and journal articles, and a great thank you goes out to all of those who provided comments and input in these contexts that helped to shape the work in this book. Finally, Daniel's wife and son have been immensely patient and supportive of the time he has poured into writing this book over the many tedious and stressful months of lockdowns and school closures, and he is forever in their debt.

We are grateful to Katie Bishop from Oxford University Press, who believed in our project and worked with us at the proposal stage, and Henry Clarke, who helped us to bring it to completion. We also owe a debt of gratitude to countless anonymous reviewers of our papers and the book proposal. In the times of the pandemic, we remind ourselves that the peer-review process in science and research, however imperfect, is one of the things that is saving humankind from extinction.

List of Figures

List of Tables

List of Frequently Used Abbreviations

ABCP	asset-backed commercial paper
ABS	asset-backed security
AUM	assets under management
CDO	collateralized debt obligation
CDS	credit default swap
DAMP	digital asset management platform
ETF	exchange traded fund
FABS	financial and business services
FC	financial center
FDI	foreign direct investment
FIRE	finance, insurance, and real estate
GFC	global financial crisis (2007-2009)
GFN	global financial network
IPO	initial public offering
OJ	offshore jurisdiction
RMBS	residential mortgage-backed security
SIV	structured investment vehicle
SOE	state-owned enterprise
WG	world government

1

Global Financial Networks: What They Are and Where They Come from

1.1 Money and Finance: An Unfinished Research Agenda

"Money Makes the World Go Round." How money does that, and with what consequences, are questions that have preoccupied much of science and literature for much longer than the musical *Cabaret* has been around. Different thinkers and disciplines have offered different answers. For Marx and his followers, it lies in the pursuit of profit by capitalists and their accumulation of capital, which can only be maintained at the expense of people (treated as labor) and the natural environment (raw materials), and is unstable, unequal, and unsustainable (Harvey 1982). For Keynes and his followers, the key to understanding money and its impact is the process of debt creation by banks, which by its nature repeatedly leads to asset price bubbles and crises (Galbraith 1975; Minsky 1986). In mainstream economics, much research focuses on the efficiency with which money and its derivatives are traded in financial markets (Mishkin 2006).

Money has also long been an important topic in the social sciences and humanities. Political economists and scientists have examined the relationship between money and power within the international monetary and credit system (Helleiner 2014; Strange 1986). Historians have studied the evolution of these systems, conducting detailed studies of financial innovations, products, firms, and financial centers (Cassis 2006; Kindleberger 1984). Anthropologists and sociologists have sought to uncover the roots of money and debt as social relations (Graeber 2011; Ingham 1996), approaching money using concepts such as assemblages and financescapes, and stressing its complexity, fluidity, and relationship with globalization (Appadurai 1990; Zaloom 2005). Philosopher and sociologist Georg Simmel (1978) has argued that money defines our relationship with the world, and that, as such, understanding money can help us to understand our lives. Interest in money has also spawned interdisciplinary research, including studies of financialization, which examine the causes and consequences of the increasingly central role of money and finance in the economy, politics, and society (Engelen et al. 2011; Epstein 2005).

Sticky Power. Daniel Haberly and Dariusz Wójcik, Oxford University Press.
© Daniel Haberly and Dariusz Wójcik (2022). DOI: 10.1093/oso/9780198870982.003.0001

In human geography, the intellectual home of the authors of this book, research on money and finance has been influenced by all of the above intellectual currents, and has produced a distinctive body of work, referred to as financial geography (Clark and Wójcik 2007; Martin and Pollard 2017). This can be defined as the study of the spatiality of finance, guided by three basic questions. First comes the *what* question. What is the spatiality of finance? What spatial forms, structures, and manifestations does finance take? This question is about mapping finance in the broad sense of the word "mapping." Second comes the *why* question. Why does the map of financial phenomena look the way it does? How can we explain the spatiality of finance? This question requires the study of the forces that shape the geography of finance, including the behavior of agents, as well as the investigation of economic structures, institutions, and ideas. This implies that while finance is a fundamentally economic phenomenon, social, political, and cultural geographies are also indispensable to the understanding of financial geography (Hall 2018).

Most important in financial geography is the *so what* question. In other words, what are the consequences of the spatiality of finance for the economy, society, and (increasingly) the environment? Finance, or more precisely the money that it produces, comprises the lifeblood of economic circulation, and is crucial to economic growth and innovation. Its role as a store of value is key to inequality, and its cyclical expansion and contraction plays a decisive role in the mechanics of economic crises. Finance also has a major impact on the natural world via its control over investment, and new financial instruments and markets have increasingly been applied to, as well as distorted, the pursuit of environmental sustainability objectives (Knox-Hayes 2016).

One of the key themes in the fields of both financial geography and financial history is the study of financial centers (Cassis and Wójcik 2018). Just as pyramids are the defining symbols of many ancient civilizations, and cathedrals are associated with medieval Europe, the skyscrapers decorating the skylines of large cities are the symbolic trophies of 20th- and early 21st-century capitalism. The main tenants are financial and related firms, piled on top of each other in the quintessentially geographical pursuit of maximizing their centrality within the commanding heights of the economy. These firms are not only banks and other financial institutions. They also include corporate law, accountancy, and business consultancy firms, as well as collections of these types of professionals running the head offices of nonfinancial manufacturing and services companies. This concern with the function and position of financial and related services firms and organizations, and the role of financial centers as hubs for their activities, runs throughout this book. Our goal is to view these centers within a bigger picture composed of their relationships with other key actors and places in the world economy.

Despite the enormous body of work on money and finance, the focus of modern research on these topics is, in our view, too narrow. Figure 1.1 shows the results of a simple exercise. With the help of Web of Science, we retrieved a list of all articles

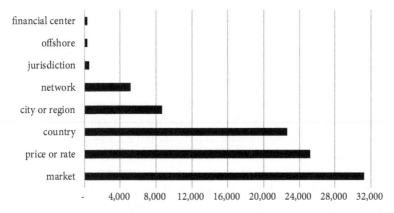

Fig. 1.1 Coverage of selected topics in scientific publications on money and finance, 1970–2020

Note: The graph shows the number of scientific works (articles and books) that cover selected topics out of a total of 159,592 works that use terms finance, financial, money or monetary in the title. It covers all works captured by Web of Science, irrespective of the language of publication. To identify coverage, we conducted searches using US and British English spellings, as well as translations of the above terms into other major languages.

Source: authors based on data from Web of Science.

and books published in the last fifty years that use the terms finance, financial, money, or monetary in the title, to see what key concepts they focus on. As can be seen, markets and prices reign supreme in this literature, and country is the principal geographical scale of analysis. Far less attention is given to cities, regions, or networks. Terms such as offshore, jurisdiction, or financial center, which are all central to the conceptual framework developed in this book, hardly register in the figure. In all, out of nearly 160,000 scientific publications focusing on finance and money, these terms are mentioned in the title, abstract, or keywords of only 279, 491, and 273 works, respectively. The narrow focus of research on money and finance is worrying in its own right, but gets even worse when we consider it as a reflection of, and a contributing factor to, a narrow approach to financial policymaking. This primarily focuses on national markets, prices, and rates, while paying far too little attention to the nuts-and-bolts geographic architecture of finance as defined by financial centers, offshore jurisdictions and structures, or even just cities and regions in general. This lack of attention is extremely ironic when one considers that terms such as "Wall Street" or "The City" are constantly used as a shorthand for the financial sector in general.

In this book, we offer the concept of the global financial network (GFN) as a novel way to analyze finance and its position in the world economy, that is grounded in an interdisciplinary body of ideas from not only economic geography, but also law, economics, economic sociology, and political economy. It is a conceptual framework that seeks to problematize how both public and private actors, operating across specialized production sites, come together to "manufacture" the institution of money in the world economy. It also seeks to cast new light on the way that this global financial assembly line has perpetuated itself historically as an architecture of power that, via its control over the institution of money, pervades and shapes virtually every aspect of our civilization.

In the following section of this introductory chapter, we outline the basic logic of how GFNs operate, before moving on to examine how a centralized structure of power that we dub *the* Global Financial Network (GFN), singular, is produced as an emergent property of the interaction between GFNs. As we show, this centralized Global Financial Network possesses a paradoxical "sticky power" that allows it to perpetuate its influence and character across deep historical timescales—despite its being nothing more than an accretion of far-flung agencies and places, and notwithstanding the fundamentally abstract immateriality of finance itself. The final part will explain the focus of the book and briefly introduce its structure.

1.2 Global Financial Networks and the Production of Money

Money can be analyzed from many different directions. In this book, however, we analyze money as, above all, a *product* that needs to be manufactured out of specific types of inputs, by specific sets of actors, through a sequence of specific production stages. The *global financial network* framework that we propose here—with its roots in the broader economic geographic analysis of the global *production* networks that multinational firms construct to organize supply chains (Coe et al. 2004; Coe et al. 2014)—is designed to capture the roles, relationships between, and geographies of the key inputs, actors, and production stages involved in the manufacturing of money.

Crucially, we argue that *all* of the instruments or "financial products" that the financial sector generates, buys, and sells need to be regarded as, in their own way, forms of money, which play the same basic role of collapsing the time gap between the past, present, and future—thereby making the expected wealth of the future available today as purchasing power. More specifically, all financial instruments, from bank deposits, to stocks and money market fund shares, to options and credit default swaps, are really just different forms of *credit* money; or, in other words, just one type or another of an *IOU* that can in various ways be converted into other types of IOUs, as well as (directly or indirectly) into purchases of goods and services. At the same time, however, some forms of money are more "money-like" than others; as defined on a sliding scale by the extent to which a financial instrument can be quickly and reliably exchanged for other financial instruments, and/or goods and services, at a well-defined and reasonably assured rate. Whether an instrument is officially labeled as "money" is not necessarily all that relevant to its position on this scale of moneyness. Most people would much rather have their

GLOBAL FINANCIAL NETWORKS 5

salary paid in shares of Apple than in Venezuelan bolivars, and the executives of companies such as Apple are indeed lucky enough to have much of their salary paid in company stock.

Money represents a claim on the future—and directly creates the future that it claims. Via the production of money, the future effectively bootstraps itself into existence, in capitalism, by converting future expectations into neatly packaged instruments that can be used (directly or indirectly) for current transactions; and that can above all be used to undertake the investments that *lead* to the realization of the future expectations that originally underpinned the production of these money instruments. As Schumpeter observed, this process whereby a particular human imagination of the future bootstraps itself into existence via the financial system's production of "certificates of future services or of goods yet to be produced" (Schumpeter 1934, 101), provides the central motor for capitalism's dynamism when it is plugged into technological and organizational innovation and entrepreneurship. However, as theorized in detail by Schumpeter's student Hyman Minsky, the fundamental uncertainties surrounding the future expectations that underpin the manufacturing of credit money, also causes its manufacture to misfire on a frequent and often monumentally destructive basis.

To see how this works, one can look at the case of the recently collapsed Greensill Capital in London. Greensill's business was trade finance. As we discuss in chapter 2, this is one of the oldest parts of the financial system, and indeed was, via the development of merchant banking and bills of exchange, at the very center of how western finance as we know it today came into being. Trade finance solves one of the most fundamental problems that businesses face; namely that they have to spend money to pay their suppliers before they can earn money by selling their own products to customers. Like the medieval Italian merchant banks who dealt in bills of exchange, Greensill helped businesses deal with this problem, in this case by packaging the future promises of companies' customers to pay them, or "trade receivables," into securities.[1] These could in turn be sold to investors to allow companies to, via Greensill, obtain the "cash" they needed to pay their suppliers now, and thereby fulfill their contracts with customers later. In practice, of course, the "cash" obtained in this way simply consisted of other financial instruments, including the shares of the same money market mutual funds that purchase the securities issued to finance firms' supply chains. In the case of Greensill, much of the paper issued to fund trade finance was sold to Luxembourg-domiciled money market funds operated by one of the world's leading investment banks, Credit Suisse.

In theory, trade finance should be one of the most boring parts of finance. However, Greensill had figured out a way to make it interesting. Namely, whereas the whole idea of trade finance is supposed to be the obtaining of finance against

---

[1] In addition, Greensill provided "supply chain" finance where companies borrow to pay their suppliers.

sales that have *actually been contracted*, Greensill was allowing and indeed encouraging its clients to obtain finance against completely hypothetical future sales contracts—often naming "customers" that companies didn't even do business with, but hoped to do business with at some point—which Greensill would classify as trade receivables to package into securities to sell to Credit Suisse's funds in Luxembourg. By allowing its clients to roll over these short-term securitized debts indefinitely—or at least until the hypothetical future sales contracts backing them materialized—Greensill in turn allowed its client companies to use this short-term credit as a source of long-term funding to undertake the investments that would, everyone hoped, eventually allow these hypothetical future sales to materialize (Levine 2021a). Smoothing things over was the fact that the Anglo-Australian Greensill was obtaining billions of dollars of bond insurance from a rogue Australian unit of Japanese insurance giant Tokio Marine, meaning that the latter was absorbing much of the credit risk of the paper being sold to Credit Suisse's funds (Griffin and Browning 2021).

In the case of Greensill, as well as its client companies and potentially thousands of their employees along with Tokio Marine and Credit Suisse and the investors in its and other money market funds—who, in a fun additional twist, were sometimes the same companies whose trade was being financed by these funds (Beardsworth 2019)—this didn't work out so well. When Tokio Marine realized what was going on at its Australian subsidiary, it pulled the plug, and the whole magical assembly line collapsed. More often than not, however, these sorts of contortions actually do end up working; or at any rate end up being very lucrative for those who are in the business of manufacturing the instruments that make them possible. The reason why this business is so lucrative is that it is very difficult to do. More specifically, it is very difficult to produce IOUs which are more than just worthless pieces of paper; not simply with respect to the solidity of the expected future cash flows backing these instruments, but even more importantly with respect to the question of whether people can actually be convinced to buy them.

We argue that there are four key categories of actor and place that come together to produce the "moneyness" of financial instruments—thus allowing financial instrument issuers and holders to command present-day purchasing power either directly, or indirectly through instrument conversion into more "money-like" instruments. Given enough leverage, credit money can move the world. However, it needs, in a literal sense, a "place to stand," which is provided by the architecture of global financial networks. To summarize, *financial centers* (FCs) are needed to house the markets that allow financial instruments to be reliably valued and exchanged for one another (i.e. rendering them liquid), and more broadly to generate the magical substance of "credit" through the centralized integration of trust and information. *Offshore jurisdictions* (OJs) support the optimization of the financial legal "coding" process (Pistor 2019), whereby instruments are packaged as credible contractual devices that afford their holders both maximal legal flexibility to achieve particular aims, and maximal legal protection of their claims. *Financial and business services* (FABS) firms serve as trusted financial intermediaries, engineers, and standard setters, who play a crucial role in resolving the informational and relational dilemmas inherent to financial market operation, and in managing esoteric legal contractual coding and creative accounting strategies spanning large numbers of jurisdictions. Finally, what we dub *world governments* (WGs), with a high capacity to project extraterritorial authority, extend their indispensable umbrellas of sovereign "protection" over all of these geographically far-flung financial actors and centers. This involves, most importantly, picking up the pieces when the world of private markets and contracts inevitably misfires, thereby creating a bedrock of confidence that money can be constructed upon.

We define global financial networks (hereafter GFNs) as the networks of these four key types of actor and place—financial and business services (FABS) firms, world governments (WGs), financial centers (FCs), and offshore jurisdictions (OJs)—that come together to manufacture the product of money in the world economy. Figure 1.2 offers a simple graphic representation of GFNs and their position in the world economy, highlighting the way that they sit astride the

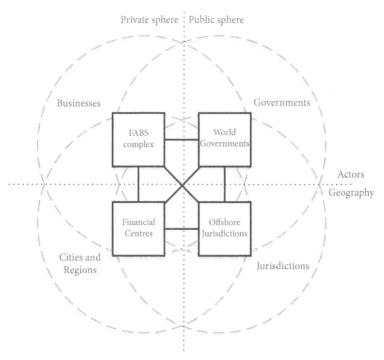

Fig. 1.2 Global financial networks—a conceptual framework
Source: authors.

interfaces between public and private agency and geographic structure. In what follows, we introduce each building block of GFNs in turn, as well as their mutual interlinkages.

The financial system revolves, first, around the operation of markets. Markets give money, conceptualized here in the broad sense of financial instruments in general, its meaning and power, by allowing these instruments to be valued in terms of and exchanged for both one another, and for "real" assets, goods, and services. Crucially, markets are not abstract forces, but rather concrete institutional systems. The places that house the financial professionals, firms, and other organizations who together *comprise* financial markets, are called financial centers. Due to the basic logic of how markets operate, all of these actors tend to crowd together geographically. Financial centers thus tend to be housed in, and indeed to reinforce the growth of, relatively large cities. Proximity makes collaboration, sharing knowledge (including privileged market information), and cultivating and maintaining trust-based relationships easier. Locating in big cities offers proximity to individual and institutional customers, including wealthy individuals, large companies, and governments, and enhances the benefits of shared labor, infrastructure (including transport and communications vital to financial services), knowledge, and big city amenities, such as sophisticated cultural products (Sassen 1991; Taylor 2004). All of these aspects of agglomeration are crucial in finance. Indeed, money is ultimately just a representation of social trust, as grounded in flows of information, and by supporting information flows and trust, financial centers effectively allow money as we know it to exist.

To be sure, there are costs associated with colocation and agglomeration in big cities, with congestion leading to higher costs of labor, land, and office space, longer commutes, and lower air quality. Such costs, however, do not undermine the existence of financial centers, but rather help to foster their multiplicity, producing interconnected networks of centers specializing in different markets and products. These networks are inherently hierarchical, with leading "world cities" at their apex, and successive layers of lower-tier regional centers, down to the proverbial main street bank office, sprawling out below them. Apart from relieving the congestion costs of agglomeration in leading financial centers, such lower-tier financial centers cast informational and relational networks across the broader nonfinancial economy, that allow the leading centers to access information from and influence this broader economy. Importantly, as shall be discussed in the book, new information and communications technologies have tended to expand these networks by creating new types of financial centers that operate in conjunction with older financial centers. New technologies are not rendering financial centers obsolete. Indeed, far from flinging financial centers apart, technology directly expands the geographic size of the market hinterlands that can be dominated by the most important global financial hubs at the expense of lower-tier centers—with

New York and the San Francisco Bay area, for example, increasingly emerging as key complementary nodes in a transcontinental American FinTech axis.

To have any credibility as financial instruments, assets and liabilities must be formally structured as contracts, which are in turn packaged into financial entities that we refer to as investment vehicles. Whether taking the form of multinational corporate holding companies, personal trusts, or any number of other devices, we can think of these as legal "buckets" that are used to purchase and house assets issued by other entities, and to issue liabilities that can be purchased by yet other entities and investors. Such entities include a profusion of different types of corporations, trusts, and partnerships, which are established for a wide variety of purposes. They all have to be booked somewhere for accounting purposes, and registered somewhere for legal reasons, and along with contracts moreover have to be subject to the laws of a particular jurisdiction. The owners and managers of an entity, or parties to a contract, can if they so choose register these in the same jurisdiction where they reside or work, or where the underlying assets held by an entity are located. However, they very frequently choose a jurisdiction with none of these substantive attachments.

Offshore Jurisdictions (OJs) are specialized jurisdictions that host the registration and booking of financial entities and contracts whose owners, managers, contracting parties, and/or assets are located elsewhere. We prefer to use the term OJ rather than tax haven or offshore financial center, as these places are not just about tax or regulatory arbitrage as narrowly defined, but rather about offering financial entities and contracts what can be described as a multidimensional legal, regulatory, and fiscal "flexibility" (Palan et al. 2010; Sharman 2006). They are not so much black holes in the global financial system, as they are toolboxes that play a pervasive role in the structuring of legitimate and illegitimate activities alike, with the boundary between the two often not altogether clear.

OJs can exist at the national or subnational level. The state of Delaware, for example, can function as an OJ within the USA, attracting literally millions of business incorporations, above all because corporation law is a predominantly state-level affair in the USA. Hong Kong functions as an OJ within China, due to its separate regulatory, fiscal, and legal system, with the latter based on English common law and equity. As these cases demonstrate, the most important OJs often do not conform well to the popular imagination of "offshore." The Netherlands, for example, is arguably the single most important hub for offshore company formation at the international level, surpassed only by Delaware when intranational shell company use is brought into the picture. In many cases, OJs exist only as an offshore *facility* afforded to certain designed activities, in which capacity they can be set up by virtually any government anywhere—with examples including the New York International Banking Facilities or Japan Offshore Market.

Together, financial centers and offshore jurisdictions constitute the key *geographic* building blocks of the GFNs that manufacture money—which respectively anchor the human relational geography of the production of financial instruments on the one hand, and the abstract legal and accounting geography of financial instruments themselves on the other hand. Meanwhile, a multitude of different *actors* are involved in producing these instruments across both types of production site. We classify the two key categories of these actors on a broadly private versus public sector basis—keeping in mind the ambiguity and overlap between these sectors—as Financial and Business Services (FABS) firms on the one hand, and World Governments (WGs) on the other.

Looking at the private sector, FABS firms are the leading firms in banking, insurance, real estate, investment management, and other financial activities, as well as in law, accounting, and business consulting services. FABS firms are the master weavers of GFNs. They connect cities, regions, countries, and jurisdictions into flows of money, data, professionals, and knowledge (Taylor 2004), and play the leading role in financial innovation, with new financial products and services arising out of the interactions between FABS and their individual and institutional customers, as well as with governments (Bernstein 2007). Taken together, FABS constitute a complex, wherein the activities of many firms traditionally seen as "nonfinancial" are just as important as narrowly defined financial sector firms. Law firms, for example, play an indispensable role in the structuring of assets and liabilities into credible and trusted packages, as well as in the structuring of contracts more broadly. Meanwhile the whole concept of "value" in finance is ultimately something that is socially constructed—and frequently manipulated—by accounting firms. Consulting helps businesses to optimize, and maintain an alignment between, their operational and financial strategies. Finally, sitting at the apex of the FABS complex are investment banks (including as parts of broader universal banks), which play a central role in virtually every aspect of the manufacturing, valuation, trading of securities, and in establishing and enforcing the key institutions, relationships, and standards within financial markets broadly.

The FABS complex is not simply a collection of individual firms. It rather has an overarching governance structure composed of the international organizations that represent and set standards for groups of FABS firms and professionals: with examples including the International Accounting Standards Board (IASB) or the Global Financial Markets Association (GFMA). The IASB, in charge of International Financial Reporting Standards, is dominated by professionals from the "Big Four" accounting firms—PwC, KPMG, Deloitte, and EY (Braithwaite and Drahos 2000; Büthe and Mattli 2011). Meanwhile, the GFMA is a global financial sector lobbying organization, which emerged after 2008 out of a merger of North American, European, and Asian lobbying groups. Taken together, these and other associations give the FABS complex an international political and institutional coherence—particularly in relation to the setting and enforcement of international rules and standards—that may either challenge or complement, depending on the context, the influence of public authorities.

Public authority itself remains critical to the operation of GFNs. Indeed, while financial globalization is typically portrayed as threatening the territorially rooted power of national governments, one of our main arguments is that this represents a false dichotomy for diagraming the relationship between finance and state power. First, finance is, out of all sectors of the economy, probably the single most dependent on state support. Indeed, the level of state support that can be obtained, above all in the acid test of a crisis, is often the most important long-run determinant of whether a particular financial firm or business model is successful. To revisit the case of Greensill Capital, for example, the company seemed to have had an ace in the hole, politically, via its relationship with the British Prime Minister David Cameron. This relationship began during Cameron's time as PM, when Greensill's founder Lex Greensill acted as a "special adviser" to the government (setting up an NHS pharmacy supply chain finance program which Greensill then operated)—and continued after Cameron left office, when he was hired as a Greensill "consultant" who apparently stood to earn millions of pounds from employee stock options (held via an offshore wealth manger in Jersey) in the event that the firm went public (Makortoff et al. 2021; Stewart and Makortoff 2021). Ultimately, though, government support for Greensill ended up not being forthcoming in amounts sufficient to save the firm, notwithstanding the lobbying efforts of Cameron to get Greensill exceptional access to Covid pandemic emergency lending facilities between March and June 2020, and the fact that he apparently met with a receptive ear in the former Goldman Sachs investment banker Chancellor of the Exchequer Rishi Sunak, who in his own words "pushed" the Treasury on Greensill's behalf (Walker 2021).

Finance is not only intrinsically dependent on government support, but governments themselves actually have a much stronger capacity, than is often acknowledged, to monitor and police the behavior of global financial actors—given the extent to which the authority of governments themselves is global in reach. Indeed, every time a US military transport plane lands in, for example, Ramstein Air Base in Germany, or Okinawa, or a US drone blasts a convoy of vehicles to pieces in Yemen or Pakistan, or the National Security Agency uses Silicon Valley tech firms as a global surveillance network, it makes a mockery of the whole concept of a *territorial* state that is simply at the mercy of global forces stretching beyond its borders. Crucially, however, not all governments have such global reach or influence, whether in the military, political, or financial spheres. Rather, there is a steeply hierarchical pyramid of global geo-financial power, atop which sits what we dub *world governments* (WGs).

WGs, as we understand them, encompass both national governments and non-state supranational actors such as the EU or Bretton Woods institutions. While the national governments included in our definition of WGs, as well as to some extent the EU, exercise de jure sovereign authority over their respective territories, what matters most to GFNs is not really conventionally defined *territorial* national economic and political power and sovereignty. Rather, what is most important to "world governmentness" is the possession of instruments of extraterritorial influence. These instruments are usually, in an indirect sense, rooted in generalized economic, political, and military power. However, they are in a direct sense semiautonomous from this broader power, being rather grounded in concrete institutional levers. Extraterritorial surveillance and regulatory capacity is one aspect of this; for example as stipulated multilaterally for banking by the Basel Accords, or claimed unilaterally by the United States with respect to the global tax affairs of its citizens abroad. Above all, however, power at the apex of the pyramid of WGs is linked to the reserve-currency-issuing power of leading central banks—and most importantly the US Federal Reserve, and to a lesser extent the European Central Bank—which exercise life-and-death control over the very lifeblood of global financial circulation (Helleiner 2014; Tucker 2018). Indeed, while money consists in a direct sense mostly of *private* IOUs, the credibility and stability of these IOUs is grounded in the common coordinate system of leading international reserve currencies, as regulated and backstopped by powerful central banks and broader WG authorities.

Effectively acting as deputies of the reserve-currency-issuing governments in the money creation process are quasi-governmental multilateral institutions such as the International Monetary Fund and World Bank (Woods 2006). Somewhat lower down the pyramid (at least for now), are governments such as China, who project global financial and monetary influence by amassing foreign assets and currencies issued by the USA and other leading reserve-currency-issuing states, even while also, in the case of China, seeking to boost their own long-term position as reserve currency issuers. Notably, this group of WGs encompasses some states, including Persian Gulf oil exporters and Singapore, which are relatively weak in conventional national economic or political power terms, but have a disproportionately high institutionalized capacity to project global financial influence as investors. This influence is felt widely. The world's largest venture capital fund, for example, Softbank's $100 billion Vision Fund, is primarily an investment conduit for the governments of Saudi Arabia and Abu Dhabi, that has intermediated Gulf state backing to numerous companies including Uber and WeWork, as well as Greensill Capital.

Most WGs, regardless of their level of power, do not hold any *formal* global governmental responsibility; although WGs in a position of global economic and political hegemony, such as the US since WWII, may acquire elements of *de facto* global governance responsibility out of self-interested necessity, or simply by default. Rather, what defines WGs is the global reach of their influence, which in practice overlaps with, interacts with, and in some cases conflicts with, that of other WGs. These interactions between WGs and other less geographically mobile states define a global political web, which is, in effect, the "real" form of global political organization. This actually existing global political network stands in sharp contrast with the cartoonish myth of the neatly bounded Westphalian nation-state system, which has never actually existed either today or historically (certainly not during either the 19th-century age of European global imperialism, or the ongoing age of US global hegemony, which does not really recognize the independent sovereignty of other states at all). Crucially, the state in this context cannot be analyzed in any sort of a coherent way as a geographic container or "scale." Rather, states fundamentally need to be conceptualized as *actors*, or more precisely as *actor-networks*, wherein the boundaries between the agencies of multiple states as well as non-state actors (including non-state WGs) are always inherently blurry.

There are relationships and interactions between WGs, FABS, FCs, and OJs within each building block of GFNs, but there are also crucial interlinkages between these different building blocks in the context of the production of money in the world economy. FABS and financial centers exist in a definitional relationship across the actor–geography boundary, given that financial centers are concentrations of FABS firms. The relationship between FABS and WGs is multidimensional and intimate. Governments share the creation of money and credit with banks and other private financial institutions—providing the foundation of monetary reserves atop which private monies are constructed, and often directly owning or co-owning FABS firms themselves. Meanwhile, the very existence of law, accounting, and consulting firms is largely a product of the need to negotiate government taxes, laws, and regulations. Of course, the influence works in both directions, with FABS firms involved in the making of laws and regulations, lobbying governments, and sponsoring political parties. This is underpinned by personal connections, with people moving between the government and FABS sector through a "revolving door," as highlighted by the use of terms such as "Government Sachs" to refer to Goldman's influence in the US Treasury, not to mention the case of Greensill Capital in the UK.

All jurisdictions are subject to a government, but OJs exist, counterintuitively in a particularly close relationship with WGs. For starters, the preponderance of leading OJs are former or current Dutch, US, and above all British colonies, with the offshore world sometimes being described as "Britain's second empire" (Palan et al. 2010). More broadly, we argue that OJs tend to transfer power and authority to the most powerful WGs from the governments of other, weaker states. The latter find that a growing proportion of their "domestic" economy is structured, from a formal legal standpoint, in various offshore jurisdictions outside of their borders. However, this places these same activities under the de facto or de jure influence of WGs with extra or multijurisdictional reach. The states that gain influence, by default, are usually the UK, as the colonial administrator of a large proportion of the global offshore network, and the USA, by virtue of its extraterritorial surveillance capacity and regulatory bully stick, and status as the world's leading reserve currency issuer. However, China has also been particularly creative and proactive at leveraging the offshore world to advance its policy objectives, whether via the use of offshore holding and listing structures by state-owned enterprises, or the establishment of offshore RMB markets by the "big four" state commercial banks (Hall 2017a). These strategies have resulted in some odd arrangements. Most of the largest Chinese companies, for example, are controlled by central or local Chinese state shareholders. However, many of these same firms (or parts thereof) are incorporated in the Cayman or British Virgin Islands, through vehicles that are subject to the ultimate judicial authority of the Judicial Committee of the Privy Council of the United Kingdom.

OJs could not exist without FABS. As already mentioned, OJs require some local FABS presence, but what is more important is their engagement with the global FABS network anchored by leading financial centers. When oligarchs, say from Russia, are interested in moving their wealth offshore, they do not start by visiting "small island" OJs. Instead, they approach (or are approached by) a FABS firm in Moscow, or better in London, who will present them with a menu of options that make use of various OJs (Seabrooke and Wigan 2018; Shaxson 2011). These OJs are, in effect, extensions of the leading financial centers and FABS firms themselves; indeed, the categorical boundary between OJs and financial centers is itself extremely fluid, and rather ambiguous. Leading financial centers, to varying degrees, often perform the role of OJs themselves, with London, Hong Kong, and Singapore being particularly important examples of such "midshore" centers.

The final relationship requiring explanation is that between world governments and financial centers. This is forged by FABS, but also has direct manifestations. It is not a coincidence that, in most countries, the political capital is also the leading financial center. In China, for example, Beijing has in many respects remained the Mainland's de facto financial capital by virtue of the state's ownership of most of the financial system, despite efforts to promote the securities market-focused Shanghai. Financial and political power are never too far apart relationally, even if not always geographically. The financial sector, for its part, needs to manage the ever-present threat posed to it by political power (via regulation, taxation, etc.), and is at the same time existentially reliant on political power for its survival during financial crises. Meanwhile, governments rely on the financial sector to help deliver the goods of economic growth and wealth creation to sustain their political popularity and legitimacy, and to mobilize the resources, via sovereign borrowing, that they need to pursue their political agendas more broadly.

1.3 From Global Financial Networks to the Global Financial Network

Crucially, GFNs are permeated by powerful interlocking centripetal forces that tend to weld them together into centralized, functionally integrated structures. Indeed, at the global level, all GFNs together can be considered to comprise a *single* integrated global financial *network* (GFN). The GFN can be defined, at the broadest level, as the sum of all GFNs. However, the GFN is also much more than simply the sum of its parts, rather operating as a functionally integrated and centralized system. Locating the actual center of power within the GFN is complicated, as the logic of centralization within it does not simply operate according to a single functional or geographic dimension. Rather, it operates according to what can be described as a logic of multidimensional *centralized specialization*. Within this logic, the various key functions in monetary production are carried out by different *specialized* actors and places. Simultaneously, however, the performance of each particular function (and segments thereof) tends to be highly *centralized* within and controlled by a fairly small number of leading places and actors. Furthermore, and even more importantly, the networks that link these actors and places together tend be characterized by an overarching logic of cross-functional relational centralization.

This juxtaposed variegation, specialization, and centralization within GFNs and *the* GFN is perhaps the single most important characteristic of global financial organization. On the one hand, the existence of the GFN, as a relatively well-defined structure with a unitary internal coherence, stems from the inherently inexorable tendency toward functional and geographic integration and centralization in finance. Financial markets, simply put, function "better" when they are "bigger," leading to a powerful winner-take-all dynamic of market share concentration among financial centers. Indeed, at any given moment historically, one can identify one or two financial centers that clearly dominate the GFN geographically. Moreover, within these leading financial centers, one can usually identify a handful of leading FABs firms that play what can be described as a quasi-monopolistic "platform" role at the center of market operation itself, with some version of investment or merchant banking usually in the lead. Reinforcing the GFN's centralizing tendencies is the winner-take-all nature of sovereign reserve currency issuer status, which tends to bring the leading financial centers and FABs firms into a close relationship with one or two (and most often just one; see Kindleberger 1986) dominant WGs, who preside politically over the GFN (Cohen 1998; Wójcik et al. 2017). Similarly, network effects and entrenched standards in the realm of legal contract, and the intrinsic connection of law to the conurbations of public and private power linking FABs firms, financial centers, and WGs, foster geographic centralizing tendencies even within the offshore elements of the GFN—with specific areas of "paper" activity concentrating in particular OJs which dominate their respective specialties.

Ultimately, all of these centralizing tendencies are reflections of the basic need for finance and money—as inherently subjective and relativistic institutional and relational systems—to establish a single shared "reference frame" for the determination and representation of value. A financial system (and economy more broadly) essentially cannot operate unless there exists a more or less singular point, in an institutional and relational sense, where everyone can come together to determine what everything is worth in terms of everything else; and, even more importantly, to determine what it even means for things to be worth something. At the level of financial (credit money) instruments themselves, all of this comes down to questions of information, trust, and credibility, and it is ultimately via the centralization of control over these that the GFN, and the various actors and places within it, derives its power. In other words, the GFN does not derive its power from the possession or allocation of money or capital, in the sense of some external thing that is stored within or intermediated through the "vaults" or valves of global finance. Rather, the GFN's power derives from its control over the networks of information, and systems and standards of trust and credibility, that allow money and value to exist at all.

The GFN thus in many respects weaves the fabric of reality itself within global capitalism into a single cloth, and those who sit at the center of the GFN have the power to consistently bend reality in their favor. Indeed, even the basic distinction between profit and loss itself in capitalism does not exist at all until somebody forces this issue to be resolved at a particular time and place, and on particular terms, all of which are inherently fungible for those with the correct positionality, and a good accountant. More broadly, if you think about the mental frameworks that we use to understand the world economy—such as BRICs, emerging markets, frontier markets, return on equity, price/earnings ratio, shareholder value, or value at risk—they have been disproportionately conceived and popularized by FABS firms, the master weavers of GFNs.

As such, the GFN, with its elite apex of leading WGs, FABS, FCs, and OJs, influences all other governments, businesses, cities, regions, and jurisdictions economically, politically, socially, and culturally. It shapes the very opportunity set of strategic options and operational modes available in the world economy—and even more importantly, the way that these options and modes are even conceptualized to begin with. However, the way that this power makes itself felt is complex, and in many respects paradoxical. Indeed, the centralized edifice of the GFN is not only internally characterized by, but ultimately dependent on and produced by, the geographic, relational, and institutional variegation of the GFNs, plural, that comprise it. The power of the GFN is, above all, directly predicated on local connectivity, and its power ceases to exist at all in the absence of connectivity with, and indeed coauthorship by, the diverse places, knowledge bases, political authorities, and firms that make up GFNs.

1.4 Global Financial Networks in Historical Perspective

Money, as noted earlier, effectively comes from the future in a sort of causal Möbius strip, allowing the future's expected wealth to be spent and invested today, and thereby creating the future expected wealth that money represents. What this really means is that money is, above all, a vehicle for human agency to change the future. However, the paradox of money is that the institutional and relational systems that produce it are extremely durable historically. They don't just passively persist, but actively reproduce their own power over long periods of time, in a logic of circular cumulative causation.

We argue that the primary reason for this historical "sticky power" of the systems that produce money is, counterintuitively, precisely the fact that money itself—as nothing more than a representation of future expectations—is so inherently abstract and insubstantial. This creates a powerful countervailing imperative for the production of money to be rooted in relationships of *trust* that need to be earned over very long periods of time, and are moreover deeply co-constituted with the institutional "legacy standards" through which they originally developed. These connections and institutions take a long time to build, and once built they tend to last (Cassis and Wójcik 2018). Furthermore, the fact that money is simply conjured out of thin air from future expectations, rather than intermediated from the past, directly bolsters the GFN's resilience to historical traumas, as the old money belonging to the key places and actors within it can be largely wiped out (e.g. as in the City of London in the first half of the 20th century) without seriously damaging the relationships and institutions that allow them to produce new money. Figure 1.3 diagrams this general logic of how the future, in the form of expectations, and the past, in the form of the institutional and relational systems of the GFN that package expectations into liquid and credible instruments, come together to produce money.

More broadly, we argue that the basic organizational *logic* of GFNs—including the four-pronged configuration of WGs, FABS, FCs, and OJs—is neither historically novel, nor historically accidental. Rather, the way that GFNs are organized is strongly conditioned by the logic of how money is produced in capitalism, and their general organizational contours emerged, at least in the West, more or less in tandem with capitalism itself out of the Middle Ages. This is not to say that GFNs have not changed historically. However, these changes have mostly involved

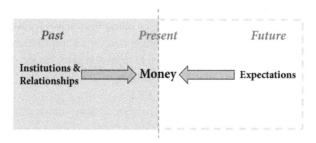

Fig. 1.3 The temporal logic of monetary production
Source: authors.

evolutionary mutations of longstanding tendencies and patterns, rather than revolutionary breaks with the past. Indeed, both the basic organizational logic of GFNs, and the power of specific geographic structures and even actors within GFNs (as well as *the* GFN), tend to reproduce themselves over remarkably long timescales, notwithstanding the typical intuitive association of finance with fast-paced change and mobility. The contemporary offshore private banking hub of Geneva, for example, was established as Europe's leading "exchange fair" (effectively a medieval offshore market) by Italian merchant banks in the 15th century—exploiting the legalization of usury in the 1387 town charter—and from the 17th century became a key haven for French flight capital that was operated largely by expatriate French Huguenot bankers, and bolstered by banking secrecy laws instituted in 1713 (see chapter 2).

Probably the single most important historical transition that has occurred in the development of GFNs is their integration into *the* GFN itself, in a singular sense. Complex systems of interconnected public and private credit money, supporting long-distance trade and economic activity, and intertwined with the power of states, have an ancient history not just in Europe but throughout major world civilizations (Graeber 2011). Trade, moreover, has been deeply globalized for centuries. However, the existence of *the* GFN, as a single integrated global network of credit relationships and financial markets, really only dates from the 19th century, when the world's various overlapping regional financial networks (presided over by various governments, merchant diaspora communities, etc.) were effectively welded together at the colonial barrel of a gun—and above all by the British Empire, including its "informal" elements in Latin America and elsewhere.

Crucially, this colonial production of *the* GFN did not entail stamping out or supplanting the older regional and ethnic financial and commercial networks of colonized places. Rather, these older networks were woven together within a common centralized structure of political power, legal and accounting standards, and financial markets presided over by multinational intermediaries—reflecting the more broadly paradoxical way that the centralized global power of the GFN is continuously constructed by, as well as strategically co-opted by, the decentralized agency of actors throughout the world. This paradox has been sharpened as countries in the global south, such as China, have become increasingly powerful economically and politically. Far from liberating themselves from the financial legacy of empire, such countries have usually leveraged and reproduced this legacy strategically to help advance their own rise, as represented by, for example, China's support for the development of offshore RMB markets centered on Hong Kong, Singapore, and London (Töpfer and Hall 2018).

The most recent chapter in financial economic history, which started with the global financial crisis of 2007–2009, can also be interpreted through the lens of the GFN. The subprime bubble at the root of the crisis was centered on the US

Sunbelt. However, the transformation of this regional bubble into a global financial crisis was the work of many hands spread across various key nodes in the GFN, the relationships between which, notably, still quite strongly reflect America's own history as a British colony. At the center of the crisis—and functioning almost as a single transatlantic financial center (see chapter 4)—were New York and London, which were home to the headquarters of the most important FABS firms, and above all the investment banks, that fueled the housing bubble with credit and financial innovation. These investment banks—such as the New York–headquartered Lehman Brothers, whose bankruptcy in September 2008 sparked the global "financial earthquake"—implemented the shadow banking innovations at the heart of the crisis by creating hundreds of financial vehicles registered in OJs, with Delaware, the (UK-governed) Cayman Islands and (City of London offshoot) Dublin in the lead (BCBS 2009). Finally, as is well documented (Sorkin, 2009; Tooze 2018), in those fateful weeks and months the fate of the USA, and by and large the world economy, was decided in meetings between the representatives of the US government (with Hank Paulson, the Treasury Secretary and Tim Geithner, the President of the Federal Reserve Bank New York, in the lead), and the bosses of the largest US investment banks. Ultimately, the Fed's support was handed out quite liberally to not just American, but also foreign, and in particular British banks (see chapter 2 Figure 2.3), reflecting the continued strength of the Anglo-American postcolonial financial relationship, even within a now inverted international power relationship.

1.5 Problematizing the Global Financial Network

If we went back in time to late 2008, when financial markets were tumbling down, and asked people what they would expect finance to look like a decade or so later, what would we hear? Many would expect smaller financial institutions, which are no longer too big to fail, a more regulated and less powerful financial sector overall, and a shift of financial power away from the leading financial centers and governments of the Anglo-American world to China, in particular. Some would also expect new financial technologies to disrupt and undercut the power of established financial actors and institutions in general, and to hollow out the dominant financial centers in which they congregate. Others would claim, at an analytical level, that we urgently need new ways of conceptualizing and studying finance, which are less obsessed with markets and prices, and pay more attention to questions of society, power, inequality, and development. One of the key goals of this book is to compare such expectations to reality, and take up the intellectual challenge of these questions, by employing the lens of the Global Financial Network as a new framework for problematizing finance and its evolution; and, ultimately, for problematizing the question of how to go about reforming a system that, at some level, never really seems to change, for century upon century.

Following on this brief introductory sketch of the concepts of GFNs and *the* GFN, in the next chapter of the book we take an extended look at the building blocks of this system: from the standpoint of both their roles in financial production, and the historical processes whereby they have assumed their contemporary shape. The remainder of the book then builds on this as a foundation to analyze more recent developments in global finance. Chapter 3 examines the power of investment banks, both in the run-up to and since the global financial crisis. It shows how they established themselves at the top of FABS hierarchy, and how they have restructured themselves over the last decade as their power and position has been challenged. Chapter 4 focuses on the leading financial centers of New York and London, charting the rise of the transatlantic "NY–LON axis" as the command center of global finance, and examining its role in the global financial crisis and subsequent decade.

Chapters 5–7 are devoted to OJs and offshore finance, and their relationships with the power of WGs, FCs, and FABS. In chapters 5 and 6 we zoom in on the intersection of OJs, FCs, FABS, WGs, by both examining the use of OJs by financial firms prior to the global financial crisis, and the manner in which the crisis subsequently impacted the world of offshore banking. Chapter 7 then maps the global network of OJs using data on foreign direct investment, identifying the global and regional components of this network, and highlighting how they have been built up through long-term historical relational layering processes.

In the following two chapters, we ask whether and how the rise of new global financial players, technologies, organizational practices, and regulatory landscapes are changing GFNs. In chapter 8, we examine China's attempts to strategically harness and repurpose the GFN, asking whether it has been able to turn the tables on postcolonial financial structures originally designed to drain its wealth into the west. This is followed by an examination in chapter 9 of the impact of new developments in information and communications technology on the asset management industry. We look at the winners and losers created by the rise of these new technologies, at both the firm and geographic level, and ask to what extent they have challenged traditional patterns of entrenched incumbent power in finance. Finally, chapter 10 concludes by applying insights from the GFN framework to the difficult question of financial reform.

Our approach in this book is interdisciplinary, combining insights from economic geography with political economy and economic history, as well as other social sciences. The book is based on mixed methods research, including hundreds of interviews with FABS executives and government officials in financial centers around the world. This is combined with quantitative analyses of original large datasets, including those on turnover, profits, employment, remuneration, financial transactions, and corporate structures and ownership. The analysis is multi-scalar, ranging from case studies of individual organizations, through cities and countries, to global networks.

Empirically, the book shows that the power of the GFN is very "sticky"—both in the sense of the established structures of the network tending to be very historically durable, and in the sense that it tends to ensnare successive ascendant centers of economic power within its embrace. This does not mean a lack of change. FABS today, for example, do an increasingly large amount of business in and out of Asia, where financial centers are growing even while those in Western Europe are stagnating. The uses and organization of offshore finance are evolving, as the international fiscal and regulatory landscape changes. Power within the FABS complex has partially moved away from investment banks like Goldman Sachs, who increasingly share power with gigantic asset managers like Blackrock and the state investment arms of countries in Asia, the Middle East, and elsewhere. FinTech investment is booming, and has led to the emergence of new types of financial actors and places.

At the same time, however, the architecture of the GFN retains a powerful odor of old money about it. It has a strongly Anglo-American flavor, underpinned by the power of the US government and its currency, US banks, rating agencies, and consulting firms, US and British law and accountancy firms, the New York–London "NY-LON" axis of leading financial centers, and a global archipelago of British territories and former colonies that comprise the backbone of the offshore system. China, for its part, rather than directly challenging established GFN structures, mostly seems to be entering and attempting to co-opt them via the internationalization of its banks, state-owned enterprises, and currency—all of which has mostly been mostly mediated through Anglo-American OJs and financial centers, and largely advised by the Anglo-American FABS complex. New developments in FinTech, meanwhile, similarly appear to be reinforcing more than challenging the existing concentrations of economic activity and power in leading financial firms and centers—defying predictions that finance will be "democratized" through technological disruption.

Our book contributes to the debate on the evolution and distribution of power within the world economy. Our thesis on the stickiness of power in the GFN contradicts predictions of a rapid shift of financial power from West to East, or a technologically driven diffusion of power away from traditional financial centers and elites. Indeed, the main way that old centers of global financial power reproduce their influence is precisely through the forging of relationships with ascendant hubs of economic and technological dynamism, whose own growth thus becomes mediated through and reinforces the established structures of financial power (Nye 2015). Furthermore, the historical novelty of most aspects of contemporary finance tends to be enormously overstated. Most assertions that are made regarding the ostensible newness of phenomena such as "globalization," "financialization," or "offshore" finance are basically the product of historical optical illusions and short memories. Broadly speaking, it is difficult to identify a time in the history of capitalism (in the sense of the specific "world system" emerging out of Europe) when this system did not revolve around the central axis of a multi-jurisdictionally differentiated yet functionally integrated GFN (including its more regionally limited European predecessor), with both offshore and onshore elements, that was operated and presided over by some complex of leading FABS firms (usually merchant or investment banks) and powerful state patrons. Indeed, the basic operational and organizational logic of the GFN is in many respects not so different today than it was in the context of the earliest stirrings of western capitalism in medieval Europe. Moreover, the roots of the dominance of the most important financial centers and relationships in the GFN date back centuries in most cases, remaining remarkably durable even as the cast of dominant political and economic powers, and the technological and organizational underpinnings of economic activity, have undergone dramatic upheavals.

Ultimately, a recognition of the tenacity of these structures opens the door to more effectively designed approaches to reforming them, as well as advancing our understanding of why prior attempts at reform have, in various respects, either succeeded or failed when viewed on various timescales. As we note in the book's conclusion, there seems to be a functional unity and historical continuity to the GFN that in many respects runs even deeper than capitalism itself. Indeed, even seemingly basic systemic distinctions between capitalism and noncapitalism(s) become extremely blurry in relation to the concrete power structures and institutional arrangements of the GFN. Socialist, post-socialist, capitalist, and (historically) feudal political economies rub together cheek and jowl within the arena of global finance, and the shadow of both state power, and private greed and "animal spirits," looms pervasively over all in a manner that transcends both national borders and systemic classifications. Most importantly, what we call "capitalism" is really a social system that revolves around *money*, not capital, and money, at the end of the day, invariably ends up wielding just as much power over socialist as capitalist societies. As the Soviet Union discovered, one can start off leading socialist revolution in the morning, before going on to help invent the London Eurodollar market at lunchtime, and finally ending up shipping the people's wealth off in bulk to Kensington and Chelsea by bedtime.

"Thinking big" from this perspective, in a policy reform sense, may paradoxically require "thinking small." This does not indicate a lack of ambition; rather, it means focusing attention on the nuts and bolts of how institutional, regulatory, and fiscal arrangements are actually set up in finance—as opposed to pursuing apparently grander systemic goals that are actually less likely to pose a meaningful long-term challenge to the inherited structures of global financial power, due to the inherently ambiguous nature of grand systemic distinctions themselves in this context. Most importantly, we argue that the emphasis of reform needs to be on proactively building up and stewarding the institutional underpinnings of the financial system that we actually *do* want—as an inherently powerful and indispensable social technology—as opposed to just trying to stamp out the practices that we *don't* want. Institutions in finance are built to last, and once established to the point of indispensability, cannot be easily torn down. Those who would reform finance need to use this fact to their advantage.

2

The Paradox of Sticky Power

All the money and all the banks in Christendom cannot control credit

J. P. Morgan

2.1 The Manufacturing of Money and the Collapse of Time

If capitalism can be defined as a social system that revolves around the accumulation of money, then finance can be defined as the set of institutions within capitalism responsible for the manufacturing of money. The term "manufacture" here has two different meanings. First, there is the figurative meaning wherein clients entrust their money to financial firms in the hope that they will turn it into a larger amount of money. More important, however, is the literal meaning of manufacturing, wherein the financial sector creates money itself as an institutional device.

Money is one of the more difficult social institutions to define. At the most basic level, money is typically defined as something that *acts* simultaneously as a medium of exchange, unit of account, and store of value. Beyond this, however, there are broadly speaking two different perspectives on what money *is* as an institution. On the one hand, some view money as an "exogenously" given scarce *commodity* (e.g. precious metals), that has the qualities of being easily and reliably exchangeable for other commodities, and can be expected to hold its value over time. On the other hand, others view money as fundamentally a form of *credit* that is "endogenously" created in the course of economic transactions themselves, and which is defined by the fact that it can be reliably used both to record and neutralize debts (Bell 2001; Ingham 1998; Innes 1914 Palley 2002; Wray 1992; 2000).

Importantly, the distinction between these two forms or interpretations of money is not really clear-cut. Rather, most monetary systems operate via a combination of endogenous credit money on the one hand, that is created more or less directly by the demand for money, and monetary reserves (i.e. "high-powered money" or "hard cash") on the other hand—which may be more or less endogenous and elastic from the standpoint of the monetary system as a whole, but are basically exogenous from the standpoint of individual participants in it. Furthermore, the distinction between these two components of the monetary

Sticky Power. Daniel Haberly and Dariusz Wójcik, Oxford University Press.
© Daniel Haberly and Dariusz Wójcik (2022). DOI: 10.1093/oso/9780198870982.003.0002

system is generally ambiguous, with different monies or money-like instruments arranged hierarchically along a continuous spectrum running from relatively low-powered endogenously created credit money, to higher-powered forms of pseudo-exogenous reserve money (Bell 2001; Palley 2002; Wray 1992; 2000). Within these hierarchies, the credibility and operation of the former is more or less directly or indirectly conditioned by the way that it references and is grounded in the latter.

With this ambiguity in mind, we propose an open-ended and flexible definition of money as a *more or less liquid financial instrument with a more or less credible guarantee of value*—thus allowing it to more or less reliably fulfill the medium of exchange, unit of account, and store of value functions. Crucially, all forms of money are social constructions, whose significance as an institution—whether or not represented by physical tokens—resides in an abstract ideational space (Graeber 2011; Ingham 1996). Furthermore, there is no clear-cut definition of what sort of ideational instruments constitute money. Rather, various financial instruments can only be benchmarked according to a relative and ultimately subjective scale that defines how easily they can be—or rather how easily they can be expected to be—exchanged for various other types of instruments at a more or less reliable rate. This exchange rate can be fixed, through various mechanisms, in relation to some other instrument. However, the value of any particular money instrument, or indeed even of money itself at the most abstract level, can never be fixed in any generalized universal sense, with the monetary credible guarantee of value thus being an inherently relative, context-dependent quality.

As observed by Marx, the basic imperative of capitalism is to invest a certain amount of money now, in order to obtain a larger amount of money in the future. The rub, however, is that once you have invested your money, you no longer possess it for the period that it is invested—which in turn translates into inflexibility, opportunity costs, and, ultimately, risks. Broadly speaking, the purpose of the financial system is to eliminate this dilemma—in other words, *to allow investors to have their money and invest it too*—by manufacturing abstract ideational representations of uncertain future cash flows and asset values that can be used as monetary instruments in the present day. Crucially, the financial system does not really "invest" money, in a meaningful sense, *in* underlying productive assets and activities in this context. Rather, money and finance reside fundamentally in a separate abstract realm of existence that is constructed in reference to, and allows for control to be exercised over, these underlying productive assets and activities. At the same time, however, the paradox of finance is that this realm of abstraction cannot simply be regarded as some extraneous set of "fictions" that are bolted onto the "real" logic of capitalism. Rather, as described by Minsky (1992a), a capitalist system *is* fundamentally a financial system, wherein the compulsion to continuously compact the future into an immediately accessible present monetary value, represented through abstract constructs, runs just as deeply as the profit motive itself. Indeed, the very medium of exchange within capitalism, whereby transactions are conducted, and out of which profits are ultimately accumulated, itself consists of the abstract monetary representations of future expectations that are manufactured by the financial system.

Capitalism thus operates in what can be described as a state of temporal-causal singularity. In other words, it is fundamentally defined by the way that the "time machine" (Goetzmann 2016) of finance and money causes the past, present, and future to continuously collapse onto one another, such that even seemingly basic assumptions—for example, that the past causes the future, as opposed to vice versa—cannot actually be taken for granted. It is within this context, that we set out to ask in this chapter what seems like it should be a simple question, but actually turns out to be fairly complicated. Namely, how and why is it that the shadow of the past does in fact seem to loom so very long across the present-day organization and operation of the global financial system—and more specifically, the structure of geographic and relational power in this system?

2.2 The Conjuring Trick

What makes this question a difficult one is the basic logic of the *demand-driven* process wherein money is brought into existence spontaneously—or endogenously—in the expectation of *future* profits. More specifically, the form of money that is endogenously created in this manner is credit money, or "a *debt* issued primarily to transfer purchasing power from the future to the present" (Wray 1992, 301). Most importantly, this creation of credit money *does not* entail the intermediation of existing funds from savers to borrowers by the financial system. Rather, the financial system continuously creates new credit money instruments "out of thin air" to meet the demand for credit from borrowers. In the most basic example, when a commercial bank makes a loan to a borrower, this loan is not funded by existing deposits. Rather, the bank simply creates a new (or expanded) deposit in the name of the borrower, with the newly "minted" credit money in this deposit itself providing the funding (i.e. the liability side of the bank's balance sheet) for the new loan (i.e. the asset side of the bank's balance sheet). In other words, newly created credit money is actually "intermediated," in the first instance, from borrowers to themselves,[1] and only subsequently passes

---

[1] For example, when a bank lends $100 to a borrower, four bookings happen simultaneously. The $100 loan is credited to the bank's balance sheet as an asset (i.e. money owed by the borrower to the bank), while a $100 deposit belonging to the borrower is debited to its balance sheet as a liability (i.e. money owed by the bank to the borrower). At the same time, on the borrower's balance sheet, the $100 loan is debited as a liability, while the $100 deposit is credited as an asset. The borrower has thus, with the help of the bank, essentially just borrowed $100 from themself; with these funds consisting of new credit money that the bank has "minted" out of thin air through the act of lending itself. In reality, these funds are nothing more than a ledger entry that the bank adds to its books at will; there

into the hands of other parties—the so-called savers—when borrowers spend the borrowed money on various purchases.

The financial intermediation process thus runs in the opposite direction to the typical idea of savers' funds (i.e. "old money") being intermediated to borrowers (see Wray 1992)—and is indeed, in the final analysis, a process in which the so-called savers are basically *consuming* what comes off the end of the monetary production line in capitalism, rather than providing the *investment* that goes into it.[2] As described by Minsky (1992b), financial firms themselves are fundamentally "merchants of debt" in this context, who continuously compete with one another to develop and manufacture new types of innovative credit money instruments that are as attractive as possible to both borrowers and savers. In principle, there are two ways that this process of innovative monetary "debt minting" can occur. The first, as in the simple example of bank money creation above, is through what is described as "intermediated" finance, in which some financial firm remains interposed, over the long run, between borrowers and savers. In this context, the expansion of credit actually entails a double process of debt creation. First, there is a short-term, liquid money-like credit instrument that is loaned to borrowers (e.g. bank deposits)—and ultimately passed on from them to savers—and second there is a longer-term credit instrument that is retained between financial intermediaries and borrowers (e.g. bank loans), whose terms of repayment are usually stipulated in the form of some larger future amount of relatively liquid short-term credit instruments. Counterintuitively here, as noted above, the original loan from the intermediary to the borrower is actually created in the form of a debt from the intermediary to the borrower (e.g. bank deposit), with the intermediary earning money in this arrangement due to the fact that its own debts are a more money-like (i.e. liquid and reliably redeemable) instrument—and thus a lower interest/higher priced instrument—than the borrower's debt that it is owed.[3]

Meanwhile, the second type of monetary manufacturing proceeds through what is described as "disintermediated" finance. In theory, this is distinguished from intermediated finance by the fact that it only involves a single process of debt creation—i.e. of debt instruments issued by ultimate borrowers that are purchased and held directly by ultimate savers—as opposed to a double process of debt

---

is no intermediation to the borrower of previously existing money that some other saver previously deposited at the bank.

[2] In broader macroeconomic terms, investment generates both expanded economic output (growth in demand and supply) and endogenous monetary expansion, with savings appearing as an accounting identity byproduct of this.

[3] For example, if a bank charges 3% interest on loans, but only pays 1% interest on deposits, it will earn a 2% annual return ("spread") on every dollar of new credit money that it "mints"—in the form of bank deposits credited to borrowers—through the act of lending to borrowers. Once created, these deposited funds move around via transactions to various other accounts belonging to various other people, at various other banks; however, the basic spread is more or less maintained, from the standpoint of the banking system as a whole, via interbank lending and clearing.

creation of credit that is both owed to and by a financial intermediary. In practice, however, the distinction between intermediated and disintermediated finance is extremely ambiguous, and they are typically intertwined. First, the purpose of issuing a disintermediated debt liability onto the market is usually to obtain some more money-like (i.e. liquid and credible) credit instrument, typically owed by a financial intermediary (bank deposits, etc.). What this usually means is that the intermediary that helps the borrower to underwrite and place the "disintermediated" loan will also either have to itself directly provide, or alternatively indirectly arrange the obtaining of, some form of intermediated credit money for the borrower. Such financial intermediary-issued credit money is also frequently obtained against existing debt instruments (e.g. via bill discounting in merchant banking). Moreover, the very distinction between intermediated and disintermediated credit is inherently ambiguous, as disintermediated loan underwriters who are in theory selling loans onward to other investors will often in practice remain interposed in various ways—often via the provision of some form of either explicit or implicit loan guarantee—in order to make these credit instruments more money-like, and thus attractive to buyers/savers. Putting this together with the need for borrowers to obtain intermediated forms of credit instruments for most transactions (bank or money market fund deposits, etc.), what this translates into is the pervasive construction, throughout the history of western capitalism, of so-called *shadow banking* arrangements that blur the boundary between disintermediated as opposed to intermediated credit (Gorton and Metrick 2012; Pozsar et al. 2010). More often than not, from the avoidance of medieval usury laws and deposit banking restrictions (see Kohn 1999c and Munro 2003), to the undercutting of Basel capital requirements (see chapters 5 and 6), such ambiguity is deliberately manipulated for purposes of regulatory arbitrage.

Most importantly, there is no fundamental qualitative difference between money as opposed to non-money financial instruments—rather only differences in instrument *moneyness*. Indeed, the instruments playing the role of "credit" money in a particular context do not necessarily even need to be structured as credit or debt as narrowly defined to only include obligations with fixed terms of repayment. Rather, they can also include what is conventionally referred to as the separate category of equity instruments (e.g. stock), but are actually just credit instruments with variable terms of repayment[4]—with a whole spectrum of instruments such as "preferred" stock or "contingent convertible" bonds, falling somewhere in between what is traditionally understood, in a narrow sense, to be either debt or equity. Like any other financial instrument, equity may be more or less money-like depending on the level of liquidity and credibly assured value it possesses. The equity of a small, privately held firm is about as far down on the hierarchy of moneyness as is possible. However, the stock of large publicly traded

---

[4] That is, via dividends, capital gains, and residual claims in the event of bankruptcy.

corporations is routinely used as a form of scrip in corporate mergers and acquisitions and the payment of executive salaries, and can be easily traded, borrowed
(e.g. for short-selling purposes), etc., like any other money instrument.

Ultimately, the financial impulse in capitalism to endogenously manufacture
an ever-growing volume of more or less money-like credit instruments, in order
to allow for the exploitation of perceived investment opportunities, is a manifestation of what Keynes described as "animal spirits"—or the willingness to
take risks in the expectation of gain (Akerloff and Shiller 2009). Notably, from
a geographic and historical standpoint, this implies that the most exuberant and
prolific loci of innovative financial monetary production should generally not
be—as argued, for example, by Arrighi (1994)—the "old money" centers of past
economic growth and dynamism. Rather, the most intense proliferation of techniques for manufacturing *new money*, in a literal sense, will tend to occur in
the places that are currently experiencing the most dynamic and innovative processes of broader economic development—where the combination of underlying
investment opportunities, and animal spirits risk appetite, is most intense.

The historical record essentially bears out this tendency for the most intense
processes of innovative financial instrument production and risk-taking to be situated, at least at the national level, within the most dynamic centers of *current*
as opposed to *past* economic dynamism. Indeed, as Sylla (2002a, 277) puts it,
"The most successful economies of modern, and perhaps earlier, economic history appear to have had 'financial revolutions' that created innovative financial
systems *before* they became leading economies." In the Middle Ages, the ability of
successive Italian city-states to take command of the most lucrative international
trading routes, as well as the highest value manufacturing activities of the day, was
deeply intertwined with their advanced development of credit instruments such
as the bill of exchange and deposit banking (including proto-central banking; see
section 2.6), as well as breakthroughs in the legal organization of the firm (e.g.
partnerships and other structures) and accounting (e.g. double-entry bookkeep-
ing; Braudel 2019; Fratianni 2009; Munro 2003). Subsequently, the ability of the
Netherlands[5] to wrest control over the most important segments of international
trade and manufacturing was likewise strongly enabled by "paper" financial innovations such as bearer securities and joint stock companies (Carlos and Neal
2011; Gelderblom and Jonker 2004; Munro 2003; Neal 2000). Likewise, the door
to the British Industrial Revolution was opened by the so-called financial revolution that swept through Britain in the late 17th and 18th centuries, which entailed
an interconnected proliferation of joint stock company and securities market development, note-issuing fractional reserve banking, and the establishment of a
structural connection between all three of these and the national debt via the Bank

---

[5] Keeping in mind that the economic and financial heartland of "the Netherlands" was, up until the
Dutch revolt (or more precisely the 1585 fall of Antwerp), actually located in present-day Belgium.

of England (BoE) and other sovereign debt purchasing corporations (Cassis 2006; Neal 1990; 2000; Neal and Quinn 2001). Nineteenth-century US industrialization was spearheaded by an even more enthusiastic embrace of the corporate legal form and securities market—first as devices for state-directed developmentalism, and eventually as a radically commodified engine for private wealth generation (Davis et al. 2003; Navin and Sears 1955; Roy 1999)—with governments at various levels furthermore experimenting, throughout this period, with an endlessly shifting kaleidoscope of national and state-level monetary and banking arrangements (Sylla 1982; 1985). In fact, the USA was already a remarkably prolific center of financial and monetary innovation for roughly a century before independence (Sylla 1982). Today, the world's most dynamic center of not only "real" economic growth, but also risk-taking animal spirits and financial innovation, is arguably Mainland China, which has increasingly leapt ahead of the rest of the world in key areas of FinTech such as the development of digital mobile payments and central bank digital currencies (Gruin and Knaack 2020; Jia and Kenney 2016; Töpfer 2018; Walter and Howie 2011).

Importantly, each of these innovative breakthroughs in the historical development of financial monetary production have had as their side effect, and indeed to a large extent been realized through, an explosion of financial speculation and instability (see Kindleberger and Aliber 2005). Britain's economic development in the 18th and 19th centuries proceeded through an endless chain of leveraged speculative bubbles from the South Sea Company to canal and railroad manias, powered by a succession of dubious and often fraudulent stock market and shadow banking schemes (e.g. the repurposing of the Hollow Sword Blade Company as a de facto bank in the South Sea bubble, the funding of mid-19th-century railroad construction by short-term contractors' bills of exchange and finance companies, etc.; Cottrell 1975). The bursting of each of these bubbles left chaos and misery in its wake; as one 18th-century observer put it, "England is the country in which the spirit of adventure and speculation has done most to promote crises and depressions" (quoted from Kindleberger and Aliber 2005, 61). The 19th-century United States was no different, generating a whole series of speculative manias in a violent cycle of economic boom and bust. More recently, the world's primary economic growth motor, China, has spawned a series of real estate and other asset bubbles over the past fifteen years that put to shame anything seen in the West in the lead-up to the global financial crisis—with, for example, $50m^2$ apartments in Tianjin, where the average salary is only slightly higher than US minimum wage, now selling for >US$ 900,000 (Xie and Bird 2020)—with the Chinese government only managing to prevent the onset of actual financial crises through the consistently proactive provision of backstops (Walter and Howie 2011). Like 18th-century Britain or the 19th-century US, the line between "animal spirts" and outright fraud and criminality in Mainland finance is ambiguous at best. The boom in Mainland digital initial coin offerings (ICOs) a few years ago, for example, was so rife with abuses that these instruments were quickly banned altogether by the People's Bank of China (Wildau 2017a). Ultimately, however, the historical pattern seems to be one of a basically symbiotic codevelopment of "real" processes of technological innovation and capital investment, and financial innovations that push endogenous credit-money instrument production to ever-greater extremes of abstraction and fluidity.

How the inherited historical position of established financial centers and actors can be perpetuated in this context is not immediately obvious. One does frequently find cases of outright national debt bondage involving chronically insolvent low-income borrower states, wherein a demand for fresh borrowing is continuously created simply by the crushing weight of interest payments themselves. However, the inherently stunted growth prospects of such places limits the long-term contribution they can make to the business of the leading financial centers. The business of these centers is rather primarily built upon, and historically mostly reproduces itself through, relationships with the most dynamic and successful economies. From the standpoint of these dynamic economies, it is not altogether clear why the centers of established financial power should be needed at all—not simply due to the apparent ability of ascendant centers of growth to internalize financial innovation, but also due to the logic of how "real" economic growth seems to occur. With respect to the latter, while growth accounting is an extremely fraught exercise (see Felipe 1999; Hulten 2001), work in this area broadly suggests that the primary driver of economic growth is not usually capital formation, but rather organizational and technological restructuring and innovation, recorded as total factor productivity growth.[6] While this type of restructuring and innovation requires inputs of labor, equipment, etc., to undertake, it yields an expansion of output far in excess of these inputs (Hulten 2011). For economies undergoing developmental "catch-up," what is needed from this standpoint is not really infusions of money or capital, but rather the ability to acquire and ultimately generate know-how (technological and organizational capabilities, skills, etc.; see Amsden 1989; Chang 2002). More broadly, while economic development does require capital-intensive investments in infrastructure and heavy industry, as well as imports of technology embodied in capital goods, successful late industrializers do not really seem to develop on the basis of net infusions of foreign capital imports. Rather, they mostly rely *in net* on their own savings to support aggregate capital formation, and from a balance of payments standpoint cover the cost of critical imports (e.g. capital goods) with exports—even while also becoming deeply enmeshed in relationships with established foreign financial centers.

---

[6] The observed predominance of total factor productivity growth can arguably be seen as a direct empirical manifestation of a broadly Schumpeterian economic growth dynamic centered on innovation (Samuelson 2009).

Indeed, a look at the historical record indicates that the net transfer of "real" capital investment or productive resources plays at most a secondary role in shaping the development of international financial relationships. For example, if one looks at the three most important "late" industrializers of the past 300 years (see Chang 2002), one sees the British government and para-public corporations raising large amounts of funds on the Dutch financial market in the 18th century, US corporations and state and local governments raising funds in London in the 19th century, and Mainland Chinese private and state-owned firms raising funds on US financial markets in the late 20th and early 21st centuries (Braudel 1992; Arrighi 1994; Eichengreen 1995; Neal 1992; Pan and Brooker 2014; Wójcik and Burger 2010; chapter 8). Presumably, if the need to import "real" resources/capital to support development were the key factor here, one would expect, due to the increasing developmental gap between leaders and laggards historically, that net imports of capital would be highest for contemporary China in this sequence, and lowest for 18th century Britain, with the 19th century USA falling somewhere in the middle. However, this is not what one sees.

If one looks at foreign *direct* investment (FDI) inflows, which in theory may involve an actual transfer of technological and organizational capabilities as opposed to just money, one does indeed see this becoming more important over time historically, with foreign multinationals playing a particularly important role in China's development (broadly following the "investment development path, described by Dunning and Narula 1996—keeping in mind, as we discuss in chapters 7 and 8, that a huge percentage of China's inward FDI is actually just offshore "round-trip" investment by its own firms and citizens). However, FDI inflows are only weakly related to the net directionality of integration into global financial flows. Indeed, one sees China running large trade and current account *surpluses* throughout most of its period of rapid development, implying that the aggressive overseas capital raising efforts of its private and state-owned firms are, in macroeconomic terms, bringing coals to Newcastle. China has been re-exporting all of its massive gross capital inflows, plus additional domestic savings above and beyond these capital inflows, resulting in a net negative overall contribution of foreign investment (inward and outward) to capital formation.

Looking back earlier, the USA seems to have roughly maintained balance in international trade for the first two-thirds of the 19th century—during which time chronic goods trade deficits were offset by large shipping service export surpluses (not least in the China opium trade; see chapter 4)—before moving into a situation of increasing overall trade surplus after the Civil War (Lipsey 1994). While the USA did run a persistent *current account* deficit throughout the 19th century, this was basically a result of inward foreign investment and American overseas borrowing, rather than a cause of it—i.e. the deficit resulted from the international imbalance in investment income itself. Moreover, the *net* capital imports that financed this US current account deficit (as opposed to gross foreign investment in the USA) were not particularly important macroeconomically, never amounting to more than 6.2% of US gross capital formation in any given decade from the

1830s to 1890s (apart from a spike in federal borrowing during the Civil War), and usually quite a bit less than this (Lipsey 1994). Indeed, 19th-century America was not really built with British capital so much as it used London as a developmental credit card "as a convenience" (Jenks 1951, 388), with net capital imports at most providing a balance of payments shock absorber during a few particularly intense bursts of railroad construction and wartime spending (Fishlow 1985; Lipsey 1994). From the standpoint of technology acquisition, the role of capital goods imports in US industrialization was non-negligible. For the most part, however, technological capabilities were acquired through skilled labor inflows (including as a mechanism for intellectual property theft from Britain; see Chang 2002; Jeremy 1977), with even FDI, such as it existed, consisting mostly of entrepreneurial immigration (Lipsey 1994).

Going back even further, the datasets needed to reconstruct Britain's net balance of payments in the 18th century, during its period of large-scale borrowing in Amsterdam, are rather problematic (see Nash 1997). However, it looks like the UK's external accounts were probably generally in surplus during periods of peacetime (reflecting mercantilist balance of trade priorities), but would swing into deficit during wartime (Nash 1997)—with Dutch investment predominantly concentrated in British government securities (including indirectly via stock in para-public corporations that acted as sovereign lending vehicles; see section 2.6), and in a net sense thus providing liquidity that smoothed out the impact of spikes in British military spending. Wars were extremely frequent, and the UK's outstanding external debt in Amsterdam thus became quite significant (Nash 1997; Wright 1997). However (contra Brezis 1995), there is no reason to think that this had much to do with the process of industrialization—wherein Britain was, by the early 18th century, the place where all of the key innovations were originating—except indirectly insofar as it helped the UK to gain an edge in international military struggles that in turn helped to open up export markets, etc. (Esteban 2001; Nash 1997). Even with respect to the latter, Esteban (2001) estimates that the UK was by the 1770s already able to run a current account surplus, and thus act as a net capital exporter, even during wartime (apart from 1808–1815), with overall military expenditures (including by parastatal corporations) largely balancing out their own current account impacts by opening India up to colonial wealth extraction.

In all, the story of economic and financial development seems to be largely one that entails the proliferation of progressively more fluid and abstract processes of financial innovation—which create increasingly frictionless mechanisms for conjuring credit-money out of thin air—that both foster and develop in conjunction with processes of "real" technological innovation and economic growth that seem to themselves have a rather transcendental "something for nothing" quality centered on total factor productivity growth. With respect to the latter, although places that are undergoing economic "catch-up" do need to acquire know-how from more advanced economies, it is difficult to draw much of a direct connection between this, in and of itself, and the need for financial dependence on these more advanced economies. The most critical aspects of technology, and technological catch up, are basically embodied in human capital/know-how and organizational capabilities, and *successful* development generates (and to a large extent requires) snowballing increases in export earnings that can self-fund necessary capital goods imports from a net macroeconomic standpoint. Indeed, taken as a whole, it seems that the logic of how finance operates within capitalist development should give the latter an inherently forward-looking, and basically democratic or at least meritocratic quality. Resources should, in theory, basically just spring spontaneously into the hands of the most dynamic (or at least charismatic) people and places that are most able and willing to make effective use of them. At the most general level, the opportunities and potentialities of the future should always take precedence over, and never be subservient to, the inherited power structures of the past. "Old money," in short, should have very little durable influence in the face of the creative potential of "new money."

2.3 The Search for Solid Ground

Ultimately, we argue that effectively problematizing the reproduction of inherited structures of global financial power cannot really be done from a "real" developmental functionalist standpoint that analytically prioritizes questions of capital formation and, broadly speaking, resource allocation. Rather, the durable power of established financial centers and structures needs to be understood in terms the advantages they offer *for the purposes of conducting financial business itself*, and more specifically for the manufacture, sale, and purchase of financial instruments. At the same time, this itself presents a paradox in light of the relative ease with which the most dynamically innovative and growing economic actors and places can, and historically have, taken the lead themselves in developing new forms of financial engineering. What this means is that the fact that new money in capitalism does live, to a pervasive extent, under the shadow of old money, must be linked to the presence of some institutional, political, or broadly sociological missing ingredient *within* the logic of financial innovation, that upstart architects of new money cannot provide themselves.

We argue that this missing ingredient can be conceptualized, at the most basic level, as the need to ground the capitalist impulse towards innovative endogenous credit money *quantity production*, in the imperative of monetary *quality production*. In other words, the apparently boundless potential of financial innovation to support monetary production is constrained by the bottleneck of needing to produce instruments that possess the crucial qualities of *liquidity* and a *reliable guarantee of value*. Most importantly, there is an inherently conservative and centralizing logic to this process of monetary quality production—or more precisely to the combination of subprocesses that comprise it—wherein the very fluidity and abstraction of innovative credit-money production drives a countervailing search for some form of solid ground on which to build this production. This "solid ground" of monetary quality production—not least in the literal sense of the pieces of land where this production is concentrated—thus becomes a scarce and valuable commodity, that confers tremendous power on those who hold it, or who are even just lucky enough to be located adjacent to it. However, this bonanza also tends to, in turn, lock the places receiving it into a characteristic trajectory of conservative and backward-looking institutional, political, and economic development—which is paradoxically intensified the more that the new centers of growth seek validation in their connection to the old.

Notably, Keynesian economic theory has a well-developed idea, at an abstract level, of what this "solid ground" looks like. Specifically, the behavior of a capitalist economy is seen as being conditioned by the tension between the "animal spirits" underpinning risk/return-seeking endogenous credit-money production and investment on the one hand, and "liquidity preference" on the other—i.e. the countervailing impulse to mitigate risk through the holding of "higher-powered," i.e. more liquid and credible, money instruments ("hard cash," etc.). In Keynesian theory, the emphasis is on how this tension evolves cyclically over time in a pattern of alternating, self-reinforcing booms and busts (as well as the chronic problem of liquidity preference, i.e. cash hoarding, acting as a black hole for effective demand for goods and services). As observed by Minsky, this cyclical logic cannot simply be conceptualized in terms of the alternation between risk-seeking credit expansion and "flight to quality" deleveraging within the existing institutional parameters of the financial system. Rather, the evolution of the institutional architecture of finance—including public regulatory and backstopping arrangements—needs to itself be regarded as being conditioned by, and in turn conditioning, the coevolution of animal spirits and liquidity preference in Minskian "super-cycles" of financial innovation, instability, and crisis (Ferri and Minsky 1992; Kindleberger and Aliber 2005; Minsky 1992b; Wray 1992; see also chapter 6).

The basic argument that we make in this chapter is that the implications of this dialectical relationship between the impulses toward monetary quantity and quality production are also expressed, and need to be understood in terms of, much broader features and tendencies in the organization and evolution of the financial system—including at a geographic level. Specifically, one needs to step back to consider, at a very basic conceptual level, what is entailed by the simultaneous production of monetary quantity on the one hand and solid ground (or monetary quality) on the other, and how this production process is made possible by, and reflected in, the geographic organization and evolution of the financial system.

Crucially, as noted above, the endogenous production of monetary *quantity* by the financial system is, in and of itself, very straightforward. Financial innovation is easy—scam artists do it all the time, in endlessly creative ways. Anybody can simply print off various types of paper IOUs, and try to get other people to either directly accept them as payment for goods, services, and debts, or to convert them into other instruments than can be accepted for such payments. The key question however, and what is highly doubtful in the vast majority of situations, is whether anyone else can actually be convinced to accept these IOUs (Minsky 1986).

We argue that there are three specific stamps of monetary quality assurance that are needed to actually get such IOUs accepted. First, there needs to be some institutional mechanism that assigns these IOUs a credible value in relation to other financial instruments, and that allows them to be reliably exchanged or redeemed for these other instruments. Second, the IOUs themselves need to be packaged into a credible legal structure that gives those holding them some assurance that they will actually be able to enforce payment (or realize any other rights attached to them), and that affords recourse to some reliable mechanism for dispute resolution in the event of non-payment (whether due to unwillingness or inability) and other problems. Third, there should, at least ideally, be some additional safety mechanism—that originates from some source other than the IOU-issuing party, and ideally from beyond the sphere of private contract altogether—which provides an enhanced guarantee of instrument value in the event of altogether unforeseen and uncontrollable circumstances.

The argument here is that the geographic organization and evolution of what we dub the global financial network (GFN) needs to be understood in terms of the way that various actors, institutions, and places specialize in providing these three basic components of financial monetary *quality* production, in relation to the process of endogenous innovative credit-money *quantity* production. Historically, there have been some changes in the way that these roles are performed, as well as the manner and places in which the GFN itself is constituted. In general, however, the tendency toward functional and structural continuity and durability within the GFN has been much more marked than the tendency toward change. Specifically, one sees a relatively consistent, even if dynamically unstable mixture of first-order and second-order dialectical processes reflected in the structure and evolution of the GFN.

With respect to the first-order impulses, these entail (1) the emergence of a hierarchical network of financial centers to relieve the interconnected informational and relational dilemmas associated with the production of financial market efficiency and liquidity, (2) the emergence of specialized offshore jurisdictional spaces of private legal–contractual financial production that tend to become partially dissociated, to varying degrees, from, the geography of either financial market efficiency and liquidity production, or of the underlying "real" economic activities referenced and controlled by the financial system, and (3) the emergence of close linkages between these centers of liquidity and legal production, and the centers of political authority necessary to provide additional backing (in various ways) to monetary production and accumulation. Meanwhile, the key second-order dialectical processes entail the emergence of rather counterintuitive mutually reinforcing relationships between (4) the development of liquid and efficient markets, and the development of monopolistic "platforms" that control key nodes in the operation of these markets, and (5) the offshore impulse toward the privatization of legal space, and the centralization of political authority in the hands of the small number of particularly powerful states that are able to incorporate this offshore legal space into their sovereign "protection rackets." Each of these processes are examined in turn, in the following sections.

2.4 Market Machines

The ability of the financial system to produce high quality money instruments is rooted, first, in its ability to ensure that these instruments can be easily exchanged for one another (and for nonfinancial assets and good and services) at a reliable and well-defined price. In other words, the financial system needs to be structured to produce *liquidity*—i.e. ease of exchangeability of various financial instruments for one another—and *efficiency*—i.e. the ability to reliably and consistently value these financial instruments in relation to one another.

Playing the central role in liquidity and efficiency production are financial markets. A financial market is, in effect, a sort of accidental computer, wherein liquidity and efficiency are generated as a kind of waste *byproduct* of the attempts of individual market participants to engage in speculative price arbitrage. In other words, liquidity and efficiency are generated by the continuous attempts of market participants to outsmart one another in assessing whether the current market consensus has priced any given asset too high or too low in relation to its likely future prospects, and either selling or buying it accordingly—and thus causing its price to converge toward its predicted fundamental value. The logic of this accidental process of market liquidity and efficiency production is inherently self-reinforcing. Within it, the volume of speculative market "churn" both conditions the level of market liquidity, and the speed with which any *obvious*[7] asset price misalignments can be arbitraged away. Meanwhile, the volume of speculative market churn is self-referentially conditioned by market liquidity, which is itself conditioned by the extent to which speculative price arbitrage makes it possible for market participants to quickly agree on well-defined fair asset valuations (see Tobin 1984; chapter 9).

---

[7] In other words, financial markets can be and often are extremely efficient in relation to the level of knowledge of their own participants—i.e. in terms of their ability to achieve a price consensus between these participants—even if their absolute level of efficiency is hugely imperfect when judged by their ability to *correctly* determine or predict the "fundamental" value of assets; see Tobin (1984).

Crucially, even while individual speculators are engaged in a zero-sum competition with one another to identify and exploit price misalignments, the way that speculation generates financial instrument moneyness has a positive sum logic at the level of the market as a whole. In other words, as soon as different financial instruments can be reliably valued in terms of, and rendered easily exchangeable for each other, they all collectively acquire a more money-like quality—even if some instruments always remain, in relative terms, more money-like than others. The ability of markets to coproduce liquidity and efficiency in this manner is, above all, a joint function of the total number of buyers and sellers in them, and the total amount of information that these market participants can bring to bear on the pricing process. Given that the latter is itself mostly a function of the former, what this means is that the single most important determinant of both the liquidity and efficiency of a financial market is simply its size. This leads, crucially, to a powerful snowballing tendency toward market centralization in already-dominant financial centers. However, this centralizing tendency is always counterbalanced against the need for financial markets to access information distributed throughout the "real" economy. The result is the formation and persistence of lower-tier regional feeder financial market centers that both extend and draw upon the informational reach of the dominant market centers in a hierarchically networked relationship (Clark and Wójcik 2007; Fratianni 2009; Grote 2009; Kindleberger 1973; Neal and Quinn 2001; Poon 2003).

The development of these networks of connections, both hierarchically between leading and lower-tier financial market centers, and horizontally among the leading centers, is shaped by multiple factors. However, trade and migration flows play an especially important role in laying down these connections, with the most successful financial centers usually developing in cities that are simultaneously leading commercial and multiethnic cultural entrepôts. The success of such places is not just built on economic openness, but also on a cosmopolitan cultural and religious openness that allows them to attract a diversity of diaspora communities, who bring with them access to far-flung commercial and financial relationships. The historical development of these interconnected networks of migration, trade, and investment, is often intertwined with political relationships; for example, between the leading financial centers of European colonizers, and their former colonies (Braudel 1985; Kindleberger 1973; Neal 1990; Neal and Quinn 2001; Palan et al. 2010).

Lying at the center of both the internal operation of, and the external relationships of financial centers, is the bringing together of information and trust to produce credit. "Credit," crucially, always carries a double-meaning that refers to both financial instruments themselves, and the assessments of issuer credibility in which they are embedded. What financial centers are essentially selling to the clients who use them, in the context of credit production, is access to the networks of information gathering, processing, and trust that allow IOUs to become something more than worthless pieces of paper. This instrument credibility is, ultimately, a self-referential product of the continuous mutual acceptance and validation of IOUs themselves, by various issuers, as made possible by the role of markets in mediating financial instrument valuation and exchange. In other words, financial centers do not provide access to some preexisting pool of money; they rather allow credit money instruments to come into existence, and to be ascribed value and credibility, by acting as centralized informational and relational brokers. As Cassis (2006, 22) notes of London in the early 19th century, for example, "The financial capacity displayed by the city was less of a quantitative nature—in other words, linked to the amount of capital available—than qualitative, through the trust it generated on account of the prestige of its largest banking houses and the networks of relationships that it could bring into play." London's role here frequently involved the brokerage of relationships between ultimate investors and borrowers who were both located outside of the City. When the Anglo-Dutch merchant bank alliance of Barings and Hope & Co. helped France to finance its Napoleonic war indemnity, for example, they actually ended up largely placing these loans to investors in France itself (Cassis 2006).

The role that financial centers play within capitalism is thus fundamentally one of completing a series of relational circuits between various issuers of IOUs, so as to render these instruments mutually credible and acceptable; with the degree of instrument credibility/acceptability, as computed and effected through markets, expressed as a yield or interest rate. What financial centers are not really doing is providing *capital* in a meaningful sense. This distinction is particularly important from the standpoint of economic "peripheries," as the resources or wealth necessary to support local investment are, as noted in the earlier discussion (see also Hirschman 1958; Rosenberg 1960), in theory usually available locally in some real aggregate sense. The issue is that the relationships and institutions whereby they are mobilized and coordinated end up needing to be mediated through the market machines of the dominant financial centers. This is a particularly acute and visible issue for the poorest and least developed countries, which often run "real" macroeconomic surpluses, but are unable to directly mobilize these for local investment due to the magnitude of capital flight to foreign financial centers. Ndikumana and Boyce (2018), for example, estimate the combined flight capital of African countries to be roughly US$1.8 trillion, which dwarfs their total external debt of US$500 billion.

Notably, as the bidirectional nature of these investment positions implies, the term capital flight here is itself something of a misnomer. The primary problem is rather one of a local relational disarticulation of the financial and monetary system in peripheral economies, wherein foreign financial centers and actors end up being pervasively (and often more or less exploitatively) interposed between local actors and activities. This local relational disarticulation is, ultimately, directly encouraged by the very existence of foreign financial centers that offer more attractive channels for both borrowing and saving than the comparatively underdeveloped local financial system. It is thus an inherently self-reproducing phenomenon. Importantly, and notwithstanding the specific political problems created by border-crossing financial flows for many countries, the basic logic of how this works must be conceptualized outside of the confines of *national* functionalist thinking (Wójcik and Burger 2010). All that Nineteenth-century US railroad promoters cared about when selling their bonds in London, for example, was the fact that they could get a better price for these securities in the largest and most liquid financial market, regardless of whether it happened to be located within or outside of the USA (Chambers et al. 2018).[8] The fact that a national border has been crossed in such a situation simply does not matter (assuming that one is disregarding, for now, *political* and *regulatory* factors); this is no different from the basic logic of why a firm in Ohio would choose to raise or invest money in New York as opposed to Cincinnati. In other words, what matters most is the gravitational pull exerted on both issuers and investors by financial centers themselves, and the gross relational interconnectedness and institutional dependency, more than the net capital flows, that result from this pull.

In short, all else being equal, "bigger" financial markets and financial centers produce "better" money—in the sense of relatively more money-like financial instruments that can be easily traded for other instruments at a relatively predicable (or at least mutually agreeable) value. However, the ability of these "big" financial markets and centers to operate depends on the strength of their network contacts with—and thus ability to draw on an interconnected combination of information and credit/trust from—both lower-tier regional financial centers, and other leading global centers. In the contemporary world, this process is mediated through, and in turn shapes, the so-called world city network (see Bassens and van Meeteren 2015; Coe et al. 2014; Sassen 1991; Taylor et al. 2014). Beyond this broad dialectic of basically symbiotic centralization and decentralization in financial market formation, moreover, the ability of financial centers (and financial systems broadly) to produce liquidity and efficiency is also conditioned by concrete institutional structures. These include both informal and formal arrangements—spanning local social networks, associations, etc., to securities (and other types of) exchange platforms (see section 2.7), as well as the whole apparatus of financial market regulation and supervision (whether state imposed or privately self-imposed; Bassens and van Meeteren 2015; Davis et al. 2003; Poon 2003; Wójcik 2011a).

Furthermore, just as there is a basically ambiguous and codependent relationship between intermediated and disintermediated forms of credit creation, the operation of markets is deeply entangled with the operation of vertically integrated

---

[8] As described by Chambers et al. (2018, 4082), this entailed a logic of "corporate arbitrage" wherein "U.S. railroads in a search for cheaper debt financing expanded their listing activity in London in response to increasing yield spread difference [in comparison to New York and other US financial markets]."

financial firms—and above all various types of banks—which internalize elements of the process of market liquidity and efficiency generation (Cassis 2006; Kindleberger 1973; Wójcik 2011a). Most importantly, banks (whether conventional or shadow, commercial or investment/merchant) are typically responsible for the initial creation, valuation and placement of newly created financial instruments— whether issued by banks themselves, or on behalf of a third party—that become subsequently traded on markets, as well as for the provision of the credit lines to market participants (including speculators, and banks themselves) that lubricate the churn of transactions generating market liquidity and efficiency generally (Minsky 1992c).[9] In both capacities, banks serve as particularly crucial clearinghouses for information centralization, and well as application (e.g. by valuing the various forms of collateral against which credit is offered). Most importantly, banks, as trusted issuers of the most widely respected private credit money instruments, play a key role in mediating the direct convertibility of the relatively less money-like financial instruments traded on and valued by markets, into the relatively more money-like instruments issued (or at least guaranteed) by banks themselves. In this sense (contra varieties of capitalism arguments, e.g. Hall and Soskice 2001) there is no basic separation between "bank-based" versus "market-based" financial systems. They are rather (as e.g. Hilferding 1981 observed; see also Carlos and Neal 2011; Dixon 2012) two sides of the same coin of financial system operation, and typically only become distinguished from one another as a result of state policies that deliberately seek to foster the development of one at the expense of the other (e.g. breaking up the "big banks" versus deliberately centralizing control in the hands of these banks, and thus typically the state; Carlos and Neal 2011; Höpner and Krempel 2004; Kandel et al. 2019 Ozawa 2001; Simon 1998).

Crucially, the financial sector, and financial centers, cannot fulfill the functions of liquidity and efficiency production simply by operating in a closed self-referential loop of *financial* market information-processing activities. Rather, the operation of both financial and nonfinancial firms and activities hinges on the networks of relationships that allow nonfinancial firms to access the money manufacturing machine on the one hand, and that allow financial firms/markets to monitor and where necessary intervene in the management of the actors that they finance on the other. At the center of these relationships is not just the financing of capital formation—which in firms like in countries tends to be mostly internally generated in a net sense (see Corbett and Jenkinson 1996)—but also, and indeed typically more so, the functions of *liquidity management* (i.e. of cash balances and credit lines) and *capital monetization* (i.e. maximizing and rendering accessible the

---

[9] Minsky (1992c, 112), for example, describes how fund managers in post-1980 US "money manager capitalism" became dependent for trading liquidity on excessively leveraged dealers (investment banks), with the latter thus becoming the "main financial houses" even as they were in turn "beholden to banks for continued refinancing."

value of the firm). With respect to liquidity management, businesses simply cannot operate in a world of credit money-based transactions without being deeply
integrated into the liquidity machine of financial markets—typically via intimate
and durable relationships with various types of banking (including shadow bank)
intermediaries. Meanwhile, the owners of firms have powerful incentives to "mon-
etize" the capital structure of these firms by maximizing the market liquidity and
value of their shares and bonds (and other liabilities); which in turn calls into play
networks of relationships with an array of additional intermediaries, including in
the area of corporate governance.

In practice, the network-relational character of financial power manifests itself
as a two-way geographic pull between the dominant financial centers, and nonfinancial sector command and control activities—wherein the gravitational pull
of the former tends, in general, to ultimately drive geographic shifts in the latter
more than vice versa. In this respect, the so-called contemporary financialization
of corporate governance in the Anglo-American world, in particular, has been well
documented and heavily analyzed (in relation to the rise of shareholder value, etc.;
see: Bassens and van Meeteren 2015; Epstein 2005; Krippner 2005)—including
insofar as it has driven direct shifts in the geography of corporate control (e.g.
Boeing's move from Seattle to Chicago; see Muellerleile 2009). Ultimately, however, it is doubtful that there ever actually was, or that there even could be a form
of capitalism that was *not* deeply enmeshed in relationships with financial firms
and centers. A central role of finance within nonfinancial activities is simply baked
into the nature of capitalism as a system of monetary production and accumulation, even if there is quite a bit of qualitative diversity in the way that this role is
structured in various contexts.

This inextricable co-constitution of nonfinancial and financial activity in
capitalism, as mediated geographically through financial centers, is too often
unrecognized–and is indeed often largely airbrushed out of the histories of the
world's leading economies. With respect to the UK, for example, as observed by
Gerschenkron (1962) the Industrial Revolution proceeded with relatively little
direct external financing of early manufacturing investment itself. Crucially, however, as described by Chapman (1979) (see also Knafo 2008), the industrial fixed
capital of British manufacturers, through the mid-19th century, was typically
dwarfed by their working capital, and in the latter area they were in fact deeply dependent for liquidity on access to trade credit—most importantly in the financing
of international import and export operations. In the case of the Lancashire cotton
textile industry at the heart of the Industrial Revolution, one manifestation of this
was a series of efforts to promote the development of Manchester as a financial
center. However, the local financial institutional ecology remained relatively
fragile and unstable, and the relational pull of the City of London, particularly in
relation to the power wielded by the Bank of England, remained irresistible, and
ultimately overpowering. The exuberantly manufactured Northern paper—bills

of exchange, regional joint stock bank liabilities, etc.—was simply never as good as London paper, and inevitably ended up needing to be validated by London. As one Bank of England official complained of the Bank of Manchester in 1841 "their depositories, instead of [being filled] with solid or convertible securities, are absolutely crammed with parchments, and I have no doubt that they are at this moment the most extensive mill owners in this country" (Chapman 1979, 60). What often appeared to be particularly important were relationships of trust—as conditioned by various prejudices, personal backgrounds, and connections, etc.—that determined whether the London financial establishment (merchant banks together with the BoE) deemed Northern entrepreneurs, both industrial and financial, to be "names of sufficient standing" (Chapman 1979, 61) worthy of support during the acid test of a liquidity crunch. Meanwhile, "wild speculative men" who had "risen from nothing," with "aspiration beyond their means" (Chapman 1979, 63) were cut loose.

In the USA, similarly, the stereotypical idea of the late 19th- and early 20th-century rise of the autonomous managerialist industrial firm, supposedly free from shareholder or broader financial influences, is deeply misleading—and indeed could in many respects not be any further from the reality of how American big business actually developed. Most importantly, the early 20th-century managerialist "separation of ownership and control," identified by Berle and Means (1932), did not entail a *self-contained* model of corporate managerialism. Rather, as Means described in detail in a 1939 investigation for the National Resources Committee, what it entailed was the rise of a managerial and financial elite organized into *inter-corporate* "interest group" networks who controlled most of the largest corporations in America without actually owning most of their stock (National Resource Committee 1939). Indeed, the development of large American manufacturing corporations, in the late 19th and early 20th centuries, was for the most part mediated through their integration into Japanese Zaibatsu or Keiretsu-like hub-and-spokes networks centered on wealthy families, financiers, and investment banks—bound by densely interwoven relationships of credit, minority equity holdings and cross-holdings, and interlocking directorships (Coffee 2001; De Long 1992; Kandel et al. 2019; Lash and Urry 1987; Pujo 1913; Tabarrok 1998). These networks were centered, most notably, on the Mellons, du Ponts, Rockefellers, and—most importantly—the vast sprawling structure of JP Morgan's "Money Trust" (or as Means called it the "Morgan-First National interest group"; National Resource Committee 1939). The latter largely controlled access, during a crucial period, to both New York Stock Exchange IPOs by the largest firms, and the transatlantic connection between New York and the old money capital markets of Europe (and most importantly London), and was also to a large extent directly responsible for the broader corporate reorganization and long-term corporate governance oversight of the large American industrial "trusts" (see

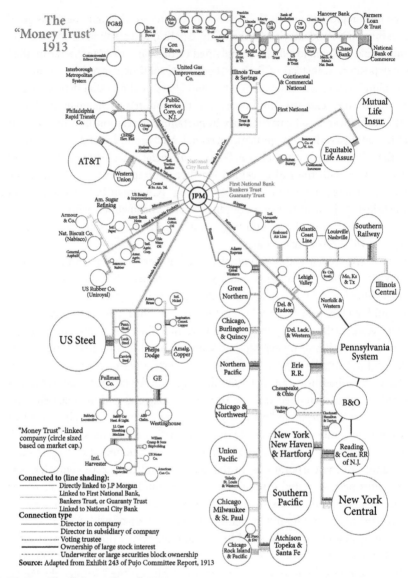

The "Money Trust" 1913

Fig. 2.1 The "Money Trust," 1913
Source: authors.

section 2.7). The remarkable scope of the networks of relationships thereby established, centered on Morgan and allied financial institutions, is shown in Figure 2.1 (based on the 1913 Congressional Pujo Committee investigation).

Probably the most important example of the development of the large American industrial corporation is provided by General Motors, which was in many respects the heart of the American economy throughout much of the 20th century. GM's founder, Durant, had originally made his fortune in the carriage industry in Flint, Michigan. From there, however, he moved to New York to start his own securities firm, before drawing on his Wall Street financial connections and expertise to assemble GM through a series of acquisitions of automotive firms back in Michigan (Dale 1956, 36). At its most ambitious, the plan put together by Durant with JP Morgan and fellow automotive industrialist Ben Briscoe was to consolidate the entire American automotive industry into a giant monopolistic "trust," with the help of financing arranged by Morgan. The resulting group was to be modeled after other Morgan-backed groups such as US Steel and General Electric. This plan fell through after Ford held out for an unacceptably high cash sale price (Pelfrey 2006). However, GM was nevertheless organized through the typical New Jersey shell company structure of the trusts (see section 2.5), and ultimately came under the control of the du Pont family and JP Morgan after the founder's freewheeling stock and leverage-based expansion schemes created repeated financial difficulties (Dale 1956; Sloan 2015). Thereafter, GM became part of a du Pont family-controlled business group held together mostly by minority but controlling equity ties—that were ultimately forcibly severed by Federal anti-trust action in the 1950s and 1960s—which also included the United States Rubber Company (Uniroyal), the chemicals firm of du Pont proper, and a joint venture (Ethyl Corp.) with Standard Oil of New Jersey that developed and controlled the innovation of leaded gasoline (National Resources Committee 1939; Rutter 1964; Sloan 2015; Stocking 1958).

According to longtime GM CEO Alfred Sloan (2015, 147), "the outstanding benefit General Motors derived from the du Pont association—apart from their general position as a responsible shareholder serving on the board of directors—was in the financial area. A number of du Pont men experienced in accounting and finance came to General Motors in the early years and assumed key positions." Under du Pont family rule, management made it crystal clear that "the primary object of the General Motors Corporation … is to make *money*, not just to make motor cars" (Link 2013, 3). Each division of GM was expected to stand on its own feet as an independent profit center to ensure that returns on capital were maximized, and to enforce this, divisions billed each other for inputs at market rates using an internal corporate credit money ("settlement certificates"). Major investment decisions were made by a finance committee dominated by the du Ponts, on which JP Morgan was also represented (Sloan 2015; Stocking 1958). According to Sloan (2015, 154):

> by establishing good working relationships with a large number of banks we were
> able to develop extensive lines of credit which could be drawn on if the need arose.
> By reducing our cash balances in banks, this system also enabled us to invest

the excess cash, principally in short-term government securities. Thus we earned an income on money formerly kept as cash and so increased the efficiency with which we used our capital.

Meanwhile, Sloan sought to align managerial and shareholder interests through a succession of executive stock purchase and bonus schemes (Holden 2005). The shareholder value GM delivered was impressive, with the firm paying out 70% of its total cash earnings as dividends between 1909 and 1940 (Maielli and Haslam 2016).

Geographically, GM was characterized by a bipolar corporate governance structure split between New York and Detroit—with the relationship between these poles not always amicable, and power swinging back and forth between them (Freeland 2001). With one foot planted on Wall Street, GM made an early direct entry into financial services itself by founding the New York–based GMAC in 1919, whose provision of consumer credit facilities gave GM an important sales edge over Ford, in particular (Maielli and Haslam 2016; Tedlow 1988). Meanwhile, in its home region, GM sought to prevent the total Great Depression–era collapse of financial services by cofounding the National Bank of Detroit in 1933 (*New York Times* 1933).

Notably, in the case of the largest industrial firm and fortune to emerge in America in the late 19th and early 20th centuries, Standard Oil/Rockefeller, the entire apparatus of command and control was packed up and moved, in the 1880s, from its initial home in Cleveland, to Wall Street. This occurred in conjunction with a legal reorganization of Standard Oil that moved its nominal seat to the paper incorporation hub of New Jersey (Yergin 1990; see also section 2.5). Having relocated to the center of US financial power, the Rockefellers proceeded to conquer large swaths of it, most notably through the establishment of control over the (also Morgan-invested) National City Bank of New York (i.e. Citibank; largely through intermarriage with the Stillmans), the Equitable Trust Company, and (via the latter) Chase Bank (Tabarrok 1998). In contrast to Morgan, which mostly managed the liability side of firms, the Rockefellers' and Standard Oil's relationships with banks developed on the asset side—with the management of the same cash reserves that insulated Standard Oil from reliance on bank credit lines (see Yergin 1990) supposedly catalyzing the development of its relationship with City in the late 1800s (Tabarrok 1998). The relationships forged were enduring; members of the Rockefeller family would head Citibank until 1967, and Chase until 1980 (Cattani and Tschoegl 2002; Sampson 1981).

In fact, it is very difficult to identify any sort of "non-financialized" era of business in 20th-century America, as opposed to a period between the New Deal and ca. 1980 when business was simply a bit less *ruthless* due to the influence of labor unions, increased regulation, etc. Once liberated from Wall Street domination by various regulatory and court actions (most importantly the 1914 Clayton Antitrust

Act, 1933 Glass Steagall Act, 1938 Chandler Act, 1956 Bank Holding Company
Act, and 1957–1965 breakup of the du Pont family empire; De Long 1992; Kandel et al. 2019; Kovacic and Shapiro 2000; Rutter 1964; Simon 1998; Stocking
1958) the major industrial firms immediately proceeded to turn themselves, via the
conglomeration movement, into octopus-like financial holding operations largely
concerned with the buying and selling of other companies (Lazonick 1990; Malkiel
2019). The priorities of these groups fundamentally revolved around Wall Street;
as Malkiel (2019) puts it, the whole idea was that "the acquisition process itself
could be made to produce growth in earnings per share," with the "managers of
conglomerates [tending] to possess financial expertise rather than … operating
skills." Ironically, the investment bank that would later help break up the conglomerates actually became part of an industrial conglomerate itself in 1970, when
Firestone Tire purchased a controlling stake in Drexel, turning it into Drexel Firestone (Robards 1972). Meanwhile, it was to a large extent the major American
industrial firms, via their expansion of commercial paper-based funding (led from
the 1920s by GMAC; Hurley 1977), that pioneered the development of the shadow
banking machine that would later become plugged into the US mortgage market
(see chapter 6). As early as 1940, GM's financial assets, including the commercial
paper-funded assets of GMAC, were already larger than its tangible assets (Maielli
and Haslam 2016); in other words, seven decades before its ill-fated involvement
in the subprime mortgage crisis, GM was well on its way to becoming a shadow
bank that also sold cars.

These sprawling industrial–financial octopi retained close connections to their
traditional Wall Street and regional bank patrons, with the post-WWII structure of the interlocking directorate actually changing surprisingly little from the
days of the Money Trust.[10] As of 1968, JP Morgan (then called Morgan Guaranty) retained three shared directors with GM and GE, and two with US Steel—all
of which it had originally helped to create—and Morgan was still at the center of the US director network in 1982 (Davis and Mizruchi 1999; Levine 1972).
While the power relationships involved were more horizontal than vertical at this
point, these interlocks provided an architecture of information flow and cooperation that supported bank–industrial financial relationships (Davis and Mizruchi
1999; Dooley 1969; Patman 1968). Bank financing of conglomerate acquisitions,
and bank dominance of corporate pension fund management—with the latter
frequently (from an effective control standpoint) making banks the largest shareholders of industrial firms—were particularly important areas of post–WWII
relational deepening, which actually prompted a great deal of regulator alarm
in the 1960s and 1970s (Kotz 1979; Lybecker 1973; Patman 1968). Meanwhile,

---

[10] The Clayton Antitrust Act only banned interlocking directorships between competing firms in
the same industry, and thus did not affect interlocks between financial and nonfinancial firms (Dooley
1969).

nonfinancial corporate cash reserve management seems to have been the most important source of demand driving shadow banking innovation by banks themselves; from the development of the repo market by investment banks in the 1950s (Minsky 1957), to Citi's popularization of commercial bank-issued negotiable certificates of deposit in the early 1960s (Summers 1980). Simultaneously, the offshore Eurodollar market exploded in size in the 1960s above all as a mechanism for the major Wall Street banks (again led by Citi) to do business with their American multinational corporate industrial clients overseas (Helleiner 1994; Shaxson 2011). The "NY–LON" axis at the heart of the GFN (see chapter 4) thus reinvented itself largely to cater to the needs of American industrial multinationals, with Wall Street emerging as the center of shadow banking, and London as the center of offshore banking.

2.5 The Legal Assembly Line

In short, capitalism is fundamentally a financial affair, that more or less by definition *must* revolve around the centralized market machines of the leading financial centers to allow for the monetary instruments via which it operates to be produced, exchanged, and accumulated. However, while the production of liquidity and efficiency by markets and intermediaries is a critical component of what finance *does*, this is not actually what finance broadly, or money specifically, *is*. Rather, financial instruments, as well as the institution of capital broadly, are composed of bundles of abstract accounting and legal–contractual constructs— or what Pistor (2019, 2) describes as "assets plus legal code," or more specifically "assets placed on legal steroids" (Pistor 2019, 11). In other words, finance is fundamentally a system that seeks to represent, organize, and control the underlying "real" economy through abstract legal and accounting constructs, with the whole vast apparatus of financial markets, intermediaries, etc. to a large extent just a means to the end of manufacturing these constructs.

At a basic level, financial legal production can be described in terms of a two-pronged logic of (1) creating legal–contractual packages, or investment vehicles (including the legal components of firms themselves), to house bundles of assets and liabilities, that allow for the rights and obligations, risks, etc. associated with them to be distributed among various parties in clearly defined ways, and (2) creating legal–contractual instruments attached to these asset and liability-holding compartments, that render various elements of the rights and obligations of the parties to them freely exchangeable on financial markets (whether through sale or redemption; Wójcik 2012). As described by Pistor (2019), the legal "steroids" that foster capital accumulation basically entail the creation of structures that systematically concentrate the upsides of rights and obligations—ideally in the form of simultaneously greater potential for gain, limited liability for loss, and market exchangeability (i.e. money-like constitution) of instruments—in one set of hands, while externalizing the downsides in other sets of hands. The latter, in general, consist of the general public, often represented collectively via the supporting role of the state. Closely intertwined with the construction of these legal "steroids" are the creative possibilities of accounting; in other words, the strategic exploitation of the ambiguities surrounding the basic question of how and what to count as assets or liabilities, or profits and losses, and when.

There are a number of different ways in which this asymmetrical distribution of legal–contractual upsides and downsides, coupled to creative accounting, can be effected. However, from the standpoint of the geographic organization of the financial system, what is most important is that the devices via which finance, and indeed capital itself are constituted in a legal–contractual and accounting sense, basically reside in an abstract ideational reality that does not necessarily correspond to the geography of the real physical world—including the geographic distribution of the key decision-making actors within the financial system itself (Picciotto 1999). The resulting legal–geographic fungibility is crucial to the logic of financial legal production, as elements of this production typically require a highly specialized legal, regulatory, and fiscal environment that is often difficult to achieve within a "normal" social and political context. On the one hand, this production requires a legal framework that recognizes, and basically gives free rein to, what can be described as a condition of hypercommodification in socioeconomic relations—wherein anything and everything can be represented in forms that allow it to be negotiated, bought, and sold, through processes of market exchange characterized by maximal freedom and sanctity of private contract. On the other hand, this production requires an exceedingly strong protection of private property rights, and specifically of the rights attached to the most abstract and complex forms of *financial* property, which face a pervasive risk of disruption from a whole array of directions ranging from the legal standing of creditors' rights, to taxation (Haberly 2021; Palan 1999; Picciotto 1999; Pistor 2019).

The impulse for the financial sector, and indeed capitalism more broadly, to seek a special, privatized legal zone of extreme private contractual freedom and property rights protection, manifests itself in the recurrent historical emergence and reproduction of the so called offshore system. As can be seen in Figure 2.2, which shows all of the world's stocks of bilateral international direct and portfolio investment and bank lending and deposits as of 2018, offshore is not some footnote to the organization of the global economy. Rather, as Maurer (2008, 160) puts it, "offshore in many ways *is* the global economy," at least at the level of the legal vehicles whereby it is structured. The People's Republic of China, for example, could be parked inside of the Cayman Islands in the figure, while the Benelux countries are almost as large as the United States. In fact, were state-level data on this available, the United States itself would likely appear as a massive offshore booking hub at the heart of the figure, with the majority of its investment stocks nominally registered in or through the state of Delaware.

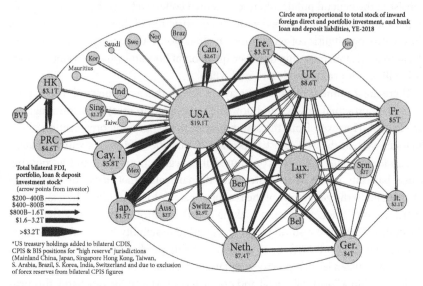

Fig. 2.2 The world map of international financial legal production, 2018
Sources: authors; data from IMF CDIS; CPIS; BIS LBS; US Treasury.

Crucially, law itself fundamentally resides, insofar as it possesses any binding enforceability, within the state as an institution. Consequently, the construction of "offshore" entails, in practice, an attempt to construct a wall *within the state* that partially insulates a privatized zone of contractual law, from the messy complexity and contestation of "onshore" politics (see also Haberly 2021). Given the basic co-constitution of law and politics, the impulse to construct this wall is inherently self-contradictory. However, there are two ways that it can be partially simulated. The first is through the creation of "offshore facilities," which are specialized legal jurisdictional platforms for designated "foreign" or "international" activities and actors, so defined as to be of limited relevance to the world of "local" politics. The second is through what can be dubbed "offshore states," whose overall architecture is constituted so as to insulate, as much as possible, the legal realms of private contract and property from either tyrannical or mass participatory democratic political disruption. Broadly speaking, the first of these represents a specialized zone wherein "the more mobile economic sectors are provided with a separate regulatory space," while "the state can carry on discharging its traditional roles as though nothing had happened" (Palan 1999, 19–20). Meanwhile, in the second, the state itself is transformed into a "fast and flexible private lawmaking machine" (Shaxson 2011, 184).

In practice, this is an extremely delicate balancing act, as the transgressing of the boundary between "fast and flexible private lawmaking" and outright corruption directly threatens the basis of rule of law on which the financial sector depends. Successful offshore states often have specialized technocratic institutional carve-outs within the state structure that help to square this circle. For example, the Bank of England was able to act, to some extent, as a quasi-autonomous state within a state in promoting the development of the offshore Eurocurrency markets both in the UK itself, and its overseas territories and dependencies, after WWII (see chapter 5; Hampton 1996; Shaxson 2011). Meanwhile, in the world's most important shell company incorporation jurisdiction, Delaware, the legislature has for decades maintained a tradition of essentially rubber-stamping the annual company law revisions submitted by the corporation law section of the Delaware State Bar Association. Delaware has, moreover, also preserved the (elsewhere discarded) tradition of maintaining a separate court of chancery specializing in matters of *equity* (i.e. contractual fairness), which basically operates as a parallel legal system serving the business incorporation sector (Strine 2005).

Typically, the ability of offshore states to function effectively or sustainably hinges, fundamentally, on their being relatively small in population. This allows for the maintenance of a tightly knit, stable local political consensus around the position of the offshore sector, and maximizes the per capita level of local economic spillover benefits—or, as critics would say, the level of local economic structural capture—that can be generated by serving a given-sized external market for financial services (Bullough 2019; Christensen and Hampton 1999; Shaxson 2011; Strine 2005). In the contemporary world, the UK seems to be more or less at, or even beyond, the absolute practical size limit for a polity to politically *sustain* something like the character of an offshore state in relation to finance. On the other hand, offshore facilities can be and routinely are set up by more or less any type or size of polity, with most large economies in the world offering at least some such facilities. Importantly, offshore states and offshore facilities are in practice often combined and blurred, with even the most quintessentially offshore states (including the proverbial "small islands") usually putting in place regulatory "ring fences" to maintain a separation between the offshore sector and local economic activities (Shaxson 2011; see also chapter 5). Indeed, the long-term political stability of the most successful offshore states to a large extent directly rests, paradoxically, on their ability to (as Polanyi would have noted) "embed" specialized hypercommodified legal–jurisdictional spaces within a highly cohesive local social context (e.g. small Continental European welfare states) that could potentially be destabilized by the offshore sector, if left unprotected from it.

Together, offshore facilities and offshore states comprise what can be described as offshore jurisdictions (OJs). Crucially, regardless of how such jurisdictions are constituted, offshore typically appears, from an "onshore" standpoint, to be a zone of regulatory and legal *subtraction*. However, on the terms of its own logic of operation, offshore fundamentally needs to be conceptualized as a zone of intensified private legal–contractual institutional *construction*, or what Le Marchant (1999) dubs a "laboratory of financial innovation." Above all, this entails providing a specialized framework of law, as well as a toolbox of specific recognized flexible legal forms (e.g. for entities, contracts), that create the maximum scope for private actors to develop creative strategies for the "coding" of innovative contractual arrangements (see chapter 6). The demand for this type of flexible legal environment is pervasive, as deep-pocketed private actors can, as Pistor (2019) observes, typically earn a more reliable return on their "investment" in state power by employing teams of lawyers to create and defend innovative contractual devices in the realm of law, than by venturing into the messy and unpredictable political realm of legislation. Such a flexible legal environment is particularly crucial to financial innovation, as the primary bottleneck to the production of monetary quality in this context is usually as much one of contractual legal design and standing, as of the design of market architecture, statistical algorithms, financial technologies, etc.

The role of what can be broadly described as offshore jurisdictions (OJs) in breaking the legal bottlenecks in financial innovation, and in the "coding of capital" broadly, is extremely old. Indeed, as far back as the Middle Ages, the operation of commerce and finance in Europe, within a profoundly decommodified socioeconomic order, was essentially dependent on the ability of merchants to conduct business within the framework(s) of the Law Merchant, rooted in the "offshore" jurisdictional spaces and legal forums of the fairs and free cities (see section 2.8). This special legal regime for business and finance, designed by merchants, and rooted in jurisdictions directly controlled by merchants, provided streamlined alternatives to medieval dispute resolution mechanisms such as, for example, trial by combat or ordeal—which were, needless to say, bad for business. Just as importantly, it provided the basic foundation of legal standing for the key types of contracts and entities used for the organization and conduct of business (instruments such as bills of exchange, various types of partnerships and company), and provided a legal basis for what were often radical concepts of financial relational commodification—for example from the 1400s in relation to (now taken for granted) ideas of debt security negotiability (Kadens 2004; 2015; Munro 2001; 2003; Pirenne 2014).

This medieval lineage of specialized "offshore" commercial law has been passed down to the present day via English common law and equity, into which medieval Law Merchant was directly incorporated as a source of legal precedent via a series of court decisions in the 17th and 18th centuries (Baker 1979). This legal framework has, even while evolving over time, essentially continued to function in its original medieval role, and remained rooted in an uneven geographic patchwork of legal–jurisdictional places. Neal and Quinn (2001, 9) describe, for example, how in the 17th and 18th centuries "merchant-controlled cities of Amsterdam,

Hamburg and London, the Law Merchant governed the settlement of disputes arising from protested bills of exchange. By contrast, in the royal cities of Paris and
Madrid, the often arbitrary law of the monarch could disrupt the web of credit
that supported Western Europe's prospering trade." More recently, this medieval
commercial legal heritage has, in conjunction with various repurposed elements
of English common law (e.g. related to trusts; see Pistor 2019), evolved into a
number of specialized, and even more flexible variants in the various nodes of
Britain's "offshore archipelago" of current and former colonial territories (Palan
et al. 2010; Shaxson 2011). Cayman Islands law, for example, provides a particularly favorable environment for the domiciliation of complex legal–contractual
arrangements (e.g. securitizations) due largely to its affirmation of extreme principles of private legal–contractual freedom—for example, the absence of a concept
of legal "substance over form," the provision of statutory backing for complex arrangements of contractual payment prioritization, and a mostly contractual à la
carte regime of bankruptcy resolution (see chapter 6).

Since the 19th century, several US states have also developed their own "offshore" branch variants of English common law and equity—with key innovations
largely centering on pushing the boundaries of the commodification of the corporation as a legal entity, as well of that of other entity types such as the trust or
partnership (Arsht 1976; Hansmann 2006; Strine 2005; Yablon 2007). New Jersey,
located just a few minutes away from Manhattan by boat or rail, played a particularly important role as a paper legal platform for American business in the
19th and early 20th centuries. In 1841, it seems to have been the first state to
generally adopt a "plutocratic" corporate voting principle of one vote per *share* as
opposed to the hitherto prevailing US "democratic" model of one vote per *shareholder* (or various hybrids between the two; Dunlavy 2004). Later, in the 1880s,
New Jersey granted the sprawling multistate industrial "trusts" a legal refuge from
anti-trust actions by various state governments, by creating the device of the holding company (basically the prototype of the offshore "shell company") with the
unconditional right to own other companies—which most importantly could be
projected across state lines (Collins 2013; Roy 1999; Yablon 2007). The ability of
massive industrial groups to trade in their legally shaky, trust-based structures for
New Jersey holding company-based structures, also opened the door to their listing directly on the New York Stock Exchange, thus helping to drive a centralization
and expansion of the US securities market (Navin and Sears 1955).

By the end of the 19th century, most of the largest US firms had reorganized themselves under New Jersey holding companies, often in conjunction with
broader restructurings led by Wall Street investment banks such as JP Morgan (see
section 2.8). Moreover, after New Jersey reformed its corporation laws in 1913,
American business simply moved its legal base next door to Delaware. This had
essentially copied New Jersey's corporation law in an effort to capture the paper incorporation business, and has managed to remain to the present day the

jurisdiction where most major US corporations are incorporated—essentially by offering a stable zone of escape from the messy and complicated world of big-city-dominated democratic politics in the states hosting major financial centers, which can flexibly and reliably cater to the needs of business and finance (Mahoney 1966; Arsht 1976; Palan et al. 2010). In the late 20th century this position, notably, placed Delaware at the center of an important series of private legal battles surrounding an escalation of the commodification of the corporate form via the rise of hostile takeovers. Delaware's role here has been a complex one that underscores the open-ended logic of the legal–contractual sandbox provided offshore; with the fate of American corporations and their employees largely being determined, for the past several decades, by the outcome of private legal arms races playing out in the arena of Delaware, as opposed to public regulation either nationally or in other states. Prior to the early 1980s, Delaware company law's embrace of private contractual freedom tended to favor hostile bidders, due the state's failure to impose the sorts of restrictive anti-takeover statutes implemented in other states in the 1970s (Black 1977).[11] Later, however, the same principle tended to uphold the legal standing of takeover defenses (e.g. poison pills) put in place by companies in response to the takeover wave of the 1980s, to protect managerial power; with power later swinging back to shareholder groups (coordinated by activist investors and proxy advisers; see section 2.8) able to organize to amend company bylaws, to have such defenses removed (Jacobs 2011).

The other side of the offshore coin of extreme private legal–contractual freedom is the quest for extreme forms of private property rights protection. One key area in which these two come together is in the emphasis of offshore jurisdictions, in general, on the protection of creditors' rights—which is an area of private property rights protection that is both particularly crucial to finance, and particularly contentious and constrained in "onshore" political contexts. In addition to the structure of bankruptcy law (see chapter 6 and Pistor 2019), and the rights of creditors to enforce payment of transferred debt securities (negotiability; see Munro 2003; Pistor 2019), the legality of lending with interest itself has historically been a perennial attraction of the offshore legal menu, wherein creditors' rights and private contractual freedom intersect.

The role of what can be described as offshore jurisdictions in enhancing regulatory "flexibility" in this area dates back in Europe to the Middle Ages. Crucially, prior to the 15th–17th centuries (or even later depending on the jurisdiction) the ecclesiastical and secular usury laws that pervaded Europe did not simply ban lending at excessive interest, but rather banned lending at any interest whatsoever (Munro 2003). In theory, this should have been more or less fatal to the entire existence of the European credit system. However, regulatory workarounds were

---

[11] This notably, became moot in 1983 with the US Supreme Court *Edgar v. MITE Corp* ruling, which overturned most state-level anti-takeover statutes (Wardwell 1983).

developed centered on the bill of exchange[12]—which if structured properly could render lending with interest "technically legal" (or least not demonstrably illegal). This device became the core of what was essentially an elaborate system of medieval and early modern European shadow banking, dominated for centuries by various Italian merchant banks (Munro 2003; Usher 1934). Playing a central role in lubricating this system were the "exchange fairs" set up by the leading Italian banking houses at a number of locations throughout Europe (e.g. Geneva, Lyons, Besançon, Piacenza, and various cities in Champagne), under the sponsorship of various local authorities (Braudel 1985; Edwards and Ogilvie 2012; see section 2.8). Beyond providing a financier-designed and controlled legal enclave to facilitate international bill clearing, enforcement, and contractual dispute resolution (subject to some version of Law Merchant), the fairs typically offered "a sort of extra-territorial exemption" (Kohn 1999a, 18) from usury laws. This allowed for any residual debts remaining after bill clearing to be openly repackaged and rolled over as interest-bearing loans (*deposito*), helping to streamline the operation of the international credit system (Boyer-Xambeau et al. 1994). *Offshore banking*, in the special jurisdictions of the exchange fairs, and *shadow banking*, via bills of exchange, thus developed in a symbiotic relationship with one another. Notably, like the modern offshore Eurocurrency markets (see Pezzolo and Tattara 2006 for a direct comparison), the exchange fairs served mostly as hubs for abstract paper operations booked in various currencies, with contemporary observers remarking that "nothing was rarer than money at these clearing fairs" (Boerner and Hatfield 2017).

Much more recently, in the 1970s, skyrocketing nominal market interest rates, precipitated by skyrocketing inflation, caused US banks to slam up against all manner of statutory caps on both deposit and lending interest rates. On the deposit side, the avoidance of these caps (e.g. regulation Q) was a key factor that accelerated the expansion of both shadow banking within the USA, and the offshore Eurodollar market outside of the USA (Cook and Duffield 1979; Palan et al. 2010). Meanwhile, on the lending side, South Dakota became the nominal center of the American credit card industry in 1980 after it amended its usury laws to eliminate interest rate caps for banks. This allowed Citibank to locally implant a model of banking regulatory jurisdictional ambiguity it had pioneered in the offshore Eurodollar market (Shaxson 2011; Vanatta 2016). Not to be outdone, Delaware quickly followed suit.

Also critical to offshore, from the standpoint of private capital's own understanding of what is meant by private property rights protection, is at least partial

---

[12] That is, a payment device where party A ("drawer") orders party B ("drawee") to pay party C ("payee") a certain amount of money on a certain date (where A and C are often the same party, e.g. a company making a sale to another company B which thus owes A/C money). A check is a type of bill of exchange drawn on a bank that is payable on demand; where, e.g. A is you, B is your bank, and C is your electrical utility.

freedom from state taxation. One aspect of this is the facilitation of outright tax avoidance and evasion, which is indeed probably the single most widespread purpose for which the offshore system is used today (Cobham and Jansky 2018; Palan et al. 2010; Zucman 2015). However, as we discuss in chapter 6 (see also Wainwright 2011), tax avoidance is not always an end in and of itself offshore. Rather, offshore "tax neutrality" also often enables the use of innovative private contractual coding to achieve non-tax related goals, as many types of complex structures and deals are simply not financially viable unless tax "leakages" can be eliminated from all of their intermediate stages. The world's largest shell company hub, Delaware, for example, is of limited usefulness as a corporate tax haven due to US state-level formulary apportionment-based corporate taxation (Clausing 2016); however, the menu of entities that it offers are extremely useful as tax-neutral fiscal pass-throughs in all manner of different applications. Securitizations, for example, are usually only viable if the numerous entities and transactions involved are structured as tax-neutral devices that pass tax liabilities along entirely to ultimate investors; in the context of which Delaware, or in many cases Cayman Islands vehicles, are particularly useful (see chapter 6 and Wainwright 2011).

Finally, it is also important to note that in the western world historically, and still in much of the world today, businesses (and business owners) often have legitimate concerns about the political and legal risks of arbitrary property expropriation by the state (see section 2.8). Offshore jurisdictions have thus, both today and historically, often operated in something of a normative grey area wherein they are simultaneously used by the same actors for genuine property rights protection purposes, along with (and in some cases not clearly distinguishable from) various abusive and often illicit purposes. Such ambiguities are particularly evident in, for example, the role of Cyprus in relation to business in the former Soviet republics (Nougayrède 2013 2019).

Crucially, while the offshore world is anchored by specific offshore jurisdictional places, it ultimately functions as an integrated network-relational space that transcends any one of these places—and, indeed, the basic distinction between "onshore" and "offshore" in any clear-cut geographic sense (as discussed in chapters 5–7). Most importantly, the fact that abstract offshore legal devices reside in an altogether separate plane of existence from the "real" world of people and things, means that they actually pervasively coexist with, and have the potential to directly influence, the real world at any given geographic location—or in many cases multiple locations at once (Picciotto 1999). Offshore, in this sense, is not "somewhere else"; it is all around us. For example, the Cayman Islands domiciled vehicles that issued most of the collateralized debt obligations (CDOs) implicated in the global financial crisis simultaneously resided, from a substantive standpoint, within both the global financial command center of Wall Street, and the suburban landscape of the American sunbelt. Indeed, as we discuss in chapter 6, most of these vehicles were actually established in ways that allowed them to, for various purposes, exist simultaneously in multiple jurisdictions even in a nominal legal sense (often via Caymans issuer/Delaware co-issuer arrangements).

This sort of interdimensional geographic porthole character of the offshore world is critical to its operation, as the ability of "real" financial centers to function as sites of financial innovation often hinges on their ability to operate *within* an offshore legal space, while the ability of offshore jurisdictions to serve as flexible sites for creative legal–contractual innovation hinges on access to the skills and markets of "real" financial centers (Coe et al. 2014; Wójcik 2012). Crucially, however, these networks cannot simply be taken for granted to be able to automatically touch down out of their abstract offshore plane of legal reality into any given location onshore. The porthole to the offshore world must rather be opened through specific legal gateways—from the various types of charters granted by medieval sovereigns to cities and merchants (both local and foreign), to contemporary networks of international trade and investment agreements and tax treaties, and facilities such as the US portfolio interest exemption. These networks of interjurisdictional legal gateways, importantly, tend to be embedded in broader overarching political relationships—e.g. between colonizer states and their networks of overseas colonial dependencies (see chapter 7; Palan et al. 2010; Papke 2000; Pistor 2019).

Ultimately, both the network-relational nature of offshore, and the ease with which ostensibly "onshore" states can themselves create offshore facilities, means that the distinction between offshore and onshore is inherently murky—with the condition of interjurisdictional mobility and ambiguity itself, as opposed to any particular list of jurisdictions, ultimately defining offshore as a *space*. In particular, the fact that offshore platforms are generally remote-controlled from substantive financial centers means that both, in effect, typically operate under hybrid legal regimes. Historically, for example, the Medici organized their banking empire as a network of partnerships spread across various jurisdictions, including exchange fair platforms such as Geneva, even while contractually subjecting these partnerships to the Florentine merchant court as a legal forum for intragroup matters (de Roover 1946; 1963). Today, a combination of New York and Delaware law applies to many structures, deals, and activities involving vehicles that are legally domiciled in the latter, but substantively managed from or conducted in the former (Eisenberg and Miller 2006). More broadly, the law of the dominant substantive financial centers is pervasively exported, and combined in various ways with the laws of offshore incorporation jurisdictions, by actors who may have little or no substantive presence in either place. Today, exported New York and English law primarily play such a role (see Knuth and Potts 2015; Pistor 2019). Historically, the medieval Law Merchant seems to have largely consisted of exported Italian commercial law, that was applied directly or adapted in various ways in other contexts, and thus took on an international character (see Kadens 2004; 2015).

This basic condition of offshore–onshore ambiguity and juxtaposition is also critical in relation to the definition of tax and regulatory jurisdiction, as it implies that most of what happens "offshore," in a legal–jurisdictional sense, can be, and frequently is, taxed or regulated by onshore states (e.g. on an actor home state or substantive host territorial basis)—provided that onshore states have the administrative capacity and/or political clout to actually do this (see chapters 5 and 6). The United States, notably, can often claim and assert such extraterritorial regulatory and fiscal jurisdiction more or less unilaterally, for example in relation to the information exchange agreements it has imposed on the vast majority of the world's financial firms in conjunction with the 2010 Foreign Account Tax Compliance Act (FATCA) (Bean and Wright 2015; Emmenegger 2015; Lips 2018; see also section 2.8). Most often, however, extraterritorial state authority relies on the negotiation of multilateral frameworks (whether treaty or "soft law" based), often mediated by international organizations, wherein states agree on key shared principles governing the geographic reconfiguration of sovereignty. Examples include the various Basel Accords and Concordats in relation to the principle of home state consolidated capital supervision of international banking groups (see chapters 5 and 6; Herring 2007; Kapstein 1991), and a succession of OECD frameworks that have established key principles in relation to controlled foreign corporation (CFC) rules and other aspects of multinational corporate and personal taxation (e.g. Common Reporting Standard for information exchange; Lips 2018; Palan et al. 2010; Picciotto 1992; Vlcek 2007). Ironically, as we discuss in chapter 6, financial devices are often created offshore (e.g. the aforementioned Caymans-based CDOs) because some particular aspect of being offshore (tax efficiency, particular points of law, etc.) helps their users to conduct other types of arbitrage *within extraterritorial* onshore regulatory frameworks (e.g. Basel consolidated capital rules).

Notably, the fact that the "offshoreness" of a polity is largely predicated on its smallness, means that the most important substantive financial centers, which are typically located in large cities riven with social and political tensions, are not always optimally positioned to play an offshore role. The nature of politics in South Dakota or Delaware, for example, is actually much better suited to support an offshore legal and regulatory environment than politics in New York (Bullough 2019). However, the distinction between offshore paper, and onshore substantive financial centers, is nevertheless quite blurry, with the latter usually assuming, to the greatest extent that is politically feasible, a "midshore" character (see chapter 5). In this capacity, substantive financial centers offer aspects of or facilities within local law, regulation and taxation that provide greater levels of flexibility and property rights protection, in relation to particular activities, than can usually be found elsewhere. The midshore jurisdictional compromise, in leading financial centers themselves, features prominently throughout the history of western finance. According to Munro (2014a), medieval and early modern

Italian city-states and Holland were just about the only places in Europe that did not maintain restrictive international exchange and capital controls. Moreover, as noted above, medieval Italian city-states acted as the principal homelands and hubs for Law Merchant–based financial legal innovations directed at circumventing ecclesiastical usury laws—even as their merchant banks developed and made use of more quintessentially offshore exchange fair jurisdictions that afforded even greater legal and regulatory flexibility, and lay outside of the incessant maelstrom of urban social and political conflict in the Italian cities themselves.

Later, in the 15–17th centuries, the Netherlands (including Antwerp) and England simply legalized usury outright (replacing interest bans with interest caps), and expanded the liquidity of paper debt instruments by legally recognizing bearer securities (opening the door to e.g. bank notes), helping to pave their way to the center of European finance (Munro 2003). In the 18th century, the ability of Amsterdam to serve as the dominant market liquidity machine in Europe seems to have been further aided by the fact that it allowed types of forward derivatives contracts on public securities that were banned in Britain and France (Carlos and Neal 2011). Even as London displaced it as the central global financial clearinghouse in the early 19th century, Amsterdam remained in relative terms a "lightly regulated market" (Cassis 2006, 12) that played a key role as a site for the listing and trading of foreign securities, which as of 1840 comprised around 80% of the stocks listed there. Making Amsterdam even more attractive as a midshore trading hub was the fact that the derivative instruments in which it specialized could be structured in a tax-neutral way that avoided stamp duty (Cassis 2006). Similarly, as New York surpassed London as the world's leading financial market after WWII, the latter moved increasingly into a midshore role centered on the lightly regulated Eurodollar market—with New York itself, from the 1980s onward, to some extent also assuming such a role within the context of its International Banking Facilities (IBFs).

2.6 Safety Net

The elements of financial market liquidity and efficiency production on the one hand, and legal–contractual optimization on the other hand, are the two most immediate requirements of monetary quality production. However, they are by themselves not fully sufficient as foundations for this process. Specifically (as we discuss in chapter 9), no matter how informationally efficient markets are from the standpoint of their ability to incorporate future expectations into current prices *based on the level of information and knowledge possessed by their own participants,* the actual level of knowledge about the future that these participants possess is inherently imperfect. In other words, even if the "information arbitrage efficiency" of a market is relatively high, a market's efficiency is invariably quite low when defined in terms of "fundamental valuation efficiency"—i.e. the ability of markets to *correctly* predict and price future events (Tobin 1984). This uncertainty, in turn, undermines the credibility of the legal–contractual packaging of the financial instruments that are valued and traded in these markets. It ultimately makes no difference how thoughtfully or elaborately a contractual structure is designed, or how reliable or efficient the legal system for enforcing it is; if the ability of parties to actually honor their obligations is simply, as is often the case, rendered impossible by unforeseen circumstances, then the entire edifice of law and contract is liable to come abruptly and uncontrollably crashing down (Pistor 2013).[13]

What this means is that the process of endogenous credit instrument creation (defined broadly so as to include all more or less liquid financial instruments) needs to be grounded in some underlying bedrock of stability that possesses a quasi-exogenous quality in relation to—i.e. that can somehow operate beyond the parameters of—both market operation and private contract. In practice, these quasi-exogenous anchors come in three key varieties: rents, reserves, and backstops.

The first of these, "rents," are in some respects the weakest of the three as far as the preservation of financial stability is concerned. However, the role that they play is so pervasive that they are arguably just as important as the other two in terms of their overall impact. Broadly speaking, a financial instrument can be said to be grounded in rents insofar as the underlying future cash flows or asset values backing it can, to at least some extent, be viewed as a "sure thing" due to their being partly insulated from the vagaries of market forces. Both today and historically, a crucial component of this has generally been literal land rent value, which, as long as it is not excessively leveraged (needless to say an important proviso), has always been seen as a reliable bedrock on which to ground the production of liquid financial instruments (Kohn 1999b; Pistor 2019). The medium for a huge proportion of transactions, in most economies, is essentially just land that has been transformed into money through the magic of mortgaging, which goes on to circulate as bank deposits, mortgage-backed securities, etc. Notably, the most concentrated and stable land rents are usually found in the leading financial centers themselves, which in this sense automatically generate, internally, a crucial source of readily available large-scale stable collateral for their own credit-production activities (which, as noted by Pirenne, has been an important phenomenon since the Middle Ages; see Pirenne 2014, 165).

---

[13] Indeed, as observed by Pistor (2013, 315), any attempt to fully enforce all legal contracts during periods of financial crisis "would result in the self-destruction of the financial system."

Apart from land rents, the other major sources of rents providing a relatively stable backing to the production of liquid financial instruments, are monopoly and state protection rents, which are in most cases at least partially connected to one another. What makes these particularly important is the fact that financial investors usually have fairly little interest in becoming associated with real productive activity—which is an inherently uncomfortable alien territory for capitalism compared to its "home ground" of mercantile and financial arbitrage and speculation (Braudel 1985)—unless production can be somehow packaged into an at least quasi-monopolistic, rentier form. The goal here is not simply, or even always primarily, to maximize the level of profits that can be earned in the future; rather, backing the issuance of financial instruments with rents is a way to maximize the market value of these instruments right now.

As noted by Schumpeter, this has particularly important implications for the logic of entrepreneurship. Specifically, the ability of innovative firms to raise capital by issuing financial instruments (both on the market and via banks) is strongly predicated on their potential to earn monopoly profits by dominating a new area of activity (Schumpeter 1934; 1942). "Pure" Schumpeterian innovation rents, however, are in many respects fairly weak (as well as a priori uncertain) in and of themselves, and in practice the state typically plays a critical role in creating and protecting the rents (including innovation-linked) that back the production of profits and financial instruments. Historically, the financial revolution in 18th-century Britain largely revolved around the issuance of liquid securities by chartered corporations (including the Bank of England as well as colonial trading companies) backed by specific state-designated monopoly privileges (Neal 1990). Later, the development of both large-scale markets in industrial securities, and large-scale bank lending to industrial companies in late 19th- and early 20th-century Germany and the USA, was initially limited mostly to monopolistic manufacturers able to consolidate and operate behind tariff barriers (Hilferding 1981; Minsky 1992c; Navin and Sears 1955). More recently, the developmental states of East Asia brought this process of rent-induced financial production under the (partial) control of the government (Amsden 1989; Johnson 1982; Ozawa 2001). In postwar Japan, for example, industrial firms could essentially throw caution to the winds in drawing on state-subsidized credit to engage in bubble-like leveraged investment in state-designated priority industries, based on the understanding that the first-mover market shares thereby claimed would subsequently be protected by state-sanctioned cartels (Johnson 1982). Today, state-protected intellectual property rents—often enhanced in value via offshore legal packaging structures—provide a particularly crucial bedrock for global, and in particular American financial production, with "intangibles" now likely accounting for greater than 80% of S&P 500 market capitalization (Ponemon Institute 2019).

Crucially, while rents both mitigate the underlying credit risks attached to, and maximize the underlying cash flows backing financial instruments, they do not deal with the problem of liquidity risk—i.e. the prospect that those who hold these instruments will all suddenly seek to sell or redeem them at once. This poses a particularly severe problem given that the very promise of liquidity that makes instruments more money-like directly intensifies the risk of snowballing mass redemptions of these instruments (i.e. "runs"). Dealing with this problem requires two additional exogenous (i.e. non-contractual or market-based) supports for financial monetary production: namely reserves and backstops.

Reserves, or "high powered money" (Bordo 1990; Wray 2000), are a type of monetary instrument whose value and liquidity are somehow strongly protected from the vagaries of market-risk and contract, and which are as such used as a basis for the denomination and redemption of endogenously generated private credit money (or money-like) instruments. By either indirectly ensuring access to or directly keeping reserves on hand, financial actors (and the financial system as a whole) establish a more or less credible basis for the promise that the weaker instruments that they issue will actually be convertible into, or will at least hold their value in terms of, this reserve standard. Ultimately, the feature of reserve money that gives it credibility is the fact that its creation is an exogenous process from the standpoint of private financial actors themselves, that lies beyond their control. There are basically two types of reserve money in this sense: precious metals, which cannot be created at all but rather only physically dug out of the ground, and state credit money, which by definition can only be created by the government (Ingham 1998; Wray 2000).

In theory, state credit money—whose value derives from the fact that private actors require it to pay their debts (i.e. taxes) to the state (Innes 1914)—provides a much more flexible and powerful reserve foundation for the financial system than bullion. Most importantly, the supply of state credit money can be regulated as opposed to fluctuating semi-randomly based on mineral prospecting and production. However, the ability of state credit money to actually fulfill a reserve function depends, in a literal sense, on the quality of the state's credit, which until recently was generally (and in much of the world still is) abysmal. Indeed, throughout the history of medieval and early modern Europe, the state itself was basically the main source of systemic credit risk in financial markets, via unending strings of sovereign defaults by nearly all governments (Braudel 1985; 1992; Roos 2019).

In some sense, state credit money always existed in the form of the frequently debased coinages that medieval and early modern European governments issued for their populations to use for transactions and tax payments, and jealously guarded behind capital and exchange controls (see Munro 2003; 2014a; Neal 1992). The financing of sovereign borrowing, moreover, was always a staple rentier income stream for the financial sector (largely via privatized tax farming), and from the 15th century, sovereign debt came to serve as an important backing for financial instrument production via the transposition of devices originally developed for land finance (the precursors of sovereign bonds; see Munro 2003). However, what most states could not do, until relatively recently, was repackage their own debts *as* a form of state credit money that possessed sufficient credibility to serve as a high-powered monetary reserve. Rather, the credibility of state coinages as a reserve money, for high-level international financial transactions, historically rested mostly on their actual precious metal content, which needed to be assayed for coins to be usable as a reserve money (with values frequently being computed in terms of some other "imaginary" unit of account money; Kindleberger, 1984; Neal 1992). One really critical point here is the importance of not conflating credit money in general, with state credit money specifically, as credit money usually consists primarily of *private* IOUs, regardless of what sort of reserves these IOUs are grounded or denominated in (see Graeber 2011). Indeed, narrowly framed theories of both commodity money and state credit money are in this respect both rather problematic, insofar as they both place excessive emphasis on reserves as opposed to the bulk of the actual financial and monetary system.

The use of bullion as a foundation for reserves did not fully disappear until the 1970s, when the USA closed the gold window once and for all (at least to date). However, the shift from the use of precious metals to state credit money as a reserve money was a gradual one, that was, importantly, also intertwined with the development of the state's role in providing backstops to the financial system. In the West, at least, this transition began in the mercantile city-states of northern Italy in the late Middle Ages (Ingham 1996). These were confronted by a double problem, namely that the private deposit banks at the center of the local payments system were constantly failing—thus wreaking havoc on the local financial system and economy (see Kohn 1999c; Mueller 1997; Usher 1934)—and the fact that the state often needed to raise large amounts of money on short notice to fund wartime spending (which imposed a particularly intense fiscal burden on these very small states; Molho 1995). The solution was to create (proto)-central banks, which were guaranteed by the government to ensure the integrity of the payments system on the one hand, and which, in addition to holding bullion, could flexibly purchase and hold large amounts of government debt on the other. In Venice, these payments and sovereign finance functions were separated into two different public banks; in Genoa, however, they were brought together into a single institution, the Casa di San Giorgio (Braudel 1985; 1992; Fratianni 2006; 2009; Taviani 2015; Ugolini 2017).

The crucial bottleneck hindering the broader adoption of this system was, as noted above, the fact that the state's promises to repay, or at least service the interest on its debt, had to be credible. In this respect, Italian city-states were centuries ahead of the major European territorial states; not least because their governments were usually directly controlled by the same merchants and financiers that they owed money to (Fratianni 2006; Ingham 1996; Roos 2019; Taviani 2015). Ultimately, the full combination of central banking innovations that these Italian cities pioneered in the Middle Ages would neither be implemented nor seriously improved upon elsewhere until the late 17th and early 18th English/British "financial revolution" that followed the Glorious Revolution of 1688.[14] With the backing of a newly empowered Parliament, that strongly represented commercial interests, and controlled a rationalized, centralized, and credible fiscal apparatus—and England moreover now temporarily merged, via the Dutchman sitting on the throne, into the same state as Europe's premier financial market in Amsterdam—this political upheaval directly opened the door to the foundation of the Bank of England in 1694 (Braudel 1985; 1992; Cassis 2006; Neal 1990; 2000).

In an innovative public financial architecture, the Bank of England financed its purchases of sovereign debt by issuing paper bank notes that could circulate widely as state credit money (Ugolini 2017). Just as importantly, the bank's stock functioned as an additional money-like tradable instrument that allowed the government to perform a massive sovereign "debt-for-equity swap" operation (Quinn 2008). The combination of the credibility and tradability of the bank's stock (and the stock of trading companies also financing the UK national debt, e.g. the South Sea Company), was particularly important in allowing the British state to conjure into existence a deep international credit line that could be tapped during periods of intense warfare; as these securities were in high demand, and were extensively traded and speculated upon, in Amsterdam in particular (Carlos and Neal 2011; Wright 1997). Ultimately, the bank played a critical role in both supporting a radical expansion of the scale and complexity of the British financial system, and in helping to finance the accumulation of what was even by present-day standards a staggering national wartime debt load. The latter, by the early 19th century, reached roughly 250% of GDP (Ventura and Voth 2015)—prompting endless prophecies of doom about the inevitability of national insolvency, that were incessantly reiterated by deficit critics despite never being borne out (Braudel 1992). This borrowing was facilitated by the suspension of bank note gold convertibility between 1797 and 1821, during which time Britain operated on basically a modern fiat state credit money reserve system; with the credibility of this system being reinforced in 1799 by the creation of the world's first personal and corporate income tax regime (Braudel 1992; Cooper 1982; Neal 2000).

The Bank of England, importantly, did not simply passively administer the provision of reserves to the broader financial system, but also intervened when necessary to support this system as a "lender of last resort"—via a circular process of issuing expanded BoE liabilities to allow it to lend to private financial institutions, who could in-turn use this funding to purchase the BoE's expanded liabilities. It thus actively accommodated and responded to the liquidity needs of

---

[14] In this respect, the 1609 Amsterdam Wisselbank was a far less sophisticated and multifaceted institution than the Bank of England, and in some respects even the Casa di San Giorgio, as it was created purely as a centralized clearing and reserve depository bank which for the most part only held bullion as an asset, and did not play a role in sovereign finance (Neal and Quinn 2001).

both the government and the private financial sector (Bordo 1990; Kindleberger and Aliber 2005). Notably, the 1844 Bank Act, which sought to limit the Bank's ability to expand its note issue beyond the value of its gold reserves (plus a fixed ceiling of sovereign debt holdings), in theory constituted a major step backward from the standpoint of the management of such an active monetary and liquidity support policy. However, the act also promoted a sharpening of the distinction between the role of the Bank of England (or at least the note-issuing department thereof) as central bank (even if still a privately owned one), and Britain's other banking institutions, wherein the latter conducted deposit banking, as opposed to issuing notes, while holding their reserves at the Bank of England (Eltis 2001; Knafo 2008; Polanyi 2001). Furthermore, the discipline that the limitation of Bank of England balance sheet expansion was supposed to have imposed on the British banking industry was thrown to the winds whenever a serious financial crisis erupted. In such situations, the Bank Act was simply suspended to allow for an elastic expansion of Bank of England liquidity support (Eltis 2001; Kindleberger and Aliber 2005; Polanyi 2001)—or, more precisely, an expansion of liquidity support to the "names of sufficient standing" discussed in section 2.4. Too big to fail was alive and well in the 19th century; in 1890, for example, the Bank of England and the Chancellor of the Exchequer jointly intervened to save Barings by guaranteeing its liabilities and orderly reorganization (Fishlow 1985).

The repeated 19th-century suspensions of the Bank Act, and more overt interventions such as the rescue of Barings, marked the beginning of a long historical line of failed, and as Polanyi and Minsky would point out, fundamentally chimerical attempts by central banks around the world, to impose discipline on the credit creation activities of banks via market-based as opposed to administrative or regulatory mechanisms. Crucially, however, the institution of the central bank has proven to be almost infinitely elastic and resilient in its ability to expand its protective umbrella over both the state and private financial sectors, even when the high-powered reserve money that it issues has assumed an entirely state-credit-based form. Ultimately, as discussed in section 2.8, the key question under this arrangement is essentially just who gets access to, and under what conditions, the protective umbrella that is provided by the most powerful reserve-currency-issuing central bank(s), that are backed by, and in turn back, the credit of the most powerful state(s) (Kindleberger and Aliber 2005; Pistor 2013).

2.7 The Gatekeepers

Together, the processes of financial market liquidity and efficiency production, legal–contractual packaging, and the provision of various quasi-exogenous anchors for financial asset value and stability, can be seen as the three basic building blocks of monetary quality production. However, the logic of these three components of monetary quality production, both individually and in combination, is also surrounded by a number of important paradoxes. Two of these stand out as particularly important from the standpoint of the present analysis.

The first is the fact that the development of competitive markets, capable of generating financial instrument liquidity and efficiency, can never really be extricated from the persistence, and indeed the active production of, various noncompetitive monopolistic elements. This is linked, at one level, to the pervasive dependence of financial instrument production (as well as underlying profit generation in general) on the backing of various rentier or at least quasi-rentier assets and cash flows. However, it also stems from a deeper paradox in the mechanics of how markets generate liquidity and efficiency, which can be dubbed the "platform paradox." This paradox results from the fact that markets, far from being some default mode of socioeconomic organization, are extremely complex institutions, which need to be constructed in a way that renders manageable a whole host of interconnected informational and relational overhead and transaction costs. There are two basic dilemmas in this respect. The first is that the process of price discovery itself is expensive. Moreover, as markets become more efficient (i.e. better at discovering prices), the cost of price discovery continuously increases, even while the rewards of price discovery continuously decrease (Fama 1995; Grossman and Stiglitz 1980; Lo 2004; see also chapter 9). Meanwhile, the second dilemma is that the more liquid a financial instrument becomes, i.e. the more heavily it becomes processed by the blender of financial market trading and intermediation, the harder it becomes for those holding it to actually keep track of and exercise influence over the underlying "real" activities referenced by it; whether home mortgages blended up and packaged into securities, or blue-chip corporations owned by dispersed shareholders (see Berle and Means 1932; Jensen and Meckling 1976; La Porta et al. 1999 Shleifer and Vishny 1997).

In practice, the resolution of these informational and relational dilemmas nearly always implies that more market, in one sense, must to at least some extent be supported by less market in some other sense. This goes beyond Braudel's (1985) characterization of the home of capitalism as the monopolistic "anti-market" of restricted competition (see also Arrighi 1994 and Wallerstein 2004); rather, it implies that the institution of the market itself is to a large extent grounded in the anti-market. More specifically, the ability of markets to function as decentralized information processing and resource allocation machines, is basically conditioned by the availability of some *centralized* informational and relational nexus—or "platform" (see chapter 9). In some cases, the way that this occurs is extremely obvious. In some financial systems, for example, nearly all activity is mediated through a handful of enormous universal banks, which are able to efficiently centralize both the collection and processing of information (regarding credit risks, investment opportunities, etc.), and the relational monitoring and in-fluencing of clients (most importantly borrowers, whether corporate, household, or sovereign; see Hall and Soskice 2001; Zysman 1983). However, the impera-tive to achieve some form of informational and relational centralization is no less present—and is indeed if anything more acute—in what appear to be more superficially "market-based" arrangements.

One crucial manifestation of this, is the inexorable geographic tendency toward the emergence of a centralized hierarchy of financial centers. These are able to both generate and reap powerful spatial informational and relational efficiency rents simply by virtue of their ability to bring large numbers of well-informed actors together, into close proximity with one another. In this respect, Bassens and van Meetern (2015, 754) describe the network of world cities at the heart of the global financial system as "an obligatory passage point for the relatively assured realization of capital." Furthermore, even the most liquid and efficient competitive financial markets invariably both generate, and to a large extent rely on, various types of monopolistic (or at least oligopolistic) choke points that help to relieve—but can also ruthlessly exploit—market informational and relational overhead costs. In the case of securities market, one key such choke point is the securities exchange itself. Notably, historically, the most successful exchanges in-variably developed as basically exclusionary, cartel-like organizations, from the standpoint of which financial institutions (and financiers) were able to govern and play various key lucrative roles within them. Both the London and New York Stock Exchanges, for example, developed along these lines. This was not simply a ques-tion of rent generation and exploitation. Rather, the absence of effective systems of state regulation that could monitor and police private behavior, and most impor-tantly introduce and enforce some basic standards for market transparency, meant that any securities market that developed along less exclusionary lines was in-evitably plagued by massive reputational and governance problems, that ultimately sabotaged its development (Davis et al. 2003; Neal 2011; Stringham 2002).

The central role, and potential insider abuse of such securities exchanges, underscores the inherently fine line between what can be described as the transaction-cost-reducing role of the monopolistic market platform, and the rent-concentrating role of such platforms. Closely linked to the development and operation of securities exchanges in this respect, as well as the various dilemmas and abuses associated with them, are investment/merchant banks. These control the process of securities manufacturing and initial valuation and sale, and play a crucial role in the making of markets in existing securities. This multidimensional role, in turn, translates into a tremendously powerful position as gatekeepers and intermediaries across a whole array of areas including the monitoring and advising of corporate governance, strategy, and organization, the management of client as-sets, and, most importantly, the linking of securities issuers and investors together (see Fernandes and Giannati 2014; Jones 2003; Wójcik 2011; chapter 3). Further-more, investment banking is usually linked more or less directly or indirectly to commercial banking (or shadow banking substitutes), which allows investment banks to manage the creation of credit needed to supply liquidity to all of these various parties.

In theory these roles, like that of the securities exchange, entail a "utility-like" function of providing a neutral platform to help reduce market transaction costs. In practice, however, the fact that investment banks intermediate between dif-ferent types of clients whose business is of uneven value to these banks, with investment banks furthermore also typically (at least prior to the Volker Rule in the USA) trading on their own accounts as well, opens the door to potentially massive abuses and conflicts of interest (Avei et al. 2018; Mehran and Stulz 2007). More broadly, brokers and investment managers/advisers often appear to siphon off more income from clients in fees than they actually generate for clients in added value (Fama 1995; Malkiel 2013). As described by Gennaioli et al. (2015, 92), the business of these intermediaries is essentially based on reaping positionality-derived informational and relational rents, wherein they "help investors make risky investments and are trusted to do so even when their advice is costly, generic, and occasionally self-serving."

Notably, client disillusionment with the rent-extracting nature of the securities industry has increasingly fostered the rise of so-called passive investment man-agers. These focus entirely on driving down the transaction and overhead costs in markets to the absolute bare minimum, and returning the savings to their clients, by employing extremely cheap algorithms to simply "buy the market" (Malkiel 2013). Paradoxically, however, as we discuss in chapter 9 (see also Fichtner et al. 2017), this drive to reduce market informational and relational overhead costs has ultimately encouraged the emergence of an increasingly monopolistic landscape of passive investment advisers, due to the imperative of maximizing cost savings through economies of scale. This centralization tendency, moreover, appears to also be occurring in other areas of FinTech development. This, like the digital economy broadly, tends to be characterized by a counterintuitive symbiosis be-tween the creation of increasingly liquid and efficient markets on the one hand, and the growing concentration of monopoly power in the hands of the platform providers that operate and oversee these markets on the other (see discussion in chapter 9).

So far, these examples of the platform paradox all involve situations wherein financial firms act directly as market-makers or intermediaries. However, the fact that this paradox ultimately concerns the resolution of informational and rela-tional dilemmas *surrounding* market operation, means that many of the most powerful platform providers are not actually directly involved in market opera-tion. Rather, they act as standard setters, code enforcers, and information brokers. The highly concentrated passive fund management sector, for example, is guided

THE PARADOX OF STICKY POWER   69

in its operation by an equally concentrated index-provider sector (Petry et al. 2021). Moreover, the market share of even the largest passive managers is dwarfed by the "proxy advisory" firms that tell institutional investors, who in most cases could not care less about corporate governance, how to vote as shareholders. In this sector, two tiny and basically unknown firms—Institutional Shareholder Services and Glass Lewis—hold a virtual duopoly within the United States, via which they exercise an almost ludicrous amount of power over US corporate governance (Copland et al. 2018). Corporate management consultancy, more broadly, is also a highly lucrative and concentrated sector, which is dominated by a handful of major standard-setting and enforcing players (Froud et al. 2000; Jones 2003). Also highly centralized, from a market power standpoint, are the various firms which assess and code the credit risks of various borrowers and instruments. The most well-known and historically important of these are the major rating agencies (Sylla 2002b; White 2010). Increasingly important, however, is the gargantuan AI-powered risk-management platform Aladdin, which is sold by the world's largest passive fund manager, BlackRock, to other fund managers on a subscription basis, and now guides the allocation of somewhere between $US20 and $US30 trillion in assets (see Beales 2020, Massa 2020, and chapter 9).

Finally, the legal–contractual "coding of capital" also creates a strong impetus toward monopolistic market platform development, which is directly intertwined with the logic of formation of the other types of platforms described above. In particular, anything involving the crafting and administration of complex multinational legal–contractual structures, linking together various offshore and onshore jurisdictional components, requires access to highly specific and esoteric sets of skills and relationships that are controlled by a tiny number of elite firms. Particularly important, in this respect, are the so-called Magic Circle of London corporate law firms, and the "Big Four" global accounting firms (Flood 2007; Galanter and Robers 2008; Murphy et al. 2019; Pistor 2019; Sikka 2008; Wainwright 2011).

We dub this whole interwoven conurbation of market-marking and standard-setting gatekeepers the "financial and business services" (FABS) complex.[15] While its architecture has become increasingly elaborate over time, the basic contours of how this complex is organized and operates are very old. In the late medieval and early modern period, the leading merchant banks of various Italian city-states were for centuries the dominant market-makers and standard setters of European finance. The Genoese, for example, were able to establish a central position within European finance in the 16th century largely via their shrewd design of the abstract paper booking platforms and clearinghouses of the Besançon and Piacenza

---

[15] Other terms that have been used to describe the same basic concept are "advanced business services" (see Coe et al. 2014; Wójcik 2012) or "advanced producer services" (Bassens and van Meeteren 2015; Sassen 1991; Taylor et al. 2014). We call this sector "financial and business services" to emphasize the paramount role of finance in these activities.

exchange fairs (Arrighi 1994; Braudel 1985; 1992; Roos 2019; see section 2.8). This system was characterized by a sharp duality between the decentralization and liquidity of the offshore wholesale markets hosted by the fairs, and the concentration of power in the hands of the firms that were able to determine and exploit the parameters of their operation. As Braudel (1992, 157) describes it, "the focal point of the whole system was not even the city of Genoa itself, but a handful of banker-financiers (today we would call them a multinational consortium)." Via their design of the "Piacenza fairs, the capital of the Italian cities was all drained toward Genoa. And a multitude of small investors, Genoese and others, entrusted their savings to the bankers for modest returns" (Braudel 1992, 168).

Similarly, in the 18th century, a handful of leading Dutch and Anglo-Dutch merchant banking houses served as the key coordinators and gatekeepers within the Amsterdam–London dyad that emerged as the heart of the European financial system (Carlos and Neal 2011; Cassis 2006). Like the Genoese financiers of the 16th and 17th centuries, their ability to assume a central trusted role in the management of "other people's money" was a particularly important component of this influence. According to Carlos and Neal (2011, 36), the:

> major merchant bankers in Amsterdam ... did very well indeed during the stock market manias that swept through Paris and London in the years 1719–20, but mainly by providing safe havens for flight capital from France ... firms such as Andries Pels & Sons, Clifford & Company, de Neufville and, by the middle of the eighteenth century, the house of Hope became the icons of patrician capitalists. It is the interaction between the leading stockjobbers in London and the leading merchant bankers in Amsterdam that illuminates the complementarity of the two financial centers—London, focused on developing the financial products most attractive for public investors, and Amsterdam, managing private portfolios in search of high, secure returns.

More recently, in the late 19th and early 20th centuries, Wall Street law firms and investment banks, and most importantly JP Morgan, effectively restructured and centralized the larger part of the organizational and legal institutional fabric of American big business (Coffee 2001; De Long 1991; 1992; Navin and Sears 1955; Pujo 1913; Yablon 2007). This involved, first, the major Wall Street law firms taking the lead in "actively drafting" (Yablon 2007) the 1880s corporate holding company legislation of New Jersey, in response to demands from their financial and nonfinancial corporate clients. Morgan (with other Wall Street investment banks and law firms) would then manage the New Jersey (and later Delaware)-based corporate restructurings and the NYSE IPOs of these firms—and thereafter retain a long-term influence over their management through a combination of direct or indirect (e.g. voting trust) equity holdings and board representation, to ensure the maximization of shareholder value.

As described by Coffee (2001), while this entailed a monopolistic concentration of corporate control, it also catalyzed the development of a liquid American securities market characterized by dispersed ownership, which in the course of Morgan's corporate restructurings and listings passed out of the hands of founders and into the hands of fragmented stockholders. What was particularly important in allowing Morgan to catalyze this restructuring of American business (e.g. in relation to the turn-of-the-century industrial merger wave, and the financing/restructuring of railroads before this) was its unusually strong reputational standing and connections on both sides of the Atlantic as an *Anglo-American* investment house (Carosso 1987). This allowed it to present a rare credible and trusted face for the wild west world of American business in the old money centers of Europe, with Morgan's power largely deriving from the extent to which it could thus simultaneously act as a key gatekeeper for US corporate access to the New York and European capital markets (Coffee 2001; De Long 1991; Hannah 2007; 2011; Navin and Sears 1995). Indeed, JP Morgan ultimately "[saw] himself as the bearer of the sound London practices of an ethical conservative banker to a new venue where they were badly needed" (Hannah 2011, 117). In some sense, a new institutional gold standard was thus created for financial and corporate governance rationalization, whose purpose was ultimately to ensure that the long-term interests of dispersed and footloose shareholders were represented in Morgan-linked firms (see Coffee 2001). As the president of the New York, New Haven, and Hartford Railway once famously boasted, "I wear the Morgan Collar, but I am proud of it" (De Long 1991). By the same token, however, this entailed a tremendous extraction, centralization, and abuse of wealth and power, via the construction of monumental monopolistic rent-production machines—not simply in any one industry, but rather sprawling across huge swaths of multiple interconnected industries and critical infrastructure systems.

2.8 The Racket

The ultimate political fate of Morgan's seemingly unstoppable offshore monopoly rent machines—whose very success at employing New Jersey–based legal structures to sidestep a succession of state-level anti-trust actions, ultimately called forth a crushing consolidation and application of US federal regulatory power (Collins 2013; De Long 1992; Kovacic and Shapiro 2000; Yablon 2007)—underscores the second key paradox in the development of the financial system. This is the fundamentally chimerical nature of the impulse of financial firms (or other actors) to somehow liberate themselves from the political complexities of dealing with the state, by seeking refuge in a literally or figuratively "offshore" realm of private legal–contractual freedom and ironclad property rights protection. At a basic level, law itself cannot exist in any meaningful (i.e. enforceable) form without the backing of state power. Beyond this, however, the process of financial monetary production itself is inevitably both dependent on, as well more or less vulnerable to the interference (and in some cases predation) of, what Tilly (1985) dubs the "protection racket" of the state.

This dependence on state "protection," is to a large extent a direct result of the need for the financial sector to establish an exogenous foundation for the credibility of financial instruments beyond the vagaries of market forces or private contract. The critical role of the state in mediating the production of monopoly and other types of rents that ground the process of financial monetary production—as well as the underlying production of profitable cash flows in capitalism—is one key component of this. Furthermore, to the extent that financial firms want to move beyond the primitive and unstable world of bullion-based reserves, they need to have access to some powerful state. More specifically, no matter how badly wealthy investors or multinational firms want to reduce their tax burden, the very value of the instruments that they produce and purchase is fundamentally predicated on the existence of some powerful state tax authority that can provide credible backing to state credit money—and that, just as importantly, possesses a central bank in control of the production of state credit money that can swoop in to rescue both market participants, and the finances of the state itself, in a crisis. Access to such a safety net, crucially, is not simply a matter of survival for financial firms, but also of profitability, as it allows the financial system to operate at much higher levels of leverage, maturity and liquidity mismatches, and broadly speaking risk, than would otherwise be possible (Farhi and Tirole 2012). Last but not least, capital, in general, ultimately needs a strong state protector simply to shield it from the predatory danger emanating from other states—as well as to, if possible, serve as a predatory ally that can open up profitable opportunities for "primitive accumulation" (Arrighi 1994; Tilly 1985; Wallerstein 2004).

The ability of finance to construct and move throughout a multijurisdictional network-relational offshore world does not fundamentally alter any of the basic facts of this dependence on the state. Rather, the net effect of finance's ability to transcend the narrowly defined geographic jurisdiction of any particular state, is simply the concentration of global authority in the hands of the limited number of exceptionally powerful states that are in a position to enroll border-crossing financial networks within their umbrella of "protection." Consequently, just as the paradoxical effect of market development is the fostering of concentrated nodes of monopolistic private power, the paradoxical impact of the political and legal unbundling of the state into offshore and onshore spheres—driven by the inherently inverse relationship between the scope of the freedoms and rights that private capital can carve out within a particular jurisdiction, and the geographic size of that jurisdiction—is actually the emergence of ever-more pervasive, intrusive, and globally centralized conurbations of *transnational* state political power. Within these conurbations of power, the offshore and onshore faces of the capitalist state are continuously brought back together into a symbiotic, even if uneasy alliance with one another (see also Haberly 2021).

The general logic of how this works has operated more or less continuously since the earliest beginnings of western capitalism in the Middle Ages. As described by Pirenne (2014), states and merchants both occupied an extremely weak and constrained social and political position in this context, with power rather primarily being distributed throughout a profoundly decommodified, conservative, and decentralized matrix of landed feudal and ecclesiastical institutions. Profit-making activities in general were a moral anathema, and (as noted above) technically illegal when they involved the basic financial operation of lending at interest, while merchants to a large extent had a free-floating semi-vagabond status at the margins of society and respectability (Graeber 2011; Pirenne 2014). Crucially, however, this disconnection of merchants from the rigid matrix of medieval feudal society also presented an opportunity to not just merchants themselves, but also the initially weak monarchical states. For the latter, building relationships of protection and patronage with merchants afforded an opportunity to cultivate an independent source of state revenue and borrowing capacity that lay outside of the control of the sprawling feudal landed hierarchy, which could be used to hire military forces answerable only to the monarch. Meanwhile, for the merchants, this arrangement offered freedom from the stifling and rigid environment of feudal society, and its replacement with a more streamlined and flexible relationship with the state as patron and protector (Pirenne 2014).

Over the long run, merchants and states thus used each other as battering rams to break down the constraints imposed by feudal society on the expansion of their own wealth and power—a process that, as North (1993, 4) describes, ultimately revolved around the merchants' role in financing a "kaleidoscope of endless warfare at every level."[16] Playing the central role in mediating this exchange of "protection and justice for revenue" (North 1993, 5) between states and merchants were, from the outset, two quintessentially "offshore" jurisdictional institutions: namely the free city, and the fair. The fairs were basically the forerunners of the modern offshore facility (see Pezzolo and Tattara 2006), and were special jurisdictional zones that were set up by public authorities, at various levels, to allow for long-distance commercial and financial activity to be conducted under special sets of rules. In practice, these rules centered on some version of the Law Merchant, administered by a fair court, and where necessary enforced in fair matters by the broader court systems of the authorities hosting and sponsoring the fairs (Boyer-Xambeau et al. 1994; Edwards and Ogilvie 2012; Kadens 2004; 2015; Pirenne 2014). The fairs, essentially, provided a comparatively liberal institutional environment

---

[16] Keeping in mind that it was not always *kingdoms*, per se, as opposed to particularly powerful duchies, etc., that served as the nuclei for long-term state formation

with far-reaching exemptions from the pervasively restrictive regulation and protectionism in surrounding areas, that by the same measure was circumscribed in a way designed to minimize the fair's disruption of broader local economic and social relations. Like offshore facilities today, this role was controversial, with one critic of the fairs (as late as the 18th century) summarizing their role as the "[granting of] special privileges and franchises ... to trade at particular places, whereas it is laden down elsewhere by dues and taxes" (Braudel 1985, 92).

While the fairs initially developed as free trade zones, some of them (as described in section 2.5), evolved into specialized international financial wholesale platforms, or "exchange fairs." These were set up and operated by the leading international Italian merchant banks as special financial jurisdictions under the sponsorship of various hosting governments, and became the central European hubs for bill of exchange-related international clearing and wholesale market activities. Crucially, notwithstanding the attempts of some to theorize the fairs as a sort of libertarian fantasyland of purely private rulemaking beyond the reach of the state (Milgrom et al. 1990), the operation of both the fairs, and Law Merchant more broadly, were ultimately grounded in their connection to and backing by public authorities (see Kadens 2004; 2015). The original exchange fairs emerged out of the Champagne trade fairs in the 12th century, and apparently derived a competitive advantage from the willingness of the counts of Champagne to act, in some cases extraterritorially, as debt enforcers on behalf of international merchants and financiers (Edwards and Ogilvie 2012). In the early 1400s, the leading European exchange fair moved to Geneva under the sponsorship of the dukes of Savoy (with usury having been legalized in Geneva under its 1387 charter; see Innes 1983), before the French monarchy managed to lure the center of international Italian banking to the exchange fair in nearby Lyons. This was done by providing the Lyons fairs with sweeping exemptions from usury laws, capital and exchange controls, and taxes (tolls, etc.), as well as by strategically deploying economic sanctions against Geneva designed to disconnect it from the crucial French market (Boyer-Xambeau et al. 1994; de Roover 1963.

Meanwhile, the free city was essentially the forerunner of the modern "offshore state," wherein the merchant community was given a corporate charter that granted them substantial leeway to write and enforce their own laws locally. This allowed the cities to, in conjunction with the fairs, function as comparatively liberal legal and regulatory enclaves of commercial and financial capitalism. However, the rights awarded by the state also came with strings attached, most important among which was helping the state to fund its military spending by raising large amounts of money from the cities, on demand, via fiscal levies or borrowing. Crucially, the corporate charter of the free cities nearly always specified various lucrative privileges in matters of trade, which were exploited monopolistically via guild associations, and later via joint stock companies (Burell 2011; Davies 2012;

Ogilvie 2014; Pirenne 2014). The free cities thus basically acted as fiscal and financial funnels that concentrated monopoly profits into the hands of merchants and financiers based in semi-autonomous offshore jurisdictional spaces, and placed the resulting financial firepower at the disposal of the sovereign. Meanwhile, as for the system of fairs, the fact that a clearly demarcated legal–jurisdictional line was, at least in theory, drawn between the world of commerce and finance in the cities on the one hand, and the realm of feudal agrarian society on the other, created a buffer against various types of sociopolitical frictions. Thus, in addition to fueling the growth of the "protection racket" of the state, the free cities also provided an early geographically mediated pathway for the Polanyian "double movement" of dialectical state-led commodification and *social* protection, smoothing the political road to the ascendance of capitalism over (or more precisely within) the feudal social order (see Haberly 2021).

Notably, whereas the free cities remained caged within, and indeed directly fueled processes of state-making in the consolidating monarchies of Western Europe (particularly France and England), in the messy European political and economic heartland of the Holy Roman Empire, the most successful cities basically broke away as (de facto or formally) free agents (Tilly 1989). In many cases, this entailed the formation of multi-city confederacies such as the Hanseatic League, Switzerland, and the Netherlands. However, regardless of how far they strayed from the political obligations specified in their original charters, the basic reality remained that the offshore half of the capitalist state—i.e. the freewheeling enclaves where capitalists could write their own rules—could not sustainably survive or function without engaging with and at some level sheltering within the umbrella of onshore state political and military protection. To be fair, these cities and city-state confederacies in some cases managed to become leading naval and maritime trading powers in their own right, and indeed the dominant *global* naval and maritime trading power in the case of the 17th-century Netherlands. However, the very fact (as described in section 2.4) that the intensely liberal offshore characteristics of these polities could only be sustained politically and socially within a relatively small state package, imposed structural limitations on this independence, which became progressively more acute as the territorial monarchies grew in power (Braudel 1992; Tilly 1989). Given that the onshore territorial powers, for their part, retained a profound need to tap into the liquidity manufacturing capabilities of these offshore states, the stage was thus set for an endlessly shifting historical musical chairs of border-crossing offshore–onshore "*liaisons dangereuses*" (Tilly 1989)—wherein the free agent cities of Central Europe, and their merchant communities, attached themselves to, and in turn helped to fuel the expansion of, the state-making protection rackets of larger and more powerful neighboring monarchies (Braudel 1992).

The Plantagenet English monarchs, for example, developed close trading and financial relationships with, and granted various privileges to, both the Hansa and

Florentines at various times (Palais 1959). The latter were handed control of the English wool trade and export duty revenues in the 14th century, in exchange for sovereign loans used to finance the Hundred Years War, with the two largest Florentine banking houses ultimately collapsing after the English crown defaulted on its loans (Munro 2014b; Roos 2019). Meanwhile, the tiny maritime republic of Genoa, while a naval force to be reckoned with, was on land "congenitally weak" and "constantly surrendering to other powers, either forcibly, voluntarily or out of prudence" (Braudel 1992, 158). Ultimately, it was pulled into a close relationship with the Habsburg monarchy in the 16th and 17th centuries after the latter helped to drive out French occupation of the city. This relationship involved the Genoese managing the bottomless wartime liquidity needs of first the Holy Roman Emperor Charles V, and then his Spanish successors, by centralizing the credit networks of northern Italy and placing them at Habsburg disposal via the exchange fairs established first at Besançon (under direct Habsburg jurisdiction) and later at Piacenza (initially under papal jurisdiction, and then under the duke of Parma, who acted as the Habsburgs' main military enforcer in Northern Europe; Arrighi 1994; Braudel 1985; 1992).

Meanwhile, the Genevan private banking sector, which was from the 17th century dominated by French Huguenot protestant merchants who had fled religious persecution under Louis XIV, rose to prominence in a paradoxically close political relationship with the same French crown that had been persecuting these merchants; playing an important role in financing France's wars from Louis XIV himself to Napoleon (Cassis 2006). This relationship with Louis XIV was so politically embarrassing and destabilizing, in protestant Geneva, that it seems to have motivated the original legislation of banking secrecy there in 1713 (Faith and Macleod 1979). For the most part, this lending involved the offshore "round tripping" to the French crown of flight capital that had been illicitly siphoned out of France itself.

This was never far away either geographically or politically, with France assuming joint responsibility with Bern and Zurich for guaranteeing Geneva's political stability in 1738, and helping its ruling oligarchy to put down a local rebellion in 1782 (Faith and Macleod 1979; Seaward 2017; Venturi 1991). As noted in section 2.7, a great deal of French flight capital also apparently ended up in Amsterdam, which together with Geneva acted as the main foreign markets for British sovereign debt securities in the 18th century, while also contributing substantially to French sovereign finance (Carlos and Neal 2011; Cassis 2006; Wright 1997). This implied, notably, that the French crown was not only being financed by the offshore wealth of its own citizens, but also in a roundabout sense fighting against this wealth in its wars with Britain.

In an equally awkward situation, the central role that the Dutch had come to play in providing trade credit in Habsburg Spain, during the rule of Charles V over both countries, was apparently not actually severed by the Dutch revolt against the Habsburgs (Braudel 1992). Moreover, after the Genoese tired of dealing with Spain's endless sovereign defaults in the 1620s, the Spanish crown seems to have shifted largely to borrowing from its former Dutch subjects—returning full circle to the days when Charles V himself had promoted the development of the local government debt securities market in the Netherlands to deepen his own sovereign borrowing capacity (Braudel 1985; Munro 2003; Neal 1990). As for Geneva's relationship with France, financial secrecy was critical to greasing the wheels of these politically awkward financial relationships, with Portuguese New Christian merchants apparently acting as front men for the Dutch in Spain (Braudel 1985).

Over the long run, both Switzerland and the Netherlands would end up neutralizing themselves politically largely to facilitate their ability to serve as platforms for such politically fraught international commercial and financial activities (Cassis 2006). However, for such small states to chart an independent course on the arena of international finance, without the benefit of the at least de facto protection of some powerful patron state, was a dangerous game. During the American revolutionary war, for example, the scale of neutral Dutch financial and material support for the United States and France prompted Britain to declare war on the Netherlands; which was a shock and a debacle for the by then militarily weak Dutch (Carlos and Neal 2011; Cassis 2006; Wilson 1941). Shortly thereafter, both the Netherlands and Switzerland were occupied by France during the Napoleonic wars; which had particularly disastrous consequences for Amsterdam's position as a financial center, from which it never fully recovered, due to the partial severing of its connections with the world beyond Continental Europe, and in particular Britain (Cassis 2006; Neal 1992). During WWII, in contrast, the fortunes of these two neutral entrepôts diverged. While the Netherlands was invaded and occupied once again, Switzerland managed to avoid this fate, rather being strong-armed into serving as an international financial hub for the Axis powers—for which it furthermore managed to politically head off the postwar retaliation that the Allies originally planned against its banking sector, largely by providing generous loans to Britain and France (Guex 2000).

Notably, even while the medieval offshore system was enrolled into increasingly modern state-making processes *inside* of Europe, a new global offshore system of trading hubs was steadily advancing *outside* of Europe with European commercial expansion. Anchored by such commercial and financial strongpoints, the European empires—culminating in the globe spanning edifice built by Britain—sprawled out as vast clanking messes of chartered corporate, federal, feudal (e.g. via local vassal potentates), treaty-stipulated extraterritorial judicial (e.g. in China), and direct rule, ringed by vaguely defined informal peripheries of gunboat diplomacy. In the Caribbean, for example, "free ports" were designated by Britain and the Netherlands in the 17th and 18th centuries to normalize already de facto state-sponsored smuggling activities directed primarily at Spain's colonies in Latin

America (Hunt 2013). Meanwhile, European commercial and imperial expansion in Asia was for centuries mediated through a constellation of special jurisdictional zones. Some of these were created and operated on the terms of Asian governments themselves, for example in Guangzhou or Nagasaki prior to the mid-19th century. Others were seized by force, for example the European-administered "treaty port" enclaves established throughout China in the 19th century, the last of which persisted until the end of the 20th century (Bickers and Jackson 2016; Taylor 2002).

Like the Caribbean free ports, this East Asian colonial offshore archipelago grew out of industrial-scale European state-sponsored criminality, centered in the 19th century on the opium trade. "Legitimate" finance followed in its wake (Bickers and Jackson 2016). Hong Kong, granted a corporate charter in 1843, and from its inception constituted as an open "free port" where British merchants (i.e. international drug dealers) could avoid what they dubbed the "arbitrary caprice" of Chinese jurisdiction (Tsang 2007, 21), rose to particular importance as a regional commercial, financial, and political strongpoint. The development of this role was strongly conditioned by Hong Kong's relationship with another treaty port enclave, Shanghai. Shanghai become the leading securities market in the greater China region, even as this market was closely linked to Hong Kong as a legal base—with not only the Hong Kong and Shanghai Banking Corporation (HSBC), but also the Shanghai Stock Exchange itself, being legally incorporated in Hong Kong (Fan 2010).

Additional details on the historical coevolution of the offshore and onshore faces of the capitalist state can be found in Haberly (2021), as well as in chapter 5 (for offshore banking) and chapters 7–8 (more broadly). The bottom line, however, is that the discombobulated apparatus of the medieval European state—characterized by a semi-articulated hodgepodge of offshore and onshore political and legal spaces—never actually evolved into a cartoonish Westphalian nation-state form wherein the various functional components of the state were simply welded together into neatly self-contained political monoliths. Rather, the fragmented and jumbled structure of the European medieval state simply mutated and expanded, over the centuries, into equally complex and messy multilayered structures in the form of globe-spanning multinational European empires, which in the wake of decolonization were in turn absorbed into (or at least had to contend with) a new global American imperial political structure. The latter, crucially, promoted the spread of national self-determination, even while pretty much openly rejecting the idea that this conferred an *unconditional* sovereignty on nominally independent states that placed their internal affairs outside of the sovereign prerogative of the United States. Indeed, since WWII, the USA has consistently claimed, and frequently exercised, the ostensible right as "leader of the free world" to intervene wherever it wants, whenever it wants, and however it wants, whenever another state refuses to bend to its will. Most importantly, this global sovereign prerogative is not only regarded as legitimate by the USA itself, but also by large numbers of other countries, who have long been not only willing to affirm and acquiesce to it, but also to actively support and even try to help save the edifice of American authority whenever its strength is in doubt.

Ultimately, as underscored by the contemporary USA, the capitalist state is not really a territorial political geographic association at all. It is rather a free-range political–economic actor network (see Haberly 2011) and "legal fiction" (Picciotto 1999) that has grown and mutated over the centuries through a succession of increasingly powerful and centralized, but still highly complex, hierarchical, and vaguely bounded forms—all of which have, in their own way, a broadly imperial character. Throughout the evolution and growth of these messy variegated imperial structures, the medieval invention of the offshore system has continued to function basically as originally created and intended. In other words, it has continued to serve as a zone of private legal–contractual freedom and property rights protection that appears to lie outside of the reach of "the state" from the standpoint of smaller and weaker polities, but is actually to varying degrees under the protection and at the disposal of whatever imperial authority is in a position to provide or claim such protection. This is not to say that this is a situation that is always, or even usually produced *intentionally*. Rather, the fact that it has been so persistently reproduced over such long historical timescales stems from the power of its structural logic; wherein capital continuously concentrates its legal footprint within tiny jurisdictional platforms that it can easily control, but which, due to their tiny size, are incapable of providing "protection" to the capital they host, or even to themselves.

Today, the USA is (still for now) the overwhelmingly dominant authority that presides over and provides "protection" to this system. Indeed, the global tax haven system, operating through shell company devices pioneered by the trusts in 19th-century New Jersey, largely acts as a giant global financial vacuum cleaner for the concentration and sheltering of intellectual property–based profits by US multinational technology and pharmaceutical firms—made possible by the US government's aggressive international advancement and protection of IP law, and its role in financing most of the key underlying technological innovations themselves (Bryan et al. 2017; Mazzucato 2013). These offshore IP repositories in turn act as vast holding bags for debt securities purchased with retained profits—with about 40% of US corporate offshore bond portfolios recycled right back into lending to the US government (Pozsar 2018)—and provide the underlying rents backing trillions of dollars of corporate securities issued by Silicon Valley and other knowledge-industry firms in the USA. In net, this structure basically converts the US multinational corporate avoidance of *foreign* taxes on IP-generated profits, into US taxable investor capital gains (and following the 2017 Tax Cuts and Jobs Act immediate US corporate tax liabilities; Davis 2019)—and possibly also lowers US federal borrowing costs by creating a captive offshore market for government debt securities (see Pozsar 2018). Essentially, it is the direct functional successor of the

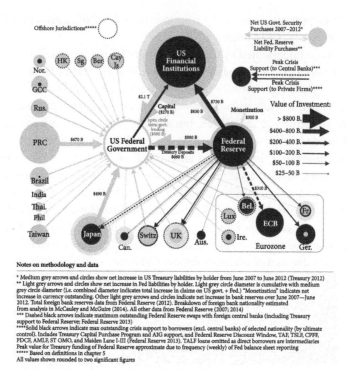

Notes on methodology and data

* Medium grey arrows and circles show net increase in US Treasury liabilities by holder from June 2007 to June 2012 (Treasury 2012)
** Light grey arrows and circles show net increase in Fed liabilities by holder. Light grey circle diameter is cumulative with medium grey circle diameter (i.e. combined diameter indicates total increase in claims on US govt. + Fed.) "Monetization" indicates net increase in currency outstanding. Other light grey arrows and circles indicate net increase in bank reserves over June 2007–June 2012. Total foreign bank reserves data from Federal Reserve (2012). Breakdown of foreign bank nationality estimated from analysis in McCauley and McGuire (2014). All other data from Federal Reserve (2007; 2014)
*** Dashed black arrows indicate maximum outstanding Federal Reserve swaps with foreign central banks (including Treasury support to Federal Reserve; Federal Reserve 2013)
****Solid black arrows indicate max outstanding crisis support to borrowers (excl. central banks) of selected nationality (by ultimate control). Includes Treasury Capital Purchase Program and AIG support, and Federal Reserve Discount Window, TAF, TSLF, CPFF, PDCF, AMLF, ST OMO, and Maiden Lane I–III (Federal Reserve 2013). TALF loans omitted as direct borrowers are intermediaries. Peak value for Treasury funding of Federal Reserve approximate due to frequency (weekly) of Fed balance sheet reporting
***** Based on definitions in chapter 5
All values shown rounded to two significant figures

Fig. 2.3 The post-GFC US global financial "protection racket"
Source: authors.

medieval chartering of free cities as state-promoted engines of offshore monopoly rent concentration, that ultimately operate at the state's disposal.

Indeed, all of this machinery of US corporate offshore tax avoidance remains within the scope of US sovereign prerogative to control, and its parameters have for decades frequently been adjusted, while never being radically scaled back, by changes to US Controlled Foreign Corporation (CFC) laws (mostly recently in the 2017 Tax Cuts and Jobs Act, which did not in fact, as is often claimed, change the USA to a territorial corporate tax system; Barry 2019; Davis 2019; Engel 2001; Kamin et al. 2019; Picciotto 1992). Meanwhile the Internal Revenue Service has steadily expanded the scope and intrusiveness of a vast international apparatus of tax surveillance and enforcement, which now forces most significant financial institutions on earth to directly report tax information to the US government, to ensure that US citizens are not hiding money overseas (Bean and Wright 2015). This apparatus has been particularly successful at breaking down the walls, from a US government standpoint, of Swiss banking secrecy (Emmenegger 2015).

This US apparatus of global extraterritorial fiscal terror in turn directly underpins the state credit money credibility of the dollar as the reserve currency on

THE PARADOX OF STICKY POWER 81

which the global financial system is constructed—with the Federal Reserve frequently stepping in, whenever needed, to act as a global lender of last resort to backstop the stability of this system. In the most notable example, this entailed underwriting a global bailout of the Eurodollar market (spread across various offshore small island vehicles and European countries) during the global financial crisis (Helleiner 2014; McDowell 2011). Notably, as shown in Figure 2.3, the peak value of Fed GFC liquidity support to *foreign* financial institutions actually exceeded its peak support to US firms (black circles/arrows in the figure); with foreign banks in turn helping to fund the Fed's expansion of liquidity by accumulating excess reserves at the Fed (light gray circles/arrows in the figure; estimated based on McCauley and McGuire 2014). At the same time, however, as we discuss in chapters 5 and 9, the inherent nexus between the state's capacity (and willingness) to backstop the underlying *solvency* (as opposed to simply liquidity) of national financial firms, and the state's ability to itself to draw directly on the shock absorber of central bank financial support, means that American financial firms ultimately came out of the crisis in a far stronger position, in general, than most of their foreign peers (particularly in Europe).

In fact, the position of the Federal Reserve and New York at the center of the global monetary system is so powerful that the USA is able to leverage it as a shutoff value to disconnect other countries or firms, more or less at will, from the global financial system as a whole (*Economist* 2020). Beyond advancing various geopolitical strategic agendas (in relation to e.g. Iranian sanctions), the threat of disconnection from the US dollar payments system provides leverage to enforce international firm and jurisdiction-level compliance and cooperation with the global US fiscal and financial surveillance state, with the help of international organizations such as the Financial Action Task Force (FATF) (Bean and Wright 2015; Emmenegger 2015; Sharman 2009). Meanwhile, developing countries are forced to accumulate vast reserve hoards of US treasury bonds in an attempt to bolster the stability of their monetary and financial systems against the threat of shocks and crises which to a large extent originate from within the USA (see Aizenman and Lee 2007). Indeed, the worse the news is from the USA itself, the more this often prompts a "flight to quality" in assets that drives the value of the dollar *upward*. The dollar surged, for example, as the global financial crisis unfolded in fall 2008 (partly due to the surge in foreign treasury security purchases shown in Figure 2.3), notwithstanding the fact that this crisis directly originated in the USA. In classic protection racket fashion, both the disease and the cure are thus provided, and the more easily dollar-denominated credit is created and sloshes around in the offshore system, the stronger this protection racket becomes. Ironically, the main threat to it, at least for the time being, is basically the increasingly arrogant and erratic behavior of the USA itself, whose ham-handed attempts to assert its own "interests" abroad are increasingly ripping down the international institutional foundations—and even more importantly the international political legitimacy and alliances—that underpin its own systems of global rule.

2.9 Graveyard of Empires

Taken together, the combination of processes examined in this chapter gives the global financial system a paradoxical character. On the one hand, money and finance exist in a fundamentally abstract ideational realm. Monetary instruments are simply conjured into existence as needed, in endlessly innovative paper or electronic forms, in an endogenous process that arises out of economic activity and investment itself. However, the very abstraction and immateriality of these constructs creates a countervailing imperative to continuously affirm and ground their credibility in multiple interconnected respects. Taken together, these interconnected elements of the impulse to seek "solid ground" foster the emergence of highly centralized and durable conurbations of public and private gatekeeping actors, as well as places—which we dub the GFN. For issuers, receiving the network's key stamps of approval of reliable instrument valuation and exchangeability, optimized legal packaging, and political protection, renders their creation of credit money instruments *credible*—in other words, allows them to produce monetary quality. The availability of deep pools of credible financial instruments, which can be both readily purchased and disposed of, in turn pulls investors into the network; thus in a circular logic ensuring that a market exists for these instruments, and ultimately allowing both their issuers and holders to command purchasing power for purposes of commerce, investment, or consumption.

The paradox of finance is that other actors and places must ultimately pass through and pay a substantial toll to the narrowly guarded gateway of the GFN, simply to unleash the inherently unbounded potential of abstract financial creation and innovation—both constructive and destabilizing—that intrinsically resides within their own hands. This paradox is also deeply reflected in the historical evolution, or more specifically the historical *accretion* of the geographic structure of the GFN. In this respect, notwithstanding the popular idea that finance is somehow the most inherently footloose and mobile sector of the economy geographically, an examination of the geographic structure of the financial system, and how it has developed over time, suggests that the situation is actually almost the exact opposite. In other words, finance actually turns out to be the most geographically immobile, inertia-prone, and in general conservative component of the world economy, precisely because of its need to ground its own inherent fluidity and abstraction in apparently strong and credible traditions, institutions, and relationships. Notably, as we show in chapter 9, this has particularly important as well as counterintuitive implications for the impact of information and communications technologies on finance, as these actually seem to have an inherent tendency to reinforce, rather than overturn, the existing dialectical logic of financial system centralization and conservatism.

This paradoxical emergence of profound forms of geographical fixity and continuity *out of the very abstraction and immateriality of finance* is also evident in the differential speeds of evolution of the GFN's various subcomponents. In this respect, what is particularly striking is that what would appear to be most abstract and fluid component of the landscape of financial production—namely the offshore realm of private legal–contractual game-playing and arbitrage—actually turns out to be, in many respects, the most geographically durable component of the GFN (see chapter 7). To put this more precisely, anybody can easily set up a low tax de/unregulated offshore platform. However, very few of these actually have a level of legal institutional credibility and international political legitimacy and support to attract any significant activity[17]—and these are usually either well established in terms of the commercial and financial legal, institutional and political heritage on which they build, and/or beneficiaries of strong "onshore" state patronage and protection (Eden and Kudrle 2005; Sharman 2005).

The decaying and repurposed wreckage of European empires—i.e. the various scattered autonomous and semi-autonomous micro-polities that serve as 20th-/21st-century counterparts to medieval offshore free cities—are actually the *newest* additions to the offshore system (see chapter 7). Meanwhile the older components are simply political fossils that have been passed down directly from the Middle Ages. The world's leading multinational corporate shell company hub and banking secrecy jurisdictions, for example, namely the Netherlands and Switzerland, are simply confederations of medieval free cities—subsequently politically unified in the case of the Netherlands, but less so for Switzerland—which have both functioned as leading offshore or midshore financial hubs for centuries (e.g. ca. 600 years in the case of Geneva). These operate alongside leftover medieval feudal offshore microstates such as Luxembourg, Monaco, and Liechtenstein which are essentially modern-day versions of the landed feudal principalities (counts of Champagne, dukes of Savoy, etc.) who in centuries past competed to draw the leading Italian merchant banks into their exchange fairs by offering the most favorable possible legal, regulatory, and fiscal environment. Luxembourg and Liechtenstein, moreover, have strong political ties to the Netherlands and Switzerland respectively. Luxembourg is basically a "spinoff" of the Netherlands (both Habsburg and Dutch) which exited a personal union with the Dutch crown in 1890, and remains strongly tied to the Netherlands (and Belgium) via the Benelux

---

[17] Indeed, the system is increasingly "pruned" of smaller and more disreputable players by the enforcement and standard-setting efforts of organizations such as the FATF, largely in accordance with US strategic security priorities (war on drugs, terrorism, etc.; Sharman 2009; Vlcek 2007).

association; while Lichtenstein operates in a monetary and customs union with Switzerland, which also runs much of its foreign policy. Probably the oldest, and in some respects most important (at least in symbolic terms) medieval offshore political entity, however, is the Corporation of London—i.e. "the City" proper or Square Mile. This is simply a living medieval free city, whose special freedoms and privileges predate the Norman Conquest (in a literal legal sense since *time immemorial*), and which has never been fully incorporated politically or administratively into the UK. In fact, the City still operates under a version of medieval corporatist guild-based government, wherein locally operating firms—including multinational financial firms—actually command a larger number of votes in municipal elections than resident human beings (Shaxson 2011).

Somewhat more ephemeral than the architecture of the offshore system is the architecture of imperial political power that more or less by definition *must* undergird the integrity of the global financial system. At any given moment, the dominant world government(s) (WGs) can project and mobilize tremendous financial and monetary power via their role as the "protectors" of the GFN, with the greatest influence frequently being derived from the offshore jurisdictional components of the system that host activities beyond the reach of other weaker centers of political authority. However, such dominant powers come and go historically, while the network remains. Indeed, the dominant political powers at any given moment are also themselves invariably largely dependent on and constrained in various ways by their relationship with the network. This is, not least, because they themselves have historically had to pass through and restructure themselves according to the standards and codes defined by the narrow gateway of the GFN, and in the wake of this remain, like the users of proprietary software packages, more or less permanently under the influence of legacy standards and relationships mediated through the network. This process of assimilation lays the historical groundwork for successive powers to ultimately become incorporated, over the long run, into the network as durable gatekeeping nodes themselves, even as their political power wanes.

In this respect, the present-day US-dominated global financial network remains, to a large extent, strongly anchored by and mediated through not only the post-imperial structures of the previously dominant global financial power, Britain, but also those of the preceding power, the Netherlands—both of which function as leading offshore/midshore hubs themselves (from the Eurodollar market to Dutch Sandwich profit-shifting structures), and moreover administer critically important "offshore archipelagos" of overseas colonial dependencies (Palan et al. 2010; Papke 2000; Shaxson 2011; chapter 7). These network structures developed historically around a deeply interconnected triangle of not only financial, but also political relationships. The rapid deepening of the financial relationship between the UK and the Netherlands was kicked off in the late 17th century by the personal union of the two countries under the rule of William III (Neal 1990). Meanwhile, the

US–UK financial relationship has been mediated by the political dynamics of US initial decolonization from, and gradual reverse colonization of, the UK. At the same time, the dominant US financial center, New York, was originally a Dutch colony, and the early post-independence financing needs of the USA were mostly met by Amsterdam (see Hamilton 1790). Indeed, in the late 18th and early 19th centuries, one of the largest asset classes in Amsterdam was apparently various types of repackaged low-grade American paper debt, that had been purchased at a discount by Dutch mutual funds, and in turn pooled and securitized to allow investors to reduce their exposure to the risk of default by any one of the underlying American securities (Rouwenhorst 2016).

In other words, the GFN is to a large extent a graveyard of dead empires and other fossilized political legacy structures that continue to exercise power over, even while being fundamentally dependent on, the protection of, the living. Notably, there are some strong affinities between the process described here, and the model of financially mediated historical economic and political hegemonic succession developed by Arrighi, building on Braudel (and Marx). However, the historical developmental logic of the GFN to a large extent seems to be the mirror image of the idea that an economic developmental exhaustion of—or "overaccumulation" of capital in—the old money centers, causes a ballooning "financial expansion" that spills over into financing capital formation in the ascendant centers of economic growth (Arrighi 1994; Arrighi and Silver 2001). Finance fundamentally does not entail the intermediation of money or capital accumulated out of the profits of the *past*. It rather conjures abstract credit money instruments into existence out of thin air in expectation of *future* profits, which will themselves ultimately be earned and denominated in credit money instruments. This conjuring act is a Keynesian *demand-led* process whose impetus does not primarily arise out of the "old money" centers, but rather the places experiencing the most dynamic and exuberant processes of real growth, which is where the most pronounced speculative bubbles invariably develop. It is this boiling caldron—or, as one mid-19th-century UK Treasury official colorfully described the United States, "monetary cesspool" (Eltis 2001)—of financial and entrepreneurial animal spirits in the ascendant centers of economic growth, that is impelled to seek solid ground in the norms, gatekeepers and places of "old money," thereby reproducing the latter's historical power.

These established financial places and gatekeepers may or may not be located within, as opposed to across national borders, in relation to the bubbly centers of economic dynamism. Most often one sees a networked combination of intra and international connectivity. The subprime bubble, for example, emerged out of the context of a genuine regional economic growth miracle in the US Sunbelt; with Arizona and Nevada both averaging 6.1% real annual GDP growth, and California and Florida averaging 4.8% and 4.7% growth, in the decade from 1996 to

2005 (BEA 2021). This was powered by a combination of high-tech manufacturing and services growth—with Arizonan and Nevadan manufacturing growing at blistering annual rates of 8.9% and 9.4% (BEA 2021), and California spawning the information age economy as we know it, during the period above—and rapid urbanization, which followed an extremely energetic quasi-developing world pattern characterized by massive inflows of rural labor, in this case from Latin America. Within the bubble that emerged out of this regional miracle economy, the primary drivers of monetary *quantity*-production through mortgage origination were mostly upstart Sunbelt financial firms led by Countrywide and WaMu, who were rapidly expanding and willing to aggressively take risks. These were in turn plugged into a far-flung network of securitization-based monetary *quality* production spread across Wall Street, Delaware, London, and UK overseas territories such as the Cayman Islands, that was operated by tangled daisy chains of more established financial firms, and grounded in promotion by and backstops from Washington, DC other capital cities (Aalbers 2009a; 2009b; FCIC 2011; French et al. 2009; see chapters 3–6).

At the end of the day, things did not work out well for Countrywide or WaMu, not to mention to the inhabitants of the Sunbelt. Crucially, however, as far as the ultimate post-crisis solidity of mortgage-backed securities themselves was concerned, this system of monetary quality production actually worked perfectly. "Toxic" securities were rendered sound simply by virtue of the way that they passed through the magical gateway of institutional and political power (including access to backstops) represented by the GFN, even as the erstwhile miracle economics of the Sunbelt unraveled. Similar instances of this type of disconnect are in anything but short supply; as illustrated by, for example, by the repeated divergence of fortunes between the inhabitants of developing countries, who after foreign borrowing-fueled national economic growth spurts find themselves subjected to merciless austerity, and the overseas bondholders of these countries.

Perhaps the most striking, and in many respects paradoxical contemporary relationship between an ascendant center of economic dynamism, and the inherited structures of the GFN, is that of contemporary China. Aside from accounting for more than one-quarter of worldwide 21st-century GDP growth (compared to 17% for the USA; World Bank 2020), China is not only one of the world's largest net capital exporters, but also probably the single most exuberant boiling cauldron of financial animal spirits and innovation in the world today; particularly in cutting-edge areas of FinTech (Gruin and Knaack 2020; Jia and Kenney 2016; Töpfer 2018). It is also home to the world's four largest banks by assets (Sanders 2020), and is second only to the USA in total stock market capitalization (including Hong Kong accounting for 14% vs the US 40% of the world total; WFE 2020), with Beijing furthermore now a close second place to the San Francisco Bay area globally in terms of overall venture capital financing by urban area (Florida and Hathaway

2018). Politically, China is fiercely independent, and not in a position to be bullied or dominated by other powers. However, as we discuss in the later chapters of this book, China's financial development has been, and continues to be, profoundly mediated through the inherited structures of the GFN, and in particular a combination of the New York capital market and investment banking community, and Britain's offshore "second empire." These structures have (as we discuss in chapter 8) played a leading role in restructuring and shaping the strategies of both the private and state sectors in China, with the largest IPOs in New York in recent years being largely undertaken by Chinese firms—which now account for around 6% of total US stock market capitalization (USCC 2020). Meanwhile, the former (and to a large extent current) British empire not only effectively provides, via incorporation hubs such as the Cayman Islands, the "Delaware(s)" of contemporary Chinese corporate legal organizational and governance (Maurer and Martin 2012; Nougayrède 2019; Sutherland and Ning 2011), but has also to date almost entirely mediated China's efforts to build the RMB into a global reserve currency—which are primarily centered on offshore RMB markets in Hong Kong, Singapore, and London (Lim 2019; Töpfer and Hall 2018; Walter and Howie 2011).

Importantly, as Arrighi and Braudel point out, the "old money" centers often fall back lazily on a disproportionate reliance on financial business, as the center of underlying economic dynamism shifts elsewhere. However, it makes less sense to explain this in terms of an overaccumulation of capital in the old money centers that spills over into financial expansion, than in terms of a shift in their comparative advantage toward an exploitation of the lucrative rents afforded by their GFN positionality. As Braudel notes, for example, the wealth of Genoa in its heyday "came not so much from gold or silver as from the possibility of mobilizing credit" (Braudel 1992, 166) while:

> the Italian merchant who arrived empty-handed in Lyons [the chief international financial center of France] needed only a table and a sheet of paper to start work, which astonished the French. But this was because he could find on the spot his natural associates and informants, fellow countrymen who could vouch for him and were in touch with all the other commercial centers in Europe—in short, everything that goes to make up a merchant's credit.
>
> (Braudel 1985, 167)

Notably, while individual financial firms obviously need to make a profit, there is little or no relationship between the ability of financial centers to generate and reap GFN positionality rents, and their status as net capital exporters or importers. Switzerland is a net capital exporter, but so are (probably) (see section 2.4) most countries in sub-Saharan Africa; meanwhile the UK is a net capital importer. The reason for this inconsistency is simple; financial centers do not provide capital, they create, buy, sell, repackage, and trade credit instruments, and their balance sheet in relation to the outside world has both an asset side and a liability side, most often simultaneously with the same counterparties. New York City does not provide capital to America. Indeed, as illustrated by, for example, the UK and London in the wake of WWII, the accumulated financial wealth of the local capitalists themselves in established financial centers can be largely wiped out of existence, without fundamentally impairing their position in the global financial network. The City is perfectly happy to operate with money belonging to, and indeed to a large extent to be operated by, Americans, petrostates, or anybody else. The house always wins, regardless of who is playing.

Ultimately, it is precisely the fact that financial power actually has fairly little to do with the immediate possession of capital or money, but is rather rooted in the difficult-to-replicate nexus of historically accreted capabilities and relationships required to *manufacture* high-quality money, that makes this power so historically "sticky." Money comes and goes, but financial power remains. It is not simply handed off like a baton from declining to rising economic and political powers, but is rather an institutional and relational craton at the heart of capitalism that accretes and is carried over across multiple "hegemonic cycles." Indeed, the logic of comparative advantage in financial production is both so tenacious, and so lucrative, that some have compared it to a "resource curse" (i.e. "finance curse"; see Christensen et al. 2016) that structurally traps small economies home to disproportionately large financial centers—even if the trap itself is quite a comfortable and stable one compared to the vicissitudes of natural resource dependence. Sticky power thus works in two directions, both ensnaring ascendant centers of economic dynamism within the relational structures of the GFN, and making it difficult for the old money centers at the heart of the GFN to relinquish this position, even if they wanted to. As Braudel (2019) puts it, "a financial center can generally be counted on to survive."

3

The End of Investment Bank Capitalism?

An Economic Geography of Financial Jobs and Power

3.1 Introduction

Economists, and particularly financial economists who have diagnosed the causes of the global financial crisis (GFC) 2007–2009, cannot come to terms with the role of financial firms and professionals. In contrast to the media, who are eager to criticize banks and bankers, economists have typically looked for the causes of the crisis in more abstract structural factors such as the failure of unrestricted financial markets (Stiglitz 2010), irrational behavior by investors (Shiller 2008), or global trade and financial imbalances (Rajan 2010). Attention to banks and bankers seems to be inconsistent with the received wisdom in economics, according to which the past three decades or so have seen a process of disintermediation, wherein the central role of banks in collecting deposits and granting loans has been replaced by investors and borrowers exercising direct access to capital markets (Mishkin 2006). Building on the received wisdom of disintermediation, the narrative of the GFC in economics focuses on the interconnected and complex nature of finance. Financial institutions and markets, so the narrative goes, have become more interconnected, and financial instruments have become more complex, increasing the severity of "tail risks" (events with a low probability but potentially disastrous consequences), also referred to as "black swans" (Taleb 2008). Governments, regulators, and scientists, so the story goes, did not keep pace with such developments, and hence the crisis resulted. The rhetoric of disintermediation, and its younger sister complexity, makes the financial system appear to be made of abstract market forces and anonymous actors, whose identity, by implication, becomes a relatively unimportant issue (Christophers 2009).

A large scholarship, however, has opposed the view of the financial sector as a mere intermediary which is fading into the background of the economy via a purported process of disintermediation. Political economists and other social scientists, particularly on the radical side of the field, have for a long time placed the financial sector at the center of power relations in the USA and world economy—as reflected in such terms as the Wall Street–Treasury–IMF (International Monetary Fund) complex (Bhagwati 1998), or the new Wall Street system (Gowan 2009),

Sticky Power. Daniel Haberly and Dariusz Wòjcik, Oxford University Press.
© Daniel Haberly and Dariusz Wòjcik (2022). DOI: 10.1093/oso/9780198870982.003.0003

as well as the broader literature on neoliberalism (Harvey 2011). More broadly, a burgeoning interdisciplinary field of financialization studies has documented and issued warnings about the excessive and harmful role of finance in economic and social life; with the GFC being framed as a culminating moment in this process of financialization (Engelen et al. 2011; Epstein 2005; Froud et al. 2006; Savage and Williams 2008).

While the GFC has served as at least a potential validation of critical political economy and financialization studies, a general problem shared by both approaches is their underspatialization of finance, with insufficient attention being paid to space and place in the analysis of both processes and effects (French et al. 2011). How does financialization spread across space? What role do particular places play in this process? What is the impact of financialization on particular places? Most importantly, given that finance, in a broad sense, inherently lies at the heart of capitalism, *what does financialization actually mean?*

The objective of this chapter is to contribute to studies that seek to more rigorously define and spatialize our understanding of financialization, by examining employment, remuneration, and power in the US financial sector. The chapter deconstructs the evolution of the US financial sector over the past several decades using a forensic "onion-peeling" technique. Following a conceptual overview in the following section, we start by analyzing financial sector employment between 1978 and 2008 in the United States as a whole, and in its leading financial center—Manhattan. This analysis pins down the securities industry as the specific subsector of finance that has been central to the phenomenal growth of finance's overall claim on the US payroll, as well as a major contributor to growing income inequality across the USA, between Manhattan and the rest of the United States, and within Manhattan. Next, we analyze the structure of the securities industry, identifying investment banking as its commanding heights, and sketching the factors that contributed to the phenomenal rise and transformation of investment banking over the thirty years leading up to the GFC. The next part considers the growth of the securities industry in major economies outside of the United States, highlighting the international spread of investment bank capitalism. This is followed by a summary of the role of investment banking in and after the GFC, which concludes by asking whether and in what respects the postcrisis period has been characterized by an erosion of investment bank power.

The main implication of this investigation is that the study of investment banking is critical to understanding the past four decades of the history of capitalism and the global financial network, not least in relation to both the causes and consequences of the GFC. Indeed, we argue that much or perhaps even most of what has been broadly dubbed "financialization," can be more precisely described as the rise of *investment bank capitalism* as a specific paradigm of *how* finance operates in the USA and elsewhere. The chapter has normative implications, in addition to supporting the conceptualization of power as something that is made and remade through the specific agency of key actors, rather than only existing as something structural and independent from anyone's will (e.g. as underpinned by, for example, the position of the financial sector at the center of "circuits of capital"; Allen 2009). It documents how investment bankers became the elite movers and shakers of finance in recent decades, and how they used their central role within the global financial network to pervasively skew rewards in their own favor, even while generating massive negative externalities for society more broadly. This reading of finance opens up space for political engagement and raises very specific questions about the potential end of investment bank capitalism and the future beyond it.

3.2 An Economic Geography of Financial Jobs and Power

Employment and power are both central foci for research in economic geography. An emphasis on employment can be grounded in the Keynesian tradition, which treats it as a key analytical and policy priority. Gainful employment is the principal way that people and societies sustain themselves, and the creation of new jobs generates multiplier effects for the rest of the economy (Skidelsky 2010). Positivist quantitative economic geography, which focuses on the location of economic activity, has conducted mapping studies of employment and factors that affect its distribution (Dicken and Lloyd 1990). Meanwhile, an interest in power can be rooted in the Marxist tradition, viewing economic activity as being underpinned by social and political relations, which, by their nature, involve unequal power relations (Singer 2000). Marxist economic geography, in particular, has directly problematized how such unequal power relations are produced by and inscribed in space (Harvey 1973).

In this chapter, we apply to the financial sector Massey's (1995) call to link these two strands of analysis by examining power through the lens of the geography of employment patterns. Power in this context is understood broadly as the economic, political, and cultural influence of the financial sector, with a particular emphasis on the soft power of consent, persuasion, and intellectual leadership, rather than simply corruption or coercion (Arrighi 1994). Power and its spatiality can be gleaned from the analysis of trends in employment and remuneration, as well as from a functional analysis of relationships within and outside of the financial sector. This inquiry is enhanced by the analysis of the impact of regulation and technology, ultimately helping to identify and locate the part of the financial sector, and the geographic locations, where power is concentrated.

The chapter presents a mesolevel approach to analyzing employment and power in finance. This can be seen as lying between the microlevel approach of anthropology, focused on the everyday life of finance (Langley 2008; Martin 2002), and the macrolevel approach of political economy, with its emphasis on financialization and neoliberalism (Arrighi 2010). The use of a mesolevel approach is not novel in itself. Indeed, the principal research strategies employed in the established literature on geographies of finance, have involved breaking down national financial spaces (or systems) into subsectors, groups of companies, and centers of financial activity, and studying them through intra and international comparisons (Clark and Wójcik 2007; Leyshon and Thrift 1997; Martin 1999). What is original, however, is the linking together of the analysis of employment, remuneration, and power in a historical and spatial context, and the application of this analysis to investment banking.

This mesolevel approach to the analysis of the geography of finance, inspired by Massey (1995), has three key advantages. First, by combining the analysis of spatial patterns and power relations, it considers both structure and agency without privileging one over another. Second, by focusing on employment and remuneration, it roots finance in the real economy, rather than cultivating a view of finance that is disconnected from the real economy, which leads almost inevitably to the neglect of space and place. Indeed, the financial system itself is ultimately an enormous human machine, as opposed to just a bag of free-roaming incentives and prices, and to be effectively understood it needs to be problematized as such a human machine; as represented, in a direct sense, by the geography of financial employment.

Crucially, as we will show, investment banking—or precisely investment *banks* and *bankers*—need to be viewed as not only the elite of the human machine of the financial sector itself, but also of the entire financial and business services (FABS) sector. No other professional group in this sector, or indeed in the economy as a whole, is rewarded so highly or has a comparable level of access to and interaction with corporate executives or policymakers. It is thus only through a focus on the rise and influence of this elite within an elite of the FABS sector that the evolution of finance in the USA and elsewhere over the past several decades can be effectively understood.

3.3 The Rise of the Securities Industry

To situate investment banking within the US financial sector and economy, we investigated the transformation of US financial sector employment and payroll patterns between 1978, on the eve of the regulatory watershed of the Reagan era, and 2008, the peak of the GFC. The financial sector is defined broadly to include four three-digit North American Industry Classification System (NAICS) categories and corresponding Standard Industrial Classification categories: credit intermediation and related activities (hereafter the credit sector); securities, commodity contracts, and other financial investment and related activities (the securities industry); insurance carriers and related activities (insurance); and real estate.

The credit sector is made of institutions that originate loans (whether they take deposits or focus solely on the origination of loans like mortgage originators or credit card companies). Meanwhile, the securities industry deals with the production, distribution, and exchange of securities, including bonds, equities, asset-backed securities, and derivatives. Data are from the County Business Patterns database of the US Census Bureau, which is collected on an establishment basis. To give an example, for JPMorgan, which is a bank holding company covering both credit and securities activities, the employment and payroll in each office was assigned to each location and classified according to the primary activity of the office. Employment data are for mid-March of a given year, and payroll data encompass the total annual payroll (including bonuses). No data are available on the breakdown of employment between front and back offices or between managerial and clerical levels. The data do not include self-employed individuals, employees of private households, railroad and agricultural employees, and most governmental employees. In the analysis, data have been used for all years between 1978 and 2008. However, the discussion here focuses, for brevity, on the comparison of figures from the start and end date of this period.

Analysis of this data reveals substantial changes in the organization of US finance between 1978 and 2008. Interestingly, one thing that did not change was the total share of the US workforce employed in finance (see Figure 3.1), which was 6.6% in both 1978 and 2008, and fluctuated within a narrow band of 6.4% to 7.1% between these two dates. However, this constant share of the workforce took home a progressively larger share of the US *payroll*, which rose from 6.7% to

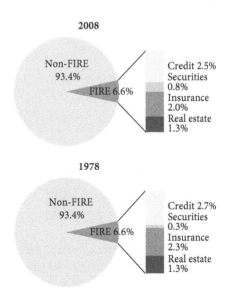

Fig. 3.1 Shares of finance, insurance, and real estate (FIRE) in US employment

Source: authors, based on data from County Business Patterns; adapted from Wójcik (2012).

11.3% (see Figure 3.2). Indeed, between 1978 and the GFC, the payroll per person (salaries) in finance lost touch with salaries in the rest of the US economy (see Figure 3.3).

What is most striking, however, is that it wasn't really finance as a whole that drove this shift. Rather, two-thirds of the increase in financial sector payroll share was accounted for by the securities industry alone, which evolved from the smallest to the biggest payer in finance, increasing its payroll share from 0.5% to 3.6% of

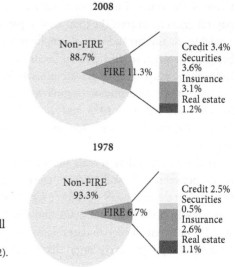

Fig. 3.2 Shares of finance, insurance, and real estate (FIRE) in the US payroll
Source: authors, based on data from County Business Patterns; adapted from Wójcik (2012).

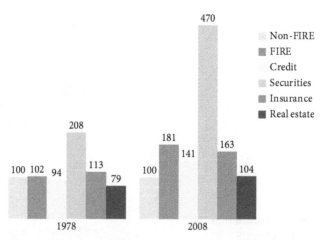

Fig. 3.3 Average payroll per person in the financial sector in relation to nonfinancial jobs
Source: authors, based on data from County Business Patterns; adapted from Wójcik (2012).

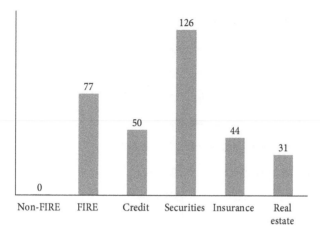

Fig. 3.4 Percentage change in the real average annual payroll per person 1978–2008

Source: authors, based on data from County Business Patterns; adapted from Wójcik (2012).

the total US payroll. Indeed, it was the securities sector that was chiefly responsible for the financial sector's overall outpacing of nonfinancial sector salaries in the USA during this period. In 1978 an average financial sector professional earned only 2% more than an average nonfinance worker; thirty years later, he or she earned 81% more. Thus, a finance worker gained, on average, a 2% per year advantage in pay over a nonfinance worker. In fact, the real purchasing power of an average US salary outside of finance did not increase at all during this period as a whole; while average real value of a financial sector salary increased by 77% (see Figure 3.4). This sounds like a lot—until one looks at the securities industry specifically, wherein average pay rose from twice that of an average US nonfinancial worker in 1978, to nearly five times as much in 2008. In fact, in 2008, there was no single NAICS category, however narrowly defined, which was anywhere near the average securities industry payroll of $189,000 (see Figure 3.5). What is even more impressive is that, in contrast to the stagnation of the share of the financial sector as a whole in US employment, total employment in the securities industry also rapidly increased at the same time that the average pay of each securities industry employee exploded; with securities sector employment rising from 177,000 to 974,000, or from 0.3% to 0.8% of the overall US workforce, between 1978 and 2008.

If one zooms in on Manhattan (New York County), the home of Wall Street, one sees further dimensions of the transformation in finance over this thirty-year period. While the share of finance in Manhattan's employment actually fell from 19.6% to 18.6% (peaking at 22.8% in 1988), the securities industry grew from the smallest to the majority employer within finance on the island (see Figure 3.6).

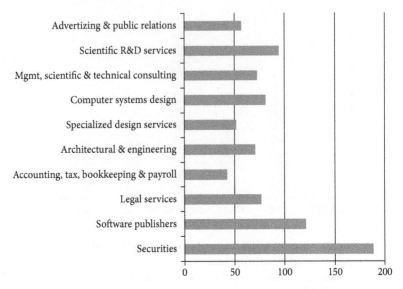

Fig. 3.5 Average annual 2008 payroll per person in selected industries (in US dollars, in 1000s)

Source: authors, based on data from County Business Patterns; adapted from Wójcik (2012).

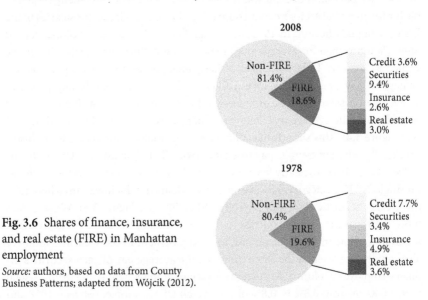

Fig. 3.6 Shares of finance, insurance, and real estate (FIRE) in Manhattan employment

Source: authors, based on data from County Business Patterns; adapted from Wójcik (2012).

In 2008, the Manhattan securities industry employed 198,000 people, more than the credit, insurance, and real estate sectors combined. The impact of the securities industry on changing payroll patterns was even more dramatic. Even while the percentage of Manhattan's workforce employed in finance as a whole actually *fell,* the payroll share of this (relatively) shrinking pool of financial jobs more than

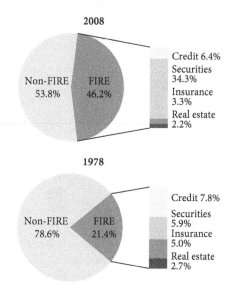

Fig. 3.7 Shares of finance, insurance, and real estate (FIRE) on the Manhattan payroll

Source: authors, based on data from County Business Patterns; adapted from Wójcik (2012).

doubled from 21.4% to 46.2%—and this was entirely accounted for by the securities industry, whose share of total pay in Manhattan rose from a mere 5.9% to 34.3% between 1978 and 2008 (see Figure 3.7). In other words, despite representing less than 10% of Manhattan's workforce in 2008, the securities industry took home more than one-third of the island's total pay, and nearly three-quarters of its total financial sector pay.

In fact, in 1978, a job in finance was nothing special from a salary standpoint, even in Manhattan. The average salary in finance was only 13% higher than the average for nonfinancial jobs (see Figure 3.8). By 2008, however, it was 273% higher, due mainly to the rise of the securities industry with its astronomical salaries. What is particularly striking is that Manhattan's share of employment within the US securities industry actually fell substantially from 36% to 20% during this period; however, its share in the US securities industry payroll remained stable at approximately 40% (see Figure 3.9). The growing disconnect between Manhattan's share of the securities industry's payroll versus its employment reflects a consolidation of the island's position at the elite apex of the industry, hosting the best-paying jobs, and coordinating the industry's expansion in the rest of the country and internationally. In 1978, the average salary in the securities industry in Manhattan was only 13% higher than in the rest of the United States; however, by 2008, it was 160% higher—underscoring the centralization of power taking place within the industry.

To summarize, the main trend revealed by the analysis of historical financial sector employment and payroll patterns between 1978 and 2008 is the phenomenal rise of the securities industry. Indeed, it would be more precise to say that the US economy became "securitized" during this period through the rise of this

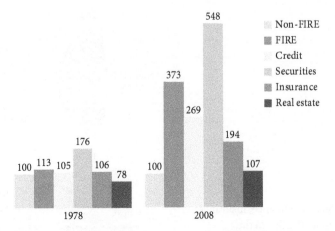

Fig. 3.8 Average payroll per person in the financial sector in relation to nonfinancial jobs in Manhattan

Source: authors, based on data from County Business Patterns; adapted from Wójcik (2012).

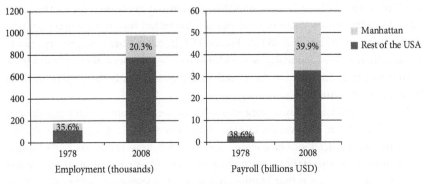

Fig. 3.9 Share of Manhattan in the total employment and payroll in the securities industry

Source: authors, based on data from County Business Patterns; adapted from Wójcik (2012).

specific segment of finance, with its center of power firmly located in Manhattan, rather than simply financialized in a broad sense. Growth in overall financial sector payrolls was actually relatively modest over this period, and growth in finance's employment share was nonexistent; in contrast, the securities sector within finance experienced explosive growth by both metrics. The analysis also indicates that Manhattan was transformed from a general financial services center into a specialized securities industry center. The booming securities industry contributed significantly to growing income inequality between financial and other jobs, between Manhattan and the rest of the United States, and within Manhattan. The industry established itself at the top of the pecking order of US industries in terms of salary, with higher levels of pay than any other professional business service, knowledge economy or creative industry.

3.4 Inside the Securities Industry

Having identified the securities industry as the engine of financialization in the USA, we now analyze its structure. Some refer to any intermediation in securities markets as "investment banking," but this is an oversimplification (Morrison and Wilhelm 2007). First, one needs to distinguish between the sell side and the buy side of the securities industry (see Figure 3.10). The sell-side manufactures and markets securities, and thus works primarily with securities issuers: including corporations issuing stocks and bonds, federal, state, and municipal governments issuing bonds, and banks originating loans to be securitized. Meanwhile, the buy-side purchases the securities that the sell-side manufactures and markets, and thus works primarily with investors, individual and institutional. In between are exchange facilitators, mainly in the form of exchanges (stock and commodity) and clearinghouses (Harris 2003). In 2008, the sell side, buy side, and exchange facilitators had 534,000, 432,000, and 8000 employees, respectively.

Defined narrowly, investment banking is restricted to the sell side, focused on underwriting the issuance of new securities; trading securities on their own account (dealing) and on behalf of others (brokerage) to create and sustain the secondary markets for securities; and rendering advisory services to issuers, including mergers and acquisitions. To be sure, there are firms on the sell side that cannot be referred to as investment banks because they focus on brokerage (e.g. Charles Schwab) or securities dealing (e.g. Tradebot) without being active in primary markets (i.e. participating in the production of new securities). Meanwhile the buy side, often referred to as the asset management industry, consists of firms that manage investment funds (pension, mutual, hedge, venture capital, and others) and investment advisers, which advise fund managers and other individuals and firms but, in contrast to fund managers, do not make actual investment decisions.

Fig. 3.10 The basic structure of the securities industry
Source: authors, adapted from Wójcik (2012).

A defining feature of the securities industry is that while investment banks operate across all parts of it, including the buy side, firms with their home on the buy side or in exchange facilitation rarely enter the sell side of the industry, and do not engage directly with the issuers of securities in primary markets. In 2009, both Goldman Sachs and Morgan Stanley, for example, were among the fifty largest fund managers in the world according to the value of the assets under their management (TowersWatson 2011). Investment banks also act as exchange facilitators, since, under certain conditions, they are allowed to internalize sell and buy orders from their customers, matching them in-house, instead of sending them to a stock exchange (Wójcik 2011a). Their monopolization of the production of securities, combined with their central role in securities market operation itself, gives investment banks privileged access to information. To put it bluntly, investment banks can reach any part of the securities industry, while other securities firms do not reach the most information-rich business segments of investment banking. This situation makes investment banking the core and the elite of the securities industry.

The earning power and geography of the investment banking industry reflect its special status as an informational and relational gatekeeper within securities markets. In 2008, the average payroll per person in investment banking (defined narrowly because data for the broad definition are unavailable) was $341,000, nearly twice the average in the securities industry overall. In fact, investment banking took home the highest payroll per employee in 2008, and enjoyed the highest growth in payroll per person since 1998, of any NAICS industry category. To put 150,000 investment-banking employees earning an average of $341,000 into perspective: in 2008, the top 762,000 tax units (the top 1% of US families) according to income (excluding capital gains) earned on average $401,000 (Piketty and Saez 2012). The investment banking sector alone thus accounts for a remarkably high percentage of the entire "1%" in America, and by extension income inequality broadly. Investment banking also exhibits the highest geographic concentration of any part of the securities industry. In 2008, more than 50% of all investment banking employees worked in Manhattan, compared to less than 20% of fund managers, and only approximately 10% of investment advisers. This figure is not surprising, given that Goldman Sachs, Morgan Stanley, JPMorgan, and Merrill Lynch (now a part of Bank of America), the largest full-service US investment banks, are all headquartered in Manhattan.

The power of investment banks extends beyond the purchasing power of their employees. At least until 2008, the leading investment banks topped the lists of the most desirable employers among graduates. Moreover, given the high-pressure working environment and high staff turnover in investment banking (McDowell 1997), it is an important feeder for the rest of finance as well as the top strata of corporate executives. Many formally independent hedge funds and other investment funds are investment bank spin-offs. Meanwhile, with respect to political power, investment banking is at the heart of the "revolving door" between Wall Street and the US government and regulatory agencies—as exemplified by Henry Paulson, Robert Rubin, and Steven Mnuchin, all of whom were Goldman Sachs executives prior to their appointment as US Treasury secretaries. This virtual hegemony within the US Treasury Department leadership of not just financial executives, or even executives from a specific segment of finance, but rather of executives who consistently hail from a single financial firm, is eyebrow raising to say the least. As *Financial Times* columnist John Gapper put it in 2008, in the midst of a series of crisis interventions by Paulson that directly benefited his former employer:

> A lot of people used to think that Goldman Sachs ran the US economy. Now we know it does…Wall Street is widely reviled at the moment, but even Wall Street is bitter about Goldman…It has become the modern-day General Motors by convincing politicians and regulators that what is good for Goldman Sachs is good for the US economy.
>
> (Gapper 2008)

Even in the UK, the current Chancellor of the Exchequer Rishi Sunak, who is the counterpart to the US Treasury Secrecy, is a Goldman Sachs alumnus. As Rajan (2010) argues, even if investment bankers assume government positions with the best of intentions and the highest level of integrity, they are likely to continue to think like investment bankers, leading to the issue of cognitive capture. Beyond this, investment banks are one of the leading donors in US politics, thus being a major contributor to the de facto legalized legislative and executive corruption that permeates US lawmaking and regulation ("Obama Top Fundraiser on Wall Street" 2007). It is estimated that the securities industry spent $500 million on campaign contributions, and $600 million on lobbying, between 1998 and 2008 (Johnson and Kwak 2010).

Beyond, as well as in conjunction with their role in directly generating a huge part of the whole broader elite of business and politics, investment banks exert power through ideas; shaping the way that the world is conceptualized both in and outside of finance. The concept of the value at risk (VaR), for example, which measures the risk of loss on a specific portfolio of assets, was developed by JPMorgan, has been used widely within the financial sector, and in 2004 was transposed into the public regulatory sphere when it was mandated as a method for evaluating market risk by the international regulatory agreement known as Basel II (Ferguson 2009). The acronym BRIC was coined by Jim O'Neill at Goldman Sachs. The term emerging markets originated from research by the World Bank, but what is probably the most influential tool for identifying and classifying emerging markets is a set of MSCI indices developed by Morgan Stanley. Investment banks have also been key promoters of the shareholder value ideology, marginalizing the interests of other stakeholders in corporations, and focusing on stock price as the ultimate measure of corporate value (Ho 2009).

The deconstruction of the securities industry presented in this section exemplifies the value of a mesolevel approach that problematizes securitization not as an abstract phenomenon mediated through abstract market forces, but rather "a product" that is manufactured by specific actors located in specific places (Leyshon and Thrift 2007; Wójcik 2011b). The section also highlights the need for an integrationist approach in geographies of finance (Pike and Pollard 2010). As we have shown, understanding the role of investment banking requires an economic, as well as a political and cultural analysis.

3.5 The Rise to Power and Transformation

As we discussed in chapter 2, the location of investment banking at the apex of financial power is far from novel historically. European finance was dominated from medieval times onwards by first Italian, then Dutch, and finally British merchant banks. These were the direct forerunners of the American and Anglo-American investment banks, led by JP Morgan, who were at the center of the restructuring and consolidation of American business and finance in the late 19th and early 20th centuries. However, the 1933 Glass–Steagall Act, which banned the integration of commercial and investment banking within individual firms, undermined the position of investment banking within American finance for decades. It was rather commercial banking that emerged out of the Glass–Steagall split in the more influential position; as indicated, for example, by the much more central position of commercial banks, than investment banks, in the post–WWII American network of intercorporate director interlocks (Davis and Mizruchi 1999; Kotz 1979; Levine 1972). Even JP Morgan, which had become the most powerful firm on Wall Street primarily as a securities underwriter, chose to reinvent itself as a commercial bank, spinning off its investment banking operations as Morgan Stanley. The investment bank Drexel also left the Morgan empire, eventually becoming, after its liaison with Firestone Tire, Drexel Burnham Lambert. Notably, even while commercial banks such as JP Morgan were banned from the sell side of the securities industry, their trust departments remained deeply involved in, and indeed dominated the buy side of the industry as asset managers for several decades (Patman 1968). In 1971, for example, the SEC found that commercial bank trust departments (including bank-managed pension funds) accounted for 59% of the total stock ownership of all institutional investors, compared to the 27% share of all other investment advisers combined, and the 4% and 3.8% shares of self-managed pension funds and insurance companies respectively (SEC 1971, table IX-1). These trust department shareholdings were, moreover, highly concentrated in the hands of a small number of leading Wall Street "money center" banks. Indeed, Kotz (1979) found that 27.5% of the largest 200 American nonfi-nancial corporations could be considered to be *controlled* by commercial banks, in 1969, via trust department shareholdings and other connections. Meanwhile, investment banks only controlled 5.5% of the top-200 US firms.

Notwithstanding its disruption of the power of Wall Street investment bank-ing, the bifurcated world of American banking that emerged from Glass–Steagall showed signs of evolutionary instability early on, as the strict regulation of com-mercial banking that also emerged from the New Deal quickly encouraged (from the 1950s) an expansion of securitized shadow banking activities aimed at cir-cumventing this regulation. The rise of shadow banking posed a challenge to the traditional long-term corporate relationship banking model of the leading money center commercial banks, including the successor institutions of erstwhile uni-versal banking groups such as Morgan. Most importantly, the bread-and-butter commercial bank business of corporate liquidity management was undercut: on the lending side, by the growing tendency of major industrial firms to directly issue commercial paper, and on the deposit-taking side by the rise of less regulated sub-stitutes for corporate cash reserve management, beginning with the development of the investment bank-operated repo market in the 1950s (Davis and Mizruchi 1999; Minsky 1957). Crucially, however, the impacts of these developments on commercial bank industrial client relationships were offset, prior to the 1980s, by the fact that commercial banks managed to grab a substantial slice of the shadow banking business themselves (particularly negotiable CDs from the 1960s), and were furthermore able to develop the offshore Eurodollar market as a largely un-regulated platform to conduct business with their major multinational corporate clients (see chapter 2 section 2.4 and chapter 5). The rapid postwar growth of corporate pension funds also reinforced traditional bank–corporate relationships, as well as the role of commercial banks within the securities industry, as com-mercial bank trust arms played the leading role in managing pension funds on behalf of their corporate clients. Indeed, the SEC's 1971 institutional investor study showed that pension funds accounted for just under one-third of total commercial bank trust arm AUM—with these commercial bank managed pension assets be-ing four times larger than what US pension funds managed in-house (SEC 1971; calculation based on tables IX-1 and III-24).

In the 1980s, however, the post–WWII pattern of incremental evolutionary change within American banking gave way to radical disruption. This was both a direct consequence of the existing tensions within post–WWII banking sector evolution, which had been building for decades, and a result of watershed shifts in US and international regulation. Perhaps most importantly, the 1980s were devastating for America's leading commercial banks, whose unstable 1960s–70s vintage offshore Euromarket-based funding models, and high-risk international loan portfolios concentrated in loans to developing countries, came home to roost in a major crisis of the American banking system. This began with the 1982 less-developed country (LDC) debt crisis, and expanded into a broader American banking crisis centered on commercial real estate and oil and gas industry lending, in particular. Meanwhile, as the importance of shadow banking-based corporate funding and cash management mechanisms, such as the (interconnected) commercial paper market and money market mutual funds, continued to grow, the leading commercial banks found themselves increasingly deserted by many of their most lucrative blue chip corporate clients. Some of the leading commercial banks in America, such as Continental Illinois, failed outright in the 1980s, and the single largest US bank, Citicorp, teetered for years on the brink of insolvency (Curry 1997; Davis and Mizruchi 1999; Davison 1997; Freund et al. 1997).

While Citi and other leading US commercial banks did mostly survive—defying pronouncements made in the early 1990s that "The banking industry is dead, and we ought to just bury it" (CEO of Norwest, quoted from Davis and Mizruchi 1999)—they only managed to do so by adapting to, and ultimately remaking themselves in the image of, a new dominant financial ecosystem. This was centered, on the one hand, on the role of the leading Wall Street investment banks as underwriters of innovative and esoteric financial products; and on the other on the diverse array of increasingly non-bank-affiliated fund managers who purchased the new products that the investment banks cooked up. Wray (2011), following Minsky, dubs this new financial ecosystem "money manager capitalism." In reality, however, the money managers played the junior role to the investment banks within it—with the latter playing the critical role in developing, underwriting, and promoting new financial products, lubricating the explosion of securities market trading, and (relatedly) operating the repo market, which grew into a sort of bottomless unregulated liquidity punch bowl at the heart of the Wall Street party.

The new Wall Street investment bank capitalism was in many respects the antithesis of the musty world of the old money center banking and corporate establishment. Whereas both commercial and investment banks had traditionally focused on cultivating long-term relationships with corporate clients (see Baker 1990; Davis and Mizruchi 1999), the shining star of the new 1980s investment bank capitalism was Drexel Burnham Lambert. This pioneered the underwriting of the junk bonds issued by private equity and hedge funds to fund their acquisition and dismantling of America's industrial titans. Even in the cutthroat world of 1980s finance, Drexel's antics eventually proved to be too much, with the junk bond king Michael Milken ending up in prison, and the firm itself collapsing after pleading guilty to several felonies (see Bruck 1988; Burrough and Helyar 1990). However, the overall structural shifts in American finance, and business broadly, proved to be durable, and indeed continued to advance during the 1990s and 2000s.

Playing a significant role in shaping the new American investment bank capitalism was the introduction of new information and communications technologies (ICT), as well as formal mathematical investment theories, with modern portfolio theory at their center. The large-scale introduction of personal computers and computer networks from the 1980s had transformative effects on investment banking. It implied, in particular, significant additional costs, a big part of which were fixed costs (setting up an internal computer network, external connections, and an IT department). The result was a ratcheting up of scale economies in a sector where even the leading firms had traditionally been small outfits in terms of employment and assets; thus creating a pressure for investment banks to merge, raise capital, and convert from a partnership-based to a corporate legal form. Investment banks thus became rapidly expanding tech giants in their own right, even while underwriting the expanding boom in tech firm IPOs. Technology also transformed the nature of skills and the labor market. Investment bankers had traditionally learned on the job, acquiring relatively firm-specific skills, which encouraged long-term relationship-building between employees and employers (Leyshon and Thrift 1997). Growing reliance on computing power, on the other hand, facilitated the use of mathematical models in finance, increasing the role of generic skills; fueling the demand for graduates in science, engineering, and technology, as well as with a formal education in finance (such as via the MBA). Changes in the nature of skills, combined with a steep demand for labor, accelerated staff turnover, and stimulated the development of high-powered incentive schemes, with a greater component of performance-based remuneration.

Regulatory shifts were also of paramount importance, as they allowed investment banks to use new technology and to respond to the increasing demand for investment services in an environment underpinned by faith in self-regulation in a competitive free market. From an indirect regulatory standpoint, the deregulation of savings and loans (S&Ls) in the 1980s ended up largely benefiting investment banks; as the S&Ls suddenly became a wide open and eager market for many of the new securities being cooked up on Wall Street, and in particular the junk bonds financing the 1980s takeover wave. This ultimately had disastrous consequences for the S&Ls themselves (Zey 1993). The 1980s partial "re"-regulation of commercial banking via the imposition of consolidated capital requirements, which were harmonized internationally by the 1988 Basel Accord in response to the debacles of the offshore Euromarket-centered LDC and broader US banking crises, also reinforced the competitive advantage of investment banks, by further encouraging the rise of securitized shadow banking activities in which they had an inherent advantage (see chapter 5). Further benefiting investment banks, and the securities industry broadly, was the introduction of 401(k) plans in 1980, which provided strong tax incentives for individuals to save outside of the channels of traditional pension funds. Investment banks could sell fund management and advisory services to cater to this rising mountain of funds, which even more importantly generated a demand for new securities, the production of which is the traditional business of investment banking.

Meanwhile, key acts of deregulation that affected investment banking directly were the 1990 Rule 144A, the progressive repeal of Glass–Steagall between 1996 and 1999, the Commodity Futures Modernization Act of 2000 (Sherman 2009), and the 2004 Consolidated Supervised Entities Program. Rule 144A, adopted by the SEC in 1990, dramatically relaxed the secondary resale restrictions on privately placed securities. This opened the door to the rapid growth of a largely unregulated Wall Street market in private securities, into which the most innovative and complex new securitized instruments (including those linked to shadow banking) were mostly issued. Without Rule 144A, it is not clear whether the most convoluted and unstable securities implicated in the global financial crisis could have been viably sold to US investors on any significant scale (see chapter 6 and FCIC 2011).

A few years later, the repeal of Glass–Steagall abolished the obligatory separation of investment from commercial banking. For incumbent investment banks, this abolition meant new competitors, but for the securities industry in general, it meant opportunities and expansion, as commercial banks—with Citigroup in the lead (see chapter 5)—grew and acquired large investment banking subsidiaries (Johnson and Kwak 2010). The SEC, meanwhile, did a staggeringly poor job of prudentially supervising the increasingly diversified and complex investment banks operating under its purview; and to a large extent did not even try, with the head of its Consolidated Supervised Entities (CSE) program at one point declaring that the "SEC's job was not to tell the banks how to run their companies but to protect their customers' assets" (FCIC 2011, 283). Finally, the 2000 CFMA prevented the Commodity Futures Trading Commission from regulating most derivatives contracts traded outside of regulated exchanges, encouraging further innovation in and a boom in the trading of derivatives, which comprised a growing core business of investment banks. New competition and the prevailing paradigm of self-regulation also contributed to and legitimated vertical integration in investment banking, including further expansion from the sell side into the buy side of the securities industry. The mixing on an increasing scale of the provision of services for both sellers and buyers of securities, as well as the mixing of trading on behalf of customers with proprietary trading, aggravated conflicts of interests; even if these conflicts of interest were ostensibly neutralized by internal controls and "Chinese walls" within investment banks and bank holding companies (FCIC 2011).

In sum, in the three decades leading up to the global financial crisis, investment banking grew in size and power within American finance, and underwent a transformation in character. In the late 1970s, investment banks were typically small partnerships, that specialized in underwriting and advisory services, offered mostly lifetime jobs that involved building long-term trust-based relationships with customers, and made relatively little use of financial "science" or technological hardware. Thirty years later, investment banking could not have looked more different. It was dominated by large multinational corporations with diluted ownership structures, some employing tens of thousands of people, which were diversified into all areas of the securities industry, and indeed finance broadly.

The focus of these giants was on trading and the engineering of new financial products, with technology and complex mathematics playing the central role in both areas. Their employees and executives were remunerated far better than thirty years earlier, and indeed better than any other US professional group of comparable size.

If we judge an economic sector by its power, pay packages, or profitability, investment banking is a good candidate for the most successful American industry of the past forty years. The nature of this success raises two fundamental concerns. First, the shift in focus from relationship-building and trust to financial engineering and trading suggests a shift to shorter-term objectives and incentives; which, indeed, are in many respects at the heart of the qualitative shifts in finance that are often described in terms of an overarching process of "financialization." To be sure, traditional investment banking activities, focused on corporate finance, remain relationship driven. However, the revenues that these traditional activities bring in have been dwarfed by revenues from trading (Morrison and Wilhelm 2007). The second problem is the extent to which the boom in the industry has been driven by its political and ideological power. In a study of US financial sector remuneration between 1909 and 2006, Philippon and Reshef (2009) demonstrated that recent high pay packages are related to deregulation and cannot be justified by factors such as the complexity and security of jobs, the level of education they require, or the use of new technology. They estimated that in 2006, financial professionals were paid approximately 40% too much. Curiously, however, they did not pay much attention to the fact that renumeration increases in the securities industry dwarfed those in the rest of finance, and indeed were essentially the sole driver of rising salaries in finance as a whole. The big question remains: to what degree has investment banking and the securities industry been successful at the expense of not just the rest of the economy and society, but perhaps even of other segments of finance?

3.6 Investment Bank Capitalism Outside the United States

While this chapter focuses on the United States, investment bank capitalism is a phenomenon that extends to other countries, and indeed is directly integrated across the US and other countries. A key moment was the 1986 Big Bang in the United Kingdom, which opened up the London Stock Market to the participation of local and foreign financial institutions beyond the traditional City merchant bank cartel. From the United Kingdom, the liberalization of securities markets spread to the rest of Europe, with securitization becoming one of the leitmotifs of European financial integration driven by the Investment Services Directive (ISD) of 1996, and consolidated through the Markets in Financial Instruments Directive (MiFID) in force since 2007 (expanded via MiFID II in 2018). The ISD introduced a single European passport for investment firms, facilitating the pan-European operations of both European and non-European firms. An investigation of cross-border corporate ownership in 2000 showed the dominance of US investors and US investment banks as intermediaries in the process of European capital market integration, leading to the conclusion that this "integration" was to a large extent really "Americanization" (Wójcik 2002). The MiFID opened the way for new trading venues to compete with incumbent stock exchanges, and in 2021 it appears that the leading owners of both incumbent exchanges and new trading venues, as well as their main customers, are US investment banks and institutional investors (Wójcik 2011a).

Ironically, even as American investment bank capitalism made deepening inroads into Europe in the 1990s and 2000s, a number of the leading Wall Street investment banks were themselves acquired by and incorporated into major European (and in particular Swiss and German) universal banks. These acquisitions spearheaded a broader push by European universal banks to remake themselves in the image of Wall Street; and resulted in several European governments ultimately having to directly bail out a large part of the Wall Street investment banking industry, via European parent banks, during the global financial crisis (see chapter 5). The transatlantic divide between American versus European investment bank capitalism thus became increasingly blurry at the level of ownership and control as well as operation. Meanwhile, beyond Europe, financial liberalization in emerging and developing markets, promoted by the IMF, as well as the Doha Round of the World Trade Organization negotiations promoting free trade in business services, opened further opportunities for investment banking (Johnson and Kwak 2010; Stiglitz 2002).

Although systematic data on remuneration in different parts of the financial sector are not available for other countries, the basic features of employment in the securities industry versus in credit and insurance, in the five largest economies outside of the United States (China, France, Germany, Japan, and the United Kingdom), as well as Switzerland, are presented in Figures 3.11 and 3.12. Because historical data for China are available only for Hong Kong, Figure 3.11 refers to Hong Kong only, while Figure 3.12 shows data for the whole of China, including Hong Kong.

The main observation is that the spectacular rise of US securities industry employment between 1998 and 2008 was not an exception internationally. Indeed, France, Germany, Switzerland, and the United Kingdom actually registered larger increases in the size of the securities industry than the USA—ranging from 42% in Germany to 98% in Switzerland. In Hong Kong, growth in credit and insurance followed that in the securities industry closely, probably because the Chinese market is still far from saturated in terms of basic banking and insurance products. Elsewhere, however, as in the USA, the rise of the securities industry overshadowed credit and insurance (see Figure 3.11). In fact, in Germany and the UK, credit and

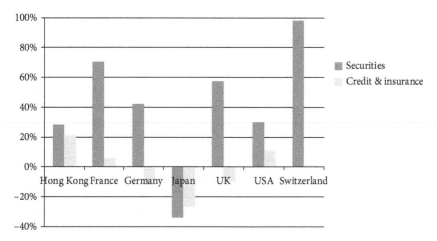

Fig. 3.11 Change in employment 1998–2008

Source: authors, based on data from the National Bureau of Statistics of China; Unistatis (France); Bundesagentur für Arbeit Statistik (Germany); Japanese Statistics Bureau; NOMIS, Office for National Statistics (UK); County Business Patterns, US Census Bureau; Federal Statistical Office (Switzerland); adapted from Wójcik (2012).

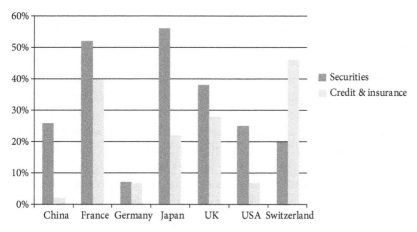

Fig. 3.12 Concentration of employment in the leading city 2008

Source: authors, based on the data in Figure 3.11. The leading cities are defined as Hong Kong SAR (China), Paris-Ile-de-France (France), Frankfurt am Main-Stadt (Germany), Tokyo–Prefecture (Japan), Greater London (UK), New York–Northern Jersey–Long Island Metropolitan statistical area (USA), Zürich-canton (Switzerland); adapted from Wójcik (2012).

insurance sector employment actually contracted. Overall, the only international exception to the success of the securities sector was Japan, where its employment shrank by more than 30%, reflecting the protracted stagnation of and predominance of public debt within the securities market after the bursting of the bubble economy (Koo 2008).

Figure 3.12 examines the geographic concentration of employment by finan-cial sector segment in various countries' financial centers in 2008. It highlights the generally much higher level of geographic concentration in the securities industry than that in credit and insurance; a pattern which, in addition to the USA, was also exhibited by China, France, Japan, the UK, and Germany (albeit weakly for the last). Tokyo, for example, accounted for 22% of Japan's employment in credit and insurance, but 56% of its securities industry employment in 2008. An even bigger discrepancy can be seen for China, where Hong Kong commanded 26% of the securities industry, but only 2% of employment in credit and insurance. On the other hand, Switzerland did not follow this pattern, and Germany did so only weakly. In Germany, Frankfurt's share in the securities industry was only 7%, just slightly larger than its share in credit and insurance, while in Switzerland, Zurich accounted for 46% of employment in Swiss credit and insurance, but only 20% of securities industry employment. Both countries, notably, have unusually ge-ographically decentralized and multipolar financial sectors broadly, with Munich and Geneva, for example, being close competitors to Frankfurt and Zurich in asset management (Klagge and Martin 2005).

In summary, a brief international overview underscores the importance of studying investment banking and the securities industry from an economic ge-ographic perspective. Notably, the basic patterns do not conform to any sort of simple distinction between securities market-based "liberal market" as opposed to bank-based "coordinated market" financial systems, as described by the va-rieties of capitalism school (Hall and Soskice 2001). First, the close pre-1980s relationships between American banks and industrial firms bore a great deal more resemblance to the bank-based coordinated market economy model, from a qual-itative standpoint, than is usually recognized. Indeed, the relational vestiges of the Money Trust were still visible as late as the early 1980s, if one looks at the structure of the US corporate director network (see also chapter 2). Moreover, the fact that bank–industrial relationships in the US company network were, in a relative sense, traditionally somewhat weaker than those in, for example, Ger-many, was mostly the result of conscious US federal regulatory interventions (see chapter 2), as opposed to being something that evolved organically on the basis of "institutional comparative advantage." Second, the rise of the securities industry since the 1980s, and of a particular set of business models within it that we dub investment bank capitalism, has been widespread not just within, but also out-side of the United States; and not least in, for example, Germany, where it has, even more than in the USA itself, severely disrupted traditional bank–industrial relationships.

An international perspective also further underscores the problems with broad-brushed conceptualizations of "financialization" as a *quantitative* as opposed to a *qualitative* phenomenon. Indeed, the traditionally enormous power wielded by leading universal banks throughout some major economies such as Germany, as both shareholders and lenders, was directly *weakened* by the attempts of banks to imitate the new American investment bank capitalism—which required putting up relational walls between financial and nonfinancial firms. Rather than some vaguely defined growing importance or power of finance, what was of paramount importance was a specific qualitative transformation of *how* finance operated and interacted with the nonfinancial sector; as represented, for example, by the declining willingness of German banks to defend longstanding industrial client firms from hostile takeovers (Dixon 2012; Haberly 2014; Höpner and Krempel 2004). This essentially mirrored, even if in a somewhat more pronounced manner, the institutional and relational shifts that had been spearheaded in the US by Drexel Burnham Lambert in the 1980s. Indeed, Davis and Mizruchi (1999) document how the traditional webs of influence of US commercial banks within the nonfinancial sector declined throughout the 1980s and 1990s, even as the new investment bank capitalism grew in power—paralleling the same basic trend in Germany. In all, even while finance as a whole did comprise a larger share of total US payroll and well as profits by the early 2000s than in earlier decades, this needs to be understood as the result of the rise of a specific set of lucrative business models, led a specific group of firms, as opposed to just in terms of the rising influence of finance generally.

3.7 The Global Financial Crisis and Beyond

The US mortgage-lending boom (including its subprime segment) and the house-price bubble of the late 1990s and 2000s were underpinned by a combination of booming economic growth and "animal spirits" in the Sunbelt, relatively low interest rates maintained by the Federal Reserve, government support for the expansion of home ownership through the government-sponsored enterprises of Fannie Mae, Freddie Mac, and Ginni Mae, and finally an explosion of "private label" mortgage securitizations enabled by financial innovation and deregulation/regulatory failure in the USA and elsewhere (FCIC 2011; Martin 2011). Importantly, even while US Federal mortgage market "parastatal capitalism" was larger in scale, it was the private label mortgage-backed securities—and the complex chains of securitization devices, such as CDOs, that they fed into—that were responsible for turning the bursting of the US housing bubble into a catastrophic global financial crisis. Moreover, it was above all the investment banking industry (including investment banking subsidiaries of bank holding companies) that bore responsibility for manufacturing and marketing these private-label mortgage-backed securities and their derivatives. Investment banks invented collateralized debt obligations (CDOs), their mutations into CDOs squared and cubed, and credit default swaps (CDS). They were the main private institutions buying mortgage and other asset-backed securities from loan originators to convert into CDOs, and they in turn exploited their global network of relationships to sell these instruments to investors around the world; paying rating agencies to positively evaluate CDOs to make them investible by pension funds and other institutional investors, and indeed often organizing training courses on CDOs for the ratings agencies (Tett 2009).

In short, investment banks were at the heart of the shadow banking activities implicated in the GFC (Pozsar et al. 2010). Apart from being the major producers and distributors of CDOs, investment banks also accumulated large inventories of asset-backed securities, CDOs, and related assets in their own portfolios. Doing so was at some level unavoidable because they had to buy pools of mortgages before processing and reselling them. Beyond this, however, investment banks also deliberately retained CDOs in their own investment portfolios, and purchased CDOs and CDSs from other institutions, due to the relatively high rates of return these instruments afforded compared to their nominally very low credit risk (and thus capital requirements). Further reinforcing the attraction of these instruments was the fact that they, as AAA-rated securities, could serve as collateral to obtain an enormous volume of cheap liquid funding via the repo market. Via these and other channels (see chapter 6), the production of these off balance sheet instruments was thus paradoxically entangled with the enormous increase in *on* balance sheet bank leverage and liquidity risk that eventually contributed to the widespread collapse of financial institutions. In all, the share of broker-dealers (investment banks outside bank holding companies) themselves in the total financial assets of the private sector rose from less than 2% in 1980 to 22% in 2007 (Pozsar et al. 2010).

In the afterword to *Ascent of Money*, Ferguson (2009) suggested that the GFC has led to the extinction of the US investment banking sector, as Lehman Brothers went bankrupt, Bear Stearns and Merrill Lynch were taken over by commercial banks (JPMorgan and Bank of America, respectively), and Goldman Sachs and Morgan Stanley converted themselves into bank holding companies. However, looking back from over a decade later, adaptation and mutation appear to be more appropriate descriptors of the fate of investment bank capitalism than extinction. First, although the standalone Wall Street investment banks have all either converted themselves into or been taken over by commercial banks, this does not necessarily imply less of an investment banking culture in finance. Indeed, the past few decades have seen many commercial banks, including Citigroup, Deutsche Bank, RBS, and Credit Suisse, permeated or even dominated by investment banking cultures, with traders and investment bankers becoming their executives. Furthermore, the bankruptcies of a few investment banks and securities firms may imply larger market shares for those left on the stage, whatever their legal format, thus reinforcing the concentration of power in the sector.

Indeed, investment banking bounced back rapidly after the GFC. As early as 2009, Goldman Sachs, Morgan Stanley, Credit Suisse, and Deutsche Bank all enjoyed their highest profit margins (net profits to revenues ratio) since the start of

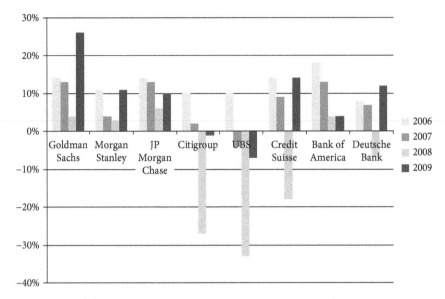

Fig. 3.13 Net profit margin of leading banks

Source: authors, based on data from Factiva Dow Jones; adapted from Wójcik (2012).

2006 (see Figure 3.13), and Goldman Sachs recorded the highest absolute value of net profits of the period 2006–2009. The securities industry in New York City reportedly lost 30,000, or 16%, of its jobs during the crisis. However, in the second half of 2010, 3,600 new jobs were added, and the overall compensation pool in 2010 was larger than in 2009 (Office of the New York State Comptroller 2011). This essentially paints a picture of rapid post-GFC industry recovery rather than retreat.

Looking more broadly since the GFC, probably the biggest potential long-term challenge to the position of investment banking has come from the growing power of the securities sector buy side—or, in other words, of the institutional investors who control financial assets. Figure 3.14 provides a picture of the post-GFC *global* centralization of ownership that has emerged on the buy side, showing all direct and indirect 5% shareholders in the world's largest 200 firms by sales in 2015. Beyond simply illustrating the tremendous concentration of power and wealth within the contemporary global financial system in a broad sense, the map underscores the extent to which this system's architecture has moved away from the comfort zone of investment bank capitalism. Specifically, buy-side concentration has resulted in the securities market itself, above all within the Anglo-American heartland of global finance, becoming increasingly "lumpy" and characterized by long-term concentrated relationships, as opposed to simply being characterized by a churning sea of fragmented positions (see Fichtner et al. 2017; Haberly and Wójcik 2017b).

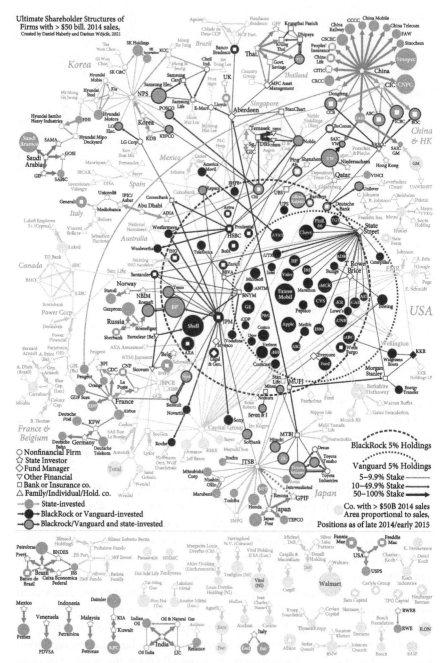

Fig. 3.14 Global company network, late 2014–early 2015

Source: authors, based on Orbis, SEC DEF-14A forms, Forbes Global 2000, company websites and reports; adapted from Haberly and Wójcik (2017b).

These increasingly lumpy securities markets may have the potential to give in-vestment banks indigestion. Indeed, unlike the early 20th-century Money Trust discussed in chapter 2 (as well the post–WWII "Deutschland AG"), wherein investment and universal banks themselves were at the center of networks of con-centrated corporate control at the buy as well as sell side, investment banks play at best a secondary or even tertiary role as shareholders in Figure 3.14. Further-more, the role that they (e.g. Citigroup or JP Morgan) do play as blockholders in the figure is mostly related to their role in operating the "plumbing" of global securities markets via the administration of American depositary receipt (ADR) programs. Rather, ownership itself is now highly concentrated in the hands of specialized institutional investors. The most important of these are first, a handful of enor-mous passive mutual fund managers led by BlackRock and Vanguard—the vast scope of whose 5% shareholdings is highlighted by the two dashed circles in the center of the figure—and, second, sovereign wealth funds (SWFs) and other state investors, who comprise a "state capitalist periphery" (Haberly and Wójcik 2017b) that reaches into the Anglo-American core of the global shareholding network from economies in Asia, the Middle East, and Continental Europe.

Passive funds and SWFs (and other state investors) can in some respects both be seen as reactions, albeit from different directions, to the practices of investment bank capitalism. The rapid growth of passive funds in many respects represents a mass collective throwing up of hands by investors, who have decided that they tend to come out ahead, net of fees, by simply buying "boring" market indices as opposed to blindly pouring funds into the Wall Street trading casino (Haberly and Wójcik 2017b; 2019). Indeed, the CEO of the world's largest passive (and overall) fund manager, BlackRock, which is a direct and indirect 5% blockholder in 28.5% and 46% respectively of the firms in Figure 3.14, has directly criticized the "gambling culture" of Wall Street (Fink 2015). Ironically, many "passive" in-vestment instruments, and in particular ETFs, are now themselves increasingly evolving into sophisticated and often speculative (including leveraged) products; as now culminating in what is literally called a "fear of missing out" (FOMO) ETF that will track "just about everything: stocks anywhere in the world, as well as SPACs, other ETFs, derivatives, volatility products and both leveraged and inverse ETFs" (Pisani 2021). However, even while increasingly departing from the basic spirit of passive investing, this itself represents an additional potential challenge to the traditional monopoly of investment banks in developing innovative finan-cial products. Reinforcing this potential challenge is the fact that BlackRock, via its enormous cloud-based Aladdin "operating system" for institutional investors, has also increasingly encroached on some of the core market "platform" activities that are the traditional bedrock of investment banking (see chapter 9).

Meanwhile, SWFs are government-owned investment funds created for a va-riety of purposes. These first rose to prominence as vehicles for OPEC states to earn a higher long-term return on their excess assets during the oil shocks of the

1970s, and have enjoyed a second period of rapid growth, led by East and Southeast Asian as well as OPEC states, since the early 2000s. To some extent, SWFs can be seen as self-insurance policies taken out by emerging economies against the vagaries of volatile global financial markets, as demonstrated most acutely by the Asian and broader emerging and transition economy financial crisis of 1997–1998 (Clark and Wójcik 2001). SWFs are mostly constructed of foreign currency reserves, which if kept parked in relatively liquid assets can be used by countries to counteract the monetary and balance of payments impacts of sudden outflows of money (Clark et al. 2010). It is ironic that although investment banks were among the institutions fleeing from Asian markets in 1997–1998, ten years later, SWFs came to their rescue with vital injections of capital during the global financial crisis. In 2008, the Government of Singapore Investment Corporation invested in Citigroup and UBS, Abu Dhabi Investment Authority and Kuwait Investment Authority also invested in Citigroup, Korea Investment Corporation and Temasek Holdings invested in Merrill Lynch, China Investment Corporation invested in Morgan Stanley, and the Qatar Investment Authority invested in Credit Suisse and Barclays (the latter with the Abu Dhabi royal family).

Importantly, SWFs, and state investors broadly, often make active and strategic investments in firms, rather than simply the arm's-length portfolio investments typical of pension and mutual funds. Such strategic investments include, for example, the acquisition of controlling stakes in the military, aerospace, and automobile sectors in which their home countries lack know-how, as well as investments in various overseas producers of critical raw materials (Haberly 2011; 2014; Haberly and Wójcik 2017b). In addition to advancing national strategic motivations, such a direct investment approach may also represent a deliberate bypassing of the lengthy, high-fee intermediation and securitization chains used within standard portfolio investment approaches—in which investment banks are the primary movers and shakers (Clark et al. 2013; Dixon and Monk 2014).

It may thus be that we are finally seeing, in the *aftermath* of the GFC, the rise of what can be truly described as *money manager capitalism*—as opposed to the *investment bank capitalism* that predominated in the years leading up to the GFC. At the same time, though, the evolving relationship between investment banks and these new private and public sector giants of the fund management industry, has the potential to be as much complementary as zero-sum. For one thing, even as institutional investor asset concentration in the hands of passive mutual funds and SWFs may shift bargaining power to the securities industry buy side, it will hardly render the sell side obsolete, and indeed may even create new niches for it. Abu Dhabi's SWF Aabar, for example, has made use of complex derivatives transactions with Goldman Sachs to limit its downside risk on concentrated strategic investments in firms such as Daimler (Haberly 2014). SWFs and other state-owned investors are, moreover, likely to continue to require the services of local relational gatekeepers to help them access developed country securities markets, and investment opportunities broadly. These do not necessarily have to be investment banks; the US$ 347 billion Saudi Public Investment Fund (PIF), for example, has mostly made its global influence felt via its backing of Softbank's $100 billion Vision Fund. However, investment banks remain extremely important. As we discuss in chapter 8, the Chinese state-owned sector has developed, and indeed to a large extent itself been constructed through, close relationships with Wall Street investment banks. SWFs (including China's), moreover, remain important shareholders in several of the largest western universal and investment banks—reflecting the ongoing legacy of their GFC rescues of these institutions (Haberly and Wójcik 2017b). Indeed, the strength of investment bank–SWF relationships is underscored, on a less savory note, by the fact that Goldman Sachs has been implicated in multibillion dollar corruption scandals involving both the Libyan Investment Authority and Malaysia's 1MDB, while Barclays has become embroiled in a corruption case surrounding its relationship with the Qatar Investment Authority; albeit with only the 1MDB allegations ultimately sticking in court (BBC 2020; Ridley 2020; Treanor 2016).

Meanwhile passive investment instruments, including ETFs, are by their very nature as much complementary as competitive with active fund management and investment banking. Indeed, ETFs cannot operate at all without the role played by investment bank arbitrageurs in keeping ETF holdings of securities aligned with the indices they track, while the new generation of zero-fee mutual funds make money by lending out securities *to* investment banks and (via investment banks) hedge funds, to support the latter's more complex trading operations (see chapter 9). More broadly, securities lending means that the portfolios of even the most "boring" passive funds are actually often in motion even while seemingly sitting still, creating grist for the mill of investment banking. Presumably, many of the products that are being shoveled into the likes of the FOMO ETF (derivatives, etc.) are also manufactured by investment banks.

Furthermore, investment banks have generally done quite well in the prevailing post-GFC environment of virtually free liquidity, which directly helps to fuel their trading activities. Shadow banking, moreover, with the investment banking sector at its center, is far from dead; as highlighted by, for example, Greensill Capital and its relationship with Credit Suisse (see chapter 1). Collateralized *debt* obligations (CDOs), disgraced by the global financial crisis, are out; collateralized *loan* obligations (CLOs), however, are in—growing rapidly over the past several years largely as a mechanism to fund aggressive corporate borrowing in the low interest rate post-GFC environment. Indeed, the CLO sector seems to have nearly become the epicenter of a major systemic crisis during the early 2020 Wall Street Covid panic, which was only averted by rapid Federal Reserve intervention (Podkul and Rivas 2020). Investment banks remain unavoidable gatekeepers within most areas of innovative fundraising broadly. The SPACs (special-purpose acquisition companies) that have recently proliferated as alternative equity funding mechanisms to

IPOs, for example, cut out investment bank IPO underwriting fees, even while creating new investment bank fee income streams that are at least as lucrative (Levine 2021b).

The investment banking sell side of the securities industry, moreover, still retains structural informational advantages over the buy side, as well as substantial market power. In a telling statement, the SEC (2020, 31) recently reported that:

> the buy-side participants with whom we have spoken worry that if they complain about information availability, or back out of an offering after submitting an order, dealers will retaliate by giving a smaller allocation in a subsequent offering.

The fact that investment banking has now largely returned to its traditional home in diversified universal banking, with JP Morgan once again sitting at the top of the Wall Street food chain, also implies a likely increase in the resilience and adaptability of the sector broadly. Indeed, if virtually the entire history of western capitalism and finance is any guide, it would seem to be unwise to bet against the continued influence and self-reinvention capacity of investment banks, over the long run.

3.8 Conclusions and Implications

This chapter has focused on the role of investment banking in the US economy over the past forty years, both leading up to and after the GFC. This is a controversial topic, with the media drumming up the culpability of investment banking with stories on exorbitant bonuses and dubious business practices, while the most influential scholarly accounts, in contrast, shift attention to the regulatory failures of governments and structural issues such as global imbalances. To provide an economic geographic perspective on the debate, we have combined an analysis of basic patterns of employment in the financial sector, with an analysis of the position of investment banking within finance, as well of as its rise to power in the thirty years leading up to the GFC, its involvement in the GFC, and its resilience in the wake of the crisis. We have demonstrated that investment banking plays the leading role in the securities industry, which was itself by far the most rapidly growing and lucrative segment of the US financial sector in the three decades leading upto the GFC. Even in the wake of the GFC, moreover, investment banking has managed to reinvent itself in ways that have mostly preserved its influence in the face of both an increasingly stringent regulatory environment, and the consolidation of the securities industry buy side in the hands of increasingly enormous fund managers and state investors.

Overall, the evolution of the US financial sector in the three decades leading up to the GFC could be summarized by one word—securitization. The process of securitization was commanded from Manhattan, which during this period could be referred to as a securities industry center specifically, as much as a financial center in a general sense. The analysis also indicates that the securities industry has been a major contributor to growing income inequality between the financial and nonfinancial sectors, between Manhattan and the rest of the country, and even within Manhattan itself.

Investment banking, functioning both independently from and within commercial banking, constitutes the elite core of the securities industry. Investment banks permeate all aspects of the securities industry and employ the best-rewarded professional group within it. The emphasis on the power and agency of specific groups of *people* here, rather than just abstract structural forces such as the capitalist profit motive, is critical. As Goldman Sachs alumnus Matt Levine (2021c) puts it:

> big investment banks are socialist paradises run for the benefit of their workers…Goldman's use of the term "partner," and its self-conscious retention of aspects of partnership culture, was a way of saying to shareholders: This is our fun little club, and we'll let you buy a stake, but don't forget that it belongs to us.

Beyond the purchasing power of their employees, the influence of investment banks extends to the politics and ideas guiding business practices throughout the economy more broadly. The power of investment banking has risen over the past forty years under the conditions of a growing demand for investment services, technological change, deregulation, and globalization. Investment banking, and the securities industry in general, has taken advantage of and adapted to these changes, making it one of the most successful sectors of the US economy. The GFC, however, revealed a long shadow to this success. Investment bankers invented many of the financial instruments that were used to intensify the turnover in the securitization chain and were at the heart of the shadow banking system created primarily for purposes of regulatory arbitrage. Their reputation and influence helped to legitimate this system in the eyes of investors, and to ensure that it was brought within the umbrella of state protection with the onset of the GFC.

The findings of this chapter speak against the often-told story on the causes of the GFC, which starts from the assumption that finance, over the past few decades, has become disintermediated, with banks becoming less important, and markets more important. In fact, as discussed in chapter 2, the basic idea of a shift or trade off here represents a false dichotomy, as the growing complexity and liquidity of financial markets is directly supported by, and in turn directly increases the power of, the key informational and relational "platform" intermediaries—including investment banks—who sit astride and manage the operation of these markets. In 2008, the United States had more people working in financial intermediation than ever before, their share of total employment was as high as in 1978, and their share of the total payroll was nearly twice as large. This situation was due primarily to the growth of the securities industry, at the core of the financial sector, which has blossomed in terms of overall size, the size of leading firms, remuneration, and power.

Most importantly, while the financial system manufactures and deals with highly abstract constructs, it also needs to be understood as a system that is operated by and on behalf of actual human beings, who are located in specific places, and embedded within specific cultural and social contexts and relationships. People who started their careers in the securities industry in the 1980s and early 1990s were the elite of a wave of yuppies who were employed in booming financial and business services. In the late 1990s, bourgeois bohemians (bobos), the elite of the creative industries, stole the limelight and attracted a lot of attention in the social sciences. Elite yuppies retreated into the shadows. But while bobos ran the facade of capitalism of the late 1990s and 2000s, elite yuppies at the peak of their careers in the securities industry were happily running the engine room, building a shadow financial system, and making fortunes on it. At the extreme, one might even argue that the creative class and industry have been a sideshow of the rise of a particular model of finance capitalism. Eighteen years ago, Wrigley et al. (2003) called for more research on investment banking as one of the keys to understanding the dynamics of capitalism. This call is now more urgent than ever.

4

The Dark Side of NY–LON

Financial Centers and the Global Financial Crisis

4.1 Financial Centers in Question

Research on financial centers (FCs) has coevolved with the broader fields of urban studies as well as economic geography and history. In one of the first accounts of the formation of FCs, Kindleberger (1973) devotes his attention to the evolution of FCs within major national economies. Only the last part of his book describes FCs in an international context, including a famously wrong prediction that Brussels would become the leading FC of Europe. Since the 1980s, however, parallel to the rise of studies on globalization, the study of the relations between cities has undergone a shift from a focus on national urban systems, to the relations between cities at an international level. A major milestone was John Friedmann's (1986) world city hypothesis. This linked word city formation to global economic restructuring, and in particular the migration of manufacturing activity from high- to low-wage regions and countries; which he argued created a demand for corporate command and control functions and producer services to become further concentrated in select elite cities. Shortly thereafter, Saskia Sassen (1991) developed the global city hypothesis, which focused on producer services firms, rather than the corporate headquarters of manufacturing and nonproducer service firms, as the main actors in global cities.

Notably, while both the world and global city concepts placed cities in the context of global economic change, they primarily stressed international competition between cities; which were in effect seen as being locked in a battle with one another over their position in the global urban hierarchy. This focus was reflected in work in financial geography examining the hierarchy of international financial centers, based on the study of individual FC attributes (Choi et al. 1986; Reed 1981). A major conceptual shift, however, followed Manuel Castells's (1996) work on the network society, which stressed the ascendance of the "space of flows" (money, people, goods, and information) over the "space of places "(cities and countries) in the contemporary world economy. This led to a retheorization of the international system of cities as a network, wherein the position and power of a city are seen as a largely positive sum function of its connectivity with other

Sticky Power. Daniel Haberly and Dariusz Wòjcik, Oxford University Press.
© Daniel Haberly and Dariusz Wòjcik (2022). DOI: 10.1093/oso/9780198870982.003.0004

cities, and the relations between cities are pictured as being characterized by a complex combination of collaboration as well as competition. A leading ongoing research program pursuing this line of analysis is the Global and World City (GaWC) project, which has conducted enormous empirical analyses covering office networks of producer services firms in hundreds of cities (Beaverstock et al. 2000; Taylor 2004). This conceptual shift from an emphasis on intercity competition and hierarchy, to networks of largely symbiotic relationships between cities, has also been articulated in works on FCs, with measures of connectivity incorporated into the rankings and hierarchies of FCs (Choi et al. 2003; Tschoegl 2000). From this perspective, international FCs are viewed as a spatially distributed network of money and power, where global and local processes intermesh with each other in a variety of ways (Allen and Pryke 1994; Amin and Thrift 1992).

This chapter builds on the network perspective on FCs, as situated within the broader GFN framework developed in this book. However, rather than looking at the global network of leading FCs in general, we focus on its single most important link—namely that running between New York and London. Recognition of the overriding importance of this connection has grown over time in studies of world and global cities. For Friedmann, New York and London were just two of six primary world cities in core economies. Slightly later, however, Sassen (1991) located only three places at the apex of the global city pyramid—with only Tokyo sharing top position alongside New York and London—and in her subsequent work (1999) she acknowledged Tokyo's relative decline among these three. More recently, work by GaWC theorists has described both the importance of and the connectivity between New York and London as being incomparably greater than any other pair of cities in the world economy. This phenomenon is referred to as the "New York–London dyad," the "transatlantic core," the "apex of globalization" or the "global twin-cities" (Taylor 2004; Taylor et al. 2011). Castells (2010) refers to New York and London as the "mega nodes" of the global network.

To study the New York–London phenomenon, this chapter first employs a historical perspective, focused on the coevolution of the two financial centers. In this respect, we build on studies of the evolution of individual centers, such as London (Michie, 1991), while also putting these in the context of the development of other international FCs (Roberts 1994; Wainwright 2011). Second, we explore the connectivity between FCs through a focus on both their *complementarities* and *commonalities*. Complementarities are understood as differences that *incentivize* interactions between centers, whereby a center can contribute something unique to others. This can be based on specialization in specific products or stages of financial intermediation, as well as access to specific markets (Clark 2002; Faulconbridge 2004). Commonalities, meanwhile, are similarities rooted in both the formal and informal institutions and cultures of FCs that *facilitate* interactions between them, supporting communication and transaction flows. As we show, such institutional commonalities are themselves strongly complementary with the functional complementarities between financial centers, with the combination of both jointly fostering a positive sum logic of mutual FC development. Notably, while the role has been documented of legal and regulatory systems, as well as of cultural factors, in the development of *individual* FCs, few studies have focused on the role of these factors in mediating the formation of relationships *between* FCs (Hall 2010; Leyshon and Thrift 1997).

Third, the chapter also investigates the role of the two centers in the global financial crisis and charts their development in the years following the crisis. This addresses an important research gap, as financial geography seems biased toward research on the growth of FCs themselves more than on the broader effects of FCs on the world around them. A notable recent exception here is work highlighting the role played by the peripheral location of Northern Rock in its demise in the GFC and the impact on the Tyneside labor market (Dawley et al. 2011; Marshall et al. 2012). French et al. (2009) stress the role of global FCs in generating the GFC in 2007–2008. Meanwhile, examining the impact of the GFC, Derudder et al. (2011) document an emerging shift of international banking centers from "West to East" in 2008. Highlighting the broader paucity of work on this area, Martin (2011) calls for efforts to analyze the geography of financial crises.

Charting the development of New York and London before and after the eruption of the GFC in 2008, a network-oriented approach is used in this chapter that at the same time does not neglect various attributes capturing the size of financial centers in favor of purely connectivity-based measures. Financial stocks and flows are anchored in particular places, being maintained and orchestrated by people (with their hardware and software) located there. Put differently, agglomeration and cluster economies matter to financial center networks and vice versa.

The chapter refers to the relationship between New York and London as the New York–London *axis*. Susan Strange applied the term axis when referring to the special relationship between the USA and the UK in matters of financial deregulation and reregulation (Strange 1998, 6). More broadly, the term axis is commonly used (although not with reference to New York and London) in international relations to refer to an agreement or alliance between two or more countries. Another meaning of the word axis, according to the Oxford English Dictionary, is "a line through the center of a rotating object." This is close to Peter Hall's observation that:

> London and New York are very special cities and in this sense represent the two poles of a transatlantic metropolis
>
> (Hall 2003, 31)

Crucially, the term axis is less neutral than dyad and brings up associations with power, which appears understudied in the literature on financial center networks. Existing work recognizes the power afforded to international financial companies via their networks and the influence of individual FCs; but what about the power of particular subsets and linkages within the network of FCs (Allen 2010)? The New York–London axis describes a special relationship between these two cities in financial matters, underpinned by the special political relationship between the USA and the UK, that is central to the operation of the GFN and the process of financial globalization. The axis can thus be understood as an element of the GFN, but is more than just a particularly strong dyadic connection in a network of flows. It has an explicit political element. The term axis is used to stress the uniqueness of the New York–London dyad among all other relationships in the GFN, and to explore its implications.

The chapter proceeds in four sections. Section 4.2 describes the historical development of the relationship between New York and London. Section 4.3 focuses on the role of this relationship in the global financial crisis. Section 4.4 analyses data on the position of New York and London in global finance, with particular attention to the impact of the GFC. The chapter finishes with conclusions and implications for literature and policy.

4.2 A Brief History of the New York–London Axis

To be understood, the rise of New York London Axis must be situated within the broader historical development of the American as well as transatlantic financial system. The United States was extraordinary precocious in its financial development. Indeed, as described by Sylla (1982), it was already a prolific center of financial innovation for over a century before independence. At the end of the 18th century—bolstered by Hamilton's interconnected reorganization of the national debt and foundation of the Bank of the United States, and the aggressive chartering of joint stock banks by states—the new republic underwent an interconnected explosion of securities market and banking development, as well as securities issuance by government and parastatal corporate bodies from the federal to local level. As early as 1800, the USA already had half of the total banking capital of England and Wales, and by 1825 it had actually surpassed the banking capital of England and Wales by a factor of 2.4 (including both the Bank of England and the Bank of the United States; Sylla 1998).

Notwithstanding the crucial role that the US federal government played as an *actor* in this context, the development of American finance cannot be effectively understood at a national level of *geographic* analysis. American financial development rather proceeded through what can be described as a government-managed "glocal" geographic logic. First, a key focus of Hamilton was bolstering the standing of US financial institutions and instruments—and above all of the US dollar and the credit of the US government—in the eyes of the "old money" centers of Europe. This, he perceived, would allow for the establishment of the international market confidence needed to support the ongoing interconnected expansion of the new nation's paper liquidity and government spending.[1] These efforts were incredibly successful, and Europeans eagerly snapped up American securities; as of 1803–1804, around half of all US federal, state, and corporate securities were owned by foreign investors, including 62% of the enormous capital of the Bank of the United States (Sylla et al. 2006).

This process of government-managed "glocalized" financial development was geographically mediated through the four great East Coast commercial cities of Boston, Philadelphia, New York, and Baltimore. These cities were the key outlets for America's exports of staples such as cotton to Britain, and the main importers of British manufactured goods. They were also the home bases for America's own global mercantile shipping and trading empires, which by the dawn of the 19th century had already established a world-circling presence, playing a major role in, for example, the China opium trade. They all had their own state-chartered banks and local securities markets, on which the US Federal, state and local securities that were being snapped up by foreign investors also traded locally, in addition to in London and Amsterdam (Sylla et al. 2006).

It was not a foregone conclusion that New York would emerge as the leader among these cities (Kindleberger 1973). New York does seem to have possessed, as early as the 1790s, the most active American securities market (Sylla 1998). Philadelphia, however, is where both the First (1791) and Second (1817) Banks of the United States were established; and was thus the political center of financial power in America until the 1830s. Meanwhile, America's first investment bank, Alex. Brown & Sons, was established in Baltimore in 1800. Finally, Boston's merchants and financiers were in many respects the most globally active of the four cities' capitalist communities, becoming, for example, the key supporting players in the China opium trade after the British (Downs 1968). Boston's merchants, financiers and entrepreneurs also led the early American industrial revolution, which they spearheaded with the help of Massachusetts state and US federal industrial policies (Chang 2002; Lively 1955).

The merchants and banking institutions of Philadelphia, Baltimore, and Boston all cultivated their own links with, and indeed to a large extent depended on, the global financial entrepôt of London and its great merchant banking houses. Of greatest importance, were the relationships that the business communities of these American cities forged with the leading British merchant bank Baring Brothers

---

[1] As Hamilton (1790) put it:

It is a well known fact, that in countries in which the national debt is properly funded, and an object of established confidence, it answers most of the purposes of money ...
It is presumable, that no country will be able to borrow of foreigners upon better terms, than the United States ... Hence as large a proportion of the cash of Europe as may be wanted, will be, in a certain sense, in our market, for the use of government. And this will naturally have the effect of a reduction of the rate of interest.

& Co., and its Dutch ally Hope & Co. These relationships were not simply important from the standpoint of the west side of the Atlantic, as Barings's (and to some extent even London's) own leadership in international finance was consolidated largely through its ties to the USA; as Valmori (2021) puts it "the U.S. market would become the company's main market." Barings helped Jefferson to finance the 1803 Louisiana purchase, and in 1817 was made the London agent of the Philadelphia-based Second Bank of United States (BUS), with Hope & Co. being granted the same status in Amsterdam. Barings helped to finance the Second BUS's initial specie reserves, and thereafter played a central role in managing the international liquidity needs of the USA, both public and private, until the BUS's charter lapsed in 1836. Barings played a particularly important role in helping the BUS to finance the international trade credit of American exporters, importers, and merchants operating as far afield as Asia (e.g. in the opium trade). It thus effectively acted as America's credit card, with the BUS's outstanding balances at Barings fluctuating year on year between net credits and debits in the hundreds of thousands and sometimes millions of dollars (Hidy 1944; see also Wallis 2001). Such transactions were of global significance; for a period in the 1830s "opium was balancing East–West trade through the American commerce in London bills" (Downs 1968, 434).

While the massive institution of the BUS in Philadelphia forged the single most important financial link to the old country in the early 19th century, Boston and Baltimore were in many respects just as well connected internationally. The US role in the lucrative opium trade, for example, was dominated by an alliance of merchants in Boston. This group of merchants had their own direct alliance with Barings, parallel to the Barings ties of the BUS in Philadelphia, that was mediated via Boston's Joshua Bates, who became a senior partner at Baring Brothers (Downs 1968). Boston was also home to Barings's special agent in the USA from 1828 to 1853, Thomas Wren Ward (Gregory 1983; Hidy 1941). Meanwhile, the most important transatlantic Anglo-American merchant (and eventually investment) banking house lineages had their roots in Baltimore; via the partnerships established in both the UK, and up and down the US Eastern seaboard, by the offspring of Baltimore's Alexander Brown (including Brown Shipley in Liverpool, and Brown Brothers & Co. in Philadelphia and New York, which eventually became Brown Brothers Harriman); and George Peabody, who, having originally built his business in Baltimore, founded the London-based George Peabody & Co (Kindleberger 1973). The latter evolved into London's J. S. Morgan when it was taken over by Peabody's partner, the prominent Boston merchant Julius Spencer Morgan, which under the leadership of his son John Pierpont Morgan spawned both the American J. P. Morgan (and via it Morgan Stanley) and the British Morgan Grenfell.

New York's ascendance over Philadelphia, Boston and Baltimore to the status of dominant US financial center emerged gradually out of a combination of favorable geography, politics, and international relationships with Britain, London, and its leading banking houses. Having already developed an enormous business financing the southern slave economy's cotton trade with Britain, New York was able to decisively outstrip its competitor cities after the 1825 opening of the Erie canal, which cemented its position as the primary gateway between the US interior and the East Coast—and thus to Europe and the world beyond (Kindleberger 1973). The Erie canal, like most early 19th-century American infrastructure projects, was a *public* project, which was built and operated as a state-owned enterprise of the State of New York. However, like all such public (and public–private chartered corporate) projects in America, it hinged on the raising of *private* funds on the American and international securities markets—and most importantly in London. In this case, the leading underwriter of New York's canal securities was Wall Street's Prime Ward & King. This firm was the primary New York–based ally of Barings, which led the marketing of canal securities in London (Burrows and Wallace 1998).

Politics intervened in the 1830s to reinforce New York's rise, with Philadelphia never recovering as a financial center from Andrew Jackson's failure to renew the charter of the Second Bank of the United States in 1836 (Kindleberger 1973). Deprived of US federal patronage and protection, the bank operated under a Pennsylvania state charter before collapsing during the financial crisis of 1839–1841—having become overextended partly by Pennsylvania's dirigiste use of it to finance a canal and railroad network that could compete with New York's Erie Canal, as well its massive operations in cotton market speculation and US state bond underwriting (Gregory 1983; Wallis 2001). There operations were centered on the BUS's own newly established London office, which allowed it to partially bypass its traditional dependence on Barings, but ultimately helped it to "stretch itself tight as a bowstring between London, Philadelphia, and the South" (Wallis 2001, 20).

While Philadelphia and the BUS self-destructed, New York's financial community consolidated its leadership in US finance largely via a three-pronged alliance with its counterparts in Boston and London, anchored by Barings and its allies Prime Ward & King in New York and Thomas Wren Ward in Boston. Through the strength of these connections linking them to Barings and New England, New York's banks were, importantly, able to maintain specie convertibility—and thus their domestic and international standing—during the crisis of 1839–1841, at a time when Philadelphia's banks were in disarray and using New York as a platform to "raid" the Northeast's specie reserves (Gregory 1983). This followed Barings's role in helping New York's banks to resume convertibility after the Panic of 1837. During this crisis, Barings had acted as a guarantor that allowed Prime Ward & King to obtain an enormous £1 million loan directly from the Bank of England, thus helping New York to quickly switch gears to receiving support from the world's most powerful foreign central bank, after Jackson abolished America's central bank (Dorfman 1951).

In the second half of the 19th century, the London-based Anglo-American merchant bank George Peabody & Co., and its successor partnerships J.S. and J.P Morgan, assumed leadership of the increasingly dominant New York–London axis, and helped to spearhead its further ascendence. Peabody and Morgan's rise was initially centered on their role as the leading marketers of American railroad securities in London, which simultaneously "laid the foundation for the rise of New York as the nation's principal capital market" (Carosso 1987, 56). Morgan's path to Wall Street dominance ran through Britain. Originally operating in New York only indirectly via its alliance with Duncan, Sherman & Company, the London-based House of Morgan planted its own feet on Wall Street in 1864, when Junius Spencer (J. S.) Morgan's son John Pierpont (J. P.) cofounded the partnership Dabney, Morgan & Co. This was reorganized as Drexel Morgan & Co. in 1871 (incorporating Philadelphia's Drexel), and finally as J. P. Morgan in 1895. The name J. S. Morgan lived on as the London half of the firm (then controlled by the New York–based J. P.), which in 1910 became Morgan Grenfell.

As late as 1902, the London Stock Exchange still had more than three times the capitalization of the NYSE (Hannah 2011), and Morgan's ability to position himself as the leading gateway to London for American securities issuers was crucial to his consolidation of his position as New York's leading underwriter. At the turn of the century, Morgan to a large extent created the market for American industrial corporate securities via his role in organizing, reorganizing, and managing the IPOs (and longer-term operations) of the monopolistic "trusts" (including U.S. Steel, General Electric, and International Harvester; see chapter 2, Figure 2.1). As well as selling securities in London, the Morgan-organized/reorganized trusts (incorporated in the "offshore" hub of New Jersey; see chapter 2) were almost invariably listed on the NYSE, helping to consolidate its position as the command center of American capitalism (Navin and Sears 1955). Morgan, like Barings before it, ultimately came to play a quasi-public role on both sides of the Atlantic; providing an emergency loan (with the Rothschilds) to the Cleveland administration that allowed it to maintain dollar gold convertibility during the Panic of 1893; organizing the Wall Street response, during a period when the USA still had no central bank, to the Panic of 1907; and later mediating a historic reversal of the net direction of credit flow between the USA and Britain, by becoming the sole purchasing agent for the British (and French) governments in the USA during WWI, in which capacity Morgan also organized bank syndicates that underwrote billions of dollars of bonds issued by Britain and France in the USA to pay for these purchases (Carosso 1987; Frieden 1988).

Despite the steady expansion of the US economy, and a gradual decline of the British Empire and economic prowess accelerated by WWI, New York never consistently surpassed London as a global FC. Even in the interwar period, cooperation between the centers was intense, as the USA tried to help Great Britain to restore the gold-sterling standard, by maintaining low interest rates and an artificially high dollar to pound exchange rate. According to Michie (2006), this helped to fuel a lending boom in the USA, which, being followed in turn by the Great Crash and the Great Depression, ultimately slowed down the growth of New York as an FC. Meanwhile, on the other side of the Atlantic, the dogged 1920s attempts to restore the gold-sterling standard at the prewar exchange rate, entailed more or less directly sacrificing the competitiveness of British manufacturing to the interests of the City.

With the breakup of Morgan's transatlantic Money Trust, the advent of increased financial regulation from the New Deal era, the establishment of the IMF and the World Bank after the Bretton Woods Conference in 1944, and the US federal centralization of power within the Federal Reserve system formerly delegated largely to the Federal Reserve Bank of New York, the center of power in US finance partially shifted from Wall Street to Washington, DC. London did not flourish either, having been partially destroyed physically during the war, and struggling after its conclusion with depression in the British and European economies, the breakup of the British Empire and sterling zone, and the fall in the international standing of sterling. These shifts in power were not altogether accidental; as US Secretary of State Henry Morganthau put it, US policy in the immediate postwar period consciously aimed to "move the financial center of the world from London and Wall Street, to the US Treasury" (Shaxson 2011, 87). Public and domestic finance dominated over private and international finance on both sides of the Atlantic from the 1930s to late 1950s, marking the lowest point of the NY–LON axis in its 20th-century history. The UK's attention was largely consumed by balance of payments problems, both during and after the war. Meanwhile, the USA sought to assist the UK and its other allies with these problems largely through official channels, from Lend-Lease during the war to IMF lending and the Marshall Plan after the war. New York was a larger FC than London during this period, but its power was almost entirely centered on the US domestic market. Indeed, although the international power of Wall Street was contained, the domestic power of New York was consolidated, as securities market regulation contributed to the demise of regional exchanges, as well as the nationwide expansion of New York–headquartered brokerage firms such as Merrill Lynch (Michie 2006).

From the late 1950s, however, the rise of the Eurocurrency markets breathed life back into the axis. The key initial decision was the agreement of the Bank of England in 1958 to allow British banks to take deposits and make loans in foreign currencies—and above all US dollars (Strange, 1997). This was followed by a series of decisions that allowed foreign banks (and within certain parameters British merchant banks) to conduct foreign currency activities outside of the scope of capital controls or regulatory oversight (see chapter 5). Although its initial development in the 1950s had been pioneered by British merchant banks and Soviet state-owned banks (see chapter 8), the rapid expansion of the London Euromarket in the 1960s was driven primarily by the activities of US banks, led by Citi, who made use of London as an international platform to escape US capital controls, as well as regulation generally (see chapter 5). The impacts of this expansion of US bank activity in London were felt on both sides of the Atlantic. As Susan Strange put it from a US standpoint:

> Who can say that the internationalization of American banking would have taken place so fast and furiously if London had not been there, ready and waiting with 'Welcome' on the mat?
>
> (Strange 1997, 38)

Meanwhile, from a British standpoint:

> London regained its position as the center for international financial business, but this business was centered on the dollar and the major players were American banks and their clients
>
> (Walter 1991, 182)

In the late 1960s, 80% of Euromarket borrowing and lending worldwide was conducted through London (Cassis 2006). In the 1970s, London consolidated its position as the main hub for US banks serving US corporations operating in Europe, as well as for recycling petrodollars. The 1970s also witnessed the shift from fixed to floating currencies, which unleashed an explosion of international foreign currency trading, speculation, and hedging activities concentrated in New York and London. The IMF, in Washington, DC, thus ceased to be the central arbiter of the global exchange rate system, with this role rather shifting to private firms and markets in the axis.

After the chaotic 1970s, financial deregulation in the USA and the UK in the 1980s helped the axis to boom. The 1986 UK regulatory "Big Bang" unleashed a new wave of US banks entering and consolidating their role in the London securities sector. It also accelerated the transition in London from a culture of class privilege to "smartness" and open hiring practices, making it more like New York (Leyshon and Thrift 1995). Canary Wharf, a new prime location for finance, was built in the early 1990s on top of the postindustrial ruins of the London Docklands, and came to be occupied mostly by large institutions, thus operating more like New York than the traditional City, with its myriad of small financial firms (Amin and Thrift 1992). During this same period, Tokyo challenged the axis, but it relied mainly on the Japanese market, forging relatively few links with foreign institutions. Investment bankers in Tokyo never lost a sense of inferiority in relation to Wall Street and the City (Miyazaki 2003), even as Japanese firms grabbed headlines around the world by splashing borrowed money on international trophy acquisitions. In 1991, Tokyo imploded under the weight of a real estate bubble and has not recovered as a financial center since.

Accelerated EU financial integration in the 1990s and 2000s consolidated the role of London as a center of European wholesale finance and as a gateway into Europe for US financial institutions. There were fears of Frankfurt challenging London, but these underestimated the power of London and ignored the role of the axis. London became the center of financial transactions in the euro, and a wave of mergers and acquisitions following the launch of the euro offered lucrative deals for London-based investment banks. London also became the agent of Wall Street's shareholder value revolution of the 1980s and 1990s, which spread to Europe in the late 1990s and early 2000s (Wójcik 2002). Security concerns after 9/11, and the more stringent reporting requirements imposed in the USA by the Sarbanes–Oxley Act, further reinforced the position of London in the axis. New York, however, also boomed as a FC, as further deregulation paved the way for unprecedented profits and bonuses for Wall Street investment banks (see chapters 3 and 5).

Throughout its history, the development of the New York–London axis has been underpinned by strong commonalities and complementarities. The cities share a common language and common law (literally), and a strong tradition of economic and political liberalism; creating a fertile ground for belief in the self-regulation of business and finance, as well corporate governance and accounting standards geared toward business owners rather than other stakeholders (Morck 2005). Peck and Tickell (2002) refer to New York and London as the principal sales offices of neoliberalism (alongside Chicago and Washington, DC). New York and London form the financial axis of the Anglo-American (Anglo-Saxon) culture. Their political, cultural, and business elites interact closely, leading to a whole lifestyle based on a fusion of London and New York (Smith, 2005). This inspired the term NY–LON, coined in a Newsweek's article which stated that:

> as different as New York and London are, a growing number of people are living, working, and playing in the two cities as if they were one
>
> (McGuire and Chan 2000, 42)

While *commonalities* between New York and London allow financial firms and professionals to move almost seamlessly between the two centers, lowering the cost of interactions, *complementarities* create opportunities, making interactions highly profitable. While New York commands access to the largest and most liquid domestic financial market in the world, London's physical, political, and historical geography implies access to a different time zone, European markets and global connections (for example, with India, Hong Kong, and Australia)—with much of this the legacy of empire (see chapter 7). London is the place where US banks can employ French- and German-speaking experts, who want to stay close to their home countries. Taking advantage of the sheer size of its liquid domestic market and the world's deepest pool of financial engineering talent, New York leads global financial innovation (Strange 1997). Hedge funds come from the USA, and so do venture capital and private equity funds. Most new products and methods of trading in the global securities markets have emanated from New York (Michie 2006). London, in turn, has specialized as a center where financial firms (with US banks in the lead) adapt financial innovation from the USA to foreign and international markets. A number of innovations from US retail banking, including data processing centers and telephone banking, have been adopted in the UK before spreading to the rest of Europe (Leyshon and Pollard 2000).

Connectivity between London and New York is also served by physical infrastructure. No other cities on the opposite sides of an ocean are connected by a denser web of fiber optics lines, more regular flights, or transmit more information between each other (Warf 2006). The world's first teleport, i.e. an office park with satellite earth stations connected to fiber optic cables, was opened on Staten Island in 1981, and operated jointly by Merrill Lynch and the Port Authority of New York and New Jersey (Warf 1995)—highlighting the role of finance in forging connections between the two cities. It is a combination of commonalities and complementarities that underpins this connectivity between New York and London, and their coevolution as leading centers in the GFN.

4.3 The Axis in the Global Financial Crisis

To make sense of the global financial crisis, we need to acknowledge the role of the New York–London axis. If we start with the house price bubble fueled by mortgage lending, we should note that, in the UK, property prices in London in the late 1990s started their ascent earlier, and by 2007 grew by a higher percentage, than anywhere else in the UK. In the USA, while the subprime bubble was centered on the Sunbelt, New York was also among the leading cities in terms of property price increases in the early 2000s (Martin 2011). As global media centers, New York and London are home to media companies that sustained the irrational exuberance of the bubble, perpetuating the myth of property as a safe and profitable investment—a narrative undoubtedly influenced by buoyant real estate markets in these cities (Shiller 2008). Indeed, as discussed in chapter 2, the very fact that these two cities are leading global FCs with exceptionally concentrated spatial economic rents means that their own property markets in many respects *do* largely bear out such assumptions of stability—creating a potential distortion in the mental map of the world when applied to, for example, the purchase and securitization of mortgages originated in truly irrationally frothy markets such as pre-GFC Phoenix or Las Vegas with their vast surrounding tracts of cheap desert land. This argument resonates with cultural geographies of finance, viewing financial centers as networks of actors that develop stories and interpretations of the world economy, and in turn spread these to the rest of the world (Allen and Pryke 1999). In other words, FCs play a significant part in the herd behavior, both in FCs themselves, and in the wider world, that fuels financial crises (Clark and Wójcik 2001).

Meanwhile, the areas of financial deregulation and regulatory laxity that most directly contributed to the crisis were led by the USA and the UK. The repeal of the Glass–Steagall Act allowed deposit-taking banks to develop investment banking businesses (and vice versa); the Commodity Futures Modernization Act of 2000 left derivatives and OTC markets basically unregulated; while the Financial Services Authority in the UK maintained a flexible regulatory regime, relying on self-regulation (Johnson and Kwak 2010). Active lobbying by the financial industry contributed to deregulation, with the ostensible competitive threat from foreign FCs being one of the lobbyists' major arguments. Financial companies, with investment banks in the lead, mostly operating in both New York and London, could above all play US and UK authorities against each other to advance the loosening of, and prevent the tightening of, regulatory measures in either country. The move toward "light touch" regulation was thus "a product not only of narrow sectoral and political interest but also of spatial competition" (French et al. 2009, 292).

Financial deregulation, and just as importantly the failure to adequately update regulation to keep pace with financial innovation, facilitated the expansion of the shadow banking system in both the USA and the UK; with investment banks (such as Bear Stearns, Goldman Sachs, Lehman Brothers, Merrill Lynch, and Morgan Stanley) and the investment banking arms of bank holding companies (such as JPMorgan Chase and Citigroup) being the leading players (see also chapters 3, 5, and 6). The key investment banks involved were the icons of Wall Street, headquartered in New York, with major offices and operations in London. The latter, among other specialties, established itself as the leading center of mortgage securitization in Europe, for both UK and foreign mortgages, with the help of Wall Street investment banks (Aalbers 2009b; Pryke and Lee 1995). Indeed, the securitization of mortgages, pioneered in 18th-century Prussia (Pistor 2019), was reexported to much of Europe in an Americanized form in 1986 via Salomon Brothers' office in London, which sold securitized mortgages to investors in the UK and Europe (Wainwright, 2009).

The operation of the shadow banking system through the axis can be illustrated by the New York–headquartered AIG, one of the world's largest insurance companies, which was deeply implicated in the global financial crisis. In September 2008, AIG was bailed out by the US government to prevent its imminent bankruptcy—as caused almost single-handedly by AIG Financial Products (AIG FP), a subsidiary headquartered in Fairfield, CT (an extension of the New York City region along the northern coast of Long Island Bay), but with its main operations in London. AIG FP in London was (as highlighted in chapter 6) a leader in the issuance of CDS, and the sale of CDS as well as CDOs to customers in the USA (for example, Goldman Sachs) and Europe (for example, Societe Generale). Prior to 2007, AIG

FP was not only the most profitable part of AIG, but was also referred to as the "'golden goose for the entire [Wall] Street'" (National Commission, 2011), reflecting its key role as the conduit for CDO and CDS production and distribution in Europe, and the apparently magical ability of its products to make risks disappear from balance sheets. Reflecting this status, the lowest amount of pay that the AIG FP CEO in London, Joseph J. Cassano, awarded himself annually between 2002 and 2007, was US$38 million.

Key accomplices of investment banks in the shadow banking system were rating agencies, which rated CDOs highly regardless of their underlying asset quality (and were paid for this service by investment banks), and thus made them attractive to institutional investors such as pension and mutual funds. The largest agencies—Standard & Poor's and Moody's—are headquartered in New York, while the third largest, Fitch Ratings, has its global headquarters split between New York and London. We can and should extend the list of suspects to accountancy companies, which were supposed to evaluate the financial affairs of banks and warn the public; law firms, which were signing off on investment banks' contracts as not only legal, but also undertaken in good faith; as well as management consultants involved in advisory work for corporations and institutional investors. In other words, we should consider the global financial crisis to be a failure of not only the financial sector, but of the whole FABS complex, as rooted above all in New York and London (Wójcik 2012b).

The New York–London axis was thus an important component of the multicausal mix that underpinned the global financial crisis. New York and London were not simply geographic platforms for the firms and individuals involved in the crisis, but provided social and cultural milieus in which the types of behavior fueling the crisis—an explosive combination of hubris, complacency, and greed—flourished. Just as importantly, the Ponzi features intrinsic to asset bubbles have a geographical dimension at the urban, national, and international levels, which ultimately chiefly benefited the axis (Harvey 2011; Kindleberger and Aliber 2005). It is not entirely clear to what extent, or at what stage in the subprime bubble, the firms and professionals in these cities genuinely believed the expanding mass of securities backed by US Sunbelt mortgages to be inherently sound investments; as opposed seeing them as risky investments that they could nevertheless render genuinely safe through financial innovation; as opposed to fully recognizing the risks in these activities, but simply not caring about them, as long as they could position themselves to profit in the short-term. Ultimately, though, it is not clear that this actually matters, as they had in any event, from a geographic and relational standpoint, positioned themselves at the top of the subprime securitization pyramid scheme, and thus benefited most from it. Meanwhile, those in peripheral locations far from the axis (e.g. the proverbial suckers in Düsseldorf described by Lewis 2010), joined the pyramid last and lost most. More broadly, at the national level, evidence suggests that, in the wake of the crisis, the income gaps between New York and the rest of the USA, and between London and the rest of the UK, have grown (Gaponomics 2011).

4.4 Underestimated Power and Exaggerated Decline: Stocks, Flows, and Networks

According to the GaWC global network connectivity ranking, using 2016 data on office networks of 175 FABS firms, London claimed the top spot, followed closely by New York, with the latter having 96% of London's connectivity. London and New York also claimed the two top spots in the Global Financial Centers Index launched by the City of London Corporation. The Xinhua–Dow Jones International Financial Centers Development Index launched in July 2010 as a joint venture of the official press agency of the PRC and the New York–based financial information company, placed New York ahead of London. It is not surprising that organizations from both London and New York were directly involved in these rating exercises.

A disadvantage of rating methodologies, however, is that they collapse differences in the position of individual centers into relatively small numerical differences. In GFCI 29 released in March 2021, New York has a rating of 764, while Luxembourg, ranked 17th, has a rating of 712. Rating methodologies intentionally focus on the competitiveness of FCs, rather than their size, and use measures of market sentiment, based on surveys among practitioners, as an important input into ratings. This allows for a significant degree of change in ratings and rankings over time. An enthusiast may praise this sensitivity to change in the landscape of FCs, while a sceptic may see it as an attempt to feed the media's hunger for news. Meanwhile, an opponent may say that it is an expression of financial sector interests, as it suggests that the position of FCs is fragile and may need to be protected—for example by permissive regulation.

Our argument is that such ratings greatly underestimate the dominance of New York and London in global finance, and consequently both underplay the role of the axis, and overplay its ostensible competitive vulnerability. To quantify the role of New York and London in global finance, we complement synthetic ratings and connectivity measures with easier to interpret figures on financial flows and stocks managed and controlled by these cities: namely foreign exchange turnover, interest rate derivatives turnover, external bank assets, stock trading value, as well as data on employment. The first four items cover key financial markets, while employment represents the local operational substance of (as opposed to simply transaction booking within) financial centers. To be sure, all data except for employment are only available at the country level. Nevertheless,

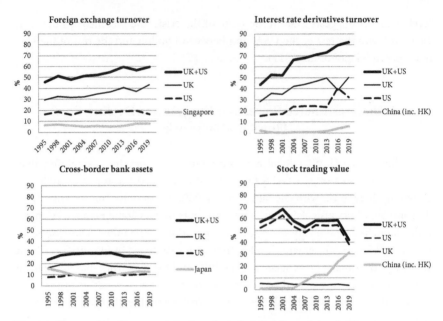

Fig. 4.1 Shares of leading countries in selected global financial activities

Sources: based on data from the Bank for International Settlements and the World Federation of Exchanges; adapted from Wójcik (2013a).

existing studies suggest that the level of concentration of the selected financial activities in New York (for the USA) and particularly in London (for the UK) is very high (Parr and Budd 2000).

As Figure 4.1 shows, the Anglo-American share in global finance in 2019 was 26% for cross-border bank assets, 42% for stock trading, 60% for forex and 82% for interest rate derivatives. The figure also shows the share of the largest market other than the USA and the UK. The dominance of the UK and US is lowest in cross-border bank assets, wherein Japan, and a number of continental European countries, all of which have powerful banks, have long also played a leading role. Anglo-American dominance has also waned at a remarkable rate in recent years for overall stock trading, in which Mainland China was roughly tied with the USA as of 2019. However, the apparent rise of China here is somewhat deceptive, as its overall stock market capitalization (even including Hong Kong) is still less than one-third of US market cap, and its actual free float capitalization is lower still. China thus has an entirely disproportionate volume of trading churn in relation to its importance in global securities markets; reflecting the incredible intensity of re-tail trading, and unparalleled fervor of risk-seeking speculative Keynesian "animal spirits" there, broadly (see chapter 2). Furthermore, China plays only a minor role in international stock trading, wherein, if one considers trading in foreign (cross-listed) stocks only, the share of the UK and the USA would exceed 80% (Wójcik

2011a). Anglo-American dominance has actually been increasing, moreover, in two other key bedrock areas of truly global financial market activity; namely forex and interest rate derivatives, wherein the combined UK and US share was quite a bit higher in 2019 than it was before the GFC. Britain/London alone accounted for almost half of worldwide activity in these areas in 2019—showing a notable rebound after a brief dip in 2016.

The often-expected decline of Anglo-American financial power is thus, at the very least, exaggerated. The figure also illustrates important generic features of the axis. Its relative strength lies in securities (including stocks and derivatives) and trading (including securities and currencies), rather in than traditional bank assets such as loans. New York and London are, after all, the centers of the investment bank capitalism discussed in the preceding chapter. This focus of the axis on securities is confirmed by Table 4.1, which presents data on financial sector employment in selected FCs. Tokyo, Paris, and leading Chinese centers may have comparable numbers of people employed in credit and insurance, but employment in the securities industry in these cities lags far behind New York and London. Even Boston and Chicago employ more people in the securities industry than Paris, while the industry is small, though growing rapidly, in Beijing, Shanghai, and Frankfurt. As discussed in the preceding chapter, the securities industry is centered on investment banking and asset management, and constitutes the elite

Table 4.1 Number of employees in the financial sector (in 1000s)

City	Securities industry		Credit & insurance	
	2008	1998	2008	1998
New York	262	217	375	414
London	123	80	209	234
Hong Kong	70	55	137	114
Boston	68	58	125	121
Tokyo	62	77	296	392
Chicago	62	43	212	224
Paris	34	26	263	276
Beijing	16	—	211	73
Shanghai	13	—	193	66
Frankfurt am Main	10	9	58	62

Note: cities are defined as: Hong Kong—SAR; Beijing, Shanghai—municipality; Paris—Ile-de-France; Frankfurt am Main—Stadt; Tokyo—Prefecture (Tokyo-to); London—Greater London; New York—New York–Northern Jersey–Long Island Metropolitan Statistical Area (MSA); Boston—Boston–Cambridge–Quincy MSA; Chicago—Chicago–Naperville-Joliet MSA. Data for Germany is for 1999 and 2008; Japan—1996 and 2006; otherwise for 1998 and 2008. The definitions of securities industry and credit & insurance industry are not fully comparable between countries.

Sources: National Bureau of Statistics of China; Unistatis (France); Bundesagentur für Arbeit Statistik (Germany); Japanese Statistics Bureau; NOMIS, Office for National Statistics (UK); County Business Patterns, US Census Bureau; adapted from Wójcik (2013a).

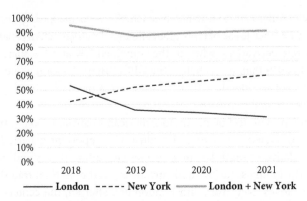

Fig. 4.2 Percentage of finance professionals surveyed who
described city as the world's leading financial hub,
2018–2021

Source: Metcalf 2021a (based on surveys by Duff & Phelps).

of the financial sector, with remuneration far exceeding that in credit and insurance or any other producer services (Wójcik 2012). In fact, between 1998 and 2008, financial firms actually shed jobs in credit and insurance in New York and London, but compensated for this by creating new (and much more highly paid) jobs in the securities industry (see chapter 3).

The single most important potential challenge to the axis in recent years has come from Brexit. Notably, however, this seems to have so far mostly prompted a shift in activity within the axis, from London to New York, as opposed to a loss of influence by the axis. As shown in Figure 4.2, 91% of financial professionals surveyed in 2021 described either London or New York as the world's leading financial hub, down only slightly from 95% in 2018; even while the majority opinion as to which of the two was more important shifted away from London toward New York. Third place position, meanwhile, remained barely visible, with Hong Kong and Singapore tied at 2.2% as of 2021.

What is particularly remarkable is that even in the midst of Brexit turmoil, nearly one-third of all financial professionals surveyed still said they thought that London, rather than New York, was the world's leading financial hub. Meanwhile, the idea of a continental European challenger arising to London, whether Frankfurt, Brussels, or Paris, remains as always the dog that will not bark. This is not to say that nothing is moving from London to the EU; however, the way that both people and money are moving seems to be designed to achieve an EU regulatory presence by moving the bare minimum of actual substance that firms can get away with. More than 99% of European share trading in London, for example, shifted to EU-based exchanges *within one working day* of the end of the Brexit transition at the start of 2021. However, three-quarters of this moved to platforms in Amsterdam (including the Turquoise Europe platform set up there in late 2020 by the

London Stock Exchange itself), which has essentially become a massive offshore share trading hub—that has now actually surpassed London to become the single largest share trading center in Europe—with disproportionately little actual local human activity (Vaghela 2021; Vaghela et al. 2021).

In other words, London's financial role in relation to Europe has become somewhat inverted, from serving as an offshore hub within the EU, to a serving a substantive financial employment hub on its periphery that makes use of EU offshore platforms to retain market access. Notably, even when firms are asked about plans to relocate *staff* to Europe, the pattern of preferring offshore platforms, suggestive of a desire to actually shift as few people as possible, persists. An early 2021 survey by EY for example, found the offshore platform of Dublin to be the top place where firms planned to relocate London staff, followed by Luxembourg, with Frankfurt and Paris only taking third and fourth place respectively (and Amsterdam, now the "number one" share trading center in Europe, in fifth place; Metcalf 2021b). This is particularly interesting given the EU's efforts to prevent firms from simply setting up "shells" in EU offshore platforms to avoid actually moving staff out of London. In fact, our conversations with industry insiders suggest that the very aggressiveness of the EU's efforts here have, atleast in some cases, simply convinced firms that trying to move anyone or anything out of London to the EU is just more trouble than it is worth.

4.5 Conclusions and Implications

The objectives of this chapter were to: highlight the historical development of the relations between New York and London as financial centers; explore the role of these relations in the global financial crisis; and shed light on the possible impact of the crisis, and subsequent events such as Brexit, on the position of the two centers in global finance. A historical analysis of the relationship between New York and London recasts the issue of interactions between FCs in terms of commonalities and complementarities. It argues that the degree of commonality, complementarity, and connectivity between the two leading global financial centers justifies the use of the term "the New York–London axis." A review of literature on the global financial crisis illustrates that, to a significant extent, the global financial crisis originated in the axis, with New York and London acting as the key decision-making centers in the shadow banking system, as well as key loci of financial deregulation. More broadly, data on financial stocks, flows and employment show that the joint dominance of New York and London in global finance must not be underestimated. New York and London still have no serious challengers in terms of the overall conjunction of multiple key global financial activities that they sit astride. Even in the wake of Brexit, London has no real peer, either within our outside of Europe, apart from New York.

These findings have implications for literature and policy. First, when we acknowledge the centrality of the New York–London axis, we can view the rise of Asian financial centers as a choice between, or a combination of, two options: namely either joining the axis, or challenging it. The GaWC research shows that after the NY–LON axis itself, the most important connections between world cities are those linking Hong Kong to London and New York (Taylor et al. 2011). In theory, a tri-city NY–LON–KONG successor to the axis could connect the leading English-speaking business centers in each of the world's major eight-hour time zones. On the other hand, a more complex alternative might emerge from deepening connectivity between NY–LON, and the triad of Beijing, Shanghai, and Hong Kong—with the latter three connected through strong complementarities in relation to the Chinese market, focusing on political, commercial, and offshore financial functions respectively (Lai 2012). There are, however, limits to either the NY–LON–KONG scenario, or the progressive deepening of relationships between NY–LON and the Chinese triad. Although potential complementarities are enormous, the commonalities between NY–LON and Hong Kong are smaller than those between New York and London, notwithstanding Hong Kong's recent British imperial roots. Moreover, Hong Kong's deepening political instability, and uncertain political and legal status in relation to the Mainland, seems likely to thwart any potential for it to move up the ranks of global FCs—or even maintain its existing position. Shanghai, meanwhile, has no hope of becoming a leading international FC as long as it is trapped behind Mainland capital controls (notwithstanding limited international stock market connect facilities), and as long as the Mainland lacks even a minimally credible rule of law. Indeed, it is not even clear if Shanghai, as opposed to China's political center of power Beijing, should be considered the Mainland's currently leading financial center (see chapter 8). Finally, Singapore—despite having institutional and political advantages over all three of these Chinese cities, and like Hong Kong also enjoying relational advantages stemming from its status as a key node in Britain's financial "second empire"—is likely to be hamstrung by its lack of direct proximity to (or location in) a major market comparable to China, the US, or the EU.

If anything, far from witnessing the rise of a new global financial multipolarity centered largely on Asia, we thus actually seem to be most likely heading toward an increasingly monopolar New York–dominated financial world (see also data in chapter 9), wherein London, closely linked to New York, still remains miles ahead of any competition for second place. A crucial implication of this remarkable durability of the NY–LON axis concerns the mobility of the firms and professionals based in the axis. It suggests, in particular, that the argument that bankers working in these centers could potentially just pack up and move elsewhere en masse is not only self-serving, but also highly exaggerated. As Allen argued, "the networks of international finance have little choice other than go through its financial district for certain types of trading and dealing" (Allen 2010,

2898). Insiders themselves admit that "only the most swingeing regulation would outweigh the City's agglomeration and time-zone benefits" (Guthrie 2011, 20). It is instructive to see thinly veiled threats made in 2011 by HSBC to move its headquarters from London to Hong Kong, and by Barclays to move to New York. Neither move materialized. Even the titanic disruption of Brexit, which has been more damaging to the City than any regulatory tightening ever could be, has so far prompted a remarkably modest actual movement of employment and substantive activity. Consequently, banning undesirable, and just as importantly *promoting desirable* financial practices in the USA and the UK, can probably achieve more than the opponents of financial reform want us to believe. Global finance starts on Wall Street and in the City of London, and global financial reform has to recognize this.

Ultimately at stake is the reform of the global financial system. Existing reform plans show little consideration of the role of FCs, and no recognition of the New York–London connection. The Financial Crisis Inquiry Report in the USA talked about Wall Street on almost every single page, but mentioned London only in the context of AIG FP. Conversely, the reports of the UK House of Commons Commission on the banking crisis used the City in their titles, but hardly mentioned Wall Street or the USA. The Financial Stability Board hosted by the BIS, the Global financial stability report of the IMF (2010), and the communications of the European Commission on financial services or supervision policy, never mentioned the words "financial center," "London," New York," "the City," or "Wall Street." In our view, notably, for global finance to change, a significant degree of change must be generated internally within the financial sector—and given the concentration of key personnel, expertise, knowledge, transactions, and power of global finance in New York and London, the axis should also be considered in the ongoing debates around financial sector change. Wall Street and the City represent communities that jointly bear significant responsibility for what has happened as well as what will happen in global finance. As *The Financial Times* put it "What is now urgently needed is some moral authority from the government and also the financial sector." Such an exhortation might seem to be almost laughable; however, one should consider that the ranks of Wall Street financiers have historically included the likes of Alexander Hamilton. Notably, a shift in stance from resisting reform, to enabling and collaborating in it, is perhaps above all a question of enlightened self-interest on the part of the financial sector itself. This is now confronted by an increasingly volatile and potentially threatening political environment within the USA and UK, that is largely a direct result of the financial sector's own destabilizing impact on society. When viewed on a scale of centuries, the GFN, and within it the position of key FCs such as London and New York, are incredibly durable. Ironically, however, history also suggests that their position over a time frame of the next few decades may be much more doubtful.

5

From the Euromarket to the Great Inversion

The Political Geographic Paradox of Offshore Banking

5.1 Introduction

While the GFN is operated by firms and professionals based in financial centers such as London or New York, the products that it manufactures consist of abstract legal and accounting constructs. These constructs disproportionately reside in an offshore legal space anchored by networks of specialized offshore jurisdictions (OJs) which afford various elements of legal, regulatory, and fiscal flexibility.

OJs are usually analyzed in terms of their negative impacts on *other* economies. These include depriving states of tax revenues, enabling illicit financial activities and corruption, undermining global financial regulation and stability, and instigating a "race-to-the-bottom" that grinds down international standards in these areas (Palan et al. 2010; Shaxson 2011). However, the leveraging of legal, regulatory, and tax advantages to attract international financial activity—even if only the nominal legal and accounting footprint of this activity—also places powerful economic, political, and potentially fiscal stresses on the states and societies hosting OJs, particularly when they are relatively small in size compared to the activities they host (Christensen et al. 2016; Shaxson and Christensen 2013).

What are particularly important, in this respect, are the implications of the basic tension between offshore as a zone of private escape from state authority, on the one hand, and the inherently inescapable dependence of private financial property on state protection, on the other. As noted in chapter 2, offshore sovereign protection costs usually fall largely onshore by default, being underwritten by the countries that host the underlying activities or assets referenced by, or that are home to the actors engaged in these activities. However, as highlighted by the global financial and eurozone crises, small states with oversized international financial sectors have also increasingly found themselves facing the nightmare scenario of having to backstop part of the vast financial "casino" intermediated through their borders (Shaxson and Christensen 2013). In cases such as Ireland and Cyprus, the economic and social consequences have been disastrous (Donovan and Murphy 2013; Michaelides 2014). Meanwhile, Iceland only avoided a similar fate by repudiating its banks' debts, and largely

Sticky Power. Daniel Haberly and Dariusz Wòjcik, Oxford University Press.
© Daniel Haberly and Dariusz Wòjcik (2022). DOI: 10.1093/oso/9780198870982.003.0005

disconnecting itself from the global financial system (Baldursson and Portes 2014). Even in the UK, the state's exposure to failing financial institutions in the global financial crisis prompted concerns of a "Reykjavik-on-Thames" (*Economist* 2009).

There is a voluminous body of case-study work examining the national historical pathways—particularly of political and economic capture—that have led to financial and fiscal disaster in specific offshore banking jurisdictions (e.g. Aliber and Zoega 2011; Baldursson and Portes 2014; Christensen et al. 2016; Connor et al. 2012; Donovan and Murphy 2013; Michaelides 2014). However, the growing tendency for OJs to become part of the collateral damage from their own activities also raises puzzling questions about the long-term structural evolution of offshore banking. Prior to the turn of the millennium, OJs mostly helped to generate financial and debt crises whose effects were felt *elsewhere*—most notably the Euromarket-centered early 1980s LDC debt crisis (Strange 1994), which left decades of economic devastation in its wake for much of the developing world. Over the past couple of decades, however, they have increasingly begun to self-destruct in devastating financial and fiscal crises of their own. The key question is what underlying global processes—if any—have led to this change? Have these countries simply been swept up in some overarching tendency toward "financialization" (Epstein 2005; O Riain 2012; Raza et al. 2016), both onshore and offshore, that has raised the stakes of hosting financial activities in general? Or are they victims of some more specific shift in the architecture of global finance? The answer to this question is not simply of consequence to OJs themselves; rather, it goes to the heart of the question of the basic stability of offshore as an institutional space within the GFN.

The remainder of this chapter is divided into four sections, which seek to answer this question by providing a novel account of the global evolution of offshore banking from the 1980s to the global financial crisis. As we demonstrate, Ireland, Iceland, and Cyprus were the most acute casualties of a broader global structural shift in the logic of offshore banking that occurred between the early 1980s and early 2000s. As shown in section 5.2, prior to this structural shift, the growth of offshore banking centers had been primarily driven by the deposit-taking and lending activities of *foreign* banks, in the Euromarket. As these banks were back-stopped by their home states "onshore," this system posed little risk to offshore host states. From the 1980s, however, widespread onshore deregulation undermined the relative regulatory advantages of the Euromarket. Meanwhile, the growing importance of home state consolidated capital supervision—coordinated via the Basel framework put in place largely to address earlier Euromarket regulatory failures—encouraged the rise of alternative shadow banking-based regulatory arbitrage strategies. In the context of these shadow banking arbitrage strategies, the regulatory significance of on/off-balance sheet increasingly superseded that of onshore/offshore in the traditional sense.

Together, these changes produced a two-fold shift in the geographic logic of offshore banking. First (as discussed in further detail in chapter 6), "small islands" (e.g. the Caymans, Jersey), increasingly shifted from hosting the deposit-taking and lending activities of foreign banks, to the off balance sheet securitization vehicles of these banks. Second, the fact that the regulatory arbitrage potential of these securitization vehicles was primarily conditioned by the *home* state capital treatment of their sponsor banks, fostered the growth of a new axis of bank *nationality*-based international regulatory arbitrage. This new logic of arbitrage involved using international mergers and acquisitions—in a logic both paralleling and intersecting with the home state-based fiscal logic of corporate tax "inversions"—to shift assets to the ownership of banks headquartered in states with relatively permissive home capital regulators (and typically also lower corporate tax rates).

As we show in section 5.3, this shift of assets to lightly taxed and regulated jurisdictions at the *home* state level—which we dub the "Great Inversion"—disproportionately encouraged the growth of the national banks of European "midshore" banking centers such as the UK, Switzerland, Netherlands, Belgium, Ireland, and Iceland. The banks and governments of these countries, in effect, took advantage of the new paradigm of home-based regulation to double down on a much higher risk trajectory of banking sector growth than they had pursued in the past. This had a major impact on the overall organization of the global banking system; all told, the growth of European midshore national banks involved, in market share terms, the reallocation of roughly one-quarter of worldwide cross-border banking assets, on a home nationality basis, from the late 1980s to 2007 (and an even larger percentage of assets at the level of the world's largest banks). Furthermore, this European midshore national bank growth was disproportionately driven by entry into the riskiest "shadow banking" activities implicated in the global financial crisis, wherein the total pre-crisis market share of these banks (most importantly British, Swiss, Dutch, and Belgian) was only slightly less than the American banks that had invented these instruments. As we show, however, this was not so much the result of a *challenge* to Wall Street investment banks from European midshore national banks, as of the latter's outright *acquisition of* a substantial number of leading Wall Street, as well as London, investment/merchant banks. These European midshore national banks were thus able to achieve, in effect, an international vertical integration of regulatory arbitrage between NYLON financial innovation capabilities, and their own home state-specific tax and regulatory advantages.

By the eve of the crisis, the old offshore misalignment between the geographies of bank nationality and jurisdiction of operation (or booking) had been largely superseded by a new misalignment between the size of multinational banking groups, and the size of their home states' economies—and in conjunction with this, between bank liability currency denomination, and home state central bank lender of last resort capacity. As we show in section 5.4, this new misalignment was fundamentally unstable, as the responsibility for backstopping the riskiest parts of the international banking system was now disproportionately concentrated on small European states with an inherently low capacity to fulfill this responsibility. In the wake of the global financial crisis, the major European midshore banking centers were thus forced to restore their national banks to health primarily by downsizing them, while also trying (with varying success or failure) to minimize broader national fiscal, financial, and economic disruption. The Great Inversion thus unwound.

We conclude in section 5.5 by suggesting that offshore banking centers face a political–geographic paradox that renders their development intrinsically unstable. In fact, this political–geographic paradox raises the basic question of how and why offshore banking can exist at all, for any length of time, on any significant scale. One of the key answers to this question is, we argue, that offshore banking is ultimately not simply an expression of the private circumvention or subversion of onshore state regulatory frameworks, but also of efforts by *onshore states themselves* to escape from the constraints imposed on their strategic freedom of action by their *own* tax and regulatory frameworks. In other words, the scope for the private sector to make use of offshore devices to subvert onshore political agency is something that is fundamentally, by definition, continuously negotiated and renegotiated politically, both onshore and offshore. At the same time, however, neither onshore nor offshore political agency is evenly distributed internationally in this process; rather, political agency is concentrated in the hands of the most powerful world governments, and their closest political allies both onshore and offshore.

5.2 The 1980s International Banking Regulatory Reconfiguration and the Decline of the Offshore Euromarket

The concepts of offshore finance, and offshore financial center or jurisdiction, are notoriously resistant to neat definition. Particularly challenging, is the fact that analyses of "offshore" problems such as corporate profit-shifting, financial regulatory arbitrage, or financial secrecy, typically show that these are dominated by what can be described as large "midshore" or "onshore–offshore" jurisdictions, as opposed to the "small islands" stereotypically associated with offshore. Well-known examples include the central role of Ireland, the Netherlands, and (formerly) Belgium in corporate profit shifting, of Switzerland and particular US states in financial secrecy, and of London/the UK in the offshore Euromarket (Cobham et al. 2015; Coe et al. 2014; Palan et. al. 2010; Shaxson 2011). Further complicating matters definitionally, as noted in chapter 2, is the fact that the logic of offshore tax and regulatory arbitrage is a network-relational one that emerges through the interaction of laws in multiple offshore and onshore jurisdictions

(Coe et al. 2014; Dörry 2014; Haberly and Wójcik 2015a; Seabrooke and Wigan 2014; Wójcik 2013a). For example, a country that serves as a tax haven from the standpoint of American multinational firms—e.g. the UK or Canada prior to the 2017 US TCJA tax reform—might not be considered such from the standpoint of other countries.

With this ambiguity in mind, the understanding of offshore employed here is a substantive one that focuses on the presence of geographic "misalignments" in international finance that are attributable to the exploitation of jurisdiction-specific legal, fiscal, and regulatory advantages. There are two basic geometries that these misalignments can take. The first, and most common geometry, is that of territorial misalignment according to a logic of host-based advantage—i.e. OJs attracting activities on a nominal territorial (booking basis) by offering local tax and regulatory advantages to foreigners. However, in many contexts one also finds an "inverted" offshore geometry of *nationality*-based misalignment, shaped by home-based jurisdictional advantage—i.e. the granting of tax and regulatory advantage to firms that are headquartered or incorporated offshore at the parent company level.[1]

The practical distinction between the classic territorial and the inverted nationality-based geometries of offshore misalignment is sometimes ambiguous—for example, in the context of many US corporate tax inversions that involve a shift in parent company incorporation jurisdiction, but not in operational headquarters (Marian 2015). However, which offshore geometry is employed often has important ramifications for firm treatment or behavior—most importantly insofar as the nationality of firms impacts their relationships with states as providers of sovereign "protection," as broadly defined (see Tilly 1985). Notably, this issue has reared its head even in cases where there would seem to be little question about a firm's substantive, as opposed to formal legal nationality. US-headquartered Broadcom, for example, which had inverted to Singaporean domiciliation in 2015, was in 2018 forced to return to US domiciliation to avoid being subjected to CFIUS[2] scrutiny as a "foreign" acquirer of American technology firms (Swamynathan 2018). Similarly, the fact that most Chinese technology firms are organized via inverted corporate holding structures—wherein the parent company is incorporated in the Caribbean (usually in the Cayman Islands)—forces most to use legally questionable variable interest entity (VIE) structures to control their own Mainland operations in strategically sensitive sectors where "foreign" ownership is banned (*Economist* 2017).

---

[1] In essence, the distinction between the "territorial" and "inverted" modes of offshore misalignment here can be framed by extending the Dunning OLI framework to tax and regulatory arbitrage, with "inverted" and "territorial" misalignments respectively driven by "ownership" (i.e. parent company level) and "location" (i.e. host jurisdiction)-based tax and regulatory advantage." "Inverted/inversion" here encompasses, but is somewhat broader than, reference to classic corporate offshore "tax inversions."

[2] Committee on Foreign Investment in the United States.

The relationship between firm nationality and sovereign "protection" is nowhere more critical than in finance. This is particularly true for banking, which is arguably more dependent on state backing than any other sector of the economy, either financial or nonfinancial (Ferri and Minsky 1992). The responsibility for backstopping international banks is, in general, assigned to various states more through messy de facto practice than through formal statute or agreement. However, it is typically the bank home state—i.e. the state where an international banking group is headquartered—that bears de facto responsibility for "bailing out" banks with fundamental solvency problems. Meanwhile, responsibility for providing short-term "lender of last resort" liquidity support is typically assigned to various central banks according to a combination of host territorial and currency denomination (Herring 2007). Contingent sovereign liabilities potentially rest with many states in this arrangement. However, the typical assumption is that the risks borne by central bank providers of lender-of-last-resort liquidity support are underwritten, in the final analysis, by the home states standing behind bank solvency on a bank nationality basis—which, depending on the currency and place of operation in question, are not necessarily the same nationality as the central banks providing liquidity support. The role of the US dollar as the leading global reserve currency, in particular, frequently compels the US Federal Reserve to step in as an indispensable global lender of last resort to support foreign banks whose solvency is backstopped, in final analysis, by their own home governments.

This de facto allocation of ultimate bank solvency backstopping responsibility to home states, on a nationality basis, poses potentially enormous fiscal risks for any small state home to disproportionately large international banks. Until the 1990s, however, this problem was mostly hypothetical, as, apart from in Switzerland, local banks were not usually the key players in offshore banking. Crucially, moreover, Swiss banks mostly attracted clients by providing secrecy to prudentially low-risk wealth management activities, rather than by leveraging prudential regulatory advantages—thus limiting the risks they posed to Swiss taxpayers.[3]

Meanwhile, the principal locus of offshore banking *regulatory* arbitrage was, until the 1980s, the Euromarket. This allowed banks to free themselves from regulations in their own home countries (primarily reserve requirements, interest rate caps, and capital controls) by operating or booking activities offshore in a host-based territorial sense (Hampton 1996). From the standpoint of offshore host states themselves, a critical attraction of this arrangement was the potential that it afforded to "ring-fence" the unregulated offshore sector—and the financial and fiscal risks that it generated—from the domestic financial system. Indeed, this logic

---

[3] As described by Guex (2000), Swiss banking secrecy (at the federal level) developed as a political compromise wherein banks were granted ironclad guarantees of client confidentiality in exchange for submitting to tightened prudential supervision.

of ring-fencing was at the heart of the prototypical Euromarket pioneered by the UK. As Shaxson (2011, 97) describes it:

> A bizarre Alice in Wonderland logic lay behind the Bank of England's decision not to regulate these markets ... If there was a run on a regulated bank in London, the Bank of England, by virtue of being its regulator, would feel some obligation to come in and pick up the pieces ... Better then, the logic went, not to regulate them.

This "Alice in Wonderland logic" only worked if there were barriers protecting the British economy (and taxpayers) from the potential liabilities associated with hosting the Euromarket. This entailed constructing two interconnected lines of defense. The first was currency denomination, with the Euromarket being limited to foreign currency activities, for which foreign central banks, rather than the Bank of England, would tend to act as lenders of last resort. Meanwhile, the second was bank nationality, with the major British clearing (i.e. commercial) banks—which the Bank of England (and potentially British taxpayers) would inevitably need to backstop in a crisis—being subjected to reserve requirements and interest rate caps from which foreign banks were exempt. British merchant (investment) banks were more lightly but not wholly unregulated (Hampton 1996; Shaxson 2011).

The flip side of this logic of Euromarket ring-fencing was an externalization of sovereign backstopping liability to the foreign home states of the banks operating in this market. In practice, this disproportionately concentrated risks in US hands, both via the Federal Reserve's de facto role as a global lender of last resort for dollar-denominated banking activities (in or outside of the USA), and the status of the USA as home state for the banks conducting the largest share of Euromarket operations (Kapstein 1991). Indeed, the risks created by the explosion of unregulated Euromarket deposit-taking and lending in the 1960s and 1970s would ultimately hit home in the USA in the form of the less-developed country (LDC) debt and US banking crises of the early 1980s, both of which had their roots largely in the proliferation of risky Euromarket financing structures (Curry 1997; Davison 1997; Strange 1994). In the context of the LDC sovereign debt crisis, US taxpayers mostly rescued the American creditor banks of developing countries indirectly via the US federal contribution to the bailout of LDC debtor states (Curry 1997). In the case of Continental Illinois, however, bank solvency problems resulted from the use of risky Euromarket wholesale financing to fund US domestic, rather than overseas lending, and the federal government was thus forced to step in to rescue one of America's largest banks directly. This incident famously led to the coining of the term "too big to fail" (Davison 1997). More broadly, as discussed in chapter 3, the banking crises of the 1980s had a fairly devastating impact on leading American commercial banks, leaving them financially sickly, in many cases, for more than a decade.

The declining effectiveness of traditional regulatory instruments, in the face of growing Euromarket arbitrage, prompted two, somewhat contradictory regulatory responses by onshore states—and in particular the USA, from the 1980s. First, the fact the Euromarket had already undermined the effectiveness of "onshore" reg- ulations, even while stealing business away from onshore banking centers such as New York, strengthened the political hand of those calling for financial deregula- tion. Combined with the general ascendance of neoliberal ideology, this helped to drive a US-led international regulatory "race to the bottom"—originally through the development of limited onshore–offshore spaces, such as the New York Inter- national Banking Facilities and Japan offshore market, and eventually through the widespread abandonment or relaxation of capital controls, interest rate caps, and reserve requirements (Roberts 1994; Shaxson 2011).

Crucially, however, the problem of international bank home state taxpayers be- ing forced to underwrite the costs of bank misbehavior—even when it occurred overseas—did not go unaddressed. The result, paradoxically, was that a far- reaching international project of banking reregulation, coordinated via the Basel Concordats and Accords, gathered strength simultaneously within the broader context of international banking deregulation. The most important principle es- tablished by Basel was that of consolidated home state supervision of international bank capitalization—or loss absorbing potential—wherein states force their na- tionally headquartered banks to internalize the costs of building loss-absorbing buffers for all of their activities, regardless of where they occur. The spread of home state capital supervision had occurred incrementally from the mid-1970s to early 1980s, both through national efforts, and multilaterally via the Basel Committee (see Herring 2007; Kapstein 1991). However, the costs imposed on US taxpayers by the LDC and Continental Illinois bailouts prompted the USA to leverage its po- litical clout to push for an international strengthening and harmonization of home state capital supervision—culminating in the 1988 Basel Accord (Kapstein 1991).

The international banking regulatory landscape that emerged in the 1980s thus differed from the pre-1980s landscape in ways that directly undermined the traditional Euromarket. Due to widespread onshore deregulation, the regula- tory advantages of offshore Euromarket deposit-taking were reduced. Meanwhile, regulatory arbitrage became increasingly targeted at *home* state capital rules— particularly via the use of securitized shadow banking instruments to move assets off-balance sheet (or otherwise reduce capital charges; Pozsar et al. 2010).

The negative impact that this international regulatory reconfiguration had on the Euromarket centers (including the UK) as sites for the booking of the con- ventional, *on-balance sheet* activities of foreign banks, is shown in Figure 5.1. This shows total global "net offshore" cross-border banking misalignment from 1983 to 2015 as a share of worldwide cross-border banking activity—with "net off- shore" defined as cross-border bank assets by residence, minus cross-border bank assets by nationality, summed across all jurisdictions for which the former was

Fig. 5.1 Aggregate "net offshore" banking misalignments (cross-border assets by residence minus cross-border assets by nationality) of all BIS reporting jurisdictions with a net offshore position (in that quarter), as a percentage of worldwide cross-border bank assets, 1983–2015

Sources: BIS Locational Banking Statistics; adapted from Haberly and Wójcik (2020).

larger than the latter in a particular year (with data from BIS locational banking statistics). This is divided by the total global value of all cross-border bank assets in that year, providing a measure of the total share of worldwide international banking activity that has been shifted, in net, to jurisdictions that serve as booking centers for foreign banks. As can be seen, the total net worldwide mismatch between where banks are headquartered, and where they book their cross-border assets, dropped from nearly half of all cross-border banking in the early 1980s, to less than one-quarter of cross-border banking by the global financial crisis. Furthermore, as illustrated in Figure 5.2, there is a strongly negative relationship at the jurisdiction level between initial net offshore misalignment, and subsequent change in net offshore misalignment (over both the entire 1983–2015 period, and the three sub-periods 1983–1996, 1996–2007, and 2007–2015 also marked in Figure 5.1);[4] indicating an international "rebalancing" of assets. Just as striking is the rebalancing at the "onshore" pole. Most notably, between 1983 and 2015, net offshore-booked cross-border lending by American and Japanese banks fell from

---

[4] Q4 1983 is the first year the BIS reports bank positions by nationality. Q4 1996 and Q4 2007 are chosen as intermediate dates due to their being the first year with data on Hong Kong positions by nationality, and the eve of the global financial crisis.

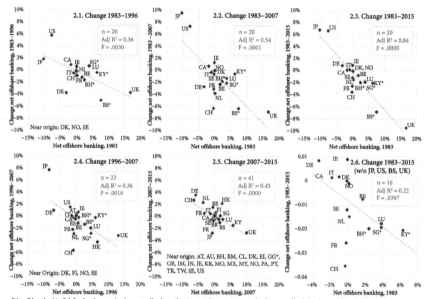

Fig. 5.2 Initial net offshore bank assets by jurisdiction (as a percent of worldwide cross-border bank assets) as a predictor of change in net offshore bank assets, 1983–2015. Countries labeled by ISO code.

Source: BIS Locational Banking Statistics; adapted from Haberly and Wójcik (2020).

74% to 21% of the value of cross-border lending conducted directly from the USA and Japan. This underscores the declining advantages for banks of conducting international operations from offshore platforms, as opposed to directly from their home countries.

5.3 Home State-level International Tax and Regulatory Arbitrage and the Rise of European Midshore National Banks: 1988–2007

This relative decline in the conventional offshore Euromarket, however, did not imply a decline in the importance of offshore banking as more broadly defined. Rather, the post-1980 regulatory reconfiguration encouraged a corresponding reconfiguration of the geographic logic of offshore banking, which became, in the lead-up to the global financial crisis, increasingly shaped by the new logic of securitized shadow banking arbitrage.

First, as we discuss in detail in the next chapter, even as offshore "small islands" declined in importance as hosts for conventional deposit banking, they became increasingly important as hosts for securitization vehicles. Most structured investment vehicles (SIVs) and collateralized debt obligations (CDOs) involved in the global financial crisis, for example, were issued from Cayman Islands vehicles (Palan et. al. 2010). Crucially, however, as described by Wainwright (2011), the domiciliation of these vehicles in offshore "small islands" was mostly motivated by tax rather than regulatory considerations. Principal regulatory responsibility for these vehicles was rather allocated to the home states of the multinational financial firms sponsoring them—with these vehicles being primarily designed to exploit gaps in home state consolidated capital rules.

In theory, the harmonization of home capital rules by the Basel Accords should have left little scope for international capital regulatory competition on a bank nationality basis. However, the fact that Basel was a nonbinding "soft law" project meant that there was in practice substantial international capital rule divergence. As described by Thiemann (2014), this divergence was far from accidental. Rather, the fact that Basel established a new international norm of home state consolidated capital supervision—but not effective capital rule harmonization—meant that it, rather perversely, directly empowered home states to leverage relatively lax capital treatment to support the global competitiveness of their own banks on a nationality basis. This entailed, in particular, fostering the ability of banks to sponsor the types of state of the art securitized instruments that would ultimately generate the global financial crisis (Thiemann 2014). The imperative to support national banks was particularly intense in Europe due to the pressure of the "American invasion" (see chapter 3), and the competition and takeovers unleashed by the 1988 European Second Banking Directive (Larson et al. 2011). Beyond a permissive home state regulatory attitude, this encouraged governments to promote, or at least allow, the formation of ever-larger national banking groups through mergers and acquisitions—both as a defensive measure against foreign takeovers, and as an aggressive measure to support bank internationalization (Epstein and Rhodes 2016).

The pressure on home states to support the growth, consolidation and competitiveness of national banking sectors was internationally widespread from the late 1980s to the global financial crisis. However, this pressure was particularly intense, politically, in what can be described as the large European midshore financial centers.[5] The UK FSA, for example, blamed its inadequate pre-crisis supervision of British banks partly on "frequent political demands for it to avoid imposing 'unnecessary' burdens which could undermine the competitiveness of UK financial firms" (FSA 2011, 11), or "harm London's competitiveness" (FSA 2011, 262). Switzerland's FINMA describes how concerns over the expansion of too-big-to-fail Swiss banks were overridden by the priority that regulation "not be allowed to jeopardise international competitiveness and Switzerland's attractiveness as a business location" (FINMA 2009, 19). In the Netherlands,

---

[5] See also Christensen et al. (2016) and Shaxson and Christensen (2013).

Engelen (2011) describes a pre-crisis regulatory and political "cognitive closure," entailing a "seduction of politics by the promises of lucrative financial gains," wherein "the Dutch Central Bank knowingly and willingly accommodated the 'regulatory arbitrage' of banks" (1790–1791). Notwithstanding the longstanding (i.e. often several centuries long; see chapter 2) support of such European midshore centers for financial services, this permissive, and indeed boosterish attitude toward the rapid expansion and prudential risk-taking of *national* banks represented a fundamental shift. Indeed, as recently as the 1980s, Swiss banks, for example, were famously conservative prudentially, while the UK was actually the leading supporter of the US push for Basel capital rule harmonization, due to the UK's desire to level the *home* regulatory playing field between British banks and their less stringently supervised onshore competitors (Hampton 1996, 65).

The underpinnings of post-1980s national bank expansion in large European midshore centers are examined in more detail in the discussion below. However, its results can be clearly seen in Figures 5.3–5.7 and Table 5.1—with the most striking national bank growth trajectories visible for the UK, Switzerland, Netherlands, Belgium, Ireland, Cyprus,[6] and Iceland.[7] Figure 5.3 shows the international banking market shares of the most important offshore (including European midshore) banking centers from 1983 to 2015, on a bank residence (host state), nationality (home state), and "net offshore" (host state minus home state) basis. As can be seen, "net offshore" cross-border booking activity by *foreign* banks (solid black lines) fell substantially as a percent of total world international banking in almost all offshore banking centers (both in and outside of Europe) between the 1980s and global financial crisis. However, the large European midshore centers simultaneously saw a rapid growth in the international market share of their nationally headquartered banks (dashed black lines).[8] This growth began abruptly in the early to mid-1990s—following the implementation of Basel (1988–1992) and the European Second Banking Directive (1988–1993)—and continued until the global financial crisis, with the global cross-border banking market share of these countries' national banks more than tripling from 11%

---

[6] Keeping in mind that Cyprus differs from these other countries insofar as it was mostly only a banking tax and secrecy haven, rather than regulatory haven (see Table 5.2), with the failure of its banks stemming from holdings of Greek sovereign debt rather than involvement in risky areas of financial innovation.

[7] As discussed below, Iceland was at this time both a corporate tax haven and a banking regulatory haven.

[8] This raises a causality question surrounding the accounting identity between national bank market share and net offshore market share, as decreases in net offshore market share can be driven by either decreases in local booking by foreign banks, or increases in overseas booking by national banks. Regressing quarterly change in net offshore booking market share on quarterly change in national bank market share (for Q4 1983–Q4 2015) indicates that net offshore position changes are mostly driven by foreign bank booking for Switzerland (r^2 0.45), Ireland (r^2 0.34), the UK (r^2 0.26), Luxembourg (r^2 0.19), and OECD offshore jurisdictions collectively (r^2 0.39). However, Belgian (r^2 0.55) and Dutch (r^2 0.67) changes in net offshore position are mostly driven by national banks.

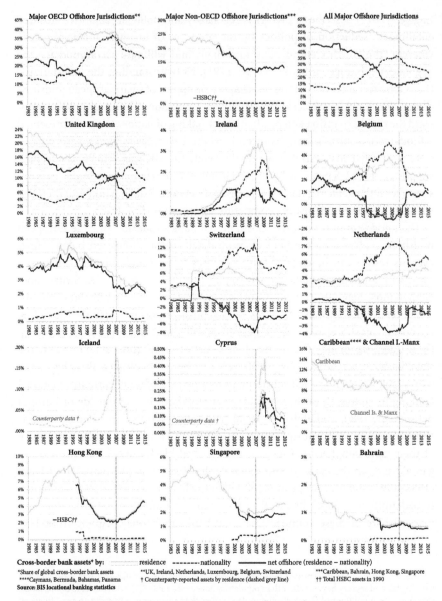

Fig. 5.3 Cross-border bank assets of offshore jurisdictions by residence and nationality

Source: BIS Locational Banking Statistics; adapted from Haberly and Wójcik (2020).

to 36% between 1988 and 2007. Importantly, as shown in Figure 5.4, European offshore/midshore national banks also grabbed market share from their onshore European peers, with Switzerland, the Netherlands, Ireland, and the UK in the lead. This confirms that their global market share growth was not simply an

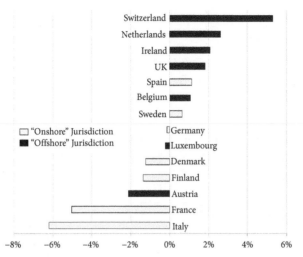

Fig. 5.4 Change in total market share of cross-border
European bank assets (by nationality), 1988–2007
Sources: BIS Locational Banking Statistics; adapted from Haberly and
Wójcik (2020).

illusion created by Europe's increasing weight in international banking (due to
EU integration and Japanese bank decline); they were rather rapidly gaining
market share within Europe, even as Europe as a whole gained global market
share.

The pre-crisis market share growth of European offshore or midshore national
banks was even more pronounced among the world's largest banks. Table 5.1 shows
the world's top-twenty banks by assets in 1980, 1990, 2002, and 2007. In 1980,
among all European midshore national banks, only two British banks made the
top-twenty list. These accounted for 9% of top-twenty bank assets in 1980, putting
British banks behind those from France, Japan, Germany, and the United States. In
2007, however, British banks dominated the top-twenty list, accounting for more
than one-quarter of its total assets. Meanwhile, Swiss, Dutch, and Belgian banks
increased from zero to four entries on the list (five prior to the mid-2007 acquisition of Dutch ABN-AMRO by Belgian Fortis and British RBS), with Britain,
Switzerland, and (pre-ABN Amro takeover) the Netherlands ranking #1, #2, and
#3 for top-twenty bank asset share increase from 1980 to 2007. Together, the large
European midshore national banks accounted for 42.5% of worldwide top-twenty
bank assets in 2007. This was almost as large as the 47.3% combined share of banks
from Japan, Germany, France, and the USA, which had a combined GDP five times
larger.

The rapid market share growth of European midshore national banks was
largely driven by mergers and acquisitions (M&As)—visible in Figure 5.3 as

Table 5.1 Nationality of world's largest twenty banks by assets, 1980–2007

1980	#	Asset %	1990	#	Asset %	2002	#	Asset %	2007	#	Asset %	1980–2007	Asset % chg.
France	4	26.0	Japan	13	68.9	Japan	4	22.6	UK	4	26.6	UK	+17.6
Japan	6	24.0	France	4	18.5	USA	4	20.7	France	3	16.9	Switz.	+8.6
Germ.	4	19.2	UK	2	8.2	UK	3	14	USA	3	14.6	Neth.	+3.9 (+7.9)*
USA	3	18.4	Germ.	1	4.5	France	3	12.4	Switz.	2	8.6	Italy	+4.0
UK	2	9.0				Switz.	2	10.6	Germ.	1	7.9	Spain	+3.6
Brazil	1	3.4				Germ.	2	10.4	Japan	2	7.6	China	+3.2
						Neth.	2	9.2	Neth.	1 (2)*	3.9 (7.9)*	Belg.	+3.0
									Italy	1	4.0	Brazil	−3.4
									Spain	1	3.6	USA	−3.8
									China	1	3.2	France	−9.1
									Belg.	1	3	Germany	−11.2
												Japan	−16.4
UK, CH, NL, BE	2	9.0	UK, CH, NL, BE	2	8.2	UK, CH, NL, BE	7	33.8	UK, CH, NL, BE	8 (9)*	42.1	UK, CH, NL, BE	+33.1

Sources: The Banker (1980), *American Banker* (1990), *Global Finance* (2002–2007); adapted from Haberly and Wójcik (2020).

Note: *Figure in parentheses estimated value for Dutch national bank groups before RBS (UK), Fortis (BE) and Santander (ES) purchase of ABN Amro (NL) in late 2007.

discontinuous growth through steep jumps.[9] Ultimately, this reflected a sorting process wherein the headquarters of combined banking groups gravitated toward jurisdictions with home state-specific tax, regulatory, and other advantages (DeYoung et al. 2009; Focarelli and Pozzolo 2008; Pasiouras et al. 2011; Valkanov and Keimeier 2006).

Figure 5.5 provides a rough assessment of the likely importance of home state-specific capital regulatory, corporate taxation, and secrecy characteristics in driving the growth of European midshore national banks between the 1980s and the global financial crisis. Importantly, tax and regulatory advantages are defined here from a strictly home state standpoint, which for taxation means an emphasis on controlled foreign corporation (CFC) rules and tax system territoriality, and for banking regulation means exclusively examining home state consolidated capital supervision (see Table 5.2 for a detailed breakdown of characteristics used to classify countries as full or partial regulatory, tax or secrecy havens). The sample of countries reporting data to the BIS on bank assets by nationality over this period is too small (nineteen including counterparty-based estimates for Iceland and Cyprus)[10] to permit useful multivariate disaggregation of the role of these factors in driving midshore national bank growth.[11] However, the simple bivariate plots

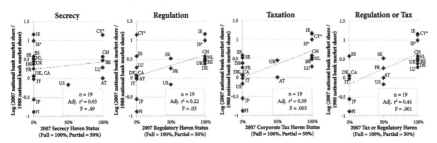

Fig. 5.5 Relationship between secrecy, regulation and tax haven status, and market share growth of national banks (% of worldwide cross-border assets) from Basel to the crisis (1988–2007)
Countries labeled by ISO code. See Table 5.2 for details of definitions and methodology.
Source: see table 5.2; adapted from Haberly and Wójcik (2020).

---

[9] Half of Switzerland's Figure 3.3 increase appears to be from acquisitions of US investment banks in 1990 (First Boston) and 2000 (Kidder Peabody, Paine Webber, Donaldson Luftkin Jeanette). Half of Ireland's increase comes from Depfa's 2002 move from Germany to Dublin. The 1996–2001 spike in Dutch and Belgian growth coincides with numerous acquisitions by ABN Amro, ING, Dexia, and Fortis (see Abraham and Van Dijcke 2002).

[10] For the purposes of the rough analysis here, using log-transformed asset growth, it is sufficient to know that Icelandic and Cypriot bank growth was exceptionally high (at least several hundred percent).

[11] Time-series panel analysis is unlikely to help due to the infrequency of national offshore characteristic change events, and firm-level analysis would mostly just obscure the home state sampling problem (and is an undertaking beyond the scope of this chapter).

Table 5.2 Selected characteristics of major OECD and EU offshore/midshore jurisdictions (shading of cells indicates jurisdiction meets a particular tax, secrecy or regulatory haven classification criteria as specified on row labels at left)

	Tax, secrecy, & reg.havens		Primarily tax havens		Primarily tax & regulatory havens		Primarily tax & secrecy havens			"Onshore" comparison jurisdictions				
	CH	BE	NL	IE	IS	UK	CY	LU	AT	US	DE	FR	IT	JP
Corporate tax haven	Yes	Yes	Yes	Yes	Yes	Part[1]	Yes	Yes	Part[2]					
2007 CIT < 20%	21%	34%	25.5%	12.5%	18%	30%	10%	30%	25%	40%	38%	33%	37%	41%
No CFC rules + territorial	Yes	Yes	Part[3]	Part[4]			Yes	Yes	Part[5]					
2009 FDI > GDP	134%	104%	255%	125%	71%	100%	834%	3371%	65%	17%	29%	41%	18%	15%
US inversions (1982–2007)	3		4	8		1								
Secrecy haven	Yes	Yes					Yes	Yes	Yes	Del.[6]				
2009 FSI > 70%	100%	73%	58%	62%		42%	75%	87%	91%	92%				
Savings dir. opt-out	Yes	Yes						Yes	Yes					
Regulatory haven[7]	Yes	Yes	Yes	Yes[8]	Yes[8]	Yes				CSEs[9]	Yes	Part		
Leverage ratio < 3% in 2007 — #1 Bank by assets	UBS <2%	Fortis 2%–4%	ING <3%	Depfa <2%	Kaup >5%[8]	RBS <3%	BOC >5%	BCEE >6%	Erste 3%–4%	Citi 2%–4%	DB <2%	BNP <3%	UC >3%	Miz. >3%
#2 Bank by assets	CS <3%	Dexia <3%	ABN <3%	AIB >4%	LB >5%[8]	Barc. <3%	Laiki >5%	Raiff ND	Raiff >6%	BOA >4%	CB <3%	CA <3%	IS >4%	MUFJ >4%
All banks lev. ratio < 4% (EU)		2.9%	3.2%	4.5%		3.7%	7.3%	6.3%	5.2%		2.7%	3.8%	7.2%	
CDOs, ABCP & SIVs — >25% bank equity (2007)	100%	45%	33%			66%				63%	106%	29%	14%	13%
Systemic impact (2007)	43%	36%	29%			66%				41%	79%	13%	6%	2%
No ABCP capital charge		Yes	Yes		Yes	Yes		Yes	Yes	No	Yes	No	Yes	
Banks fund own equity		Yes	Yes	Yes	Yes									

Offshore dependencies			1			9			1		1			.
Net offshore intl. banking position, 1988	Yes	Yes	Yes		ND	Yes	ND	Yes	-1					
National bank market share growth % 1988–2007	267	196	223	1316	895[10]	174	1,272[10]	91	-1	-31	136	80	-6	-72

Source: adapted from Haberly and Wójcik (2020).

Notes

[1] UK has been a major corporate tax haven since 2010 tax changes (e.g. ten US corporate inversions 2010–2017). Difficult to classify pre-2010; central hub of global tax haven network (current and former dependencies), and widely used as offshore FDI conduit.

[2] Minor role as FDI conduit jurisdiction.

[3] Netherlands has CFC rules, but these are largely overridden in practice by participation exemption.

[4] Ireland operates worldwide taxation system but has no CFC rules.

[5] Austria has no CFC rules, but has alternate rules serving similar purpose.

[6] US secrecy haven status at state level (mostly Delaware; also Wyoming, Nevada, South Dakota)

[7] "Regulatory haven" here refers specifically to consolidated home state capital supervision of nationally headquartered bank groups.

[8] See in-text discussion of Ireland and Iceland.

[9] US supervision of investment banks by Securities and Exchange Commission under Consolidated Supervised Entity (CSE) program was much weaker than supervision of commercial banks by Federal Reserve (see FCIC 2011).

[10] National bank growth figures for Iceland and Cyprus are estimates based on counterparty-reported assets by residence.

2007 CIT < 20%: 2007 corporate income tax rate below 20%. Source: KPMG (2018).

2009 FDI > GDP: Total outward foreign direct investment larger than gross domestic product in 2009 (first year with available IMF CDIS data).

2009 FSI > 70%: Opacity score of greater than 70% in 2009 Tax Justice Network Financial Secrecy Index (first available year)

All banks lev. ratio < 4%: Total leverage ratio of banking system < 4% in 2008 (earliest date of data availability from ECB). EU members only. Source: ECB Consolidated Banking Data.

Banks fund own equity: Pre-crisis bank capitalizations artificially inflated (and apparent leverage depressed) through equity purchases funded by loans from banks themselves (or among each other).

CDOs, ABCP, & SIVs > 25% bank equity (2007): Total value of ABS-CDOs, credit arbitrage and hybrid ABCP conduits and SIVs > 25% of the shareholder equity of national banks involved in sponsoring/underwriting these vehicles. Captures the potential risk posed by all major forms of pre-crisis securities repackaging for the banks involved in these activities. CDO data from Beltran et al. (2013). SIV and ABCP data from Standard & Poor's and Moody's. Shareholder equity data from Bankscope and company reports.

CDOs, ABCP, ... SIVs systemic impact (2007): Multiplies percentage in previous row by percentage of total consolidated national banking system assets (estimated from ECB and BIS data) accounted for by banks directly involved in securities repackaging. Gauges potential systemic risk of securities repackaging activities to the national banking system as a whole rather than only to banks directly involved in repackaging.

Leverage ratio < 3%: Largest and or second largest bank in country by 2007 assets had a leverage ratio smaller than 3% (i.e. would have been noncompliant with post-crisis Basel III leverage standard). Approximate ranges are given based on authors' calculations from Bankscope and a number of secondary sources, to reflect fluctuation over time and variation stemming from source and methodological details.

National bank market share growth 1988–2007: Q4 2007:Q4 2007 cross-border asset share by bank nationality divided by Q4 1988 share.

ND: no data

Net offshore intl. banking position, 1988: Q4 1988 Cross-border bank assets by residence exceeded cross-border assets by nationality.

No ABCP capital charge: Jurisdictions did not apply any capital charge to bank liquidity support lines to asset-backed commercial paper (ABCP) conduits prior to 2007/2008 Basel II phase-in (effectively allowed unlimited movement of assets into off-balance sheet vehicles). From Thiemann (2014).

No CFC + territorial: Territorial corporate taxation system combined with lack of controlled foreign corporation rules (gives national firms total or near-total exemption from home state taxation of foreign-source profits, including profits that are aggressively sheltered from host state taxation; see European Commission 2015). Source: EC (2015) and Deloitte Taxation and Investment Guides and Country Highlights.

Offshore dependencies: Number of overseas dependencies/territories of country ranked on 2009 Tax Justice Network Financial Secrecy Index.

Savings dir. opt out: Jurisdictions complying with Savings Directive by levying withholding tax rather than sharing taxpayer information US inversions (1982–2007): Number of US firms moving headquarters to jurisdictions via inversions through 2007. Source: Bloomberg (2017).

and regressions in Figure 5.5 suggest (tentatively) that European midshore national bank growth was likely encouraged, as would be expected, by a combination
of light home state corporate taxation and permissive home state capital supervision. Meanwhile, financial secrecy does not appear to be systematically associated
with national bank growth.

Interestingly, this analysis finds corporate tax haven status to be the factor most
strongly associated with pre-crisis midshore national bank growth. Notably, Ireland, the Netherlands, Switzerland, and (to a lesser extent) the UK are all popular
jurisdictions for corporate tax inversions, whereby firms (particularly but not
exclusively American; see Marian 2015) relocate their headquarters to low tax
jurisdictions. Figure 5.4 and Table 5.2 suggest that a similar logic of home state-
level corporate tax arbitrage, albeit undertaken in a more organic manner (i.e.
centered more on larger tax haven banks acquiring smaller foreign banks, than
on the conventional inversion pattern of larger foreign firms acquiring smaller
tax haven firms), likely encouraged the rapid pre-crisis expansion of these countries' national banks. Notably, the three sample countries with the lowest headline
corporate tax rates—Iceland (18% rate), Ireland (12.5%), and Cyprus (10%)—had
by far the fastest rates of pre-crisis national bank expansion (see also Table 5.2).
According to Engelen (2011), the Dutch SPV formation industry that had developed to serve multinational corporate tax avoidance, also directly encouraged the
expansion of Dutch banks into securitization activities that used the same basic
vehicles.

Moreover, the analysis here indicates that lax home state capital supervision
likely also encouraged European midshore national bank growth. In other words,
the conventional logic of home state-level corporate *tax* inversion appears to have
operated in tandem with an additional logic of home state-level bank *regulatory*
inversion—keeping in mind that this mostly played out through piecemeal international M&A accretion (see Valkanov and Keimeier 2006), rather than overt bank
redomiciliation (although the latter did sometimes occur; see below). Notably, as
shown in Table 5.2, the major European midshore centers do in fact appear (with
a few exceptions) to have "won" the race to the bottom in pre-crisis home state
capital supervision. Two key indicators of pre-crisis (2007/2008) home capital supervision are shown in Table 5.2: (1) bank "simple" leverage ratios (i.e. unadjusted
for self-assessed asset risks, and including off-balance sheet exposures);[12] (2) the
systemic impact (in relation to shareholder equity) of crisis-implicated securities repackaging activities on national banking systems, and absence of regulatory
restrictions on capital arbitrage via these activities (see Table 5.2). Out of nineteen sample countries, seven—Switzerland, Belgium, the Netherlands, the UK,

---

[12] See Mariathasan and Merrouche (2012) for discussion of leverage and capital ratio manipulation. In our analysis, "dangerous" pre-crisis leverage is defined based on post-crisis Basel III rules (3%
leverage ratio).

Germany, France, and Sweden—were substantially worse than the others in terms of leverage, with most of their largest banks more precariously leveraged in 2007 than the most fragile US investment bank, Bear Stearns (which had a leverage ratio of 2.7%). Meanwhile, six countries—Switzerland, Belgium, the Netherlands, the UK, Germany, and the USA—were outstanding in terms of the systemic impact of securities repackaging activities on national banking systems (and in the case of Belgium, the Netherlands, the UK, and Germany the lack of restrictions on flagrant capital arbitrage via asset-backed commercial paper (ABCP) conduits; see Thiemann 2014). Of the five countries scoring very poorly on both indicators— Switzerland, Belgium, the Netherlands, the UK, and Germany—all but Germany can be described as European midshore jurisdictions.

Neither Ireland nor Iceland performed poorly on paper in these two core indicators—apart from Ireland's largest bank, Depfa, whose leverage ratio reportedly reached a staggeringly fragile 0.83% in 2005 (Dübel 2013). However, they can be classified as home capital regulatory havens based on a well-documented litany of acute regulatory lapses, which were mostly either a part or a byproduct of efforts to boost international bank competitiveness (Benediktsdottir et al. 2011; Connor et al. 2012; Stewart 2013). The most egregious was the failure (highlighted in Table 5.2) of both countries' regulators to prevent banks from manipulating their capitalizations through loan-funded purchases of their own and each other's equity (directly or via related parties; Benediktsdottir et al. 2011; Connor et al. 2012). In Iceland, as much as 70% of bank core capital was an illusory product of this behavior, with "weak capital the key to rapid expansion" (Benediktsdottir et al. 2011). Meanwhile, the clearest demonstration of Ireland's regulatory laxity is the fact that its largest bank, Depfa, was in fact a bank from Germany—which as noted above already had highly permissive home capital supervision—whose headquarters was lured to Dublin in 2002 with the promise of even greater regulatory permissiveness and lower taxes (Dübel 2013; Stewart 2013). This "naked" tax and regulatory inversion doubled the cross-border assets of "Irish" national banks overnight (Figure 5.3).

The low scores of the large European offshore centers on home state capital regulatory metrics, and the fact that this likely helped their national banks to expand international market share, suggests a new twist in the debate over the responsibility of OJs for the crisis (Haberly and Wójcik 2017a; Palan et al. 2010; Shaxson 2011). What is especially striking is the intensity of these countries' banks' involvement in the riskiest securities repackaging[13] activities at the heart of the financial crisis (see FCIC 2011; Pozsar et al. 2010. As shown in Figure 5.6, the combined share of British, Swiss, Dutch, and Belgian financial institutions in the three most important repackaging segments—asset-backed securities collateralized debt obligations

---

[13] Off-balance sheet securitization vehicles whose assets are also securities.

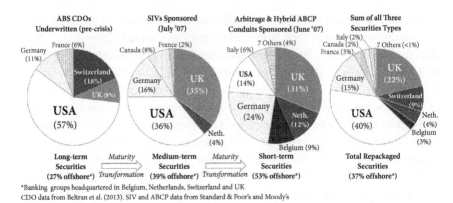

Fig. 5.6 Market shares of firms by nationality in pre-crisis underwriting and sponsorship of securities repackaging activities

Sources: Beltran et al. (2013) (ABS CDO data), Standard & Poor's and Moody's (SIV and ABCP data); adapted from Haberly and Wójcik (2020).

(ABS CDOs), structured investment vehicles (SIVs), and credit arbitrage and hybrid asset-backed commercial paper (ABCP) conduits—was approximately the same as financial firms from the USA (37% versus 40%), which had a GDP three times larger than these countries combined. Swiss banks, for example, were the second largest pre-crisis underwriters of CDOs after American banks, with a market share larger than the next two countries combined. Moreover, the market share of offshore national banks increases as one moves toward activities in the right side of the figure—reaching 53% for credit arbitrage and hybrid ABCP—which entail increasing direct balance sheet risk for sponsors (and their home states) due to the shorter maturities involved, and liquidity support required (FCIC 2011; Pozsar et al. 2012). Crucially, Figure 5.6 captures off-balance sheet instruments that may not be fully represented in other datasets (e.g. from the BIS). This suggests that the overall pre-crisis market share growth of European offshore national banks—taking into account these instruments—may have been even more pronounced than indicated by Figures 5.3–5.4 and Table 5.1.

The irony of European offshore national bank involvement in shadow banking was that the origins and conduct of these activities were, from a territorial standpoint, mostly American. In this sense, even as European midshore national banks shifted in the 1990s and 2000s toward specialization in home state tax and regulatory advantages, the Wall Street securities market partially usurped the traditional "offshore" role of facilitating *host*-based regulatory avoidance; albeit mostly through financial innovation as opposed to geographically based host regulatory arbitrage (see FCIC 2011 and chapter 6). To be fair, traditionally offshore London (and its spinoff securities market in Dublin) also had a leading position in shadow banking, from a host territorial standpoint, as one pole of the NY–LON axis. However, as discussed in chapter 4, London was increasingly a twin of Wall Street, that specialized in importing and adapting American financial products to Europe, rather than a place where American banks went to do things they could not do at home.

In fact, as shown in Table 5.3, the large shadow banking market shares of European offshore national banks appear to be largely explained by their aggressive acquisition of American and British securities firms in the 1990s and early 2000s. This suggests a logic of vertical integration (including internally within the UK) between European midshore state home capital regulatory failure, and NY–LON host financial innovation and governance failures. Remarkably, by 2007, Swiss banks had purchased a quarter (5/20) of what had been the largest US investment banks in the 1980s (by M&A advising). Meanwhile, of the eight 1982 London accepting houses (investment banks) that had come under foreign ownership by 2007, half were owned by Swiss, Dutch, Belgian, and Icelandic banks. Icelandic Kaupthing's 2005 purchase of Singer and Friedlander is particularly notable, as the latter's London-based activities directly precipitated the former's failure (Baldursson and Portes 2014). In all, European midshore national banks (including British banks) accounted for 60% (9/15) of pre-crisis foreign ownership of what had been the leading US and British investment/merchant banks in the 1980s. These included some of the most venerable names in British and American investment/merchant banking: including Barings (the remains of which were absorbed by the Dutch ING and ABN Amro), Brown Shipley (absorbed by Belgium's KBC), and Paine Webber (and via it Kidder Peabody), Dillon Read, and First Boston (absorbed by UBS and Credit Suisse).

Ultimately, where European midshore national banks were most outstanding was in the intensity of the risks they concentrated on their home states. This is highlighted by Figure 5.7. The left side shows the estimated systemic impact of securities repackaging activities (listed in Figure 5.5) on national banking systems (i.e. in relation to bank assets; see Table 5.2). By this indicator, Germany actually exhibited greater home supervisory dereliction in relation to shadow banking than the four largest European midshore centers' banks. However, the right side shows the value of securities repackaging activities as a percent of bank home state GDP. By this measure, Switzerland, the UK, the Netherlands, and Belgium easily top the scale.

5.4 The Global Financial Crisis and the End of the Great Inversion

By the eve of the global financial crisis, the old offshore misalignment in international banking—between the nationality of banks, and the territory in which they booked their operations—had been partially superseded by a new misalignment between the size of European midshore national banks, and the size of their home

Table 5.3 Ownership in 2007 of largest 1980s US and British investment and merchant banks

Parent company, 2007		Top-20 US investment banks by M&A advising, 1980–1991 (with acquisition date)	London accepting houses, 1982 (with acquisition date)	Total
Swiss	UBS	Kidder Peabody (2000), PaineWebber (2000), Dillon Read (1997)	S. G. Warburg (1995)	6
	Credit Suisse	First Boston (1990), Donaldson Lufkin & Jenrette (2000)		
US	Citigroup	Shearson Lehman Hutton (1998), Salomon Brothers (1998), Smith Barney Harris Upham (1998)		4
	JP Morgan		Robert Fleming (2000)	
German	Deutsche Bank	Alex Brown & Son (1999), Bankers Trust (1999)	Morgan Grenfell (1990)	4
	Dresdner Bank		Kleinwort Benson (1995)	
British	HSBC		Samuel Montagu (1974), Charterhouse Japhet (2000), Hill Samuel (1987), Guinness Mahon (1998)	4
	Lloyds TSB			
	Investec			
Dutch	ABN Amro		Baring Brothers (US) (2001), Baring Brothers (1995)	1
	ING			
Icelandic	Kaupthing		Singer & Friedlander (2005)	1
Belgian	KBC		Brown Shipley (1992)	1
French	Société Générale		Hambros (1998)	1
Independent in 2007		Goldman Sachs, Morgan Stanley (incl. Dean Witter Reynolds), Merrill Lynch, Keefe Bruyette & Woods, Lazard, Shearson Lehman Brothers, Bear Stearns, Financo	N M Rothschild & Sons, Shroders, Lazard, Lea Brothers	13
Defunct		Drexel Burnham Lambert		1
Total		20	16	36

Sources: US investment bank M&A data from Rau (2000). London Accepting House list from Hablutzel (1992). Adapted from Haberly and Wójcik (2020).

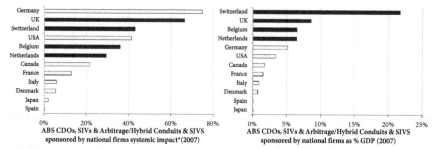

*Total value of ABS CDOs, SIVs & Arbitrage/Hybrid Conduits & SIVS, divided by shareholder equity of sponsoring & underwriting institutions, multiplied by percentage of total consolidated national bank assets accounted for sponsoring & underwriting institutions

Fig. 5.7 Total pre-crisis underwriting and sponsorship of repackaged securities by firm nationality by systemic impact on national banks (left) and as a percent of home country GDP (right). See Table 5.2 for methodological details.

Sources: Standard & Poor's; Moody's; Beltran et al. (2013); Bankscope; company reports; BIS; ECB; adapted from Haberly and Wójcik (2020).

economies, which we dub the Great Inversion. Table 5.4 shows the severity of this new misalignment in 2007. Most extreme was the overgrowth of Iceland's three largest banks, with assets equal to 741% of Iceland's GDP. Switzerland's top-three banks, however, were only slightly less distended, with a collective asset to GDP ratio of 687%, while the top-three banks of Belgium, the Netherlands, Ireland, Cyprus, and the UK had assets greater than 250% of GDP.

From a purely political standpoint, this new inverted geometry of offshore banking misalignment was in some respects more viable than the traditional logic of Euromarket regulatory arbitrage. Specifically, with primary responsibility for bank supervision now in the hands of the same home state capital supervisors with de facto responsibility for backstopping banks, the new architecture was not beset with the cross-border moral hazard—and consequent seeds of onshore regulatory backlash—of the pre-1980s Euromarket. Indeed, as can be seen in Table 5.4, offshore/midshore and onshore home states alike typically bore sole responsibility (with some exceptions) for recapitalizing their own national banks. However, this same concentration of sovereign backstopping liability in the hands of European midshore states—whose GDP was in some cases smaller than the balance sheets of individual national banks—raised the prospect that banks might not only be "too big to fail," but also "too big to save" from the standpoint of these states.

Importantly, the extent to which banks are overextended, in relation to home state backstopping capacity, is not simply determined by bank size in relation to GDP, but also the currency denomination of bank liabilities. Table 5.5 probes the impact of this through regression modeling of post-global financial crisis (Q4 2007–Q4 2012) change in the cross-border assets of banks by nationality. The first independent variable is simply total cross-border liabilities of national banks in Q4 2007 as a percent of home country GDP. Meanwhile, the other variables test the

Table 5.4 Assets of largest three national banks in Q4 2007 as a percent of GDP

Country	#1 Bank Q4 2007	% GDP	Recap.**	#2 Bank Q4 2007	% GDP	Recap.**	#3 Bank Q4 2007	Recap.**	% GDP	top-3 % GDP
Iceland	Kaupthing	394	Home	Landesbanki	226	Home	Glitner	Home	122	741
Switz.	UBS	423	Home, SWFs	Credit Suisse	253	SWFs	Julius Baer	–	11	687
Belgium	Fortis	239	Home, NL, LU, SWF	Dexia	186	Home, FR, LU	KBC	Home (Flan.)	109	534
Cyprus	Bank of Cyprus	214	Home	Marfin	203	Home	Hellenic	Home	49	466
Neth.	ING	176	Home	Rabobank	99	–	SNS	Home	12	287 (456)*
Ireland	Allied Irish	96	Home	Bank of Ireland	91	Home	Anglo Irish	Home	52	239 (305)*
UK	RBS	128	Home	Barclays	83	SWFs	HSBC	–	79	291
France	BNP Paribas	94	Home	Crédit Agricole	85	Home	SocGen	Home	59	238
Sing.	DBS	91	–	UOB	69	–	OCBC	–	68	228
Spain	Santander	91	–	BBVA	49	–	Caixa	–	24	164
Germany	Deutsche Bank	87	–	Commerzbank	26	Home	Dresdner	Home	21	134
Lux.	BCEE	117	–	Raiffeisen	12	–	SNCI	–	3	131
Italy	Unicredit	68	Home	Intesa Sanpaolo	38	Home	Monte dei Paschi	Home	8	114
China	ICBC	45	–	Construction Bank	34	–	Agricultural Bank	Home	31	110
Canada	RBC	41	–	TD-Bank	29	–	Scotiabank	–	28	98
Japan	Mizuho	35	–	MUFJ	31	–	SMFG	–	25	90
USA	Citigroup	15	Home, SWFs	Bank of America	12	Home, SWFs	JP Morgan	Home	11	38

Source: authors' research; adapted from Haberly and Wójcik (2020).

Notes

* Figures in parentheses indicate top-three bank asset–GDP ratio for Netherlands and Ireland prior to foreign bank acquisitions earlier in 2007 of ABN Amro and Depfa respectively.

** Source of global financial or eurozone crisis emergency capital injection (own home state, foreign sovereign wealth fund (SWF), or other non-home state government as indicated).

Table 5.5 Determinants of change in cross-border assets of banks by nationality, Q4 2007–Q4 2012

	Combined sample: dependencies & independent		Split sample: independent countries only				local forex liability data	
Sample size	39	39	33	33	33	33	19	19
Variables (values for Q4 2007)	Model 1	Model 2	Model 3	Model 4	Model 5	Model 6	Model 7	Model 8
All X-border liabilities / GDP	−0.040	−0.11***	−0.11***	0.15				
Net X-border foreign currency liabilities[1]/GDP				−0.27***	−0.13***	−0.065**	−0.065*	
Dependency dummy		−0.59***						
All X-border liabilities / GDP x dependency dummy		0.27***						
Euro member X-border euro liabilities / GDP						−0.30***	−0.29***	−0.19**
Foreign currency (x-border & local) & all Euro liab[2]/GDP								−0.042**
Adj. r2	0.004	0.32	0.30	0.42	0.40	0.61	0.75	0.76

Sources: BIS Locational Banking Statistics; World Bank WDI; ECB; adapted from Haberly and Wójcik (2020).
Notes
1. Includes eurozone member euro-denominated cross-border liabilities (reported or estimated).
2. Includes all (estimated) euro-denominated liabilities, cross-border, and local, of both eurozone and non-eurozone member banks.
All models use ordinary least squares regression, where dependent variable is log (2012 x-border bank assets by nationality/2007 x-border bank assets by nationality).
All independent variables only include cross-border liabilities.
* Significant at 10% level
** Significant at 5% level
*** Significant at 1% level

impact of bank liability currency denomination. Central banks have a theoretically unlimited capacity to backstop the own-currency liabilities of both banks, and the sovereigns supporting these banks. Consequently, foreign-currency-denominated bank liabilities should be more harmful to crisis resilience than own-currency liabilities (Buiter and Sibert 2011). In practice, however, this is complicated by additional factors. During the crisis, foreign currency funding pressures were alleviated by inter-central bank swap lines, and central bank liquidity support to foreign bank offices within their jurisdiction. The Federal Reserve was particularly generous in backstopping the dollar liquidity of foreigners (see chapter 2; Helleiner 2014; McDowell 2011). Furthermore, states can "self-insure" against foreign currency funding problems by accumulating sovereign wealth funds and foreign exchange reserves (Aizenman and Lee 2007). Finally, the European Central Bank (ECB) is banned from acting as a sovereign lender of last resort to eurozone states, meaning that their banks' own-currency liabilities are more akin to foreign currency liabilities once a crisis moves them onto the state's actual or de facto balance sheet (de Grauwe and Ji 2013). Complicating matters has been the eurozone's ad hoc development of sovereign lender-of-last-resort-like workarounds (Buiter and Rahbari 2012).

The impact of bank liability currency denomination is probed through two variables. The first is 2007 "foreign currency exposure"—i.e. the cross-border foreign-currency-denominated liabilities of all national banks, minus sovereign foreign exchange reserves, as a percent of home country GDP. The euro-denominated liabilities of all countries' banks, including eurozone members, are treated as foreign currency for this variable. However, euro-denominated liabilities of eurozone member banks are also included as a second variable, allowing for the disaggregation of their impact from that of true foreign currency liabilities. Finally, politically dependent jurisdictions are disaggregated from independent countries (via dummy and interaction terms in model 2, and sample division in models 3–6) to account for the formal or tacit fiscal backstops the former enjoy from colonial patrons (e.g. the 2009 UK bailout of the Cayman Islands).

Due to the limited sample of BIS-reporting countries, only a small number of variables can be tested simultaneously. Furthermore, the results should be treated with some caution due to the necessity of estimating foreign currency liabilities by nationality from foreign currency liabilities by residence for a number of jurisdictions (fully for fourteen, and partially for four, of thirty-nine). However, they are nevertheless intriguing. First, the simple cross-border liabilities/GDP variable strongly predicts post-crisis international bank retrenchment, but only for independent countries rather than dependent jurisdictions (evidenced by the variable's significance in models 2 and 3 but not 1; see also Figure 5.4). This highlights the extent to which politically dependent OJs free-ride on the explicit or implicit backing of "big brother" (Hampton 1996)—keeping in mind that none of these dependent jurisdictions (e.g. UK territories) were important sites for pre-crisis national bank growth. The second key finding is that foreign currency (defined to include eurozone-member euro) liabilities are not simply more harmful to national bank resilience than own-currency liabilities, but that the latter are not harmful at all (model 4). This underscores the shock-absorbing "money printing" capacity of central banks in relation to national own-currency-denominated liabilities. Given that central bank liquidity support was quite liberally provided to foreign *banks*, it also appears to highlight the importance for banking stability of the more narrowly nationalistic logic of central banks' sovereign lender of last resort support to home states backstopping bank solvency.

Finally, the results show that the eurozone was exceptionally toxic to large banking groups headquartered in small economies. As can be seen in model 6 (which explains 61% of post-crisis bank asset change), the euro-denominated cross-border liabilities of eurozone member banks actually seem to have been even worse than *foreign-currency*-denominated liabilities, in terms of their impact on post-crisis bank stability. This implies, at least if one simply takes results at face value, that European banks and governments would have actually been better off "dollarizing" like Panama, as opposed to dealing with the monetary doomsday machine of the ECB (keeping in mind that reforming the ECB would obviously have been preferable to either). One possible explanation is that unlike other countries' banks, all of the domestic liabilities of eurozone banks are also effectively foreign-currency liabilities for which there is no sovereign lender of last resort. However, model 8, which adjusts foreign currency exposure to include all cross-border and (estimated) local liabilities of eurozone member banks, and the local foreign currency liabilities of non-eurozone member banks (for countries with available data), indicates that this only partially explains the eurozone's toxicity to bank stability. One possible interpretation is that the eurozone's ad hoc sovereign lender of last resort workarounds may not have only been of limited usefulness (corroborating de Grauwe and Ji 2013), but actually may have amplified the crisis via self-defeating EU-imposed austerity programs, and investor uncertainty generated by protracted and acrimonious international political wrangling. This provides contextualization for the severity of the sovereign debt crises in Ireland and Cyprus, wherein the inhabitants of these countries were subjected to severe hardships by their European compatriots, after their governments overextended themselves backstopping private financial institutions.

Notably, whether the process of European midshore national bank retrenchment translated into relatively severe, as opposed to mild national fiscal pain, appears to have been conditioned by substantial country-level contingency. This can be seen in Figure 5.8, which plots the relationship (model 5 in Table 5.5) between 2007 "foreign currency exposure" and 2007–2012 change in cross-border bank assets, illustrating the post-crisis rebalancing of the misalignment between international bank size and home state backstopping capacity. What is particularly interesting is that the eurozone midshore/offshore jurisdictions (with available

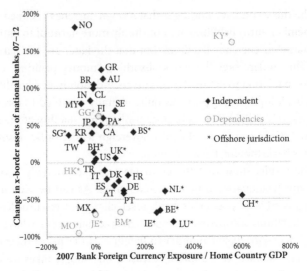

Fig. 5.8 Net cross-border foreign currency exposure of national banks in Q4-2007, and change in cross-border assets of national banks from Q4-2007 to Q4-2012. Countries labeled by ISO code.

Source: BIS Locational Banking Statistics and authors' analysis; adapted from Haberly and Wójcik (2020).

data)—Ireland and the Benelux countries[14]—are clustered closely together in the lower right corner of the figure, indicating extreme pre-crisis foreign currency exposure, and correspondingly pronounced post-crisis bank downsizing. Notably, both Ireland and the Benelux countries had their most problematic international banks—Irish Depfa, Dutch ABN Amro, and Belgian Fortis—fortuitously come under foreign ownership immediately prior to or in the early stages of their failure (see Table 5.3). Belgium—the pre-crisis assets of whose top-three banks, all of which failed, were 534% of GDP (compared to 305% for Ireland)—was particularly fortunate, as France helped rescue both Fortis, via its acquisition by BNP Paribas, and Dexia, via a highly unusual transnational capital injection (reflecting Dexia's dual nationality). With the most troubled international banks of all of these states fully or partially removed from their contingent sovereign balance sheets, Ireland seems to have been left in relatively worse shape due to the Irish real estate crash's impact on Ireland's other, more domestically oriented banks.

The peculiar crisis experience of eurozone midshore national banks—both in terms of the ECB's exceptionally severe failure as a sovereign lender of last resort, and the eleventh-hour musical chairs of bank nationality shifts—raises questions about what could have been, either for better or worse, for eurozone midshore

---

[14] Cyprus is omitted due to a lack of data on bank asset change by nationality.

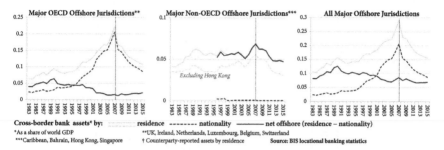

Fig. 5.9 Cross-border bank assets of major offshore jurisdictions as a percent of world GDP, 1983–2015

Source: BIS Locational Banking Statistics; adapted from Haberly and Wójcik (2020).

centers with large national banks. Ultimately, however, as shown in Table 5.6 (and Figure 5.3), the days when some of the world's largest banks were based in economies far smaller than these banks, have now come to an end. No country whose banks appeared on the 2019 top-twenty list of world banks by assets (Table 5.6) had a GDP smaller than $1 trillion, and only one, Spain, had a GDP smaller than $2 trillion. Furthermore, as shown in Figure 5.9, post-crisis mid-shore/offshore bank retrenchment is even more pronounced when cross-border assets are viewed in relation to world GDP, as this this retrenchment has been amplified, in absolute terms, by a decline in the total cross-border bank assets of all banks, worldwide, as a percent of world GDP.

5.5 The Political Geographic Paradox of Offshore Banking

In this chapter we have presented a novel analysis of the evolution of offshore banking from the 1980s to the global financial crisis, and beyond. We have shown that the traditional model of offshore Euromarket banking was subjected to a structural squeeze for nearly three decades prior to the global financial crisis. Specifically, the combination of widespread international deregulation in traditional territorialized areas of banking regulation, and the construction of a new home state-centered capital regulatory regime under Basel, reduced the advantages for onshore banks of booking conventional deposit-taking and lending offshore. Meanwhile, the logic of this new regulatory configuration encouraged the rise of shadow banking regulatory arbitrage that exploited gaps in home state consolidated capital rules.

Between the 1980s and the global financial crisis, this change in the logic of banking regulatory arbitrage prompted a geographic and functional reorganization of the global offshore banking system. This entailed small island jurisdictions increasingly becoming platforms for securitization vehicles, while large European

Table 5.6 Nationality of top-twenty world banks by assets, 2007–2019

2007	#	Asset %	2012	#	Asset %	2019	#	Asset %	2007–2019	Asset % chg.
UK	4	26.6	China	4	21.1	China	4	35.3	China	32.2
France	3	16.9	France	4	19.3	USA	4	19.1	Japan	6.0
USA	3	14.6	UK	3	16.5	France	4	16.2	USA	4.5
Switz.	2	8.6	USA	3	14.9	Japan	3	13.6	Spain	0.1
Germ.	1	7.9	Japan	3	14.6	UK	2	8.7	France	−0.7
Japan	2	7.6	Germ.	1	6.1	Spain	1	3.6	Belg.	−3.0
Italy	1	4.0	Spain	1	3.9	Germ.	1	3.4	Italy	−4.0
Neth.	1	3.9 (7.9)*	Neth.	1	3.6				Germ.	−4.6
Spain	1	3.6							Neth.	−3.9 (−7.9)*
China	1	3.2							Switz.	−8.6
Belg.	1	3.0							UK	−17.9
UK, CH, NL, BE	6	42.1	UK, CH, NL, BE	4	20.0	UK, CH, NL, BE	4	8.7	UK, CH, NL, BE	−33.4

Source: Global Finance; adapted from Haberly and Wójcik (2020).

Notes: *Figure in parentheses estimated value for Dutch national bank groups before RBS (UK), Fortis (BE) and Santander (ES) purchase of ABN Amro (NL) in late 2007.

midshore jurisdictions increasingly specialized in providing home state-specific tax and capital regulatory advantages to their own national banks as sponsors for these activities—thus encouraging a substantial percentage of the global banking system to be shifted, through mergers and acquisitions, to the ownership of these banks. The result of this Great Inversion was the emergence, by the global financial crisis, of an unsustainable new "offshore" banking misalignment between the size of these overgrown European midshore national banks, and the backstopping capacity of their home states. Following the shock of the crisis, this edifice came crashing down.

Notably, the lessons of this experience appear to have, at least temporarily and in a narrow sense, been learned. A key consideration in HSBC's recent decision not to move to lightly taxed Hong Kong seems to have been the fear that its dollar liabilities were too big for Hong Kong to backstop even with its foreign reserves (*Economist* 2016). Meanwhile, the Netherlands has rebuffed Swedish Nordea's interest in inverting to Dutch nationality, to lower its capital regulatory and tax burden, by merging with ABN Amro. As one analyst put it:

> the Dutch government would never allow ABN Amro to merge with a foreign bank looking to flee its own regulatory regime ... The Netherlands has barely recovered from ABN Amro's last adventure with banks from abroad.
>
> (De Jong 2016)

Above all, what is underscored by the story in this chapter is that banking is a particularly tension-ridden area of offshore jurisdiction specialization, due to the inescapable dependence of banks on the protection of strong state patrons. Indeed, our findings suggest that states such as Ireland, Iceland, and Cyprus were, in the wake of the global financial and eurozone crises, merely the most visible causalities of a deeper political–geographic paradox—stemming directly from this dependence of banks on state protection—which renders offshore (including midshore) banking center development inherently unstable under either a host or a home-based international banking regulatory regime.

On the one hand, when international banking regulation is dominated by host states, offshore hosts have substantial regulatory leverage to attract the operations of foreign banks backstopped by foreign governments. However, the moral hazard entailed by the fact that onshore states are forced to absorb the costs of offshore bad behavior, means that such a host-state-dominated pattern of banking regulation is politically precarious, over the long run—as it is likely to generate an onshore regulatory backlash that undermines the scope for offshore hosts to attract business. On the other hand, an "inverted" paradigm of offshore/midshore national bank development, fostered by home state-dominated regulation, is more politically stable from an international standpoint, as offshore states are mostly forced to internalize the costs of the regulatory laxity they employ to support national bank competitiveness. However, this same offshore internalization of bank backstopping costs, within states with a limited capacity to underwrite these costs, makes such an arrangement structurally unstable in the event of a financial crisis.

The obvious question this raises is why should offshore banking, as broadly defined, come to exist at all, for any significant length of time, on any significant scale? Why, in the context of a host-based regulatory system, such as that which prevailed after WWII, would a powerful "onshore" state such as the USA be willing to go along for as long as it did with allowing the flagrant offshore arbitrage of its own regulations by its own banks? Conversely, why, in the context of a home state-centered regulatory regime, such as that which prevailed under the Basel framework from the 1980s, would the governments of small countries go along with not just allowing, but to a large extent actively helping their banks to grow to such outrageously large proportions in relation to the size of their home economies—by engaging in all manner of regulatory and fiscal arbitrage—that they became a source of existential danger to the country?

One answer to these questions seems to be that much of what the offshore system does, including in relation to banking, actually does not necessarily entail the enabling of flagrant forms of *jurisdictionally based* arbitrage at all. The offshore world rather often provides a more generalized and subtle zone of institutional flexibility, that helps private actors to outflank the parameters of regulation altogether on a definitional basis via financial innovation. The role of OJs, in this context, operates at a level that would make it difficult for onshore regulators to even define the nature of the offshore problem. As we show in the next chapter, the role of offshore "small islands" in hosting securitization vehicles implicated in the global financial crisis mostly seems to have fallen into this category. These jurisdictions were basically operating *within* the umbrella of onshore extraterritorial, and in particular of US extraterritorial, regulatory oversight. Indeed, there seems to be an inherent pressure for OJs to become domesticated, over time, from the standpoint of onshore regulatory authority—a process that is particularly well advanced, in a historical sense, in US state-level "onshore–offshore" jurisdictions such as Delaware. Paradoxically, as we show in the next chapter, this process of domestication is itself quite subversive and potentially destabilizing, as OJs still ultimately retain their fundamental character as flexible zones of accelerated creative private rulemaking.

A more complicated question is why would the midshore national bank home states discussed in this chapter—places like Ireland, Iceland, Belgium, Switzerland, the Netherlands, and the UK—support a pattern of such obviously high-risk regulatory arbitrage and expansion on the part of their own national banks, which they would inevitably be forced to backstop at a tremendous cost? Broadly speaking, what this seems to underscore is the path-dependent tenacity of the political economy of what we dub the offshore state (see chapter 2), which, once entrenched, tends to opportunistically metastasize across new activities and arbitrage activities (see Christensen et al. 2016; Shaxson and Christensen 2013). In this case, the three most important centers of high-risk European midshore national bank development, in the lead-up to the global financial crisis—namely the UK, Switzerland, and the Netherlands—have all long been key lynchpins of the global offshore system. Indeed, in the case of the Netherlands and Switzerland, a clearly recognizable offshore or midshore role dates back centuries. However, none of these countries had, prior to the 1990s, a recent tradition of large-scale high-stakes risk-taking behavior, enabled by regulatory laxity, by their *own* national banks. In other words, what one sees in these countries is a very old pattern of finance-led development, reproducing itself through continuous mutation and adaptation at the level of specific strategies.

Trying to diagram how this offshore stateness produces and reproduces itself, in such a durable yet multifarious and shifting way, involves delving into a rabbit hole of contradictions. Looking at Britain in the 1950s–1970s, for example, one sees the Eurodollar market being fostered by an only recently nationalized Bank of England. This functioned as a veritable state-within-a-state, which was not so much beholden to the City of London as indistinguishable from it. The head of the Bank's foreign exchange department during the early development of the Eurodollar market was a City banker named George Bolton, who described the establishment of the Eurodollar market as "a conscious effort by a number of us to create a money market from the bits and pieces that were floating around" (quoted in Shaxson 2011, 88). The Bank was, in short, packed full of bankers, and it maintained a deep cognitive and operational congruence with the City.

At the same time, though, it is important not to discount the importance of ideology, as a semi-autonomous logic in its own right that has long transcended simple self-serving economic "interests" in this context. Rather remarkably, Hayek's Mont Pelerin Society, which led the post–WWII ideological counterattack against Keynesianism, actually appears to have received direct financial support from the Bank of England, alongside its primary backing from Swiss banks and insurance companies and the Swiss central bank; with both public and private financial institutions in Britain and Switzerland thus establishing a sort of offshore axis of neoliberalism, at an extremely early date (Shaxson 2011). Moreover, there was always more at work ideologically in the Bank of England's promotion of the Euromarket than just an embrace of the "free market," with neoliberalism always intimately wrapped up with British nationalism and imperialism. Bolton, for example, was not only "eager to help private interests skip around annoying regulations, but also deeply enamored of Britain's imperial magnificence" (Shaxson 2011, 88). Imperialism did not just exist at the level of nostalgia, but was actively reinvented in this context via the Bank's cultivation of offshore activities in Britain's overseas territories and crown dependencies (Palan et al. 2010; Shaxson 2011).

As this illustrates, there is a basic ambiguity, for countries with a disproportion-ately large financial sector, between the interests of the financial sector, and what is positioned as "the" national interest. Indeed, in the case of the UK, this ambi-guity between the impulse to promote the interests of the City, and the impulse to "make Britain great again" *through* finance, has become sharper as the promo-tion of finance has become part of the political agenda of the government proper, as opposed to primarily a project of the Bank of England. Indeed, the relationship between these impulses often seems downright tense. According to Michie (2004), for example, the 1986 Big Bang, which created a harshly competitive environment for British financial firms, was to a large extent foisted on the City by Thatcher. It was a policy that reflected a profound political commitment to the *idea* of Lon-don as a leading global financial center, but on terms that were defined by the state. More recently, one sees a similar dynamic unfolding in the context of Brexit, which has from the outset been conceived largely as a neoliberal "shock doctrine" vehicle for the rollback of regulation—that the City itself does not actually want. As Thomas (2021) described the situation a few weeks after the end of the Brexit transition period:

> Chancellor Rishi Sunak said last week that the City could expect something akin to a "Big Bang 2.0"—harking back to the Thatcherite deregulation of the finan-cial services industry… But business chiefs say there is little need for wholesale deregulation in the UK.

As Miles Celic, who heads the lobbying organization TheCity UK, puts it:

> The UK did a superb job of getting its voice heard on the regulatory debate in the EU…As such, it's not a surprise that the UK industry is broadly content with the regulation that we've just onshored—the UK was, after all, the main architect.
>
> (Thomas 2021)

As discussed in chapter 3, Sunak is himself a Goldman Sachs alumnus (not to men-tion a billionaire by marriage), whose worldview is in a broad sense clearly shaped by his experience in finance. However, the City itself seems to have very little po-litical influence within the Johnson government, and indeed has had its interests consistently ignored throughout Brexit, which has inflicted greater damage on it than any regulatory tightening ever could. The current right-wing push to ratchet up the offshoreness of the UK, to realize the vision of "Singapore on Thames," rather seems to be a fundamentally state-led ideological project, that stems from a particular skewed definition of the national interest. This remains in many respects deeply enamored with the idea of "Britain's imperial magnificence," and the role that finance has to play in this vision—with memories of British hegemony being mixed together in it with Brexiteer references to Elizabethan-era "swashbuckling" and "buccaneering."

Such a state-led definition of the "national interest," in manner that partially aligns with, but is politically semiautonomous from financial sector interests, also seems to be part of the answer to the second question that arises out of the political–geographic paradox of offshore banking. Namely, why did the USA as an "onshore" bank home state in the *pre*-1980s era not bring the hammer down on its own banks' Eurodollar market activities? This was, notably, a period when banks were not in especially high esteem politically in the USA—which was, indeed, the very reason why there was so much regulation in the USA for them to go offshore to avoid.

In fact, a large part of the answer to this question seems to be that the US federal government—or at least particular parts of the executive branch—not only did not view the offshore Euromarket activities of US banks to be a problem in the 1960s and 1970s, but actually encouraged these activities out of national strategic policy considerations (Helleiner 1994). Specifically, US policymakers kept finding that elements of their own Keynesian-era financial and monetary regulatory frameworks and objectives created various policy contradictions, both in relation to one another, and with the overarching US goal of promoting global economic integration. As a result, US policymakers, in various quarters of the executive branch, repeatedly ended up promoting or benignly neglecting the expansion of offshore activities by US banks and corporations, as way of squaring this circle.

The logic of how this unfolded—not only in relation to offshore banking, but also for broader US corporate use (and indeed development) of the global offshore system—above all revolved around the stresses surrounding the US dollar's role at the center of the Bretton Woods fixed exchange rate system. Through the 1950s, the biggest problem that arose in this system was the dollar shortage afflicting US allies and client states. As described in chapter 4, in the immediate postwar era this was mostly addressed by the USA through direct public assistance to its allies (e.g. the Marshall Plan). However, as time progressed, the USA shifted to promoting private sector mechanisms for providing the world with dollars, including by using tax inducements to encourage outward investment by US firms (Gowa 1985). In practice, these inducements largely revolved around a corporate tax framework that supported (via offshore profit tax deferral) the use of tax haven "base companies" as a de facto subsidy to outward investment—with US corporate profit-shifting subsidiaries proliferating in Switzerland and other continental European tax havens, US satellite states such as Panama, Liberia, Venezuela, Cuba, and Haiti, and also various British small island overseas dependencies (Engel 2001; Gibbons 1956; Stevens 1962). In fact, the Eisenhower administration was at one point pushing for a rule change that would have allowed US firms to access US tax deferral via overseas *branches*, which would have saved them the trouble of even having to set up actual offshore shell companies (Gowa 1985).

By the early 1960s, these and other measures aimed at providing the world with dollars had essentially worked too well, with the dollar shortage turning into a "dollar glut" that threatened the dollar's stability (Engel 2001; Gowa 1985). The Kennedy administration thus put in place the first US Controlled Foreign Corporation (CFC) rules in 1962 to end the de facto tax subsidy for *outward* corporate investment (Engel 2001; Picciotto 1992). As Kennedy put it: "since the post-war reconstruction of Japan and Europe has been completed, there are no longer foreign policy reasons for providing tax incentives for foreign investment in the economically advanced economies" (Committee on Ways and Means, 1961: 9). This, however, failed to stem the US balance of payments bleeding, and as the 1960s wore on, the USA was forced to put in place increasingly direct restrictions on outward capital flows; first by taxing them, and finally by imposing outright capital controls.

It was largely a desire by the US executive to alleviate the inconvenience to US banks and corporations caused by these taxes and controls on outward investment, that led the USA to, as Helleiner (1995) puts it, "actively support" the expanding use of the offshore Eurodollar market by US banks and corporations from the 1960s (see also Shaxson 2011; Strange 1981). Beyond providing a platform for US corporations and banks to conduct their international business with each other outside of US capital controls, the Eurodollar market was also seen, as Undersecretary of State for Economic Affairs Douglas Dillon put it, as "quite a good way of convincing foreigners to keep their deposits in dollars," and thus helping to shore up the dollar directly (quoted in Shaxson 2011, 100; see also Helleiner 1994; Strange 1981). In addition to promoting the use of London and British colonial offshore Eurodollar market centers, the US government also helped to activate the Dutch colonial offshore network; with the Netherlands Antilles being turned, from the 1960s, into an "IRS engineered" (Papke 2000) conduit for US multinational firms to channel funds raised in the Eurobond market into investment in the USA itself.

US promotional interventions in the Eurodollar market were ongoing throughout the 1960s and 1970s—perhaps most overtly within the context of the 1970s politics of offshore petrodollar recycling and LDC lending (see Spiro 1999). Of particular importance were a series of decisions by the US Comptroller of the Currency to—as the FDIC put it (see Curry 1997: 204), as a result of higher-level "political pressure"—first disregard, and then simply eliminate for developing country borrowers, the borrower risk concentration rules that would otherwise have prevented US banks from engaging in such a large-scale expansion offshore-funded dollar lending to the largest Latin American borrowers such as Brazil and Mexico (Curry 1997; Kapstein 1994; Lissaker 1977).

In other words, the LDC debt crisis—whose fallout would play a key role in prompting the USA to push, in the 1980s, for tightened home state capital supervision of Euromarket activities—was itself just as much a result of US efforts to encourage its banks' offshore lending to LDCs, as it was a result the efforts of these banks to avoid US regulation. None of this is to downplay the central role of private regulatory and fiscal arbitrage in driving the expansion of these offshore markets. Rather, the point is that these private arbitrage strategies would have likely struggled to reach the scale that they did unless the door to them was being deliberately kept open by the USA in its capacity as an onshore bank *home* state, alongside the efforts of Britain to promote itself as an offshore *host* state. As was the case on the British side, not even the support of the whole US state was needed. Indeed, as described by Helleiner (1995), the Federal Reserve was quite concerned about the scale of offshore regulatory arbitrage by US banks, and in the late-1970s lobbied for an expansion of extraterritorial bank supervision—ultimately being blocked when opposition within the USA effectively joined forces with opposition from Britain and Switzerland to its proposed model of international cooperation (Helleiner 1995).

Ironically, the only way to effectively neutralize the political geographic paradox of offshore banking seems to be to push the involvement of the state in it to such an extreme that it makes a mockery of the whole concept of offshore as a zone of private actor "escape." In fact, as can be seen in Figure 5.3, the only two offshore banking centers that have exhibited any growth since the global financial crisis (as measured by "on balance sheet" bank assets) are Hong Kong and Singapore, which are both ensconced within what can be described as a regime of offshore state capitalism. This entails far more direct support for, and indeed direct operation of the offshore sector, on the part of both the local state authorities, and foreign state patrons, than ever characterized the already semi-state-led pattern of offshore system promotion by the UK and the USA.

This offshore state capitalism has several interlocking elements. First, the foreign currency risks that offshore activities potentially pose to the finances of the offshore state are offset in both Singapore and Hong Kong by the hoarding of foreign exchange reserves (Clark and Monk 2010a). In Singapore, the largest national bank—DBS, which has played a leading role in the city-state's bid to become the "Switzerland of Asia"—is also controlled by the government as a shareholder, thus effectively canceling out any moral hazard associated with its backstopping. Second, both Hong Kong and Singapore are leading centers for the development of the offshore RMB market. This has been promoted by the Chinese government for the same reason that the US government promoted (or at least benignly neglected) the development of the Eurodollar market in the 1960s—namely to try to reconcile capital controls with a bid to preserve (or in the case of China attain) leading reserve currency issuer status. However, the way that the offshore RMB market has been cultivated by China has been far more systematic and proactive than the haphazard and accidental way that the US stumbled into embracing the Eurodollar market. Most importantly, the big four Chinese banks that have led the establishment of the offshore RMB market are directly owned by the government itself (Hall 2018; Töpfer and Hall 2018); which should in theory (even if not necessarily entirely in practice) neutralize the agency and moral hazard dilemmas inherent in any "onshore" state attempt to promote the offshore activities of its banks. This is, moreover, as we discuss in chapter 8, just one element of China's broader multidimensional offshore state capitalism.

Ultimately, it remains to be seen whether China's bid to displace the USA as the leading global reserve currency issuer will actually succeed. What is clear, however—as observed by Polanyi for economic liberalization generally—is that the ultimate result of the offshore "liberation" of markets from the reach of the state is, paradoxically, an inexorable expansion of the role of the state in supporting and operating these markets.

6

Culprits or Bystanders?

Offshore Securitization Centers and the Global
Financial Crisis

6.1 Introduction: Offshore Jurisdictions and the
Global Financial Crisis

The global financial crisis unfolded as a collapse of the shadow banking system,
wherein traditional bank lending and deposit-taking were simulated through the
production, purchase, and trading of securities (FCIC 2011; Gorton and Metrick
2010; Pozsar et al. 2010). As discussed in the preceding three chapters, this shadow
banking system had an exceedingly complex geographic structure, defined by the
interactions between multiple types of specialized financial production site, and
overlapping layers of territorial and extraterritorial regulatory authority exercised
by various governments in different capacities.

The substantive design and control of crisis implicated financial activities was
overwhelmingly concentrated, from a territorial geographic standpoint, in a handful of leading global financial centers, and above all the NY–LON axis. This occupied a dominant global position in securities issuance, trading, and development.
In the context of shadow banking, the agglomeration of financial professionals
and firms in these cities facilitated not only the flow of information within markets, but also innovation in the securitization "knowledge industry." Meanwhile, as
discussed in chapter 5, regulatory authority was distributed between the home and
host regulators of the investment and universal banks (as well as non-bank financial institutions) that played the leading role in designing, producing, repackaging,
marketing, and purchasing mortgage-backed securities; with the most important
level of prudential regulatory oversight, under the Basel framework, being that of
the home states that supervised the global consolidated capitalization of banks on
an extraterritorial basis.

As we showed in chapter 5, the growing concentration of prudential regulatory authority in the hands of bank home regulators, together with the post-1980
international race to the bottom in territorialized areas of host-based prudential regulation, combined to produce a shift in the logic of "offshore" banking
regulatory arbitrage in the lead-up the global financial crisis. As this shift occurred,

Sticky Power. Daniel Haberly and Dariusz Wójcik, Oxford University Press.
© Daniel Haberly and Dariusz Wójcik (2022). DOI: 10.1093/oso/9780198870982.003.0006

the regulatory significance (as well as total global importance) of the conventional on balance sheet offshore Eurocurrency markets declined.

Meanwhile, banks based in large European "midshore" jurisdictions—and above all the UK, Switzerland, and the Netherlands, along with other jurisdictions such as Belgium, Ireland, and Iceland—increasingly came to leverage relatively lax *home* state capital supervision (as well as tax advantages) to expand their competitive advantage within the newly emerging areas of shadow banking.

However, as noted in chapter 5, along with these large European midshore banking centers, another important category of offshore jurisdiction was also involved in shadow banking. These were the jurisdictions that specialized in hosting the legal vehicles issuing, and in some cases the exchanges for listing, the actual securities produced by the shadow banking system. Some of these securitization jurisdictions, such as Ireland, were midshore banking centers that were simultaneously used for bank home regulatory arbitrage. For the most part, however, the organization of offshore shadow banking securitization had a distinctive geography of its own (Wainwright 2011; Wójcik 2013b). The role of this distinct "paper" geography of offshore securitization remains poorly understood. It is known that securitization special-purpose vehicles (SPVs) domiciled in low-tax, "light-touch" regulation jurisdictions such as the Cayman Islands, Jersey, and Ireland, were linked to some of the most high-profile bank failures in the global financial crisis (Palan et al. 2010).[1] Furthermore, several critical accounts of the offshore world have argued that these jurisdictions were partially to blame for the crisis in a fairly direct sense (Shaxson 2011; Stewart 2013). However, analyses of the role of offshore jurisdictions as securitization SPV hosts, or sites for structured finance securities listing (e.g. Ireland) (Stewart 2013), have struggled to draw a concrete connection between the governance of these activities and their geographic domicile, as opposed to simply their existence (Palan and Nesvetailova 2013).

At most, analyses have implicated the geography of shadow banking securitization vehicles and securities exchange listings in the undermining of relatively peripheral points of European securities regulation (Stewart 2013). This is difficult to square with both the status of the United States as the homeland of the subprime crisis and shadow banking, and the more fundamental importance of prudential regulatory failure in this context. More commonly, issues of tax efficiency have been cited as primary motivations for the offshore location of securitization vehicles (Bayer and Bräutigam 2015; Gorton and Souleles 2007; Wainwright

---

[1] The failure of Northern Rock, for example, has been linked to a funding vehicle in Jersey; likewise, the failure of Sachsen LB was precipitated by the failure of a similar vehicle in Ireland, where a large number of collateralized debt obligations (CDOs) were also known to have been exchange-listed. In perhaps the most notorious incident of the crisis, the failure of German IKB partially resulted from its purchase, via a Jersey-based vehicle, of a Goldman Sachs–underwritten CDO issued in the Caymans. See Palan et al. (2010); Shaxson (2011); Stewart, (2013)

2011). However, the relationship between taxation and financial stability has not been clearly theorized in this context, with the relatively innocuous device of "tax neutrality" sometimes being squeezed into offshore financial conceptual frameworks built around the idea of overtly harmful secrecy and regulatory laxity. None of this literature has situated offshore jurisdictions within the type of ground-up analysis of international shadow banking organization and regulation necessary for their significance to be contextualized. Most problematically, we do not have the detailed empirical picture of the scale and organization of offshore shadow banking that would allow for these questions to be systematically tackled (Bayer and Bräutigam 2015). Ultimately, as noted by Palan et al. (2010) 165, "why so many SPVs were set up in tax havens is not entirely clear...nor is it clear what proportion of the structured finance market was set up offshore."

In this chapter, we seek to fill these gaps in the literature on offshore shadow banking by (1) compiling data from an array of archival sources (e.g. company registries, ratings agency reports, offering prospectuses) to construct the first detailed map of the jurisdictional geography of pre-crisis shadow banking, and (2) systematically analyzing the relevant academic, regulator, and practitioner (e.g. legal specialist) literature on the taxation and regulation of these activities to determine the potential direct and indirect bearing of their jurisdictional geography on financial stability. Specifically, we focus on the production of the short-term asset-backed commercial paper (ABCP) which constituted one of the key outputs of the subprime mortgage-backed security assembly line from the standpoint of shadow banking maturity and liquidity transformation. Prior to the global financial crisis, ABCP was seen as one of the least adventurous classes of debt instrument. However, the ABCP market ultimately proved to be surprisingly unstable, and played a central role in the run on the shadow banking system that began in mid-2007. Most importantly, from the standpoint of the study here, many of the vehicles that issued ABCP are known, at an anecdotal level, to have been domiciled in so-called small island offshore jurisdictions such as the Cayman Islands.

The evidence we present fully confirms these anecdotal reports. In fact, we show that the structured investment vehicles (SIVs), collateralized debt obligations (CDOs), and credit arbitrage conduits issuing the most problematic forms of ABCP, were disproportionately concentrated in "small islands," whereas more stable issuers were mostly based in "onshore–offshore" Delaware. However, we find that this geography is difficult to explain in terms of the traditional conceptualization of offshore banking centers, wherein they are seen as sites of direct escape from the jurisdiction of onshore authorities. The substantive onshore regulation of these activities (most importantly by the USA) was so minimal that there was very little to escape from. Furthermore, the minimal regulation that did apply to these activities had increasingly assumed an extraterritorialized form, by the onset of the global financial crisis, that projected onshore authority offshore. Given this two-pronged narrowing of their significance as sites for overt regulatory avoidance, we argue that offshore jurisdictions had, in this context, increasingly moved into a more complex normative grey area, wherein their specialization was less in the provision of overt forms of secrecy and regulatory laxity, than a flexible political and legal environment that facilitated rapid institutional innovation. This innovation could sometimes be legitimately described, at least in a narrow sense, as improving the institutional efficiency of global financial markets. However, given the endogenous crisis-generating logic of markets described by Keynes and Minsky, this apparently innocuous behavior could also have profoundly negative systematic consequences. More than pointing the finger of blame at offshore jurisdictions per se, this underscores a fundamental conundrum in financial governance.

The remainder of the chapter is divided into four sections. In section 6.2, we conceptually problematize the logic of offshore shadow banking, and situate it within a Minskian model of offshore financial institutional innovation. In section 6.3, we provide an overview of the organization of ABCP production on the eve of the global financial crisis, before revealing its detailed jurisdictional geography. In section 6.4, we seek to understand the significance of and rationale for these jurisdictional structures, through a combination of a process-of-elimination analysis of relevant onshore regulations—wherein we rule out the potential significance of most forms of direct offshore regulatory arbitrage—and a review of the relevant practitioner literature, which indicates that the hosting of these activities offshore was primarily motivated by more subtle and superficially innocuous factors such as tax neutrality, speed of entity creation, and bankruptcy resolution law. Finally, in the conclusion (section 6.5), we examine the policy implications of these findings. Specifically, we suggest that certain types of institutional "inefficiency" may need to be explicitly recognized and protected as a "Minskian Tobin tax" on financial innovation and complexity.

6.2   From Black Holes to Ball Bearings: A Minskian Model of Offshore Shadow Banking Development

Traditionally, offshore banking has primarily been seen as being motivated by the desire to directly escape the reach of onshore authorities—most importantly via the avoidance of financial regulation in the Euromarket, and the sheltering of assets from taxation in tax and secrecy havens (Hampton 1996; Lewis 1999; Palan et al. 2010; Shaxson 2011). As noted above, there have been some attempts to apply such an understanding of offshore jurisdictions as secretive, regulation-free spaces, to their role in the global financial crisis. There is reason to believe, however, that this model is a weaker fit in this context than for past financial and debt crises (Strange 1994).[2] Specifically, as we discussed in chapter 5 the structure of international

---

[2] Most notably the Euromarket-centered 1980s LDC debt crisis—see Strange (1994, 49–62).

financial regulation and intermediation had, by the global financial crisis, changed in ways that either constrained or reduced the relevance of this traditional offshore banking paradigm. First, the very success of offshore jurisdictions in historically spearheading an international regulatory race to the bottom has given the regulation-avoiding component of their business model a self-obsolescing quality. By the early 1990s, the regulatory advantage of the offshore Euromarket, in particular, had been significantly eroded (Hampton 1996). Second, even while the territorialized regulatory frameworks of the post–WWII era have been undermined by global capital mobility, and international regulatory competition predicated on this mobility, newer and less geographically limited frameworks have been expanded in their place. These have, as described in chapter 5, increasingly given states an institutionalized capacity to chase multinational firms across international borders (Phelps 2007; Weiss 1997). This extraterritorial adaptive capacity is unevenly distributed. However, what is crucial, from the standpoint of the global financial crisis, is that it is disproportionately concentrated in the hands of the most powerful countries, and in particular the United States. Offshore jurisdictions have been subjected to particularly intense international pressures by the USA and multilateral bodies (e.g. Financial Action Task Force), since the turn of the millennium, in relation to financial transparency and information exchange (Eden and Kudrle 2005; Sharman 2005; Vlcek 2007). These have been far from fully successful in an absolute sense; however, they do seem to have reduced the relative onshore–offshore transparency gap. Indeed, the USA in particular has often leveraged the same international political clout that allows it to dictate reforms elsewhere, to avoid reciprocation, and various US states have increasingly been ranked below many "small island" jurisdictions (e.g. the Caymans) on indicators of financial transparency and client due diligence (Cobham et al. 2015; Findley et al. 2012).

Even more important than initiatives targeting offshore jurisdictions specifically, is the fact that financial regulation in general has, as discussed in chapter 5, moved toward an extraterritorial paradigm designed to combat host-based interjurisdictional arbitrage. This raises the question of whether offshore activities actually operate outside of, as opposed to within, the purview of onshore regulators. The US Securities and Exchange Commission (SEC) has increasingly assumed the role of a global securities regulator (Chang 2003; Davison and Litvinoff 2013; Deacon 2004). Even more importantly, a succession of Basel Accords have redrawn the geography of international banking regulatory jurisdiction, by moving the primary locus of authority from the host states where banks operate, to the home states where they are headquartered (D'Hulster 2012; Herring 2007; Pistor 2010). The critical literature on offshore finance has understandably tended to either ignore or dismiss Basel, due to its demonstrable failure to actually prevent financial crises (Hampton 1996; Lewis 1999; Strange 1994). However, this has led it to overlook the qualitative regulatory implications of Basel for offshore centers. Indeed, the international supervisory dilemma that historically fueled off-shore banking—namely the inability of home states to control the behavior of their banks overseas—appears to have become largely inverted, with host states now often struggling to protect themselves from lax regulation by home states (D'Hulster 2012). As we showed in the previous chapter, this actually opened the door, in the lead-up to the GFC, to an expansion of new types of *home*-based prudential regulatory arbitrage by the larger European midshore banking centers such as the UK and Switzerland; however, it does not really shed light on the role of offshore "small islands," such as for example the Cayman Islands or Jersey, as hosts for shadow banking–linked securitization activities.

In fact, most analyses of the regulatory failures responsible for the global financial crisis locate these failures within the regulatory authorities of the largest developed economies—and most importantly the United States—whether in their capacity as home, host or global regulators of the largest financial firms and markets. This is particularly true for shadow banking specifically, which tended to fall outside of the scope of conventional banking regulation on an intra-jurisdictional basis (see discussion in sections 6.3 and 6.4). Indeed, the explosion of key shadow banking devices such as money market funds and the commercial paper market from the 1970s essentially represented an onshore alternative to the expanding offshore Eurodollar market, which allowed for bank deposit interest rate caps and reserve requirements to be bypassed on US soil (Minsky 1980). More recently, the exhaustive report of the US Financial Crisis Inquiry Commission identifies monumental flaws and lapses within US prudential and securities regulation that appear to explain the key shadow banking governance failures responsible for the global financial crisis (FCIC 2011). Meanwhile, analyses of the participation of non-US financial firms in crisis-implicated shadow banking activities have located the most important regulatory failures at the home state level, particularly in Europe—including on the part of the midshore home states discussed in the previous chapter (Acharya et al. 2013; Arteta et al. 2013; Thiemann 2014).[3]

This apparently superfluous nature of the offshore domiciliation of securitization vehicles from a *host* standpoint, in relation to the regulatory failures responsible for the crisis, makes the reported pervasiveness of this domiciliation something of a paradox from the standpoint of the traditional offshore banking model. Resolving this paradox, we argue, requires a normative reproblematization of the role of offshore jurisdictions in international finance. This, on the one hand, acknowledges their potential to provide services that may be (in some sense) beneficial, but, on the other, also more broadly construes the level at which these services can be considered harmful. The first requires moving away from an understanding of offshore jurisdictions that emphasizes their pursuit of particular

---

[3] For example, of European bank-sponsored securitization vehicles, see Acharya et al. (2013); Arteta et al. (2013); Thiemann (2014).

harmful policies, to a definition of offshore emphasizing a particular brand of local politics within the *offshore state* (see chapter 2). Meanwhile, the second requires adopting a Minskian conceptualization of endogenous market instability, wherein financial crisis production is seen as being primarily rooted in the private rather than public sector.

The first of these shifts is already underway in the literature on offshore political economy. Nicholas Shaxson, for example, argues that the defining feature of offshore jurisdictions is a profound condition of state responsiveness to (and often outright capture by) international financial firms, and related FABS firms in law and accountancy, wherein these polities operate as "politically stable" "fast and flexible private law-making machines" on behalf of (what we dub) the FABS complex (Shaxson, 2011,184). As he emphasizes, this role can, notably, be played by subnational as well as national political units, such as the US state of Delaware. However, this *politics*-based definition of offshore still tends to be treated in analyses as being rather interchangeable with more narrowly *policy*-based definitions, which only emphasize specific categories of directly and obviously harmful behavior. Typically, the focus is on some combination of financial secrecy and tax avoidance/evasion, with the terms "secrecy jurisdiction" and "tax haven" often used as stand-ins for the term "offshore jurisdiction" (Palan et al. 2010; Shaxson, 2011). This ambiguous juxtaposition of politics and policy-based models of "offshoreness" creates two analytical problems. First, the idea of a narrow policy specialization sits uneasily with the open-ended flexibility implied by a politically based understanding of offshore states. In this vein, Christopher Le Marchant argues that a focus on questions such as secrecy misses the more basic role of offshore jurisdictions as institutional "laboratories," "wherein the more flexible and innovative atmosphere of offshore has enabled offshore centers to invent or pioneer products and services" (Marchant 1999). Second, and relatedly, it creates an expectation that offshore practices can be easily and uncontroversially labeled as harmful. This is ill-suited to deal with the potential of jurisdictions to retreat, in the face of international reform pressure, into a more complex normative gray area.

In fact, there is reason to believe that offshore jurisdictions can, *in principle*, serve as sites for useful forms of institutional innovation. This potential legitimacy rests on the fact that actually existing economic activity has institutional overhead costs, with all institutional frameworks being, furthermore, path-dependent accretions of "second-best" workarounds to historical problems. As rightly emphasized by offshore critics, many onshore tax and regulatory costs of business have a clear and necessary social purpose. Consequently, their circumvention constitutes a zero or negative-sum wealth transfer, rather than, as claimed by offshore defenders, a positive-sum improvement of economic institutional efficiency (Palan et al. 2010). However, the situation is more complex where inherited onshore institutions impose unintentional burdens on economic activity. Research suggests, for example, that offshore jurisdiction use by Chinese and former Soviet

Union companies largely reflects the capitalist institutional legal vacuum in post-communist transition economies (Nougayrède 2013; Sharman 2012). This is not to say that offshore jurisdictions are not used for dishonest purposes, but rather that this is not always the only, or even the primary rationale for their use. Russia, for example, did not create an onshore company law until 1996, several years after the beginning of mass privatization (Nougayrède 2013). In China, meanwhile, the most widespread use of offshore jurisdictions appears to be as conduits for listings on overseas exchanges (typically New York or Hong Kong) (Sharman 2012; Sutherland and Matthews 2009). The fact that state-owned national champions account for a substantial share of these offshore-structured listings (see chapter 8), is a strong indication that the Chinese government sees them as a mechanism for enhancing, rather than undermining, the onshore institutional framework (Wójcik and Camilleri 2015).[4] Indeed, in the context of these listings, offshore jurisdictions (particularly midshore Hong Kong) arguably provide transparency, rather than secrecy, to opaque and lawless Mainland financial markets.

For countries with more developed legal systems, the potential draw of relatively strong but low-cost offshore institutional frameworks is less pronounced. However, there are often qualitative differences between national institutional regimes—e.g. civil versus common law jurisdictions—which are the product of historical path dependencies, and may have advantages or disadvantages for any particular transaction (e.g. securitizations) (Schwarcz et al. 2004). More broadly, offshore jurisdictions may facilitate the creation of flexible, à la carte contractual arrangements, in areas such as bankruptcy resolution. The latter casts a particularly long-shadow of potential litigation costs and legal uncertainty over financial activity, which may raise the present cost of finance. The avoidance of this shadow through "bankruptcy remote"[5] securitizations can thus be considered a form of transaction cost reduction, which may or may not be additionally motivated by regulatory arbitrage (Gorton and Souleles 2007). Finally, offshore jurisdictions have increasingly rebranded themselves in terms of the rather slippery concept of "tax neutrality," or the lack of additional taxation beyond what is due onshore (Gorton and Souleles 2007; Wainwright 2011). Where combined with indefinite deferral of onshore tax liabilities (e.g. by US corporations prior to the 2017 TCJA), this can be tantamount to tax avoidance. However, this is not necessarily the case for vehicles that continuously pass through cash flows from one location/party to another, which are more likely to use offshore locales to avoid double-tax "leakages" along the chain of intermediation. The purpose of such vehicles is not to avoid taxation; rather, a tax-neutral structure facilitates their creation for other purposes, such as issuing or holding securities.

---

[4] For example China Mobile, see Wójcik and Camilleri (2015, 464).
[5] That is the movement of assets and liabilities into a vehicle removed from the potential bankruptcy estate of a firm, with this vehicle typically also structured so that its own potential bankruptcy risks and costs are minimized.

That these offshore services might in some contexts be, in and of themselves, relatively innocuous, does not mean that they cannot have pernicious effects. On the contrary, it potentially makes their negative impacts more profound and intractable. In order to fully theorize these impacts, in the area of banking regulation, it is necessary to adopt an endogenous perspective on financial instability and crisis (Ferri and Minsky 1992; Keynes 1936; Minsky 1980). In an exogenous theory of market instability, crises are seen to result from limited points of failure in the otherwise sound operation of markets. In neoclassical economics, these failures are typically ascribed to excessive and or poorly designed state interventions. Right-wing pundits in the USA, for example, often blame the subprime crisis on low-income household lending quotas, and government sponsorship of Fannie Mae and Freddie Mac. In contrast, in an endogenous theory of market instability, financial crises are viewed as an intrinsic product of private sector behavior (Ferri and Minsky 1992). This idea has been notably underdeveloped in the literature on offshore political economy. This has, while debunking neoclassical critiques of "excessive" onshore regulation, constructed what is in some respects a new narrative of exogenous government-driven financial instability focused on offshore states (Palan et al. 2010, 154–158). In contrast, the endogenous perspective on offshore-exacerbated financial instability proposed here does not dispute the idea, in principle, that these jurisdictions may help to "make markets work" by streamlining their institutional overhead costs. Rather, we argue that it is precisely in this efficiency-enhancing capacity that they can potentially cause severe damage.

As theorized in the works of Keynes and Minsky, capitalist financial systems contain positive feedback loops that automatically generate cyclical boom–bust dynamics (Ferri and Minsky 1992b; Keynes 1936; Minsky 1980, 1992b). Two factors are, in combination, a particularly acute source of instability. First, the government only has limited and indirect control over monetary expansion and contraction. Money is rather an endogenous product of private sector credit creation, the volume of which primarily reflects the level of demand for capital assets. Second, the demand for debt-financed investment in capital assets is conditioned by, and in turn conditions, a combination of expected future profits and current ability to service or refinance debt payments—as determined by both asset yields and capital gains. The result is a positive feedback relationship that generates alternating periods of self-reinforcing asset price inflation and debt deflation. Crucially, according to Minsky, private actors do not simply create credit within the existing financial institutional framework, but can modify this framework through the invention of new types of credit instrument. Consequently, a process of outright interjurisdictional arbitrage, or intra-jurisdictional deregulation, is unnecessary, in principle, to regulatory failure; rather, any given regulatory framework will tend to continuously become obsolete. Indeed, as financial stability fosters the Keynesian "animal spirits" that motivate financial innovation, the very effectiveness of regulation is actually a direct cause of its obsolescence.

Ultimately, the fact that shadow banking did not so much circumvent specific banking regulations, as the traditional definition of banking itself, makes this perhaps the most compelling theory of the trajectory of shadow banking development that produced the global financial crisis (Wray 2009). Indeed, although there was a strongly laissez-faire regulatory inclination from the 1980s to 2000s, its most important manifestation was arguably a misplaced faith in the stability of new credit instruments, as opposed to the deregulation of older ones (for conventional banking, Basel actually restored oversight to the offshore prudential regulatory void that had emerged during the Keynesian era). However, what Minsky's model does not directly address, is that financial innovations designed to skirt directly relevant regulations might be obstructed by a host of other tax, legal, and regulatory issues which are entirely incidental. In other words, financial innovation is likely to be slowed by a generalized "friction" with the inherited institutional environment. It is the ability to help financial actors overcome such frictions, we argue, that has increasingly become the core specialization of the offshore institutional "laboratory" in relation to financial innovation. This is not to say that offshore jurisdictions have not in the past, and do not continue to more directly facilitate escape from onshore regulation. However, as traditionally territorialized regulatory frameworks have either been eroded by international regulatory competition and arbitrage, or replaced by more geographically robust extraterritorial frameworks, the role of offshore jurisdictions as financial governance black holes has increasingly taken a backseat to their more subtle role as financial innovation "ball bearings" (Maurer 2008).

As we show in the following sections for the case of asset-backed commercial paper (ABCP), this shift has made it increasingly difficult to characterize offshore policies as harmless or harmful at the jurisdictional level. Rather, this is contingent on their broader contextual insertion into the global financial networks constructed by private sector actors. This makes the reform of the offshore world a more complex dilemma than is typically recognized.

6.3 Mapping the Geography of Pre-crisis ABCP Production and Failure

The 2007–2009 global financial crisis unfolded as a bank run, wherein financial intermediaries found themselves unable to roll over short-term debt liabilities due to a generalized loss of confidence in borrower creditworthiness (Gorton and Metrick 2012). In contrast to a traditional bank run characterized by deposit flight, however, the crisis took the form of a run on short-term shadow banking liabilities, namely commercial paper (CP) and asset-backed commercial paper (ABCP) issued by on and off balance sheet vehicles, overnight repo credit collateralized by longer-term asset-backed securities (ABS), and shares of money market mutual funds investing in the CP/ABCP and repo markets. What renders banks susceptible to runs is the process of maturity and liquidity transformation, whereby liquid, short-maturity debt is used to fund illiquid, long-term loans. In the pre-crisis shadow banking system, the function of maturity and liquidity transformation primarily occurred through the funding of long-term securitized and non-securitized investments via the wholesale CP/ABCP and repo markets. Maturity transformation was also performed by money market mutual funds, which funded short-term CP and ABCP purchases and repo lending with very short-term, demand deposit equivalent, stable net asset value (NAV)[6] shares. In the pre-crisis subprime mortgage securitization chain, CP and repo primarily acted as working credit used by financial firms to fund loan origination and other intermediate on balance sheet stages of securitization. Meanwhile, the end product of the securitization process was typically the sale of assets to off balance sheet special-purpose vehicles/entities (SPVs/SPEs) issuing either ABCP or longer-term ABS, which could be sold to a variety of institutional investors (e.g. pension funds, mutual funds, insurance companies) (Pozsar et al. 2010).

From the standpoint of maturity and liquidity transformation, ABCP-issuing SPVs served as key shadow banks within the securitized credit intermediation chain. Importantly, as the ABCP issued by these vehicles was both very highly rated, and of very short maturity, it could be purchased by the money market funds which served as the primary "deposits" in the shadow banking system (Archarya et al. 2013; Covitz et al. 2013; Gorton and Metrick 2012; Pozsar et al 2010). Most ABCP-issuing vehicles were created and sponsored by banks, as a mechanism for reducing regulatory capital by moving assets into nominally off balance sheet vehicles. Crucially, these vehicles were "bankruptcy remote"—i.e. structured to be excluded from the sponsor's estate in the event of its bankruptcy, so that investors were only exposed to credit risk from the vehicle's own assets. However, due to the short maturity (< three months) of the paper they issued, they were also inherently dependent on explicit or implicit sponsor backstops to mitigate the risk of investor runs (Gorton and Souleles 2007; Acharya et al. 2013). Liquidity support (e.g. via liquidity put options) was most important in practice, as it amounted to a contingent promise by a sponsoring bank to repurchase securities from investors at face value, yet was typically not subject to the capital charges of overt credit support. This rendered vehicles substantively on balance sheet from the standpoint of the risk they posed to their sponsors (or third parties to whom sponsors had transferred these risks), despite being insulated from the sponsor's own credit risk.

That many ABCP-issuing vehicles were based in jurisdictions typically identified as offshore has been established at a qualitative level (Palan et al. 2010). Beyond SPV domiciliation, it is also known that many troubled structured finance securities were exchange-listed in Ireland (Stewart et al. 2015). However, neither the

---

[6] That is redeemable at a guaranteed constant face value.

detailed jurisdictional geography of this activity, nor the precise significance of this geography, has been systematically described. From an empirical standpoint, the remainder of this section seeks to understand (1) the offshore and onshore geography of domiciliation and exchange listing of ABCP-issuing vehicles by type, (2) the nationality of the ultimate sponsors of these vehicles, and (3) the jurisdictions from which vehicles were immediately sponsored. Next, in section 6.4, we examine (1) whether the offshore footprint of these activities could have potentially had a bearing on their onshore regulation, and (2) what the specialist/practitioner literature says about the rationale for this offshore footprint.

ABCP was issued prior to the crisis by several types of vehicle (see Figures 6.1 and 6.2) whose stability was a function of the sponsor backstops they received, and the type of assets they purchased. Most stable were conventional multi-seller conduits, which were engaged in the primary securitization of loans purchased from multiple originators, and typically enjoyed a high level of direct liquidity and credit support from sponsors or third parties. These conduits in most cases had little connection to US subprime mortgage lending, rather focusing on areas such as trade receivables, credit card, and auto loans (Acharya et al. 2013; Arteta et al. 2013). More mixed in their resilience were single-seller conduits that securitized loans originated by a single firm, with home mortgage origination warehousing conduits being predictably hard hit (Covitz et al. 2013).

Less stable than primary loan securitization vehicles, in general, were the various classes of vehicle (structured investment vehicles, collateralized debt obligations, and credit arbitrage and hybrid conduits) engaged in the purchasing and repackaging of ABS, including subprime residential mortgage-backed securities (RMBS). Collateralized debt obligations (CDOs) were the most systemically destabilizing vehicles, as they proved to be a fundamentally faulty statistical device that was intended to convert high-risk into low-risk securities, but in practice simply passed risk on to investors (Mendales 2009). Without the market for lower-rated RMBS tranches created by CDOs, it is doubtful that the subprime lending bubble would or could have reached the proportions that it did (FCIC 2011). While most CDOs issued long-term ABS, some also issued short-term ABCP, which typically received liquidity support from either the underwriter or a third party (Mueller et al. 2006). ABCP-issuing CDOs were among the most problematic vehicles in the crisis, as they combined the defective credit risk management of a CDO with the liquidity risk of an ABCP conduit (FCIC 2011).

In contrast to CDOs, credit arbitrage (and hybrid)[7] ABCP conduits and structured investment vehicles (SIVs) usually only purchased highly rated ABS. However, the fact that these included a substantial component of CDOs and other subprime-backed RMBS widely contaminated, and often precipitated the failures of, both of types of vehicle in the crisis. Notwithstanding their less pronounced

---

[7] Hybrid conduits typically held a mixture of loans and ABS.

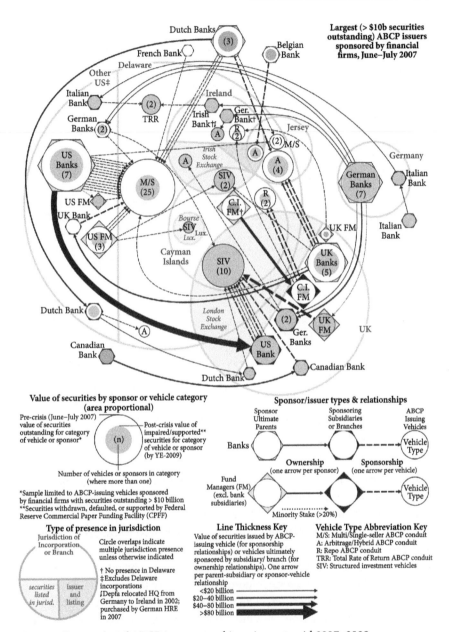

Fig. 6.1 Geography of ABCP issuance and impairment, mid 2007–2009

Sources: Moody's; Fitch; Standard & Poor's; authors' research; adapted from Haberly and Wójcik (2017a).

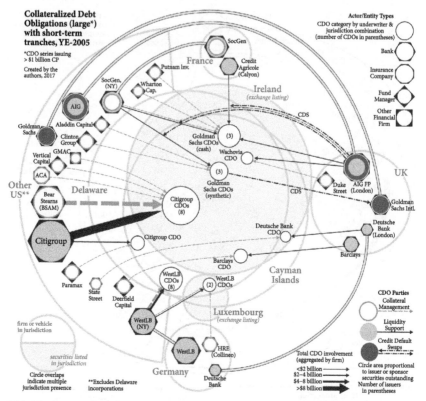

Fig. 6.2 Geography of CDOs with short-term tranches, YE-2005

Sources: Mueller et al. (2006); authors' research; adapted from Haberly and Wójcik (2017a).

maturity mismatch, SIVs were more severely impacted than arbitrage and hybrid conduits—indeed they entirely ceased to exist as a vehicle class. Unlike arbitrage and hybrid conduits, SIVs tended to lack explicit sponsor support, being rather structured as independent lenders (essentially shell banks) whose ABCP tranches were protected by a capital structure of medium-term notes (MTNs) and capital notes (CNs). This lack of explicit sponsor backstops, combined with the preprogramming of SIVs to conduct value-destroying asset fire sales in a liquidity crunch, rendered them inherently susceptible to investor runs (FCIC 2011; Arteta et al. 2013; Covitz et al. 2013). Ironically, most SIVs ultimately did receive sponsor support during the crisis, with investors typically not suffering losses (Arteta et al. 2013; Covitz et al. 2013).

Figures 6.1 and 6.2 show the first comprehensive jurisdictional maps of the largest pre-crisis ABCP issuers in these different categories. Figure 6.1 shows the largest financial firm-sponsored ABCP conduits and SIVs as of mid-2007, while Figure 6.2 shows the largest CDO ABCP programs as of YE-2005. Rankings of programs by size, and data on program sponsorship were obtained from ratings agency databases and reports (primarily Moody's, Fitch, Standard & Poor's), and cross-checked (for non-CDO programs) against the list of ABCP programs compiled by Acharya and Schnabl (2010). CDO-issued ABCP program size rankings and sponsorships were obtained from a one-off ratings agency report released in 2006 (Mueller et al. 2006), necessitating the eighteen-month discrepancy between the two figures. Notably, while the volume of CDO issuance increased substantially over the year-and-a-half separating the two figures, this tended to reproduce patterns established by YE-2005. Together, the vehicles in the figures accounted for approximately half of total worldwide pre-crisis ABCP issuance.[8]

While the data sources above typically include information on the geographic location of program sponsors (including, in most cases, the location of immediately sponsoring subsidiaries or branches), they only rarely specify the geography of securitization vehicle domiciliation or securities exchange listings. Due to a lack of public databases containing this information, we have hand-compiled it from exhaustive searches of online company registries, exchange prospectuses, and news articles and reports detailing specific vehicles. Company registry searches were based on vehicle name matches, tested against a variety of entity-type suffixes (e.g. LLC, Corp., Ltd.). Results were cross-referenced wherever possible against other sources detailing individual vehicles. Exchange listing searches were based on name-match searches for programs and the most popular structured finance exchanges (Ireland, Luxembourg, London, and New York). As we have been forced, in the absence of centralized public databases, to construct the results from a labor-intensive "collage" technique, the jurisdictional patterns revealed below cannot be assumed to be error-free with respect to individual actors or relationships; rather, they should be interpreted as a best-possible view of patterns that have to date been entirely opaque.

Figure 6.1 shows the jurisdictional structure of the largest fifty-four ABCP conduits and SIVs (outstanding securities > $10 billion) sponsored by financial firms in mid (June–July) 2007. The area of white circles is proportional to the aggregated assets of vehicle classes with a specific jurisdictional organization, and/or the combined value of vehicles sponsored by banks and fund managers of a particular nationality. Both ultimate sponsor nationality and the location of immediately sponsoring subsidiaries or branches are indicated. The area of shaded circles within larger white circles indicates the total value of impaired securities for each category of vehicle or sponsor, with impairment defined as an event of default,

---

[8] According to Moody's ABCP Program Index the sample encompassed 49.6% ($726 billion out of $1,424 billion) of all outstanding ABCP in Q2-2007. The fact that a disproportionate number of the largest ABCP issuers were "exotic" vehicles such as SIVs, repo, arbitrage, and hybrid conduits means that these are likely overrepresented in Figure 5.1 in relation to "plain vanilla" single- and multi-seller conduits. SIVs, which issued multiple types of securities, are also overrepresented from the standpoint of ABCP issuance (although their total size better reflects their systemic importance as shadow banks). As we are primarily interested in the geographies of different issuer types, rather than ABCP issuers as a whole, these sampling issues do not significantly impact the analysis.

the withdrawal of all securities by the sponsor as of the beginning of 2010, and the peak value of securities supported by the Federal Reserve's Commercial Paper Funding Facility (CPFF) (CPFF 2017).[9] The jurisdiction of vehicles or sponsors is indicated by the light gray circles, with jurisdiction of incorporation indicated where circles/wedges have a white fill, jurisdiction of exchange listing indicated by a light gray fill, and both jurisdiction of incorporation and listing indicated by darker gray fill. Vehicles or sponsors falling within multiple circles are domiciled and or listed in all of these jurisdictions unless otherwise indicated.

Several aspects of the diagram are striking. The first is the apparent (but superficial, see section 6.4) dominance of Delaware as a securitization jurisdiction, with every SIV and conduit in the sample incorporating a Delaware-based vehicle. Just as notable, however, is that most (29/54) of the SIVs and conduits in the sample were not limited to Delaware geographically, but rather extended across two or more jurisdictions with respect to domicile and or listing. As a result, the map has an interlocking Venn-diagram structure. Different types of vehicle exhibit pronounced segregation by domicile. Conventional single—and multi-seller conduits were nearly all established as Delaware-only issuer structures. In contrast, all of the SIVs were established with a lead issuer in the Cayman Islands, and co-issuer in Delaware. Meanwhile, most of the arbitrage and hybrid conduits were structured with a lead issuer in Jersey and or Ireland, and a co-issuer in Delaware. On top of these dual domicile arrangements, the jurisdiction of exchange listing added a third layer to the legal geography of securitization in many cases. In this respect, there was a sharp divide between SIVs and ABCP conduits, with all SIVs listing at least some classes of securities (in most cases on the London Stock Exchange, although in a few cases in Ireland or Luxembourg), while only two ABCP conduits were found to have exchange listings (in both cases in Ireland). Moreover, short-term commercial paper itself appears to have only seldom been listed by any type of issuer, with SIVs typically only listing longer maturity securities (e.g. medium-term notes).

Both the immediate and ultimate jurisdiction of sponsors exhibit a strong relationship with issuer type and jurisdiction. SIVs were nearly all sponsored by London-based subsidiaries and branches of non-British banks. By far the most important was Citigroup's UK subsidiary, Citigroup International (the lone UK-based US bank in the sample), which invented SIVs in the 1980s. The few SIVs whose immediate sponsors were not London-based were sponsored from New York. More broadly, 45/54 vehicles in Figure 6.1 had an immediate sponsor in either the USA or the UK. In practice, these immediate sponsors were typically (and for foreign banks operating through these countries always) based in New York or London, underscoring the dominance of the NY–LON axis in the design

---

[9] The CPFF was a Federal Reserve crisis facility provided to support the commercial paper market. See CPFF (2017).

and administration of crisis-implicated securities (see chapter 4). Of the remaining nine vehicles not sponsored from the US or UK, two were sponsored by German banks operating in Ireland (including Depfa, a quasi-German institution rescued by Hypo Real Estate in 2007), while five were sponsored by Dutch banks directly from the Netherlands. Both of these jurisdictions, notably, are leading European corporate tax havens widely used for securitizations in general (Deacon 2004). With respect to the ultimate sponsorship of vehicle types, American banks were mostly oriented toward "plain vanilla" single and multi-seller conduits in Delaware, with the major exception of Citigroup's London-managed SIV activities. In contrast, German banks—particularly the public banks (Landesbanken and IKB) accounting for 5/7 of German sponsors—concentrated on exotic arbitrage and hybrid conduits and SIVs. British and Dutch banks fell in between their German and American peers in this respect.

With respect to security impairment rates, analysis is complicated by the high collinearity between vehicle type, domicile, and sponsorship structure. The high failure rate of vehicles domiciled in Jersey, Ireland, and the Cayman Islands, or sponsored by German banks, is strongly associated with the specialization of these jurisdictions/banks in the domiciliation/sponsorship of highly failure-prone arbitrage conduits and SIVs. Likewise, vehicles with an immediate sponsor in London were likely to be highly failure-prone SIVs, which were invariably domiciled in the Cayman Islands and listed in London. Conversely, the low failure rate of vehicles with either a Delaware-only domicile, or US bank sponsorship, is associated with the tendency of these vehicles to be relatively stable single or multi-seller conduits. Such collinearity casts doubt on any simple guilt-by-association interpretation of the offshore location of crisis events, as blame for failure could theoretically be assigned to any one (or more) of these parameters.

Figure 6.2 shows the jurisdictional organization of major CDOs issuing short-term (ABCP and equivalent) securities as of YE-2005, along with the key actors involved in their operation. Due to the complexity of CDOs, only the largest ABCP-issuing CDO series (with > $1 billion in commercial paper issuance) are shown for the sake of clarity. Four categories of actor are shown. First, CDOs are aggregated and labeled based on underwriter (i.e. the investment bank which arranged their structure and marketed their securities). For cash CDOs, the involvement of two additional types of actors are shown; collateral managers responsible for the selection of CDO assets, and providers of liquidity support to short-term CDO tranches. For synthetic CDOs (in this sample entirely underwritten by Goldman Sachs), a fourth type of actor is shown, namely the buyer of credit default swap (CDS) protection (in this case Goldman Sachs itself). In addition, we show the CDS protection purchased by some CDO liquidity support providers to protect themselves from the associated credit risk.

The CDOs in Figure 6.2 can be mostly grouped into three networks. The first, and largest, is an American network of CDOs underwritten and backstopped by

Citigroup, which were mostly managed by Bear Stearns's hedge fund arm (BSAM) in the Klio CDO series. The second is a Goldman Sachs centered network of cash and synthetic CDOs, with a heavy involvement of AIG and French banks in collateral management and liquidity support. Notably, AIG assumed nearly all of the liquidity risk of the CDOs in this network, either directly as a put provider, or indirectly via its assumption of risk from Crédit Agricole and Societe Generale through CDS. Beyond the high level of French participation, this network is given a strongly transatlantic character by the fact that the associated CDS activities of Goldman Sachs and AIG were conducted by London affiliates of these firms (also see discussion of AIG FP in chapter 4). The third, and smallest major network, is likewise transatlantic, being dominated by CDOs underwritten, and in most cases managed and backstopped by, the New York subsidiaries and branches of German Landesbank WestLB. Swiss banks, notably, despite being the second-largest underwriters of CDOs generally after US banks (see chapter 5), do not seem to have been involved, on a large scale, with these particularly risky short-term-funded CDOs.

The CDOs in the sample exhibit a relatively homogenous jurisdictional structure, which resembles the SIVs in Figure 6.1. This was usually characterized by a dual Cayman Islands-Delaware issuer-co-issuer structure, with a listing on the Irish Stock Exchange (although as for SIVs, short-term ABCP tranches themselves were typically not listed). Like SIVs, the direct management of CDOs was overwhelmingly based in New York or London, albeit with a much higher concentration in the former. London appears, in relation to CDOs, to have primarily specialized in CDS underwriting. Also resembling SIVs is the near universality of failure of sample CDOs, which negates any attempt to find a straightforward association between vehicle stability and domicile or sponsoring institutions. Indeed, the activities and relationships in Figure 6.2 constituted a critical area of instability in the crisis. It was primarily the CDO-linked losses of Bear Stearns's hedge fund arm (particularly in conjunction with Citi's CDOs) which precipitated the downfall of this firm. These same CDOs also played a leading role in the fall of Citigroup (see 6.4). Finally, the sale of CDS by AIG to Goldman Sachs and its French partner banks, in conjunction with these (and similar CDO) series, was a central factor in AIG's collapse (FCIC 2011).

6.4 Problematizing ABCP Governance Failure—Offshore and Onshore

These patterns fully confirm the "staggering reports of financial activities in OFCs" (Palan et al. 2010), prior to the crisis. Most strikingly, the ABCP-issuing vehicles most directly implicated in the crisis itself, and characterized by the highest levels of crisis security impairment—specifically CDOs, SIVs, and credit arbitrage/hybrid conduits—nearly always had a lead issuer located in an offshore jurisdiction outside of the United States, and in many cases also listed securities on the Irish or Luxembourg exchanges. The Cayman Islands held a commanding lead as an offshore (non-US) lead issuer domicile, hosting forty-two vehicles in the sample (fourteen excluding CDOs), while Jersey hosted six, and Ireland hosted four. Most importantly, the fact that these lead issuers were invariably paired with a co-issuer in Delaware appears to have been of little significance from the standpoint of US regulatory jurisdiction. The sole purpose of these Delaware co-issuers seems to have been to satisfy restrictions in certain US states on the ability of insurance companies to buy foreign securities (i.e. providing a "made in USA" label for the purposes of these state regulations alone) (Lucas et al. 2006). Beyond this, the Delaware co-issuing SPVs had no tax or regulatory substance, which was rather attributed to the offshore primary issuer. Consequently, Delaware's specialization was effectively in conventional multi- and single-seller conduits, rather than more exotic vehicles.

Notwithstanding their pervasive presence in ABCP production, however, the contribution of offshore jurisdictions to ABCP-market instability appears to have mostly been an indirect facilitative one—involving a lowering of the cost of Minskian shadow banking innovations—rather than a direct enabling of regulatory arbitrage or opacity. This conclusion can be reached through both a process-of-elimination analysis of pre-crisis prudential and securities regulation, oriented toward ruling out their potential to serve as significant sites for direct regulatory arbitrage, and a review of the specialist practitioner literature on offshore securitizations. The latter emphasizes points of law, regulation, and taxation that were mostly peripheral to financial stability in a direct sense, but represented potential institutional frictions that could impede the deployment of securitized credit instruments (including ABCP) in general. As we will show, it was primarily the need to alleviate these frictions that led to the issuance of all ABCP from jurisdictions with broadly offshore characteristics—including "onshore–offshore" Delaware—as well as the concentration of the most complex ABCP issuers (e.g. CDOs and SIVs) in "small islands" (e.g. the Caymans) offering the highest level of institutional flexibility in areas such as taxation and bankruptcy treatment.

From the standpoint of a process-of-elimination analysis of the direct role of offshore jurisdictions in undercutting financial regulation, what is striking about the massive involvement of offshore jurisdictions in crisis-implicated ABCP production is how little this geography seems to have mattered within the pre-crisis regulatory architecture. On the one hand, the relevant elements of national onshore regulatory frameworks were typically characterized by a high degree of extraterritoriality, which could not be evaded through the use of paper offshore devices. At the same time, these onshore regulatory frameworks were so riddled with loopholes as to make offshore regulatory arbitrage unnecessary. Ironically, even while domiciled, or in some cases listed offshore, the vehicles presented in section 6.4 were overwhelmingly structured to operate within these onshore loopholes.

For ABCP prudential regulation, the geography of jurisdiction was primarily defined by Basel. This granted primary responsibility for liquidity supervision to host states on a territorial basis (before Basel III), while assigning primary responsibility for capital supervision to home states on a globally consolidated bank nationality (i.e. headquarters) basis (D'Hulster 2012; Herring 2007; Pistor 2010). Given that the failure of the ABCP market was, as noted in section 6.3, above all a liquidity issue, host responsibility for the former could have theoretically given the offshore domicile of SPVs a bearing on their regulation. In practice, however, the fact that very few governments, onshore or offshore, considered these vehicles to be "credit institutions" subject to direct prudential supervision, made this issue moot (Thiemann 2014). The question was not one of their offshore location, but rather their off balance sheet treatment (specifically for purposes of bank sponsor prudential regulation, which applied different criteria than vehicle accounting consolidation).

To the extent that these vehicles were constrained by prudential regulation at all, it was indirectly via the global (extraterritorial) capital charges that home regulators imposed on the sponsoring banks that provided vehicles with liquidity backstops (Acharya and Schnabl 2010; Thiemann 2014). Generally speaking, the laxity of home regulators in defining these charges was so pronounced as to render other prudential regulatory jurisdiction issues moot. SIVs operated in the most complete regulatory void, as they were only protected by implicit sponsor backstops to which no capital charges were attached. However, even explicit liquidity backstops extended to ABCP conduits by German, British, Dutch, and Belgian national banks were completely free of capital charges until the phasing in of Basel II between 2006 and 2008. This may explain why virtually all credit arbitrage and hybrid conduits—which were used as devices for the off balance sheet accumulation of third party, and in particular US mortgage-backed securities—were sponsored by banks headquartered in these countries (see Figure 6.1; also see chapter 5). Furthermore, although Basel II did introduce partial capital charges for these support lines, this was apparently more than undercut by its relaxation of risk weighting requirements, particularly for mortgage-backed securities (Acharya and Schnabl 2010; Thiemann 2014).

The pre-crisis capital treatment of bank liquidity backstops of ABCP-issuing conduits and CDOs was marginally more strict in the United States, where backstops were assigned (from 2004, following the experience of Enron) a capital charge equal to 10% of what would have been applied to the underlying assets supported (Croke 2007; FCIC 2011; Thiemann 2014). Furthermore, vehicles that were off balance sheet for capital regulatory but not accounting purposes could still be included in the calculation of bank sponsor leverage ratios. This would have significantly impacted the bank-sponsored credit arbitrage conduits popular in Europe (Arteta et al. 2013). However, it was insufficient to deter Citigroup from providing $25 billion in liquidity backstops to ABCP-issuing CDOs, the largest of which was the Bear Stearns–managed Klio series in Figure 6.2 (FCIC 2011). Most problematically, the asset risk-weightings from which capital charges were calculated did not come close to reflecting actual credit risk. Indeed, beyond backstopping the liquidity of these CDOs, Citigroup accumulated tens of billions of dollars of them on its own balance sheet at little capital cost. Compounding this problem was the willingness of the US to outsource prudential supervision to private ratings agencies, as well as to banks themselves in the form of internal models (an approach internationalized with Basel II) (Acharya and Schnabel 2010; FCIC 2011).

To the extent that offshore jurisdictions could have impeded home state prudential supervision of these activities, it seems that this would have been via their role as intermediate functional coordinating sites (particularly via subsidiaries), rather than as SPV hosts. As highlighted by Stewart (2013), there are a few cases (visible in Figure 6.1) where Ireland could have played such as role with respect to German bank-sponsored arbitrage conduits. Indeed, perhaps the clearest case of pre-crisis offshore regulatory arbitrage was Depfa's (the "Irish" nationality bank in Figure 6.1) relocation of its headquarters from Germany to Ireland in 2002 (Dübel 2013). However, as detailed in chapter 5, this actually underscores the importance of home state as opposed to host supervision under Basel. Furthermore, given that German regulation of ABCP conduits was already nil (as noted above), lax Irish regulation seems unlikely to have been an issue for this *particular* activity. Perhaps most importantly, to the extent that the host geography of direct management did impact vehicle supervision, Figures 6.1 and 6.2 suggest that this would have mostly concentrated authority in the hands of US and UK regulators, due to the securities sector dominance of New York and London.

Given that ABCP was designed to serve as a direct alternative to conventional bank deposits, prudential regulatory failure had the most substantive bearing on pre-crisis ABCP production (and shadow banking as a whole). However, the fact that this prudential regulatory arbitrage entailed the issuance of securities, rendered it potentially susceptible to second-order securities regulatory constraints. Here there appears to have been slightly more scope for offshore regulatory impacts than in prudential regulation. However, this scope was still fairly small (at least for the activities examined here) due to the fact that the relevant onshore securities regulation, like prudential regulation, was both extremely lax in substance and relatively resistant to offshore arbitrage.

Playing the leading role in defining this regulation was the US SEC, which claims an expansively extraterritorial jurisdiction (Chang 2003; Davison and Litvinoff 2013; Deacon 2004). As was the case for prudential regulation, the major lapses in pre-crisis US securities regulation stemmed from gaps within this extraterritorial onshore regulatory regime. Most importantly, the types of securities examined here were invariably sold (making use of Rule 144A; see chapter 3) in the US market via private placements subject to only minimal regulation in the form of buyer/resale restrictions (which prevented retail investor participation), and the prohibition of outright fraud (Croke 2007; Deacon 2004; FCIC 2011; Ferran et al. 2012).[10] These restrictions applied regardless of whether the issuing vehicle was in or outside of the USA. Furthermore, the jurisdictional scope claimed by the SEC for the most significant aspect of the private placement regulatory regime— protection against outright fraud—is highly extraterritorial, and cannot be avoided through paper offshore structures (Chang 2003,89; Davison and Litvinoff 2013). This was affirmed in the *SEC v. Tourre* case surrounding the Goldman Sachs- underwritten Abacus 2007-AC1 synthetic CDO, in which a US District Court upheld SEC anti-fraud jurisdiction—despite the fact that the security was sold by a Cayman Islands vehicle to Jersey-based conduit sponsored by German IKB—due to the fact that a person involved in the offer was physically based in New York (Chang 2003, Davison and Litvinoff 2013).

Approximately two thirds of outstanding ABCP as of 2007 was issued in the US market (Zakaim and Deméocq 2008). Nearly all of the remainder was issued in the European market, which seems to have absorbed a disproportionate share of the most toxic US mortgage-backed securities created in the one or two years im- mediately preceding the crisis (Lewis 2010). Importantly, it does not seem that the level of regulation of these securities in the EU market could fall substan- tially below that in the US market, regardless of whether they were issued from or listed in offshore jurisdictions. This was due to the rock-bottom regulatory standard established by US private placements, combined with the fact that the SEC claimed global jurisdiction over fraud for deals substantively connected to the USA. Figure 6.2 suggests that the latter would have been particularly perva- sive in the CDO market—where the potential for fraud was most acute—given the substantive dominance of New York in its operation. Beyond this, even secu- rities sold to non-US buyers by non-US-domiciled vehicles still typically had to be structured to qualify for a specific exemption (Regulation S) from SEC regis- tration requirements (Croke 2007; Deacon 2004). Perhaps most notably, among offshore vehicles in Figures 6.1 and 6.2, even those sponsored by non-US firms from a non-US location invariably had a Delaware co-issuer. This indicates that they were selling at least some of their securities to US investors, rather than being purely offshore market issuers that systematically avoided US market oversight. This can usually be confirmed by direct documentation (e.g. of simultaneous US and Euro CP programs). CDOs, in particular, were typically issued simultaneously into the US market as Rule 144A private placements and outside of the US as Regu- lation S offerings, with this distinction not having an apparent substantive impact on their stability or transparency. Ultimately, the key issue seems to have been the lack of a perceived need to escape from the SEC's geographic jurisdiction, with

---

[10] That is securitizations were exempt from registration under the Exchange Act at the issuance and resale level (typically via rule 144A), and from the Investment Company Act at the issuer level, see Croke (2007); Deacon (2004, 55–61); FCIC (2011, 170); Ferran et al. (2012, xviii–xix).

securities underwriters engaging in borderline fraudulent sales practices both in and outside of the US.

This having been said, offshore jurisdictions—and in particular EU jurisdictions such as Ireland or Luxembourg—could have theoretically impeded European efforts to raise securities regulation beyond the minimal level in the US private market (although in practice European governments seem to have been more concerned with maintaining competitive parity in regulatory laxity; Thiemann 2014). The European securities regulatory landscape had a three-pronged structure, revolving around national regulatory frameworks, EU-level directives, and a disproportionately powerful UK national regulator, whose influence stemmed from the dominance of London in the European securities sector. These regulatory issues were entangled with a labyrinth of country-specific tax and legal issues (Deacon 2004). Probably the most significant offshore aspect of the structures in Figures 6.1 and 6.2, from the standpoint of EU securities regulation, were the Irish and Luxembourg exchange listings (of Regulation S or dual Rule 144A/Regulation S issued securities). These effectively extended the relatively loose oversight of listings in these countries to the EU securities market as a whole, via the financial passporting regime (Stewart 2013). These listings were important in relation to the marketability of securities, given that purchases of unlisted debt securities by European institutional investors are typically limited by national regulations and or internal guidelines (in contrast to the USA) (Bartlett 2010; Milne and Onorato 2004). Ultimately, however, the level of transparency provided by these listings—as governed by EU directives (e.g. for prospectuses)—was clearly superior to the US private market (Bartlett 2010). Indeed, without the publicly available, and easily accessible (i.e. Google-searchable online) Irish Stock Exchange documents produced by many vehicles examined here (particularly CDOs), we would know much less about their organization.

The inference from this process-of-elimination analysis of the potential direct role of offshore jurisdictions in either primary prudential, or secondary securities regulatory arbitrage, is that their principal role in the activities here was a more subtle, facilitative one. This is supported by the specialist practitioner literature, which, above all, emphasizes points of taxation. This has a key bearing on Minskian shadow banking innovations (including ABCP) that use securitization to bypass regulations constraining conventional banking, as this typically requires the use of large numbers of entities and transactions that can each potentially generate tax "leakages." Unless eliminated, these leakages will tend to offset any advantages of securitized credit intermediation. Notably, from a normative standpoint, this is a clear case of tax "neutrality" as opposed to avoidance, as the goal is not to reduce onshore taxation, but rather to prevent cash flows from being double-taxed at the SPV in addition to sponsor level (BCBS 2009; Gorton and Souleles 2007; Wainwright 2011). In fact, the US Portfolio Interest Exemption directly encourages such use of tax-neutral offshore bond investment conduits, by exempting them from the withholding taxes that would normally be levied on interest payments to tax havens excluded from tax treaty networks (e.g. the Cayman Islands and Jersey). To at least some extent, the jurisdictional segregation of vehicle types in Figures 6.1 and 6.2 appears to reflect the complex criteria whereby debt instruments were deemed eligible or ineligible for this exemption. Unsecuritized US consumer loans or home mortgages were reportedly ineligible in general (Nirenberg 2013, 14), which may have necessitated the location of issuers holding these types of receivables in Delaware, rather than even more tax-friendly locales such as the Caymans (BCBS 2009). In contrast, vehicles that only purchased and repackaged securities (e.g. SIVs, CDOs, arbitrage conduits) were reportedly least affected by withholding tax issues, and had the greatest freedom to locate offshore (Deacon 2004). Notably, for Irish or UK-issued securities purchased by a non-treaty offshore jurisdiction SPV, the Quoted Eurobond exemption provided an analog to the US Portfolio Interest Exemption (although it required that these securities be listed).

Provided that withholding tax on the receipt of onshore payments could be bypassed, the location of an issuer in an offshore tax haven such as the Cayman Islands, Jersey, and (for the most part) Ireland, reportedly afforded three key tax advantages. First, withholding taxes on international payments from the vehicle could be avoided regardless of where investors were located. Second, the taxes on financial transactions (e.g. VAT and stamp duties) levied by some European countries could be avoided. Thirdly, taxes levied on profits earned by the vehicle itself could be avoided, as could most of the compliance costs associated with an onshore tax presence. These issues were not necessarily prohibitive with respect to the onshore location of vehicles—especially in "onshore–offshore" Delaware, which has aggressively sought to position itself as the "jurisdiction of choice for securitization" (Waxman et al. 2004). However, the avoidance of profit taxation, in particular, often required a careful matching of outgoing and incoming cash flows that was unnecessary if a vehicle was simply located in a zero-tax jurisdiction. In particular, the fiscally transparent devices that Delaware offered for simpler securitizations were reportedly unsuitable for the most complex vehicles such as CDOs, which were actively managed (Carden and Nasser 2007; Kothari 2006). In these cases, a zero-tax offshore domicile was especially helpful.

As shown in section 6.3, the Cayman Islands was the dominant jurisdiction for these types of highly sophisticated securitizations. In addition to offering near-zero taxation (which could be found elsewhere), the Caymans had other institutional features conducive to these arrangements. In particular, it allowed for legal certainty to be established on points important to bankruptcy-remote "robot firms" with complex liability structures. First, beyond simply offering a current zero profit tax-rate, the Caymans allowed "exempted companies" (the most commonly used securitization vehicle) to lock in this rate for twenty to thirty years (Deacon 2004). Second, Caymans law firms advertised the lack of a local legal principle of "substance over form" (Ashman and Bestwick 2003; Maples and Calder 2003; Moon 2003). This was emphasized in relation to the capital notes issued by SIVs, which were classified as debt obligations, but had a heavily subordinated equity-like payment structure. In many jurisdictions, the holders of these notes might be considered by courts to be shareholders. Additionally, the complex layers of contractual priority and subordination in vehicle payment "waterfalls" were given statutory force in the Caymans. Finally, with respect to vehicle bankruptcy treatment more generally, a notable legal feature advertised by Caymans law firms was the absence of any US or English-style mechanism for bankruptcy rehabilitation allowing obligations to creditors could be frozen or discharged (Deacon 2004; Moon 2003) (although following the crisis US courts have ruled that offshore "letterboxes" do not put vehicles out of reach of US bankruptcy jurisdiction; Svirsky et al. 2012).

A final advantage shared by popular SPV domiciliation and securities listing jurisdictions was a streamlining of approval procedures and regulations. In Jersey, security issues were subject to approvals that could take two weeks (Deacon 2004). In the Cayman Islands, however, the relevant regulation was mostly indirect, via supervision of local service providers (Maples and Calder 2003; Moon 2003). Beyond this, there were no authorization, or minimum capital requirements for SPVs, and no restrictions on their transactions and securities issues. Particularly notable, in the context of the rapidly changing landscape of pre-crisis financial innovation (particularly in CDOs), was the fact that this allowed SPVs to be set up in the Caymans within twenty-four hours (Ashman and Bestwick 2003).

Notwithstanding this "light-touch" regulation, however—as noted by many academic commentators on offshore political economy—the situation in offshore jurisdictions catering to OECD corporate clients was not one of zero regulation (Palan et al. 2010; Sharman 2012; Vlcek 2007). On the contrary, as international pressure on offshore jurisdictions has increased, a regulatory void, particularly in the area of transparency, has come to pose an increasing threat to a jurisdiction's reputation for these clients (Ashman and Bestwick 2003, Moon 2003). Any reputational damage from illicit activity, in particular, threatens the more lucrative business of crafting legal contractual devices that exploit onshore loopholes. Most critical, is the existence of a large and experienced local financial services and judicial infrastructure that can ensure compliance with any necessary onshore legal formalities. As one Cayman Islands-based lawyer describes the onshore–offshore division of labor: "How the isolation of the financial risk is accounted for and reported onshore is determined by the onshore rules. From an offshore perspective the key point is to show that an SPE is real" (Moon 2003).

What is particularly notable is that the jurisdictions in Figures 6.1 and 6.2 fall into the elite echelons of ostensibly respectable offshore locales. The dominance of the Cayman Islands in the most complex forms of securitization is especially significant, as non-OECD "small island" jurisdictions have generally had to earn respectability through substantive reforms, in contrast to OECD states which enjoy a more positive reputation by default (Eden and Kurdle 2005; Sharman 2012; Vlcek 2007). As noted in section 6.2, the Cayman Islands specifically has been ranked above many onshore jurisdictions on key points of financial transparency and due diligence, and has been particularly successful at avoiding international black/gray listing through a proactive approach to complying with OECD, FATF, and other initiatives. Meanwhile Delaware is consistently placed at the bottom of international offshore jurisdiction governance rankings (Findley et al. 2012).

6.5 Conclusion: Institutional Inefficiency as a Minskian Tobin Tax

Observing the automatic crisis-generating tendencies of liquid and efficient markets, Keynes advocated the taxation of financial transactions. The idea was that, if financial markets are endogenously unstable, stability could be improved by impeding market operation in a blanket non-specific manner. Following Tobin's advocacy of "throwing sand in the wheels of our excessively efficient international monetary markets" (Tobin 1978) via transaction taxes, these are typically referred to as Tobin taxes. What the analysis in this chapter underscores, from a policy standpoint, is that actually existing financial markets are in fact always subject to unintentional Tobin tax-like institutional obstacles and overhead costs. However, where these are felt is not simply the normal course of financial transactions, but even more so in the context of financial innovation, which invariably creates frictions between newly developed institutions and their inherited surroundings. These frictions can be seen as "Minskian Tobin taxes" that slow the tendency of financial regulatory frameworks toward obsolescence in the face of this innovation. This is particularly true to the extent that innovations require an increase in financial institutional complexity that generates a corresponding increase in institutional overhead costs.

Offshore jurisdictions appear, at least in relation to the activities examined here, to have primarily served as sites for the reduction of these institutional overhead costs attached to financial innovation. From a regulatory standpoint, this innovation was inherently subversive; however, the role of offshore jurisdictions in this subversion was mainly an indirect facilitative one that involved the provision of tax "neutrality" as opposed to tax avoidance, and the minimization of transaction costs associated with the threat of bankruptcy proceedings. Meanwhile, the black holes of regulatory failure were onshore (or in some cases midshore)—most importantly in Washington, DC, New York, London, Berlin, and Brussels. Crucially, authorities in these locations had far-reaching prerogative to regulate activates examined in this chapter, regardless of whether their geography extended across offshore jurisdictions. For the most part, however, they made only feeble efforts to exercise this prerogative. Indeed, the onshore prudential and securities regulation of these activities was so lax, from a substantive standpoint, that there appears to have been little scope for offshore jurisdictions to undercut it.

In some respects, this constitutes a radical shift in the traditional conceptualization of the role of offshore banking centers, which calls into question the distinction between on and offshore. Indeed, from the standpoint of global financial network organization, it has become increasingly appropriate to view offshore jurisdictions as spaces of institutional flexibility *within* the leading "world city" financial centers, rather than as escape routes from regulation in these centers. At a deeper level, however, this role continues to be predicated on the basic offshore political niche of catering to the rapidly evolving needs of financial firms. This often takes the form of overt legislative malleability; however, it also entails the cumulative development of a toolbox of ready-made legal devices (e.g. Delaware LLCs and Cayman Islands exempted companies and STAR trusts) that can be adapted to serve a wide variety of novel purposes. In many respects, "onshore–offshore" or midshore jurisdictions such as Delaware or Ireland have a growing edge over "small islands" in providing these services, due to both their preferential access to the largest financial markets, and the erosion of the latter's competitiveness by international regulatory extraterritoriality and reputational double standards. However, where able to avoid reputational stigmatization, "small islands" still appear to have advantages in terms of the level of institutional flexibility they can offer. Crucially, from a normative standpoint, their primary advantage for the activities examined here—at least in comparison to Delaware—seems to have been their ability to facilitate devices such as securitization tax neutrality that were regarded as more or less legitimate in the USA in principle, but were sometimes complicated in practice by the overarching logic of Federal tax and other laws. Ultimately, the relationship between these jurisdictions was as much cooperative as competitive; in the case of CDOs, for example, the Caymans provided issuers with optimal tax and bankruptcy treatment, while Delaware co-issuers and Irish exchange listings enhanced the marketability of securities in the USA and EU.

In all, these findings pose a challenge to the most widespread approach to the criticism of offshore jurisdictions. This narrative has emphasized their role in providing services that are clearly and unambiguously harmful, insofar as they directly undercut the tax base, financial stability, and financial transparency of other states. Meanwhile, it has consistently attacked the idea that offshore jurisdictions can improve the institutional efficiency of the global economy. Our analysis suggests that this is a rather dangerous drawing of intellectual battle lines, wherein offshore critics run the risk of being outflanked. Offshore jurisdictions can in principle be "cleaned up" from the standpoint of specific abusive practices—and indeed appear to be moving in this direction—yet at the same time preserve their more fundamental business model as sites for flexible institutional innovation. To the extent that they retool themselves in this manner, they may provide a legitimate service to the global economy, wherein they grease the institutional operation of markets. However, given that financial instability is an intrinsic product of market operation and evolution, this service is in fact a source of potentially acute danger.

This in no way undercuts the arguments in favor of reforms targeting overtly abusive forms of regulatory, tax and other forms of interjurisdictional arbitrage— both offshore and onshore. Furthermore, given the complexity and scope of the international governance failures that led to the crisis, it is certain that other more direct contributions of offshore jurisdictions can be found, that fall outside of our analytical scope.[11] Rather, what our findings underscore is the need for an additional layer of offshore reform analysis on top of the traditional emphasis on directly harmful effects. It is unwise to expect financial stability to be a byproduct of laws (e.g. tax codes) that were not designed with this objective in mind; rather, there needs to be a deliberately laid-out connection between policy ends and means. Such a paradigm of policy analysis needs to start from the recognition that all actually existing economic institutional frameworks are imperfect, and can potentially be improved by various forms of innovation and streamlining. Next, it needs to explicitly problematize which forms of "inefficiency" act as unintentionally beneficial impediments to the endogenous crisis-generating tendencies of markets. Once identified, such accidental impediments can, in theory, be in turn be repackaged as rationalized and targeted policies.

The proposal of specific policies that would "throw sand in the wheels" of financial innovation in a generalized manner is beyond the scope of this chapter. However, they could take the form of waiting periods on entity creation and or securities issuance (similar to the issuer "minimum duration" requirements imposed by some countries) (Deacon 2004). Another possibility is the additional taxation of complex intermediation structures involving large numbers of entities and transactions, in contrast to the current (Basel III) approach to increasing capital charges based on the size and complexity of financial firms. This existing approach is largely based on a narrow understanding of the emergence of moral hazard from too-big-to-fail status, which fails to grasp the chimerical nature of the whole concept of "market disciplining" of financial actor behavior (Pistor 2013).

Such Minskian Tobin taxes would need to have a sufficiently extraterritorial design to prevent offshore circumvention. However, this does not appear to be an insurmountable problem, given the existing tendency toward national extraterritoriality and international coordination in financial regulation and taxation. A more fundamental issue, given the "incompleteness" of any regulatory framework,

---

[11] Perhaps the most likely, given the structure of Basel, is lax host state liquidity supervision of on balance sheet bank activities—see example in Shaxson (2011, 188). Notably, Basel III has addressed this by introducing a consolidated bank liquidity coverage ratio (LCR) similar to that used for capitalization.

is the potential for offshore jurisdictions (including US states) to continue to facilitate the opening of new dimensions of institutional innovation that fall outside of the scope of these frameworks. Given that offshore jurisdictions can, almost by definition, modify their legal and regulatory frameworks more rapidly than onshore ones, it is not entirely clear how this problem can be dealt with. Indeed, as we suggest in the conclusion, the best way to reform finance may ultimately be to de-emphasize regulation altogether, and rather adopt an approach wherein public policy proactively takes the lead in financial innovation itself.

7

Regional Blocks and Imperial Legacies

Mapping the Global Offshore FDI Network

7.1 Introduction

While traditionally assumed to represent the "real" operations of multinational firms, foreign direct investment (FDI) is in reality a byproduct of multinational corporate accounting strategies, that is dominated by networks of abstract entities spanning onshore and offshore jurisdictions. The extent of this can be seen in Bureau of Economic Analysis (BEA) data on US FDI (BEA 2013), with more than half of the FDI stock of US nonfinancial firms, or 1.9 out of $3.6 trillion, attributed to overseas holding companies rather than functional subsidiaries as of 2012. More than half of the assets of these—nearly one-third of the total FDI stock of US firms—were reported in three leading OJs: the Netherlands, Luxembourg, and Bermuda (BEA 2013). Such behavior is not limited to US firms; all told, based on IMF data, around two-thirds of the world's total FDI stock is either in or from OJs specializing in the registration of shell companies. Taking into account double counting (i.e. of positions entering and leaving OJs), at least one-third, and likely closer to half of the underlying capital represented by the world's FDI is likely "offshore FDI" that lacks a direct attachment to productive activity in the economy where it is reported (Damgaard et. al. 2019; Palan et al. 2010; UNCTAD 2015; authors' analysis).[1]

Offshore FDI can in many respects be viewed as the paper legal contractual backbone of the global economy, with the structures that it represents mediating activities from the tapping of international capital markets, to corporate and individual tax avoidance, to the direct or indirect arbitraging of financial regulation, to illicit capital flight from developing countries (Baker 2005; Palan et. al 2010; Shaxson 2011). Consequently, even while FDI data tells us fairly little about the organization of productive activities in the world economy, it provides us with one of the best windows onto the global network of OJs. Notwithstanding the growing body of scholarly, media, and civil society attention paid to offshore secrecy and

---

[1] Fifty percent is a rough estimate based on our analysis of the IMF CDIS, including Dutch FDI as "offshore" (see Figure 7.1).

Sticky Power. Daniel Haberly and Dariusz Wòjcik, Oxford University Press.

tax havens, however, as well as the growing body of empirical research that has sought to unveil the various pathways and uses of offshore FDI, our understanding of offshore FDI remains limited in many respects. In particular, research on this topic faces a basic methodological challenge in trying to combine empirical rigor and detail, with a conceptual analysis of the "so what" and the "why" represented by this detail. Empirically sophisticated analyses of offshore FDI network organization run the risk, in effect, of tunneling through the subject of analysis itself, to emerge on the other side with an enormous amount of data but a dearth of meaning. Such questions of meaning are anything but resolved within this field of study. Indeed, a superficial consensus regarding the scope of the offshore *problem* belies a lack of scholarly agreement on such fundamental issues as whether offshore activity is attracted to or repelled by various types of financial regulation, or the extent to which its organization should be understood with reference to a timescale of centuries as opposed to an individual business day (Baker 2005; Palan et al. 2010; Roberts 1994; Sharman 2012; Shaxson 2011; Vlcek 2013).

This chapter contributes both empirically and conceptually to the debates surrounding offshore finance, by producing and analyzing a new type of map of global offshore FDI network organization. This new type of map seeks to systematically reveal and convey the key underlying structures that define the architecture of the network itself, by statistically reducing its dimensionality to a level that can be intuitively visualized and grasped. In other words, rather than employing quantitative analysis as a substitute for human analysis, we employ quantitative analysis to transform a complex dataset into a form that human analysis can process. Specifically, by applying principal component analysis (PCA) to International Monetary Fund (IMF) worldwide bilateral FDI data, we demonstrate that the global offshore FDI network can be described in terms of only a handful of primary underlying subnetworks linking groups of offshore and real economies, which are in turn nested within a dominant global network structure.

The structure of these networks sheds light on the processes shaping the integration of OJs into the global economy. We find evidence that an economy's engagement with OJs may be shaped by its institutional characteristics in a largely qualitative as opposed to quantitative manner, with reliance on trust and face-to-face contact apparently conditioned by the interaction between rule of law and communist history. Our results also cast doubt on the idea that the geography of the offshore world is highly footloose and technology driven, suggesting that it has rather been built up through a historical layering of political and social relationships. A fairly small number of historical processes and events appear to have been of decisive importance: the establishment of global empires by the United Kingdom, and to a lesser extent other European countries; the shift in economic and political hegemony from the United Kingdom to the United States and its allies; the collapse of Soviet communism; the rise of Chinese capitalism; and financial globalization as an overarching process.

The remainder of the chapter is organized into five sections. Section 7.2 briefly revisits the definition of offshore finance, and its situation within economic geographic theory, before examining gaps in our understanding of offshore network architecture, focusing on conceptual controversies regarding its institutional drivers and historical and relational "stickiness." Section 7.3 introduces the IMF Coordinated Direct Investment Survey (CDIS) dataset, and the use of PCA to decompose the global FDI anomaly matrix into its constituent subnetworks. Each of these networks is examined in turn in section 7.4, which closes with an analysis of the core structures linking them together. Section 7.5 then discusses the implications of these structures for our understanding of the evolution and operation of the offshore network. We conclude by discussing directions for extension of the research presented here, and its potential relevance to policy.

7.2 Offshore Jurisdictions in the Global Financial Network

The offshore world can be understood at two levels. The first is at the level of specific OJs, which specialize in providing the private sector, as well as in many cases other states, with a zone of intensified legal contractual flexibility and property rights protection (see chapter 2). At a deeper conceptual level, however, offshore is defined less by the jurisdiction within which transactions are booked or conducted, than by their conduct in a networked transnational legal space, that paradoxically emerges out of the lack of a direct legal basis for multinational activity. In other words, all aspects of *multinational* economic activity need to be, from a formal legal standpoint, located in a specific *national* (or subnational) jurisdiction—which in turn opens the door to private strategies of legal–geographic optimization wherein private actors try to strategically locate the nominal "paper" footprint of these activities within combinations of jurisdictions that afford the greatest regulatory, fiscal, or legal advantages (Picciotto 1999).

The study of these network-relational offshore legal, regulatory and fiscal spaces has in recent years gone from being a niche area of research, to one of the major growth areas in international political economy, and is closely linked to the global civil society and international public policy push to reign in harmful offshore secrecy and tax arbitrage (Cobham and Janský 2018; Damgaard et al. 2019; Findley et al. 2012; Garcia-Bernardo et al. 2017; Palan et al. 2010; Seabrooke and Wigan 2014; Shaxson 2011; Zucman 2015). However, our understanding of the geography and role of the offshore world remains in many respects ambiguous with respect to basic conceptual questions, two of which stand out as particularly important.

The first is the extent to which offshore financial ties should be regarded as relatively arm's length and footloose, as opposed to historically and relationally "sticky." Crucially, in the context of *onshore* financial relationships (e.g. within and between major FCs and their hinterlands), technology-catalyzed time-space compression has clearly not undermined the importance of difficult-to-replicate trust-based relationships, institutional frameworks, and esoteric knowledge bases (Clark and O'Connor 1997; Thrift 1994). However, there are conflicting perspectives on the extent to which this applies to *offshore* financial connections. Roberts (1994), for example, stresses the immaterial, fictitious quality of offshore finance and its potential to be controlled at a distance via electronic communications. According to this perspective, OJs serve as interchangeable platforms constantly at risk of being sidelined by regulatory developments in competitors, with the frictions imposed by time zone on real-time communication being the primary basis of geographic differentiation. In contrast to this, however, other work emphasizes the importance of deeply rooted political and institutional structures (Palan et al. 2010; Shaxson 2011). Offshore activities, according to this view, are mediated through tightly-knit networks linking specialized professionals to one another, regulators, and clients, which exhibit a high degree of geographic and historical inertia (Wainwright 2011). Looming particularly large within this inheritance is the legacy of European colonialism (Eden and Kudrle 2005; Palan et al. 2010; Shaxson 2011). Laws and institutions that facilitated the extraction of wealth by colonizers have sometimes proven to be useful for jurisdictional arbitrage, for example, UK domiciliation and Dutch holding company laws (Palan et al. 2010). More importantly, colonialism established durable networks of political, economic, and cultural ties. In contrast to arguments that London's position as an offshore hub is vulnerable to competitive deregulation (Roberts 1994), this perspective sees London as the indispensable core of an offshore archipelago of current and former colonies bound together by historically accreted relationships and institutions (Palan et al. 2010). Some have referred to this as Britain's "second empire"—albeit an empire dominated by the wealth of former colonies, rather than Britain itself (Palan et al. 2010; Shaxson 2011; Wójcik 2013a).

The second set of key debates surrounding offshore finance relates to its role in shaping the "variegated capitalisms" produced through the transnational interaction of institutional and regulatory environments (Dixon 2011; Haberly 2014; Peck and Theodore 2007). Beyond an understanding that companies and individuals use OJs to reduce their taxes, sharply contrasting interpretations exist of their institutional role. Some emphasize the provision by OJs of relatively strong institutional environments, which facilitate international investment, and offer more stringent property rights and general legal protections than many onshore jurisdictions (Desai et al. 2004; Dharmapala 2008; Hong and Smart 2010; Sharman 2012). In contrast, others see them as fundamentally specializing in the provision of financial secrecy and the facilitation of various types of malfeasance, and having a destabilizing influence on the global economy (Baker 2005; Palan et al. 2010; Shaxson 2011). Beyond their normative disagreements, these arguments imply intertwined yet distinct mechanisms through which OJs facilitate the exercise of power: one involving a manipulation of the rule of law that obeys its letter, and the other an undermining of the rule of law enabled by financial secrecy. Roberts (1994) describes this dichotomy in terms of *fictitious* versus *furtive* capital.

These questions are particularly important for developing and post-communist transition economies. While many have argued that the use of OJs by actors in these economies is related to poor domestic governance and institutional quality, conflicting interpretations exist as to whether OJs exacerbate or compensate for these problems. Some view offshore activity as primarily a mechanism for political insiders to hide the proceeds of corruption and state asset theft, and for wealthy individuals and firms to deprive developing economies and governments of desperately needed investment capital and tax revenue (Baker 2005; Brovkin 2001; Ding 2000; Oxfam 2000; Shaxson 2011). In contrast, others downplay these factors, arguing that OJs augment the competitiveness of emerging market firms by allowing them to harness stronger overseas financial and legal institutions, often by facilitating overseas listings (Sharman 2012; Stal and Cuervo-Cazurra 2011; Sutherland and Matthews 2009). Clearly all of these motivations and effects come into play in various situations; however, we know little about their relative importance, even in the context of the most heavily studied cases such as China (Vlcek 2013).

A problematic aspect of both sides of this debate is that they imply a divergence in offshore activity on the basis of national institutional characteristics, which has been more often assumed than demonstrated. To date, the strongest evidence for a general divergence between developing and developed economies relates to the role of the latter as suppliers of offshore services. The Organisation for Economic Co-operation and Development (OECD) economies are not only home to nearly all leading FABS firms, but occupy dominant positions as OJs (Tax Justice Network (TJN) 2012). This has complicated recent initiatives by the OECD and other organizations targeting offshore tax evasion and money laundering, with evidence suggesting that OECD investors increasingly prefer to use ostensibly respectable OECD midshore OJs to reduce home economy legal and reputational risks (Eden and Kudrle 2005; Haberly and Wójcik 2015b; Vlcek 2007). Ironically, this OECD "offshore club" effect (Haberly and Wójcik 2015b) appears to have occurred even as many non-OECD OJs have implemented increasing regulation to boost their reputations (Sharman 2005), with some (e.g. the Cayman Islands) being shown to exercise stronger due diligence against activities such as money laundering and terrorist financing than most OECD OJs (e.g. Delaware) (Findley et al. 2012). As such, the implications of a preference for OECD OJs are difficult to interpret from a governance perspective. Analyses of tax treaties are likewise mixed regarding whether the discouragement of illicit investment by information sharing tends to be outweighed by the attraction of licit investment (Blonigen and Davies 2004; Haberly and Wójcik 2015b; Hearson 2016; Rawlings 2007; Weyzig 2013).

That research on offshore finance has produced a picture that is increasingly detailed, yet at the same time largely incoherent, can be attributed in part to an inadequate basis for adjudication between competing perspectives. There is a wealth of case studies of OJs (Christensen and Hampton 1999; Cobb 1998; Roberts 1994; Sharman 2005; Warf 2002), and to a lesser extent their use by particular actors (Sutherland and Matthews 2009; Ting 2014; Walter and Howie 2011). At the global level, moreover, OJ rankings have been produced based on characteristics such as total assets or secrecy provision (TJN 2012). There are also a growing number of increasingly sophisticated large-scale studies of the key network nodes and pathways in offshore finance, including of offshore (or "phantom") FDI (Damgaard et al. 2019; Garcia-Bernardo et al. 2017). What has been much more challenging to produce, however, are empirically grounded studies that are not only detailed and rigorous, but that also shed conceptual light on the *meaning* of the architectures within which OJs are situated. Influential claims about the parameters of this architecture, such as the importance of postcolonial networks or longitudinal belts reflecting time zone frictions to communication, rest on shaky foundations. In a reflection of this dearth of empirics, the time zone–based map of Roberts (1994) continues to appear in *Global Shift* (Dicken 2011), despite being decades old and never having been rigorously verified. From the standpoint of operationalizing the GFN framework outlined in this book (as well as the, in this context, partially overlapping global wealth chains framework; see Seabrooke and Wigan 2014), establishing a conceptually interpretable empirical outline of global offshore network organization is a crucial starting point.

Two general approaches could be taken to this. The first approach, which has been the focus of an increasingly sophisticated body of work by researchers affiliated with UNCTAD and the IMF, is to try to look through the "fictions" of offshore FDI to understand what the "real" underlying structures of the world economy look like (Casella 2019; Damgaard et al. 2019). Here, however, we take a different, and essentially complementary approach—namely one of problematizing the fictions of the offshore world as an important legal–contractual reality in its own right. The principal building blocks of this abstract legal–contractual realm are investment vehicles (IVs), or shell companies, as they are widely known (Coates and Rafferty 2007; Coe et al. 2014; Wójcik 2013a). These take a variety of forms including trusts, international business companies, and holding companies. What they share, however, is their dissociation of the legal geography of capital from that of ultimate assets, owners, and/or management, to allow for the optimization of various regulatory, legal, and fiscal considerations and/or the enhancement of secrecy.

The geography of IVs is often extremely complex, with vehicles organized into multijurisdictional networks that serve as captive financial systems for wealthy individuals and multinational corporations (Haberly and Wójcik 2015b). There are generally incentives for these networks to be as complex as possible, as this maximizes the potential for jurisdictional arbitrage and/or the levels of secrecy that can be achieved. Among a multitude of uses (as discussed in the various chapters of this book), these networks are probably most often designed to support corporate tax avoidance, wherein profits/earnings are concentrated in low tax jurisdictions through the use of various types of "transfer mispricing," that is, the valuation of intragroup financial and trading transactions at nonmarket rates (Palan et al. 2010; Sikka and Willmott 2010). This transfer mispricing has been facilitated by, and, in turn encouraged, the knowledge economy attribution of earnings to intellectual property (IP) without a clearly defined territoriality, or a clearly defined market value (Seabrooke and Wigan 2014). Also playing an important facilitative role has been the traditionally lax, and indeed often borderline promotional attitude of the USA, in particular, toward the overseas avoidance of foreign taxes by its own firms (see chapter 5).[2]

A growing number of studies have examined offshore FDI by German (Weichenrieder and Mintz 2006); American (Desai et al. 2004; Lewellen and Robinson 2013) and BRIC (Brazil, Russia, India, and China) economy firms (Ledyaeva et al. 2013; Sharman 2012; Stal and Cuervo-Cazurra 2011; Sutherland and Matthews 2009; Vlcek 2013). These have revealed important structures, such as the centrality of the Netherlands as a tax treaty-shopping jurisdiction for OECD firms (see Weyzig 2013), and large-scale offshore FDI round-tripping (for poorly understood reasons, see earlier discussion) by Chinese, Russian, and Indian firms in their home economies via Hong Kong, Cyprus, and Mauritius, respectively, and the Caribbean. Since 2011, moreover, the IMF has released a worldwide dataset of bilateral FDI stocks, the CDIS, which allows research to be conducted on offshore FDI at the global level. Using CDIS data, we earlier conducted the first world-wide regression analysis of the determinants of bilateral FDI by OJs in onshore economies (Haberly and Wójcik 2015a). The results indicated that offshore FDI was sensitive to physical proximity and OJ ties with former colonizers, but not time zone proximity. Meanwhile, no evidence was found for variation in the level of inward offshore FDI on the basis of economic or institutional development or communist history, although evidence was found of elevated offshore FDI by OECD OJs in OECD hosts, as well as between tax treaty signatories.

While it has provided useful insights into the determinants of offshore FDI, however, regression has only a limited ability to address debates surrounding the historical and relational stickiness, and institutional dimensions of offshore

---

[2] Some aspects of IP-based offshore profit shifting by US firms were theoretically addressed by the global intangible low tax income (GILTI) provisions of the 2017 TCJA tax reform. However, these provisions, and the structure of TCJA more broadly, appear to be problematic at the level of specific design (Davis 2019). It remains to be seen whether the current US and OCED-led push to implement a 15% global minimum corporate tax rate, even assuming that US participation is ultimately approved by Congress, will be designed or implemented in a way that will substantially reign in corporate offshore tax arbitrage.

activity. These debates reflect fundamental uncertainties regarding the type and nature of the processes that have the most important bearing on offshore activity, and encompass many arguments that are only roughly defined, and poorly suited to quantification. In contrast, regression is limited to confirming/disconfirming variable effects specified in a precisely targeted manner. In the absence of correspondingly refined a priori theoretical development, and rigorous variable quantification, it is likely to yield misleading results. What is needed in this situation is a different methodology capable of shedding light on whether a factor has any important effects on offshore activity, regardless of whether the precise nature of these effects (e.g. with respect to interaction effects, quantitative expression of qualitative arguments) is correctly anticipated.

Above all, what is needed here is a methodology that problematizes the architecture of offshore FDI as a *network*. Notably, the advent of very large-scale global micro (entity)-level datasets of global corporate balance sheets, structure, and shareholders—most importantly Orbis—have allowed for unprecedentedly detailed studies of the global offshore FDI network to be conducted. The most comprehensive of these is Garcia-Bernardo et al. 2017, which highlights the central role of a few large OECD offshore (or midshore) jurisdiction "conduits"—and most importantly the UK and the Netherlands—as intermediaries between offshore shell company domicile "sink" jurisdictions (including many "small islands") and the rest of the world economy.

In contrast, here we approach the analysis of the global offshore FDI network from a somewhat different perspective, which seeks to highlight and characterize, at a stylized level, its overall pattern of network *connections*, as opposed to analytically prioritizing the network's *nodes*. Specifically, we make use of PCA to reveal the most important statistical *dimensions* or *layers* of shared connectivity within the global offshore FDI network. The result is a "digestion" of the network's structure into a fairly small number of easily visualizable key layers, that can in turn be used as a basis for a relatively open-ended and flexible qualitative assessment of the likely importance of various processes in shaping network organization and evolution. Most importantly, unlike regression, this allows for the assessment of explanatory factors to be conducted in a manner that is relatively unaffected by either high levels of a priori uncertainty within, or a limited ability to quantitively formalize, the existing conceptual models themselves.

In examining the PCA results, we seek to answer three questions pitched at a broadly qualitative level. First, how globalized is the offshore FDI network? Are all economies strongly tied to a common global core of OJs, or does the network exhibit a high degree of internal differentiation? Second, to the extent that the global network is internally differentiated, what is the geographic structure of its principal subnetworks? Third, what arguments regarding the technological, institutional, political, and relational factors impacting offshore finance are supported by the organization of these networks?

7.3 Data and Methodology

The CDIS consists of two bilateral FDI stock matrices, one containing inward FDI data reported by 83 hosts for 245 origin counterparties, and the second containing outward FDI data reported by 67 origins for 245 host counterparties (for the 2010 data analyzed here). Figure 7.1 shows all bilateral FDI positions greater than US$50 billion for both matrices, as of 2010. Two aspects of the data are striking. The first is the lack of an association between gross domestic product (GDP) and FDI stock, with offshore FDI clearly not being a peripheral distortion of the FDI network, but rather the predominant form of FDI. At the center of the network are four jurisdictions with similar FDI positions; the United States, the United Kingdom, the Netherlands, and Luxembourg. The second notable features of the data are the discrepancies between host and origin reporting. In some cases, these result from sample differences. China and Singapore, for example, participated in the inward, but not outward CDIS, while many important OJs (e.g. British Virgin Islands (BVI), Bermuda) participated in neither, meaning that only unidirectional host/origin counterparty data is available for these in each matrix. In many cases, however, governments report radically different figures for the same FDI position. While Ireland, for example, reports hosting only $19 billion of inward FDI from the USA, the United States reports an outward FDI stock of $158 billion in Ireland. These discrepancies appear to provide a window into the mechanics of offshore jurisdictional arbitrage, which largely rests on divergent definitions of nationality and residence.

While the CDIS contains an unprecedented wealth of information on global offshore FDI, its analysis is hindered by the fact that values only appear accurate (or perhaps rather are only *meaningful*) to within perhaps an order of magnitude,

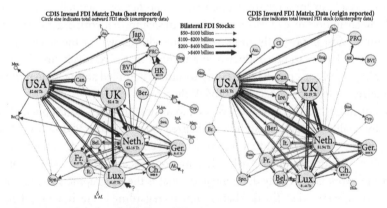

Fig. 7.1 FDI stocks >$50 billion, YE-2010

Source: IMF CDIS; adapted from Haberly and Wójcik (2015a; 2015b)

as well as the sheer scale of the CDIS, with the host-reported matrix alone containing over 18,000 country pairs. PCA is highly suitable in this context as a tool capable of extracting general patterns from this vast quantity of data while abstracting from the somewhat dubious individual figures. PCA is a statistical data compression technique that represents the largest possible percentage of variance in a high-dimensional dataset using the smallest possible number of dimensions (components). In the simplest example, most of the information in two highly correlated variables could be captured by one component roughly following the trend line in a scatterplot of the two variables. In most cases, however, PCA is used to extract the core features of datasets with more dimensions than can be easily visualized. Its applications fall into two categories. The first is the reduction of a list of variables into a smaller number capturing key common elements, for example, extracting a socioeconomic status index from household lifestyle indicators (Vyas and Kumaranayake 2006). Meanwhile, in the second class of applications, PCA is used to analyze the distribution of a single indicator within a matrix wherein one dimension (i.e. rows vs columns) is classified for the purpose of analysis as variables while another is classified as observations.

This study falls into the second class of applications, namely using PCA to reduce the complexity of a matrix of bilateral economic relationships; a technique notably explored by Taylor et al. (2004) in the analysis of world city network structure. We apply this type of PCA to bilateral FDI anomaly data derived from the 2010 CDIS. FDI anomalies are designed to capture the "offshoreness" of FDI linkages, in the absence of a clear distinction between onshore and offshore jurisdictions. Anomalies are defined as a multiple of the bilateral FDI expected on the basis of a partial gravity function, in which global FDI is assumed to be allocated in proportion to the product of origin and host nominal GDP sizes. This transformation is founded on the IMF's heuristic definition of an offshore center as "a country or jurisdiction that provides financial services to non-residents on a scale that is incommensurate with the size and financing of its domestic economy" (Zorome 2007, 12–13). By examining bilateral rather than jurisdictional anomalies, our analysis refines the IMF rubric to reflect the relational nature of offshore finance. FDI anomalies are log-transformed[3] to achieve a normal distribution, which has the added benefit of rendering PCA results relatively robust to the large margin of error of the CDIS data.

The discrepancies between the CDIS inward and outward FDI matrices mean that there is no effective way to combine them; we only use the host-reported

---

[3] Zero values present a challenge in this respect; we use an if–then statement to force zero values to zero in the log-transformed matrix. Maintaining zero values in this manner requires us to apply a large multiplier to all anomalies before log transformation to prevent anomalies smaller than 1 from assuming negative values.

inward FDI matrix (see Figure 7.1), which has superior coverage.[4] We classify hosts as variables and origins as observations.[5] Several OECD hosts share a correlated pattern of missing influential values, which if uncorrected produces a spurious component. In most cases, gaps could be filled with OECD data on the bilateral FDI of member states (which closely matches IMF data), in some cases from 2009 or 2011. It was impossible to adequately repair inward FDI data for Spain, Portugal, Switzerland, Luxembourg, Australia, Bosnia, and Bhutan, which had to be dropped as hosts.[6] The KMO test of sampling adequacy for the seventy-six hosts retained is 0.94, indicating high PCA suitability.

Figure 7.2 shows the largest FDI anomalies in the CDIS inward FDI matrix. Dominating the center is what could be described as a Caribbean offshore financial *Bermuda Triangle* consisting of Bermuda, the Caymans, and BVI. Other major OJs, including Cyprus, Mauritius, and Luxembourg, also stand out prominently. The PCA results can be conceptualized as bundles of the (log-transformed)

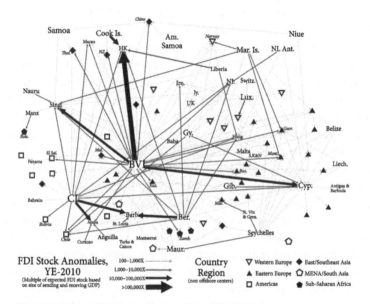

Fig. 7.2 Bilateral FDI stock anomalies, YE-2010

Source: IMF CDIS, inward FDI matrix; adapted from Haberly and Wójcik (2015a).

---

[4] The origin-reported matrix excludes many important economies such as China, Singapore, Indonesia, and Nigeria.

[5] The fact that the CDIS reports data on a larger number of origins than hosts means that the reverse assignment of variables/observations may produce poor PCA results (MacCallum et al. 1999).

[6] This was decided on the basis of a host PCA suitability index calculated as the sum of total outward FDI anomalies (outward FDI/GDP) for each missing origin counterparty, divided by the sum of total FDI anomalies of all origins. Host economies with an index less than 50% were retained; in only two retained cases was the index greater than 20%.

FDI anomalies visible in Figure 7.2, correlated across groups of hosts. Although the analysis is quantitative, the results should be seen as qualitative, providing a general map of offshore FDI network structures. While the use of FDI anomalies weights the analysis toward offshore structures, "real" FDI (to the extent that this is a meaningful concept) is still incorporated into the analysis, allowing it to capture the relationship between onshore and offshore network elements. This information may also shed light on the nationality of investors using OJs, although the results primarily identify the major offshore pipelines channeling capital into economies, without definitively revealing the identity of this capital. More generally, while the CDIS provides the best picture of offshore FDI currently available, our results should be treated as tentative in light of the limitations of the dataset discussed above.

PCA involves two successive algorithms: extraction and rotation. Extraction entails a successive selection of components (dimensions) such that each explains the greatest possible remaining variance in a dataset. Next, rotation adjusts the loadings of variables (host economies) onto a selected number of components such that each is as closely associated as possible with a single component, facilitating the visualization of the data space defined through extraction.

To gain the most exhaustive possible understanding of FDI anomaly network structure, we employ a novel iterative rotation procedure. This incrementally increases the number of (varimax) rotated components, starting from the one-component solution that generalizes network structure to the greatest extent possible, with each additional component allowing for the targeting of more specific network features. The addition of components yields diminishing returns, with the first alone explaining 41% of all variance in global FDI, and the next three together only explaining an additional 15% (see Figure 7.3 left). Subsequent components have little or no more explanatory power than benchmark components generated from random data.[7] As such, most of the variance within the global FDI anomaly matrix can be represented with four to five dimensions. Given that each additional component adds little to total explained variance, each can be thought of as a subnetwork predominantly nested inside of the networks identified using smaller numbers of components, as shown in the tree diagram in Figure 7.3.

At the highest level of generalization, all components can be seen as being primarily nested within the one-component solution, which captures nearly half of the total variance in global offshore FDI network structure. This one-component solution can be viewed, in effect, as the offshore backbone of the GFN, *singular*, in the sense of an overarching centralized relational and institutional structure at the heart of global finance. The strengths of correlation (loading) of hosts with

---

[7] This is based on parallel analysis (see Hayton et al. 2004). A fifth component had borderline meaningful explanatory power but appears somewhat noisy visually, and conveys little additional information.

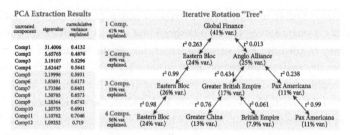

Fig. 7.3 PCA results summary

Source: authors' analysis based on IMF CDIS; adapted from Haberly and Wójcik (2015a).

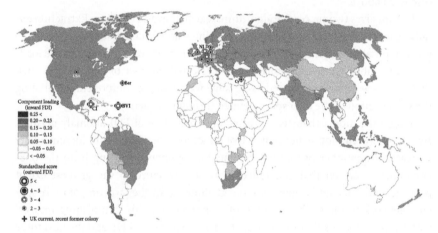

Fig. 7.4 "Global Finance"

Source: authors' analysis based on IMF CDIS; adapted from Haberly and Wójcik (2015a).

this Global Finance network are indicated by the shading in Figure 7.4, with the standardized "scores" of FDI sources indicated by circle icons. An examination of highly scoring sources suggests that the methodology here effectively targets offshore FDI. Scoring highest is BVI, followed by Luxembourg, the Cayman Islands, the Netherlands, Switzerland, and the United Kingdom. Also scoring above 2 are Bermuda, Cyprus, France, Germany, Liechtenstein, the United States, and Denmark. In all, this component indicates that the offshore FDI network is highly centralized on the supply side in northwest Europe and the *Bermuda Triangle*. However, it is remarkably homogeneous on the demand side. All major economies have loadings of between 0.1 and 0.2, and most have loadings of between 0.15 and 0.2. This indicates that the offshore FDI network is at its heart truly global, with countries having limited differentiation in engagement with it based on development, proximity, history, or other factors.

The global offshore FDI network is not entirely homogeneous, however, and it is possible to dissect its structure by examining the lower tiers of the tree diagram in Figure 7.3. New components tend to branch off from specific parents as the number of components increases, with others being retained in mostly unchanged form. As such, only six distinct dimensions of differentiation can be identified within the PCA tree; the four subnetworks identified in the four-component rotation—what we have deemed the *Eastern Bloc, Greater China, Pax Americana*, and *British Empire*—and two linking networks into which these merge at higher levels of generalization, referred to here as the *Greater British Empire* and *Anglo Alliance*.

In the next section, we examine the organization of each of these six subnetworks, and the relationships between them. Apart from describing the key features of each network, we look for evidence of the influence of factors hypothesized to impact their organization. The interpretation of PCA is based on the assumption that component structures are likely to reflect the influence of shared characteristics across variables loading strongly onto them (i.e. hosts with correlated FDI anomalies). Analytically, we also emphasize the differentiation between pairs of components produced by each of the three bifurcations in Figure 7.3, presenting the results in this sequence.[8] We focus on the association of host loadings, as well as origin scores and host–origin relationships, with factors relevant to the two key debates discussed in the previous section. Hypothetically, the Roberts's (1994) footloose/technology-driven model of offshore finance, wherein time zone is seen as crucial, should produce visible longitudinal banding. Conversely, the relationally/historically sticky model would be supported by network differentiation based on historical spheres of colonial and or geoeconomic influence (particularly of the United Kingdom and the United States), ties of shared ethnicity, and or clustering based on physical as opposed to time zone proximity. With respect to institutions, we are primarily interested in whether there is any differentiation of any kind based on rule of law or communist history, given the dearth of existing empirical evidence for this. We also seek to gauge the relative importance of the OECD "offshore club" effect (Haberly and Wójcik 2015b), as potentially evidenced by a component dominated by OECD origins and hosts.

7.4 Mapping the Global Offshore FDI Network

Figures 7.5a and 7.5b illustrate the first bifurcation in the global offshore FDI network at the two-component level of differentiation. This clearly reflects the legacy of communism and the Cold War, with the deepest cleavage in the global offshore

---

[8] The *Eastern Bloc* and *Pax Americana* networks shown are from the four-component rotated solution.

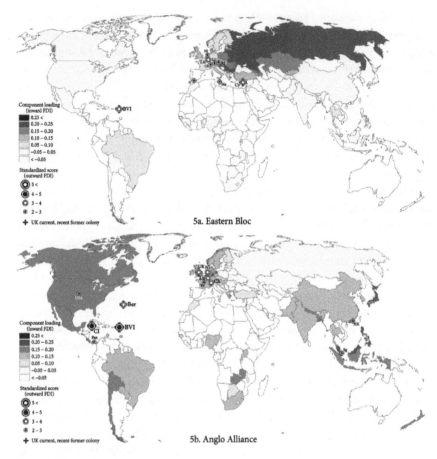

Fig. 7.5 First network pair
Source: authors' analysis based on IMF CDIS; adapted from Haberly and Wójcik (2015a).

network apparently separating a post-Soviet *Eastern Bloc* network (Figure 7.5a) from a broader network encompassing the remainder of the world's economies, including Mainland China (Figure 7.5b). The *Eastern Bloc* network is centered on the Russia–Cyprus–BVI round-trip FDI circuit, as well as the Gibraltar and Liechtenstein branches of this circuit, identified in previous research (LaFranco and Sazonov 2013; Ledyaeva et al. 2013), indicating that this is a regional rather than a distinctly Russian pattern. Among hosts, most highly loading economies share not only communist history, but also particularly low scores on the World Governance Indicators Rule of Law index (World Bank 2012). This suggests that communist history and rule of law have, in combination with one another, a substantial impact on offshore FDI. Also striking is the clustering of OJ FDI sources in close physical proximity to *Eastern Bloc* hosts. This indicates three-dimensional interactions between communist history, rule of law, and proximity sensitivity (discussed further in the next section). In contrast, Figure 7.5b shows little apparent influence of either physical or time zone proximity. At the FDI origin side, it comprises all of what Roberts (1994) described as the three major OJ clusters in the Caribbean, Europe, and East Asia, indicating that these exercise a substantial influence in each other's as opposed to simply within their own respective regional hinterlands. We refer to this network as the *Anglo Alliance* due to its internal differentiation in the three-component solution discussed below.

At the three-component solution, the *Anglo Alliance* bifurcates into the two networks shown in Figures 7.6a and 7.6b, which appear to roughly follow the post–WWII division of the nonsocialist world between US and British imperial influence. Figure 7.6a appears to be a British postcolonial network centered on

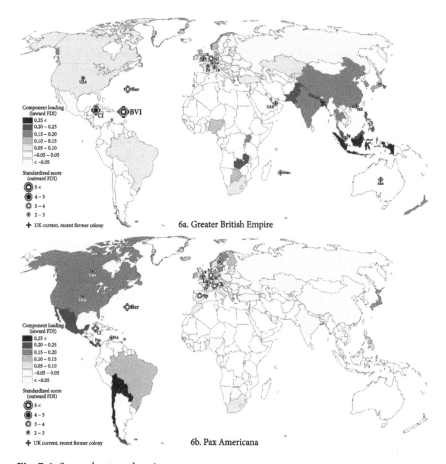

Fig. 7.6 Second network pair

Source: authors' analysis based on IMF CDIS; adapted from Haberly and Wójcik (2015a).

the Indian Ocean core of the British Empire, with the United Kingdom itself also loading relatively highly as a host. Among FDI sources, high PCA scores indicate that the UK-colonial entrepôts of Hong Kong, Singapore, the United Arab Emirates (UAE)/Dubai, and Mauritius act as key regional offshore nodes, with hosts not formally colonized by the United Kingdom—such as Mainland China—pulled into its postcolonial offshore network via their ties with these jurisdictions. Existing research on the offshore FDI of major regional economies (e.g. India, China), suggests that this *Greater British Empire* network contains a high proportion of round-trip FDI intermediated via these regional nodes, and the three *Bermuda Triangle* shell company jurisdictions (Stal and Cuervo-Cazurra 2011).

Figure 7.6b appears to reflect a US-centric sphere of geoeconomic influence, or *Pax Americana* network, encompassing the Americas, Japan, and parts of Western Europe. To a greater extent than the other components, it is unclear whether host loadings primarily reflect round-trip investment via OJs or inward OJ-mediated investment by foreign, and particularly US capital. To a large extent, the OJs scoring highly as FDI sources do correspond to the jurisdictions of choice of US multinationals, particularly in the Caribbean, where Bermuda, the Cayman Islands, and the Netherlands Antilles score highly. In general, however, the FDI sources scoring highly are suggestive of more than a purely US-driven pattern, with the diversified OECD OJs of Luxembourg, the Netherlands, and Switzerland scoring above 3. Latin American investment is particularly difficult to disentangle from that of the USA and other OECD investors, with capital in the western hemisphere appearing to flow between north and south through similar channels in both directions. Two highly scoring jurisdictions, Panama and Spain, do appear to have characteristically Latin American fingerprints, with the prominence of Spain, in particular, likely reflecting the influence of shared cultural and historical ties.[9] Spain is unusually specialized as a node in this respect, however, with both the *Pax Americana* and *Greater British Empire* networks apparently cosmopolitan in nature. Also notable in both is the lack of a clear imprint of institutional characteristics comparable to that seen within the *Eastern Bloc*, and the relatively weak impact of proximity (distance or time zone) on offshore–onshore ties.

In the four-component solution, the cosmopolitan *Greater British Empire* appears to undergo a final bifurcation largely on the basis of cultural ties, revealing a regional *Greater China* subnetwork (Figure 7.7a). Just as the nucleus of the *Eastern Bloc* network is formed by the well-known Russia–Cyprus–BVI round-trip FDI circuit, this network is centered on the even more important Mainland China–Hong Kong (HK)–BVI/Cayman Islands (CI) circuit (Sharman 2012; Sutherland and Matthews 2009; Vlcek 2013). As for the *Eastern Bloc* network, however, the

---

[9] Spain has been ranked as the world's #11 OJ (TJN 2012; Henry 2012a), reflecting the private banking activities of Santander Bank and Banco Bilbao Vizcaya Argentaria (BBVA), which enjoy regional dominance in Latin America (Guillen and Tschoegel 2000).

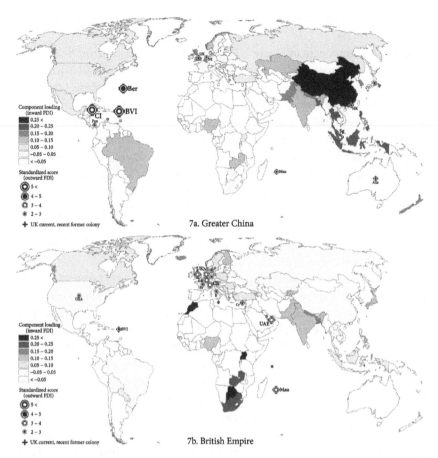

Fig. 7.7 Third network pair
Source: authors' analysis based on IMF CDIS; adapted from Haberly and Wójcik (2015a).

results indicate that this is more of a regional than a country-specific structure. While Mainland China, Hong Kong, and Macao load most strongly as hosts, Singapore, the Philippines, Thailand, Indonesia, Malaysia, and Bangladesh also have high loadings, with the first five of these standing out as having economies largely dominated by ethnic Chinese business networks (Weidenbaum and Hughes 1996; Yeung 1999). At the FDI origin side, the regional OJs of Singapore, Hong Kong, and Mauritius score highly, suggesting some influence of proximity. However, this influence is weak (at least at the level of FDI booking), with the *Greater China* network dominated by shell company jurisdictions in the Caribbean (including Panama, which has surprisingly strong Asia Pacific ties), and the Netherlands and the United Kingdom also scoring highly. In addition to round-trip FDI, it is clear that large amounts of outside capital flow into *Greater China* through these OJs, although this is difficult to gauge precisely (Vlcek 2013). Conversely, strong loadings by some hosts, such as Zambia, may largely reflect inward Chinese investment via OJs.

Finally, the component in Figure 7.7b can be described as a narrow *British Empire* network dominated by former UK colonies in South and East Africa, the Persian Gulf, and the Mediterranean (e.g. Malta) with former colonies in South Asia roughly equally associated with the *British Empire* and *Greater China*. Morocco also loads highly as a host, raising the question of whether the boundary between British and French spheres of postcolonial financial influence has blurred somewhat. At the FDI origin side, the United Kingdom scores much more highly on this network than it does on any of the others. Also scoring highly are the regional offshore hubs of Mauritius, the UAE/Dubai, and Cyprus, with this component exhibiting a higher sensitivity to proximity than most of the others. The list of highly scoring/loading FDI origins and hosts suggests a more diverse composition of capital than the *Greater China* network. Neither network exhibits any apparent differentiation on the basis of host institutional factors.

Comparing the two networks, the dominance of *Greater China* is striking, with this network much more strongly correlated (r^2 of 0.76) with the overarching *Greater British Empire* than the narrow *British Empire* network (r^2 of 0.061). This gives the impression that the UK postcolonial offshore network has been increasingly coopted by (Mainland and overseas) Chinese capital, with the narrow *British Empire* component something of a residual remaining once this dominant strand has been subtracted. Indeed, the United Kingdom itself has a higher loading as a host onto *Greater China* than any of the other components. According to Bloomberg, Mainland China, Hong Kong, Malaysian, and Singaporean investors accounted for 51% of new home purchases in central London in 2011 (Spillane 2012), a type of investment associated with the use of London financial services by wealthy clients, and often routed through offshore vehicles. Kar and Freitas (2012) further estimate that Mainland China, Malaysia, Indonesia, and the Philippines account for 60% of developing world flight capital, or a sum approximately equal to the entire US stock of outward FDI (BEA 2013). As we discuss in the next chapter, the Chinese state itself, via its state-owned enterprises, also plays a central role in Mainland China's offshore FDI.

Figure 7.8 summarizes the structure of the global offshore FDI network at the four-component level of differentiation. The network at the upper left shows commonalities between the FDI sources scoring highly on each PCA component, and can be understood as a simplified version of the network anomaly map shown in Figure 7.2. Three features, shown in the inset in stylized form, stand out prominently. First, the *Pax Americana* and *British Empire* components exhibit the densest concentration of shared connections, being linked through the United States, France, and Germany, as well as the Netherlands, Luxembourg, the United Kingdom, and Switzerland. These include the leading OECD midshore jurisdictions, with each home to not only a large offshore financial sector, but also a

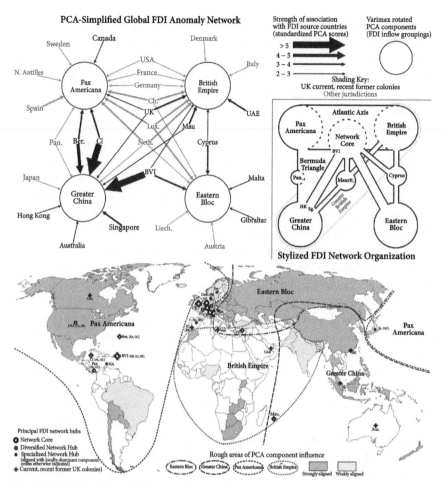

Fig. 7.8 Global offshore FDI network organization

Source: authors' analysis based on IMF CDIS; adapted from Haberly and Wójcik (2015a).

diversified array of multinational enterprises. There appears to be a direct correspondence between this *Atlantic Axis* of jurisdictions bridging the *Pax Americana* and *British Empire* components, and the situation of both within the overarching *Anglo Alliance* network. The UK and US spheres of offshore influence are relatively subtle gradations within this network.

Lying mostly within the *Atlantic Axis* is a global *Network Core* of jurisdictions linked to at least three of the four components, consisting of the Netherlands, Luxembourg, the United Kingdom, Switzerland, and BVI. The first four constitute the more offshore of the OECD midshore economies within the *Atlantic Axis*, with BVI being something of an outlier insofar as it is purely a booking rather than functional financial center and not part of the *Atlantic Axis*. Within the *Network*

Core, the Netherlands is the only jurisdiction linked to all four components, underscoring its status as the global FDI network's central hub. BVI is unusual, as it is relatively specialized toward a single component, *Greater China*, and only weakly connected to the *Pax Americana* component. It is also an oddity insofar as it lies outside of Northwest Europe, which as Figure 7.8 (bottom) indicates is clearly the dominant geographic center of the global offshore FDI network. Indeed, there is no visible OECD "offshore club" effect along the lines of that found by Haberly and Wójcik (2015b), with Europe's OECD OJs having an essentially global footprint.

BVI, in turn, forms one vertex of the *Bermuda Triangle* dominating Caribbean offshore finance, with the Caymans and Bermuda forming the other two. Presumably there are large FDI linkages between these OJs, but these are impossible to measure given that none participated in the CDIS. These jurisdictions serve as booking centers for enormous offshore capital flows, most importantly within and between the *Pax Americana* and *Greater China* networks, with BVI also having strong connections to the *Eastern Bloc* and *British Empire*. Panama, with strong ties to both the Americas and *Greater China*, can be seen as an extension of this structure.

Together, these three structures define what could be described as the primary offshore pipelines within the global economy. Also standing out as important on the basis of the PCA, however, are three secondary features. Cyprus is more important than has been appreciated during the eurozone crisis, forming a key linkage between the *British Empire*, *Eastern Bloc*, and global network core. Mauritius arguably plays an analogous role to Cyprus in linking the *Greater China* and *British Empire* components to one another and the *Network Core*. Two final jurisdictions deserving particular mention are Hong Kong and Singapore, which serve as the financial gateways to *Greater China*. Strikingly, nearly all of these major hubs and gateways are current or former UK colonies, which account for two-thirds of highly scoring FDI sources outside of Northwest Europe, and underscore the importance of Britain's offshore "second empire" (see Figure 7.8).

7.5 Determinants of Offshore Foreign Direct Investment Network Organization and Evolution

The offshore FDI network organization revealed by the PCA sheds light on debates regarding the organizational and evolutionary logic of offshore activity, painting a somewhat different picture than regression analysis of the same dataset (Haberly and Wójcik 2015b). The network is strongly globalized, with a well-defined core of jurisdictions in Western Europe and the Caribbean exhibiting a largely homogeneous global footprint. This centralized structure, however, appears to be the product of a process of slow historical accretion, rather than being indicative of a fast-paced virtual global electronic marketplace whose geography is constantly reshaped by regulatory shifts. The idea that offshore finance is organized into time zone blocks, linked to the imperative of instantaneous communications, is clearly not borne out. In the Old World, the major divide is between north (*Eastern Bloc*) and south (*Greater British Empire*), not east and west, while Japan loads more strongly with the Americas than its neighbors. Moreover, the reach of OJs is both heterogeneous—with some serving global more than regional hinterlands—and seemingly influenced more by physical than time zone distance (corroborating Haberly and Wójcik 2015b). The latter suggests an influence of long-term trust and face-to-face contact (i.e. travel).

Above all, the network structures appear to reflect a deep historical layering of social and political ties, with four processes and events standing out as most important: the establishment of global empires by European states, most importantly the United Kingdom, the shift in global economic and political hegemony from the United Kingdom to the United States and its allies, the collapse of Soviet communism, and the rise of Chinese capitalism. Strikingly, regression analysis of the same data by Haberly and Wójcik (2015b) failed to detect the imprint of any of these, apart from the narrow finding that colonized OJs have significantly elevated FDI in their colonizers. This reflects the advantage of PCA at revealing the influence of complex, imperfectly understood factors, that are poorly suited to regression model specification.

With respect to the first process, the metropolitan core of the former European imperial system is clearly the center of the global offshore network, with Britain's offshore "second empire" of singular importance. Acting as its principal nodes are an array of formerly, and in some cases currently UK-controlled entrepôt city-states ringing the world's continents, which were typically established largely to control existing commercial networks—most importantly Arab, Indian, and Chinese networks spanning the Indian Ocean and Southeast Asia. Although a mixture of local capital has once again become predominant within this region, the PCA results demonstrate that it continues to flow through this network of colonial strongpoints. Remarkably, this British financial empire does not seem to have displaced that of the previous economic hegemon, the Netherlands, but rather incorporated the latter as the single most important global offshore FDI hub. More broadly, the global offshore net cast by European colonialism can be clearly seen as being built around a much older European offshore core roughly running in an axis from the Low Countries to Switzerland. This has hosted Europe's leading concentration of "offshore" platforms since the Middle Ages, originally established largely by Italian merchant banks. These included exchange fairs such as that established in Geneva in the 15th century, which is essentially the progenitor of Switzerland's position as a leading OJ today, and the bearer-securities-based Antwerp securities market, which largely relocated to Amsterdam during the Dutch revolt, forming a key foundation for the latter's position in finance today (see chapter 2).

The second key historical influence on network organization was the shift during and after WWII of global economic and political hegemony from the United Kingdom to the United States and its network of alliances, most importantly with the declining British Empire. While the PCA results show a general division between a US-dominated western hemispheric offshore system, and a UK-colonial dominated eastern hemispheric system, these share a broad *Atlantic Axis* composed of the United States and major Western European midshore jurisdictions, which roughly corresponds to the Cold War western alliance and adjacent neutral OJs. Indeed, the *Pax Americana* and *British Empire* components do not represent a sharp divide so much as two expressions of this axis, the global footprint of which is visible in the *Anglo Alliance* component.

This narrative generally corroborates, while elaborating on and pushing further back in time, the historical–political accounts of Palan et al. (2010) and Shaxson (2011) of offshore network evolution. In contrast, the first and second components reveal structures and processes not hitherto recognized. While the activities of Russian investors in a group of OJs including Cyprus are well known, what has not been known is that these follow a stereotyped Eastern European pattern, likely produced largely by chaotic privatization programs in the 1990s. Meanwhile, the world's other major socialist state, China, is clearly the rising engine of global offshore finance. Mirroring Russia, however, what has not been recognized is that the volume and pattern of PRC offshore FDI, passing in particular through the Caribbean, is part of a *Greater China* network encompassing regional overseas Chinese-dominated economies. The Mainland, it seems, has become plugged into the offshore backbone of the regional "bamboo network" (Weidenbaum and Hughes 1996), with roots in 19th-century colonial labor and commercial policies, and older regional trading networks. Through this network, China has been drawn into the orbit of (or more precisely *back* into the orbit of; see chapters 2 and 8) the United Kingdom's postcolonial offshore system—which, in turn, appears to have been increasingly drawn into the orbit of China. This highlights the question of whether China or other emerging economies will supplant the United States as the leading source and destination of capital circulating through the UK's offshore archipelago; what does not seem to be in doubt, however, is the dominance of the archipelago itself.

The PCA results are also relevant to debates regarding the institutional and regulatory dimensions of offshore finance. Although robustly detectable in regression (Haberly and Wójcik 2015b), the OECD "offshore club" effect is apparently too subtle to be visible in the PCA results, being buried under the imprint of other factors. Meanwhile, rule of law and communist history variables, found by Haberly and Wójcik (2015b) to have an insignificant effect on offshore FDI quantity, appear to have quite important effects on its connectivity. Indeed, we find that the single deepest divide in the offshore FDI network is defined by the legacy of communism and the Cold War, as reflected in a sharply differentiated *Eastern Bloc* subnetwork.

In addition to being distinctly defined, this network exhibits unique institutional characteristics, specifically an association with weak rule of law. Taken together with the apparently unusually strong preference for physically proximate OJs in the *Eastern Bloc*, this indicates that the relational embeddedness of offshore ties may be conditioned by rule of law and communist history in a three-dimensional interaction relationship. Notably, by making use of regression analysis elsewhere (see Haberly and Wójcik 2015a), we have confirmed that such a three-pronged interaction does exist. Moreover, it also seems to extend (albeit more weakly) to countries in general, which, as their level of institutional strength declines, show a progressively stronger connection to geographically proximate as opposed to distant OJs.

7.6 Conclusions: Conceptualizing the Offshore World

The centrality of "paper" offshore structures in FDI underscores the need for analyses of the world economy that not only bridge the gap between financial and "real" activity, but also problematize the role of offshore legal constructs in defining the institutional geography of capitalism (Coe et al. 2014; Seabrooke and Wigan 2014). This chapter has made a significant contribution to this agenda, by constructing the first map of the global offshore FDI network that clearly and succinctly reveals the key features of the offshore system *as a network*. Keeping in mind the limitations of the CDIS dataset,[10] the network organization revealed by the PCA results, analyzed in conjunction with regression tests of offshore FDI determinants, helps solidify our conceptualization of the evolutionary and organizational logic of the offshore world.

First, information technology and the knowledge economy are indisputably intertwined with offshore finance, notably in the intellectual property mediated profit shifting embodied by a substantial portion of offshore FDI. However, our results cast doubt on the idea that the geographically embedded "hardware" of the offshore network itself is fundamentally technology driven and footloose. Rather, the offshore world is best conceptualized as a legal–institutional infrastructure underpinning the global economy, whose organization embodies the conservative, accretive process whereby laws, practices, and relationships have emerged and been reproduced over long periods of time by communities of experts and elites. It has a hegemonic quality in this respect, reflecting not only the economic, political, and ideological predominance of the current superpower, but incorporating a

---

[10] Most importantly, the CDIS (1) is an incomplete sample of economies, producing geographic coverage gaps in Africa and the Middle East, and constraining our ability to probe the structure of "real" economy to OJ, as opposed to OJ to real economy FDI; (2) does not disaggregate FDI by investor nationality or activity, and (3) is new, meaning that results shed light on network development only when examined through the lens of other historical research.

succession of past preeminent capitalist empires and institutions, and evidencing a potential to absorb and adapt itself to future hegemonic regimes.

At a detailed level, the relational and institutional modalities of this infrastructure appear to be heterogeneous. Notably, regression analyses (see Haberly and Wójcik 2015a) guided by the PCA results shown here, indicate that an economy's offshore ties are increasingly conditioned by trust and face-to-face contact as the strength of its legal institutions declines, and conversely by formal legal and public reputational factors, such as OECD membership, as institutional strength increases. This effect, moreover, appears to be stronger for former socialist countries than for developing countries without a history of socialist rule. At the same time, though, our results also indicate a need for caution in positing any particular narrow demand-side institutional *cause* for the existence of offshore activity broadly, and in particular either positive or negative institutional arbitrage by developing and transition economy firms. Conceptually, institutional explanations for offshore activity risk conflating distinct questions, notably the means through which capital is accumulated, incentives for capital flight/round-tripping, incentives for capital intermediation through OJs, and factors conditioning which OJs are used. Our findings only directly relate to the last of these, and are compatible with a null hypothesis of universal *incentives* for OJ use—e.g. what could be dubbed multifarious institutional "flexibility" and cost reduction—as suggested by Vlcek (2013).

Indeed, the overall picture is of an offshore world in which demand-side drivers are of secondary importance to the centralization of power on the supply side, as evidenced by a dominant *global finance* network with a largely homogeneous global footprint. Firms, wealthy families, and even governments, from all sorts of diverse contexts, in all parts of the world, in other words, make use of offshore structures for many different reasons. However, these functionally diverse structures end up being mediated through a common global offshore network core of key nodes and pathways. This centralization of supply-side power within the global offshore network, it must be emphasized, is clearly not vested in OJs themselves, but rather in the GFN more broadly, and above all in the leading FABs firms at its center (Wójcik 2013a).

From a policy standpoint, this picture casts doubt on the idea that the principal obstacle to offshore regulation is the corralling of numerous competing jurisdictions engaged in a cutthroat "race to the bottom" with one another. While this amoebic character may prevail in peripheral portions of the offshore network, this network has a centralized core likely to present a more stable target. However, core elements of this system are likely to be protected by the concentration of political and economic power that they represent. The apparently deep historical roots of these structures have particularly important potential policy implications that increase the urgency of more in-depth research on the deep historical roots of offshore finance, not just within but also outside of Europe. To the extent that offshore finance, in some form, is a deeply rooted product of the interaction of global capitalism with the sovereign state system, or perhaps of even more fundamental tensions surrounding the regulation of finance in any geographically variegated socioeconomic order, this would cast doubt on attempts to regulate offshore activity specifically, which have mostly assumed that it can be decoupled from globalization generally. In the confident assessment of one offshore professional, "There will always be an offshore sector. We are the ball bearings in the machine of the world's financial markets" (quoted in Rawlings 2005, 307).

8

"Capitalist Tools in Socialist Hands"?

China Mobile in the Global Financial Network

8.1 Introduction

China Mobile Ltd (CM) is a state-owned enterprise (SOE) created in 1997 as part of the reform of the Chinese telecom sector. Its initial public offering on the Hong Kong and New York stock exchanges raised over $4bn—then the largest amount of capital ever raised by an Asian company—turning CM into the pioneering Chinese megadeal on international capital markets, and one of China's first "national champions." CM is by far the largest mobile phone operator in the world, with nearly a billion subscribers (China Mobile 2020), and according to the Forbes Global 2000, was the world's fourth most valuable telecom company by market capitalization ($165bn); just slightly behind Comcast ($172B), AT&T ($219bn), and Verizon ($238bn). In 2016, the advertising firm WPP ranked CM as the second most valuable Chinese brand, worth over $50bn, following Tencent and ahead of Alibaba (WPP 2016). Fortune's Global 500, ranking firms according to revenues, as of 2020 lists CM as the sixteenth largest company in China, and the sixty-fifth largest company in the world overall. In short, CM is a giant at the heart of the telecom industry with strategic significance for mass media, ideology, and national security in China.

Where is CM? This basic question turns out to be surprisingly difficult to answer. The company's 2019 Annual Report states that it is *incorporated* in Hong Kong, but does not mention the location of its headquarters. The 2019 20F form, filed with the US Securities and Exchange Commission, meanwhile, states that CM has an *executive office* in Hong Kong, and regional headquarters in each of its regional mobile companies, but does not mention a central headquarters either. The FT Global 500 ranking assigns CM to Hong Kong as its home jurisdiction, as does the Forbes Global 2000. In contrast, the Fortune Global 500 lists the company under the name China Mobile Communications and assigns its headquarters to Beijing. Presumably, this refers to China Mobile Communications Corporation, the state-owned parent company of CM. However, to add to the confusion, the same Fortune Global 500 listing uses financial figures from CM and contains a link to its website. The geographical scope of CM's activities also presents a puzzle.

Sticky Power. Daniel Haberly and Dariusz Wòjcik, Oxford University Press.
© Daniel Haberly and Dariusz Wòjcik (2022). DOI: 10.1093/oso/9780198870982.003.0008

While no reports mention CM selling its services outside of Mainland China and Hong Kong, the Ministry of Commerce, in 2010, ranked the company as the tenth largest Chinese nonfinancial transnational corporation according to the value of foreign assets, and the 19th largest by total outward FDI stock. The only reason for these FDI accolades seem to be legal entities within CM's corporate structure registered in OJs, with the British Virgin Islands in the lead—a surprising association for an SOE.

The historical and strategic significance of CM in China's political economy, as well as the puzzles surrounding its geographical structure, make CM an important and intriguing case for studying the evolution, structure, and globalization of China's state-owned "national champions." As Lin and Milhaupt (2013, 697) put it, "the national champions are the fullest expression of state capitalism in China—the global face of China Inc." This is justified given that as of 2011 "more than 60% of China's largest 500 enterprises, and all of its 30 largest enterprises were SOEs" (ibid, 702). As such, "national champions" are key to understanding the Chinese corporate sector and its globalization.

Not surprisingly, the globalization of Chinese firms has attracted research in international business studies, economics, and economic geography. Existing studies focus on the determinants of Chinese foreign direct investment (Buckley et al. 2007), the internationalization strategies of Chinese firms (Nolan 2001a), the political economy of China's industrial policy (Yeung and Liu 2008), and regional development outcomes (Wei et al. 2007; Yeung 2009). However, these studies pay little attention to the financial actors and practices shaping the transformation of the Chinese corporate sector and political economy.

In this chapter we use the case of China Mobile to shed light on the emergence and evolution of China's "national champions," and their relationship with the GFN. Analyzing the case of CM through the GFN framework offers multiple contributions. While existing case studies of Chinese companies focus mainly on manufacturing, this chapter highlights the interactions between two strategic sectors of China's 12th five-year development plan—telecom and FABS. It sheds light on the key "triangle" of Chinese "foreign" investment, comprising Mainland China, Hong Kong, and the Caribbean (most importantly the Cayman and British Virgin Islands; see chapter 7). Finally, while there are studies of Chinese financial centers (Lai 2012), FABS in China (Daniels 2012), and the geography of Chinese capital markets (Karreman and van der Knaap 2012; Wójcik and Burger 2010), the GFNs concept offers a link to connect these literatures to each other and to an investigation of emerging Chinese global *production* networks.

This chapter uses secondary as well as primary data sources. To track CM's development, including the role of OJs within its corporate structure, we have used its annual reports and filings with the US SEC. To investigate the involvement of FABS in CM's development, in addition to annual reports, we have studied hundreds of pages of prospectuses prepared for CM's initial and secondary public offerings. To help interpret and augment publicly available information, twenty-four interviews were conducted in 2012–2014, with former and current officers at CM (three interviews), its services providers in investment banking, legal services, and accountancy (four), as well as experts in telecom, corporate law, accounting, and finance (seventeen), based in Hong Kong (twelve), Beijing (eight), London (three), and Singapore (one). Finally, to put CM in context, we have compiled data on other leading SOEs using annual reports available on their websites.

The structure of the chapter follows the logic of GFNs. This is first fleshed out in the context of literature on the globalization of Chinese companies in section 8.2. Section 8.3 introduces the case study, charting the evolution of CM since its inception in 1997, and its rise to the status of a "national champion," under the tight control of the Chinese government. Sections 8.4–8.6 analyze CM's engagement with the additional building blocks of GFNs (apart from China itself as a budding "world government"): FABS, FCs, and OJs. The last section concludes by examining CM, and China's relationship with the GFN in general, from a broader historical perspective—looking at how this relationship compares to earlier patterns of GFN engagement by the US and UK, as well as the Soviet Union, historically.

The main finding is that CM has not just been an active weaver of GFNs, but is also itself, notwithstanding its status as a Chinese "national champion," essentially a product of *the* GFN as a centralized nexus of global financial power. Global FABS firms—KPMG, Linklaters, Sullivan & Cromwell, and above all Goldman Sachs—were instrumental in the very conception of the company in 1997, when it was sewn together from the assets of two regional telecom organizations in southern China, and in its expansion ever since. With the help of the FABS complex, CM was born into the world at the very heart of the GFN, through registration in Hong Kong, cross-listing in Hong Kong and New York, and offshore entities in the British Virgin Islands. For the Chinese government, these operations were a means of consolidating and modernizing the telecom sector, without relinquishing control over it. Building CM into a "national champion" with a global brand and financial market profile has therefore represented a conjunction of interests between the Chinese government and FABS firms.

At the same time, however, we show that a basic tension remains, for CM and other "national champions," between their ability to construct and harness GFNs as "capitalist tools in socialist hands," and the ability of *the* GFN to remake the Chinese political economy in its own image. The outcome of this push and pull of structure and agency is uncertain; indeed, as we show in the last section of this chapter, the USSR historically wove itself into a similarly entangled relationship with the GFN, centered on the offshore Eurodollar market, in the decades leading up to its collapse. Complicating matters further is the fact that this strategic tension, permeating China's relationship with the GFN, has now also manifested itself as a second-order strategic paradox for the United States; whose increasingly aggressive efforts to disconnect CM and other Chinese national champions from the GFN could just as easily end up undermining the US position as the imperial "protector" of this network. Ultimately, perhaps the greatest irony of all is that the outcome of this struggle between the USA and China does not really seem to matter much from the standpoint of the historical accretion of financial power represented by the GFN itself—which is being actively reproduced by both countries.

8.2 China in Global Production and Financial Networks

The development of "national champions" such as CM must be situated within the context of Chinese economic reform. During the "reform without losers" phase of 1978–1992, the central government gradually relaxed its control over SOEs as part of a broader move to decentralize authority and resources to create space for development to be driven by market forces. While SOEs remained subject to the central plan, they were allowed to sell goods and services on the market after satisfying plan quotas. They were thus encouraged to "grow out of the plan" (Naughton 2006). However, under the pressure of competition from private and collective enterprises, with Township and Villages Enterprises (TVEs) in the lead, and without freedom to downsize their employment and welfare functions, SOEs experienced a dramatic decline in profitability, from 14% of gross domestic product in 1978 to less than 1% by 1996. As these financially shaky SOEs represented a major drain on government resources, a pressure arose for a more radical approach to restructuring them. This set the stage for the second phase of reform, often referred to as "reform with losers," which focused on state-sector downsizing, restructuring, and recentralization (Naughton 2006).

As observed by Nolan (2001b, 16) "By the early 1990s, a key policy slogan had become 'grasp the large, let go of the small.' The determination to build a group of globally competitive large, multiplant corporations stemmed from deep study of the development experience of successful late-coming industrializing countries and from close observation of the industrial structure of advanced capitalism." As Vice-Minister Wu Banguo stated in 1998: "our nation's position in the international economic order will be to a large extent determined by the position of our nation's large enterprises and groups" (cited in Nolan 2001b, 17). By letting the small go, "policy-makers were giving local governments much greater authority to restructure their own firms and, in particular, to privatize or close down some of them" (Naughton 2006, 156). The policy of building large, centrally controlled corporations was also a response to problems resulting from the partial plant- and enterprise-level autonomy of the first phase of economic reform. The most successful of these enterprises attempted to grow through the market, taking over weaker competitors and merging with other strong companies. This, however, represented a threat to centralized control. If local and regional companies could grow national from the bottom-up, through market mechanisms, this could undermine the influence of the central administration. Instead, by the mid-1990s, central administration took the building of "national champions" into its own hands, with the aim of conducting industrial consolidation on its own terms.

The motivation for the creation of "national champions" was thus political as well as economic. As Yeung and Liu (2008, 61) put it "Since the second half of the 1990s, the central state has intensified its efforts to re-regulate the national space-economy in order to curb the spread of Chinese style federalism." According to McGregor (2010), following the decomposition of communist regimes worldwide—spreading from Central and Eastern Europe, and nearly coming to a head in China itself—the Communist Party of China realized it needed much greater financial resources to maintain its power. Commercialization of strategic industries under state control would help generate such resources. Eventually, out of thousands of SOEs, the State Council, in two batches (1991 and 1997), selected a "national team" of 120 large enterprise groups in strategic sectors such as coal mining, electricity generation, aerospace, and telecommunication (Nolan 2001a). The selected SOEs benefited from preferential policies in terms of taxation, access to government contracts and funding from state-owned banks, and eligibility for stock exchange listing. By 2003, the national team's membership had grown to 198 enterprise groups (Lin and Milhaupt 2013).

An additional impetus for SOE restructuring came from China's accession to the World Trade Organization in 2001. As China was partially opening its door to foreign transnational companies, it encouraged its own "national champions" to become transnational companies with world-class brands. In April 2003, the State Asset Supervision and Administration Commission (SASAC) was created with the mandate to transform the SOEs under its control into fifty global TNCs featuring in the Fortune Global 500 (Pamlin and Long 2007, cited in Yeung and Liu 2008). The SASAC orchestrated a consolidation of the SOEs under its supervision, bringing their number down to 109 by 2013. Foreign listings proved instrumental in this project, as a way to raise equity in hard currency, and to establish an international corporate image and reputation. Overseas listings also helped Chinese companies to pursue outward investment via M&As, by allowing them to use their own publicly traded shares as a "money" to purchase equity in foreign companies. The use of mergers & acquisitions, instead of greenfield investments by Chinese firms as an internationalization strategy, has been referred to as a "fast lane" to the development of "national champions" (Warner et al. 2004)—and is often highly controversial, due to the state control and often opaque governance of these emerging multinationals. Many of these mergers & acquisitions have been linked to the national objectives of acquiring natural resources and technology abroad to maintain growth at home (Yang and Stoltenberg 2008). To help Chinese firms internationalize, in 2005, China's State Administration of Foreign Exchange

(SAFE) issued new regulations that facilitated the establishment of offshore holding companies as a prelude to foreign fundraising. In addition, for the first time,
Chinese firms were expressly allowed to exchange their equity for the equity of
foreign publicly listed companies in mergers & acquisitions, while Chinese accounting standards were at the same time moved toward international accounting
standards.

The legal foundations for the "national champions" policy were laid by the 1994
Company Law. This "provided a framework for 'corporatizing' SOEs, that is, converting traditional SOEs into the legal form of the corporation, more appropriate
to a market economy" (Naughton 2006, 161). A common pattern for the corpora-
tization of centrally controlled sectors, such as telecom or electricity generation,
was to transfer assets from a ministry or ministries to a state-owned holding (parent) company, to separate regulatory from commercial functions. In a second step,
more than one SOE would typically be carved out from the parent company with a
view to avoid creating monopolies. At the same time, however, this two-step process of consolidation usually also involved a Frankenstein-like piecing together
of loose national collections of local and regional enterprises. As these enterprises
had enjoyed a substantial level of autonomy since the 1980s, they would sometimes
oppose the process of SOE consolidation, as for example in the power equipment
sector (Nolan 2001a). To make the new enterprises attractive to investors, welfare
functions, such as kindergartens or hospitals, would be left under the administration of the parent company, and not transferred to the SOEs carved out from
it. Table 8.1 presents the top-ten "national champions," defined as the ten largest
Chinese companies according to revenues in 2013 that are on the list of central
SOEs controlled by the SASAC. The list does not include financial sector SOEs,
which are controlled through separate channels by China's main Sovereign Wealth
Fund (CIC). For each "national champion," the table lists the state-owned holding
(parent company), as well as the main listed subsidiary.

To problematize CM as a case study, a three-pronged approach is needed. First,
we have to look at the economic geography of CM as a *political*–economic geography. As Yeung and Liu (2008, 57) put it, "the Chinese state is strategically and
intricately enmeshed with the corporate interests of its leading business firms."
Second, we have to apply a multi-scalar approach to the problematization of this
political–economic geography, as the influence of the home country on the internationalization of its firms, in the case of China, operates simultaneously at
both the national and local governmental levels (Yeung 2000). This is particularly important in the context of the recentralization of the Chinese economy
that has been a focus of government policy since the mid-1990s, which has often sharpened central–local government tensions. Finally, we need to take finance
seriously. Notably, in this respect, while initial public offerings, mergers & acquisitions, and accounting standards are considered in the existing research as financial
instruments of *corporate* consolidation and internationalization, the agency and

Table 8.1 Top-ten national champions from outside the financial sector

Parent company	HQ	Listed subsidiary	IPO year	IPO location	IPO lead managers	Legal advisers	Auditors	Use of BVI or CI
China Petro-chemical Corporation	Beijing	Sinopec	2000	Hong Kong, New York, London	Morgan Stanley, China International Capital Corporation	Haiwen & Partners, Herbert Smith Freehills, Skadden Arps	PwC	BVI and CI
China National Petroleum Corporation	Beijing	PetroChina	2000	Hong Kong, New York	Goldman Sachs, China International Capital Corporation, Bank of China, HSBC	Freshfields, Shearman & Sterling, King & Wood Mallesons	KPMG	BVI and CI
State Grid Corporation of China	Beijing	Not listed				King & Wood Mallesons	Ruihua	BVI and CI
China Mobile Communications Corporation	Beijing	China Mobile	1997	Hong Kong, New York	Goldman Sachs, China International Capital Corporation	Sullivan & Cromwell	PwC	BVI and CI
China State Construction Engineering Corporation	Beijing	CSCEC	2009	Shanghai	China International Capital Corporation	Dacheng Law offices, Jingtian & Gongcheng, JT&N	PwC	CI

Continued

Table 8.1 *Continued*

Parent company	HQ	Listed subsidiary	IPO year	IPO location	IPO lead managers	Legal advisers	Auditors	Use of BVI or CI
China National Offshore Oil Corporation	Beijing	CNOOC	2001	Hong Kong, New York	Merrill Lynch, Credit Suisse First Boston, Bank of China	Stikeman Elliott, Davis Polk & Wardwell, Akin Gump	Deloitte	BVI and CI
China Railway Construction Corporation	Beijing	China Railway Construction	2008	Hong Kong, Shanghai	CITIC Securities	Baker & McKenzie, DengHeng Law Offices	Ernst & Young	CI
China Railway Group	Beijing	China Railway	2007	Hong Kong, Shanghai	UBS, Bank of China	Jiayuan Law Offices, Zhonglun Law Firm	Deloitte	Neither
Sinochem Group	Beijing	Sinochem	2000	Shanghai	HuaXia Securities	Tian Yuan Law Firm	Ernst & Young	CI
China Southern Power Grid Co. Ltd	Guangzhou	Not listed				Everwin Law Office, ETR Law Firm	Ruihua	Neither

Sources: authors' analysis based on data from annual reports, stock exchange filings; <http://fortune.com/global500>; http://en.sasac.gov.cn/index.html> accessed December 17, 2021; adapted from Wójcik and Camilleri (2015).

Note: The table presents the ten largest Chinese companies according to revenues in 2013 that are on the list of central state-owned enterprises controlled by the State-owned Assets Supervision and Administration Commission. The list does not include SOEs in the financial sector, which are controlled by other authorities. HQ refers to the headquarters of the parent company. Information on the IPO refers to the listed subsidiaries. Information on legal advisers, auditors, and the use of BVI or CI is valid for the end of 2013, and refers to the listed subsidiary (with the exception of State Grid and China Southern Power, for which it refers to the parent, as they do not have a listed subsidiary). The company is considered as using BVI or CI if its annual report or stock exchange filing mentions registration of the company or any of its subsidiaries in the British Virgin Islands or Cayman Islands.

transformative power of *finance itself* in these operations is given short shrift. Alon and McIntyre's edited volume on the globalization of Chinese enterprises, for example, does not even feature the word finance in the index (2008).

In contrast to most literature, Walter and Howie's (2011) *Red Capitalism* offers a bold account of the central role of finance in the transformation of the Chinese corporate sector. The authors, notably, worked as financial professionals in Mainland China and Hong Kong since the early 1990s, so theirs is an insider account. They argue that by the mid-1990s, the Chinese government had essentially run out of large nationwide enterprises that they could market to international investors. Consequently, to continue building the "national team," the government had to engage leading global FABS firms to help them create new internationally marketable national champions from scratch. In fact, they go so far as to say that the "China of the twenty-first century is a creation of the Goldman Sachs and Linklaters & Paines of the world, just as surely as the Cultural Revolution flowed from Chairman Mao's Little Red Book" (2011, 159).

According to Walter and Howie, CM was the first major successful case of such FABS-assisted national champion creation, which paved the way for other Chinese companies to follow in its footsteps, for example in the energy and financial sectors. Our objective here is to build on their discussion of CM to explore this case in more depth through the lens of the GFN framework. Importantly, the study of CM through this perspective contributes just as much conceptually to our understanding of GFNs, as the GFN perspective contributes to our understanding of CM. Financial centers, offshore jurisdictions, leading international FABS firms, and the power of the state, both territorial and extraterritorial, all feature prominently in the story we are about to tell.

The GFN framework structures the rest of the chapter along the following lines of enquiry. First, how has the Chinese government sought to employ the services of the GFN strategically in its efforts to build national champions such as CM, and how has this strategy been impacted by China's relationship with the established power of the US within the GFN? Second, what has been the role of FABS in the evolution of the company? Third, what are the interactions of CM with financial centers forged by FABS firms, and what impact have these interactions had on financial centers themselves? Fourth, what has been the role of offshore jurisdictions in the evolution of the company? Put together, these questions will help us to evaluate the formative and transformative power of the GFN in the evolution of the Chinese economy.

8.3 The Evolution of China Mobile

CM was incorporated in Hong Kong in September 1997 under the name China Telecom (Hong Kong) Ltd. The latter was renamed China Mobile (Hong Kong)

Ltd in 2000, and China Mobile Ltd (CM) in 2006. To avoid confusion, we refer to the company as CM irrespective of the period of time concerned. In 1997, the company's assets were made up of two provincial companies, Guangdong Mobile and Zhejiang Mobile, which were transferred to CM by the Ministry of Post and Telecommunications. Only seven weeks after CM was incorporated, 24.9% of its shares were offered to international investors through a cross-listing on the Hong Kong Exchange and the New York Stock Exchange. This IPO was very well timed, being launched at a time of growing foreign investor appetite for Chinese stocks, as well as international excitement about telecom stocks generally, set against the backdrop of the building dot.com bubble in the USA. It was thus enormously successful, raising $4.2bn, and being oversubscribed thirty and twenty times over in Hong Kong and New York respectively. In fact, CM's IPO raised more capital in international markets than any Asian company had raised before, despite the fact that the Chinese government retained over 75% of its ownership.

CM has subsequently expanded in a spectacular fashion (Figure 8.1). Using the proceeds from its IPO, it acquired mobile phone operators in Jiangsu in 1998, and in Fujian, Henan, and Hainan in 1999. With acquisitions in Liaoning, Beijing, Tianjin, Hebei, Shandong, Shanghai, and Guangxi in 2000, CM established itself all over the Chinese coast. In 2002 it ventured inland, with acquisitions in Anhui, Jiangxi, Chongqing, Sichuan, Hubei, Hunan, Shaanxi, and Shanxi. Finally, purchases in 2004 in the north and west of China brought CM to all thirty-one

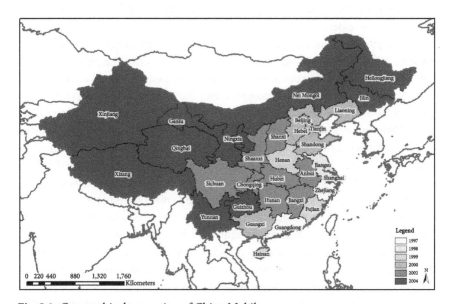

Fig. 8.1 Geographical expansion of China Mobile

Sources: authors, based on data from China Mobile 20f forms 1998–2004; adapted from Wójcik and Camilleri (2015).

Mainland provinces. Consecutive rounds of acquisitions were funded with internally generated funds, as well as further equity and debt offerings. Since 2004 the company has consolidated its domestic market position, tripling its assets, revenues, and profits in real terms, and doubling employment to 197 thousand by 2013. In 2013, CM's market share in Mainland China was 62%. In addition to mobile telecommunications services in Mainland China and Hong Kong, CM offers internet access through wireless local area networks in Mainland China. In 2013, the parent company of CM was also granted permission to authorize CM to operate fixed-line telecommunications services in Mainland China (China Mobile, 2014, 17–18).

Notwithstanding its public listings in Hong Kong and (until 2021—see below) New York, control over CM remains firmly in the hands of the Chinese government. At the end of 2013, China Mobile Communications Corporation owned 74.08% of CM's shares (72.72% at the end of 2020), and all of CM's executive directors were also executives of the parent company. Government control over CM, and the telecom sector in general, are however, like the Chinese state itself, far from monolithic. They are rather permeated by complicated and messy internal power struggles and bargaining processes between various authorities at and between the central and regional levels. CM's initial creation and listing was accompanied by a fierce, protracted battle, characterized by "intense bureaucratic in-fighting to attempt to capture the stream of rents stemming from the limited number of licenses and the absence of multinational competition" (Nolan 2001a, 801). Complicating matters was the fact that the Chinese government has aimed, since the outset of telecom sector reform, to create more than one provider; thereby forcing its telecom champions to compete with one another, even while trying to retain coherent strategic control over all of them. The creation of CM, by the Ministry of Post and Telecommunications, was preceded by the establishment of China Unicom by the Ministry of Electronics Industry together with the Ministry of Railways and other partners, and was followed, in 2002, by the creation of China Telecom by the Ministry of Information Industry—itself the product of a merger between the Ministry of Post and Telecommunications, the Ministry of Electronics Industry, and other ministries (Yu et al. 2004). Today, China Unicom and China Telecom are the main competitors of CM in the market for mobile telecom services. In theory, following China's WTO accession in 2001, foreign mobile phone companies are allowed to provide competition in China by taking up to 49% stakes in joint ventures in the sector, and operating nationwide; moreover, they should theoretically be protected by pro-competitive regulatory principles. In practice, however, this foreign competition has not actually materialized, with the telecom sector in China thus remaining a state-controlled oligopoly (Voon and Mitchell 2010).

Within CM, like most national champions, the central government, and in practice the Communist Party of China, retains the power to appoint top executives (Naughton 2006). Events in 2004 and 2008 served as reminders of this power.

In 2004, the government orchestrated a three-way swap of executives between CM, China Unicom, and China Telecom, bringing the CEO of China Unicom to CM, with the CEO of the latter being sent to China Telecom. This move was made without consulting the public shareholders of CM. In 2008 there was another reshuffle, wherein China Unicom and China Telecom were converted into full-service telecom providers offering both fixed-line and mobile services, in a move to strengthen them in relation to CM—the dominant player in the sector (Harwit 2008). Further complicating CM's governance is the significant autonomy of the firm's constituent pieces at the regional level. The thirty-one provincial mobile phone companies that constitute CM are actually separate legal entities, not branches of CM. The parent holding company of CM itself, moreover, is also organized on a provincial basis. The result is a rather odd parallel organization of both CM *and* its parent holding company at both the central and regional levels, wherein the regional executives of the parent company itself act as the executives of the regional CM companies. CM's 20F reports, which it submits annually to the US Securities and Exchange Commission, actually seems to emphasize the geographically decentralized nature of corporate governance, by mentioning its regional headquarters, in addition to its executive office in Hong Kong. It also appears that CM's regional companies have autonomy in negotiating deals with telecom equipment providers and other suppliers, as well as corporate customers (Lovelock 1997). Thus, although the map in Figure 8.1 superficially paints a picture of a premeditated and centrally planned process of consolidation, the reality is much messier. Indeed, it is unclear to what extent CM actually functions as a unified company, as opposed to a sort of loose confederation of commercialized local government agencies, that share a common brand and stock market listing.

In summary, with the creation of CM, the Chinese government built a "national champion" which conquered the Fortune Global 500 and other corporate rankings, thus becoming one of the pioneers of China's "national team" of globally significant corporations. The evolution of CM represents a process of centralization and consolidation, but it has also involved a tricky balancing act between the interests of the center and various regions; as well as between building powerful national champion firms, and maintaining the international standing and reputation of these firms—from the perspective of both foreign investors and foreign governments. Modernization, domestic expansion, and the achievement of international status arguably would not have been achieved in this case without plugging the company into international financial markets via listings on the Hong Kong and New York exchanges. These provided CM with capital via a non-*dirigiste* channel, as well as global brand and investor recognition, and internal corporate incentives for commercialization, including via the use of stocks as part of executive remuneration. In this respect CM is a pioneer, but it is not an exception. Most national champions, including eight out of the ten largest SOEs, have sold shares to the public, even while the government has retained controlling ownership (Table 8.1). Four out of the top eight have listed their shares in New York in addition to Hong Kong. In the following sections, we delve into the details of the IPO process itself, to highlight the role of the GFN and FABS complex in CM's creation.

8.4 The FABS Team

Conducted with the objective of finding investors to purchase the shares issued by a company, an IPO is a complex activity that requires the assistance of an array of FABS providers (Wójcik 2011a). Playing the leading role are investment banks. An investment bank assesses the value of the company, advises on the issue price, drafts an initial public offering prospectus (detailing opportunities and risks facing investors), and promotes the issue to potential investors. In addition, an investment bank typically underwrites an IPO, meaning that any shares unsold to investors are bought by the bank itself at a predetermined price. Acting as key assistants to investment banks are law and accountancy firms. Lawyers ensure that the issuer, the initial public offering, and the newly issued shares comply with all laws and regulations of the jurisdictions where the shares are listed, and in which they are sold. Meanwhile, accountants make sure that the issuer's financial statements included in the prospectus present a fair and true view of the company, and comply with the accounting standards of the host market.

Its dual exchange listing, unprecedented IPO size, and state control of the issuer, made CM's IPO particularly complex. The key intermediary was Goldman Sachs (Asia) LLC, which acted as the offering's global coordinator. While it technically shared this role, as well as the role of the largest underwriter, with China International Capital Corporation—a Beijing based investment bank created as a joint venture between Morgan Stanley and Chinese banks—the latter lacked an international network, and played a nominal part in the process. The IPO's underwriting team consisted of thirteen other institutions: twelve US and European investment banks, and Bank of China International (China Telecom 1997). Legal work was divided between Sullivan & Cromwell, key legal advisers to Goldman Sachs, responsible for compliance with US laws and regulations (as stipulated by the New York Stock Exchange and the Securities and Exchange Commission, among others); and Linklaters, one of the world's largest law firms, responsible for compliance in Hong Kong and internationally, outside of the USA. Amsterdam-headquartered KPMG conducted due diligence and auditing. The IPO generated hefty fees for the advisers involved, with underwriting fees estimated in excess of $200m, and lawyers and accountants charging single digit millions. This disproportionately high remuneration of investment bankers underscores the pecking order in FABS. The ultimate point of an IPO is financial, with law and accountancy performing necessary but secondary functions. It is the investment bankers who develop the closest relationships with the top executives of an issuer, and work with them on strategic issues, while lawyers and accountants do the "paperwork."

An IPO typically serves as a starting point for long-term relationships between an issuer and its FABS providers, and in this respect CM is no exception. The company has hired Goldman Sachs as chief adviser on its subsequent equity and debt offerings, as well as on its acquisitions of provincial telecom companies. According to CM's annual reports, Linklaters acted as CM's main legal adviser until 2011, with the role since taken over by Sullivan & Cromwell. KPMG has recently been replaced by PwC as CM's auditor. There are good reasons for such long-term relationships. An IPO involves an intensive exchange of tacit, commercially sensitive information, requiring trust and representing a large intangible investment, which is best capitalized on through repeat interactions. To be sure, even while serving issuers, FABS firms also have to cultivate their good reputation among investors, which can lead to difficult judgment calls, particularly in the Chinese context. For example, how well should investors be informed about who actually controls CM? Both the prospectus and consecutive 20F forms stress that China Mobile Communications Corporation, as the ultimate parent of CM, may have interests that conflict with those of CM. However, the role of the Communist Party of China in nominating top management is never mentioned. Auditors assure investors of the quality of CM's financial information, but at the same time realize that the working papers produced while auditing the company in Mainland China are subject to state secret laws, and that their disclosure to investor protection authorities in Hong Kong or the USA would violate these Chinese laws.

Considering that CM was incorporated only weeks before its IPO, and that it consisted at that time only of the assets of two regional mobile operators, what was sold so successfully to international investors was really only the *idea*, or the *promise* of a "national champion." As Walter and Howie put it "American investment bankers created China Mobile out of a poorly managed assortment of provincial post and telecom entities and sold the package to international fund managers as a national telecommunications giant" (2011, 10). Walter and Howie go even further, claiming that "Goldman Sachs aggressively lobbied Beijing using the very simple but powerful idea of creating a truly national telecommunications company. Such a company it was argued, could raise sufficient capital to develop into a leading global communications technology company" (2011, 159). To be sure, the "national champions" policy was the Chinese government's own, so it is questionable how much lobbying was required. Goldman Sachs and other FABS firms, however, helped to operationalize the policy, providing expertise and networks not available in Mainland China. In this respect, moreover, CM is not an exception. As Table 8.1 illustrates, almost all IPOs of Chinese SOEs in Hong Kong or New York have involved US or European investment banks as lead managers. All of the top "national champions" listed in Hong Kong or New York employ US or European firms as advisers, and all of the listed companies in the table are audited by one of the Big Four companies (Deloitte, EY, KPMG, PwC). It is not an exaggeration to state that China's "national team" would not exist as we know it without the "FABS team."

8.5 Financial Centers

Intermediating between CM and international investors, FABS firms have also nurtured international financial centers as nodes mediating CM's engagement with the GFN. To explore the geography of these interactions, we first need to ask where the FABS firms involved come from. While Goldman Sachs is head-quartered in New York, Linklaters in London, and KPMG in Amsterdam, it was the Hong Kong offices of these firms that were directly in charge of CM's IPO. In the case of Goldman Sachs, many bankers working on the transaction were flown in from New York and London. Sullivan & Cromwell, responsible for US compliance, did not have an office in Hong Kong back then, and operated out of their New York headquarters, focusing on relations with the New York Stock Exchange and the SEC. The actual work of Goldman Sachs, KPMG, and Linklaters on the offering was carried out both in Hong Kong and Mainland China. Accountants, in tens or hundreds, coming mainly from KPMG's Hong Kong office, carried out most of their work in Guangdong and Zhejiang, where CM's only assets were located at the time of its IPO. Investment bankers and lawyers would sometimes accompany accountants in Guangdong and Zhejiang, but spent most of their time traveling between Hong Kong and Beijing. CM itself was incorporated in Hong Kong, with its chief executive, financial, and operating officers working at least partly in Hong Kong and partly in Beijing. As the CM was controlled by the Ministry of Post and Telecommunications in Beijing, however, investment bankers and lawyers needed to work for long periods in the capital. This was complicated by the fact that, in 1997, neither Goldman Sachs nor Linklaters or KPMG had an office in Beijing.

Hong Kong, while home to CM's "executive office," was never its real decision-making center or headquarters. Moreover, its role has diminished even further with time. As the company approached the completion of its domestic expansion, by 2003, its chief executive, financial, and operating officers ceased to work from Hong Kong. The executive office reduced employment from approximately fifty in the late 1990s, to thirty-five in 2013, and refocused on investor relations, with company secretary the most senior remaining employee. Most meetings of the board of directors still take place in Hong Kong, as do conferences for financial analysts. However, all six executive directors work and live in Beijing, while only three nonexecutive directors live in Hong Kong. The location of CM's real headquarters is somewhat disguised in corporate documents. 20F forms mention the executive office in Hong Kong and regional headquarters in Chinese provinces, but neither the 20F nor annual reports refer to the company having a central "headquarters." Addresses themselves, however, give away some of the real geography. CM's Hong Kong executive office is at 60/F The Centre, 99 Queen's Road Central, occupying one floor. Meanwhile, China Mobile Communications Corporation, the parent of CM, is located at 29 Financial Street, Beijing, occupying a whole block, with a couple of thousand employees—an unsurprising number given that it constitutes the real decision-making center of a giant company.

Over time, Beijing has risen in importance as a locus of interactions between CM and its FABS team. Partly due to the presence of lucrative SOE clients such as CM, Goldman Sachs, KPMG, Linklaters, and Sullivan & Cromwell all now have offices in the capital. For investment bankers, Beijing matters as the home of the decision makers of CM and other SOEs. For accountants and lawyers what matters, in addition to proximity to decision makers, is the availability of original documentation (such as property deeds). In 2013, Goldman Sachs employed approximately 1300 people in Hong Kong—the Asian headquarters of the company—and approximately 200 in Beijing, with another 200 in Shanghai and Shenzhen together. Beijing, rather than Shanghai, was thus the center of Goldman's operations in the Mainland. Indeed, the Chairman of Goldman Sachs Asia (as of 2013) lived and worked from Beijing, positioning himself at the center of political power. Of approximately 200 professionals working for Linklaters in China, over 100 are based in Hong Kong, but Beijing is the second largest office, ahead of Shanghai. KPMG has eleven offices in Mainland China. The Beijing office had nearly 2000 staff, being larger than the Shanghai office, and growing much faster than the Hong Kong office with its 2200 employees. The chairman of KPMG China alternates between the Beijing and Hong Kong offices.

At the same time, though, the continued importance of Hong Kong as a financial center to CM's functioning must not be underestimated. In addition to hosting the executive office, the listing and trading of the company on the Hong Kong Exchange generates jobs and revenues for the city's securities industry. Furthermore, CM's public shareholders (mainly institutional investors owning less than 1% of its shares each) are mostly either Hong Kong institutions or the Hong Kong–based subsidiaries of American or European investment managers. Via incorporation and listing in Hong Kong, CM is subject to Hong Kong laws and regulations, which are closer to those found in London and New York than those in Beijing. Put differently, Hong Kong is a finance-savvy world city, and with its laws, regulations, and reputation, it in turn underwrites the reputation of CM, as well as that of many of China's other national champions registered and listed there as "red chip" stocks. It thus acts as a bridge between international finance and corporate China. It should also be noted that many professionals working with Chinese corporations in Beijing are actually employed by Hong Kong offices, commuting from Hong Kong, and having families there.

The case of CM illustrates how the creation of "national champions" has implicated China in the evolution of the GFN (Lai 2012; Zhao et al. 2004). As existing
research has demonstrated, by far most important connections of Hong Kong with
this network are those linking it to New York and London internationally, and to
Beijing within China (Taylor et al. 2011). CM is a great example of this pattern.

8.6 Offshore Jurisdictions

The rise of CM to the status of a "national champion" has not only implicated
the company in networks of relationships with FABS and FCs, but also with offshore jurisdictions. Figure 8.2 shows the organizational structure of CM based on
information in the 2012 20F report, published in 2013, which has changed little
as of 2021. China Mobile Communications Corporation—the parent of CM—
is controlled by the SASAC, which is controlled in turn by the State Council.
SASAC appoints the directors of China Mobile Communications Corporation.
However, the latter does not own CM directly, but rather via a chain of entities
via China Mobile Hong Kong Group incorporated in Hong Kong, which in turn
owns China Mobile BVI incorporated in the British Virgin Islands. It is this BVI
company that is actually the direct owner of over 74% of CM. To complicate things
further, CM owns all of its provincial operating companies indirectly via China
Mobile Communication Ltd, which is also incorporated in BVI. This is a highly
insubstantial shell, whose capital is made up of one share with a nominal value of

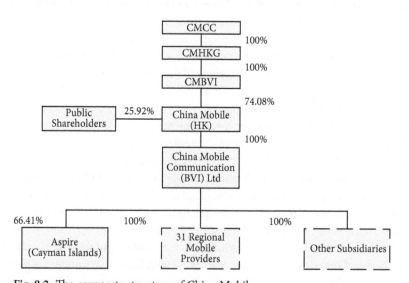

Fig. 8.2 The corporate structure of China Mobile

Sources: authors, based on information in China Mobile 20f form 2012; adapted from
Wójcik and Camilleri (2015).

$1. Via this company, CM also co-owns Aspire, a joint venture with Vodafone and Hewlett-Packard incorporated in the Cayman Islands, which owns a technology development platform operating in Shenzhen. Other subsidiaries that CM owns via China Mobile Communications Ltd are incorporated in Mainland China, Hong Kong, and BVI, and include: China Mobile Hong Kong (a mobile telecom operator in Hong Kong); various technology development platforms (one of which is co-owned by Nokia); and China Mobile Group Finance (delivering financial services to group companies).

Explaining the presence of CM in OJs is difficult. Indeed, the existing literature on the connections between the Chinese corporate sector and OJs is often inconclusive with respect to motivations. As one offshore professional said for Chinese corporate offshore structures in general, "You have to wonder why they bother" (quoted in Maurer and Martin 2012, 528). What is clear, is that such behavior is pervasive across both the private and state sectors in China; as Table 8.1 shows, almost all top "national champions" have entities incorporated in BVI and/or the Cayman Islands. Bankers and accountants interviewed did not want to comment on the issue and deferred to lawyers, while comments from the latter were limited. While the explanations suggested here are partly speculative, it is necessary to present them, given the centrality of such structures in the organization of China's national champions.

To start with, CM and many other entities in its corporate structure are incorporated in Hong Kong, due at least partly to the offshore character of the latter. Hong Kong is an attractive jurisdiction for domiciling financial vehicles due to its common law, enforced through an effective legal system, as well as its flexible regulation and relatively low tax levels, and freedom from any type of international capital controls. Mainland China offers none of these features. The question remains about the purpose of China Mobile Hong Kong Group, placed between China Mobile Communications Corporation and CM. The reason for its existence may be purely historical. In early 1997 China Mobile Hong Kong Group bought fixed-line operations in Hong Kong, but it was later decided that the listed company to be controlled by China Mobile Communications Corporation would only have a mobile license.

While Hong Kong offers some offshore benefits, the Cayman Islands and BVI are "more offshore" than Hong Kong, offering common law and political stability, but also secrecy (albeit weakening), and close to no taxation. The reason given for Aspire's domiciliation in the Cayman Islands was that it allowed a cheap potential listing of the joint venture in Hong Kong and the USA. The justification given for the existence of China Mobile BVI was that it helps CM avoid Hong Kong stamp duty charged on any potential transfer of ownership in shares. Any changes in the ownership of shares in CM attract stamp duty, but changes of ownership in China Mobile BVI, which indirectly change the ownership of CM, do not. Another possible explanation for China Mobile BVI is that it introduces a legal and symbolic distance between CM and China Mobile Communications Corporation and the Chinese government. According to Maurer and Martin (2012), Chinese companies in general view BVI as a fast, flexible, and cheap legal forum, which like the US state of Delaware, operates in relation to business matters primarily through the more convenient sphere of equity (i.e. judgements of "fairness") as opposed to common law. They paint a rather vivid picture of how this actually operates with respect to Chinese firms:

> Picture the courtroom scene. A row of four or five West Indian judges face the bar. Behind them, a slightly off-center framed picture of the Queen. At the bar, learned counsel in ribbons and robes (but no longer wigs) argue over the status of corporate entities whose names often confuse the judges, the audience, and even the lawyers themselves, since they are often identical save for a marker of the site of registration. In one sentence, there will be references to "Smith Co. BVI," "Smith Co. China," "Smith Co. Caymans," and so on.
>
> (Maurer and Martin 2012, 538)

The function ascribed to China Mobile Communications Ltd by interviewees has to do with regulation. As the direct owner of provincial companies, China Mobile Communications Ltd can enter into contracts with entities in China and abroad on behalf of provincial companies, without a long and uncertain process of seeking regulatory approval in Beijing. As also discussed in chapter 5, this highlights the way that OJs often play the role of helping governments to conditionally cut through their own "red tape" in certain situations, while still leaving regulation formally in place to apply to other situations where it may advance their goals. Similarly, although tax changes introduced in 2008 have now largely eliminated the tax benefits of FDI "round tripping," at the time these structures were established by CM, they might have afforded it tax advantages within the Mainland by giving its subsidiaries the status of "foreign invested" enterprises. Given that the Chinese government itself is CM's majority shareholder, this wouldn't really have constituted a strategy of offshore tax avoidance by CM itself, but rather—as was the case for the US treatment of its own firms' offshore structures in the 1950s (see chapter 5)—the use of the offshore system by the Chinese government to provide CM, as a national champion firm, with a de facto tax subsidy. Finally, as BVI entities do not publish any reports, they can potentially also serve as conduits for any transactions between CM and its ultimate controllers in Beijing, as well as its actual operations in the provinces. We may expect dividends to flow from CM, through the British Virgin Islands and Hong Kong entities to the SASAC. Information on how much flows upward, how much is retained at each level, and the value of funds flowing in the opposite direction, is not publicly available.

Overall, what is most interesting about these structures is how much resemblance they bear at a basic conceptual level, in terms of their apparent functional subtlety and normative ambiguity, to the securitization vehicles examined in chapter 6. The Chinese government and its national champions are, it seems, using the offshore world as (1) a cheap and flexible legal "toolbox" to construct—in literal sense, *on paper*—an institutional framework for engaging with the global economy that would be difficult to establish within the Mainland itself, and (2) a mechanism that allows China to selectively bypass its own regulations and taxes in situations when this is convenient, while still leaving them in place more broadly.

Ultimately, the key to the creation of these structures, whatever their purpose, was CM's relationship with FABS firms. All BVI entities in CM's structure use Linklaters and/or Sullivan & Cromwell as their law firms. In addition, CM pays a Hong Kong–based specialized offshore finance company for servicing these entities. Thus, FABS connect CM through Hong Kong to other OJs that are more offshore than Hong Kong itself.

Crucially, CM is anything but an anomaly in using such structures, but is rather an excellent representative of the broader picture of so-called foreign direct investment in and out of China. The British Virgin Islands represent the second largest source and destination of Mainland Chinese FDI (after Hong Kong), the second largest source of FDI into Hong Kong (after Mainland China), and the largest destination of FDI from Hong Kong. Thus, the three jurisdictions form the key triangle of Chinese FDI. The bulk of Chinese FDI is thus likely neither foreign nor direct, with the flows and stocks recorded as foreign direct investment rather largely being pure legal and accounting constructs that represent no real flows of investment, production, or service provision. At most, the FDI entering China through such structures can be considered to represent, in part, reclassified foreign (and particularly American) *portfolio* investment, picked up via offshore listing vehicles. The CM case thus underscores that China's FDI statistics have to be interpreted with even greater caution than is already the case for FDI statistics in general (see chapter 7).

8.7 China Mobile in Perspective

Th objective of this chapter was to study the creation and evolution of CM—one of China's "national champions," and one of the world's largest telecom companies—through the lens of the GFN framework, focusing on the role of FABS, FCs, OJs, and world governments (established and aspiring). This strategy was used to shed light on the globalization of the Chinese economy, a context in which the role of financial actors and practices has been understudied and rarely combined with the analysis of globalization.

The main finding of the chapter is that CM would never actually have existed at all, at least in any sort of recognizable form, without being plugged into the GFN— with Goldman Sachs, Hong Kong, and BVI playing the roles of lead FABS firm, leading FC, and leading offshore platform respectively. The depth of CM's articulation into the GFN may be surprising given that the company, although a giant in its industry, is essentially restricted in its operations to the Chinese domestic market. CM thus does not follow the typical model, whereby a mature company enters international financial markets as it internationalizes, to access additional capital. The GFN has rather assisted in the very conception of CM, as well as its domestic expansion.

While from an ideological standpoint, firms like Goldman Sachs and offshore jurisdictions like the British Virgin Islands may seem to be unlikely partners of the Chinese government and Communist Party, pragmatic considerations bring them together. By plugging CM and other national champions into the GFN, the Chinese government has "borrowed" institutions and expertise lacking in Mainland China, in order to modernize its strategic industries. This is in some respects a one-sided exchange, as the Chinese government limits the power of global financial markets over national champions, with foreign investors in companies like CM remaining only minority shareholders with no real corporate governance influence. However, even while ensuring that firms advance national policy objectives, state ownership and control are also a fundamental liability in the globalization of China's national champions. Indeed, although western FABS firms have helped to organize the Chinese state sector into giant companies that are globally significant in terms of size, when it comes to significance in foreign markets for products and services, these state-owned national champions have enjoyed relatively little success. China Mobile itself is connected to the global supply chains of telecom equipment, as well as global financial markets. However, it has struggled to break into markets outside of Mainland China. Limited operations in Pakistan are controlled by its parent company, while an attempt to expand into Taiwan, through the purchase of a 12% share in EasTone Telecoms Company, was blocked by the Taiwanese authorities. Other governments, more broadly, may leave their domestic telecoms sectors to private companies, but they still recognize the sector's strategic importance, and would find it difficult to approve a Mainland Chinese SOE's attempt to acquire significant stakes in the sector. Even trying to access global financial markets is becoming politically fraught for Mainland Chinese firms, whether state owned or private. In fact, in early 2021, all three of the major Chinese state-owned telecom firms, including China Mobile, were forced by the US to delist from the New York Stock Exchange, as part of a broader effort to limit the ability of strategically sensitive Chinese firms to tap the US capital market.

Looking more broadly, China can be described as sitting at a crossroads of historical structure and agency in terms of its relationship with the GFN. Ironically, trying to predict the implications of this relationship for China itself, politically and economically, is complicated by the sheer number of parallels that one can draw between China's current relationship with the GFN, and that of various other places at various points in history. First, as noted in chapter 2, there are significant historical similarities between China's contemporary relationship with the GFN, and the earlier relationships of the US and the UK with this system during their own periods of rapid industrialization. As noted by Lin and Milhaput (2013, 703) "China's present system of national champion capitalism bears some similarity to the US baron era: China's economy is dominated by large, politically connected conglomerates operating in a weak institutional environment without robust antitrust scrutiny." FABS, with Goldman Sachs in the lead, have helped the Chinese government consolidate the Chinese telecoms sector, just as investment banks such as JP Morgan were, with the help of their ties to London, the great consolidators of US infrastructure and industry in the late 19th and early 20th centuries (Geisst 1997). Furthermore, there are even deeper historical parallels between China today, and both the USA and the UK, if one goes back further. In the early to mid-19th century, it was above all American state and local *governments*, along with the parastatal banking and infrastructure corporations (railroads, canals, etc.) chartered by these governments, that were tapping the London capital market to support local economic development (Lively 1955; Roy 1999; see also chapter 4). These parastatal, and often partially or fully state-owned early 19th-century American banking and infrastructure corporations, plugged into the GFN, could be directly compared to contemporary Chinese national champions listed on foreign exchanges. Looking slightly earlier, one could also compare these Chinese firms to the massive parastatal trading and banking corporations set up by 18th-century mercantilist Britain, which were deeply connected to the Amsterdam securities market and Dutch (and Anglo-Dutch) merchant banks (see chapter 2).

One can also compare China's efforts to strategically harness its relationship with the GFN with more recent strategies by other governments. As discussed in chapter 5, there are particularly strong parallels between China's current strategic engagement with the GFN, and that of the USA in the decades after WWII. In both cases, one sees a government striving to reconcile a broad project of global economic integration, with the preservation of relatively tight domestic territorial economic controls and regulations, as well as broad domestic authority over monetary and financial policy levers. For China since 1978, like the USA in the 1950s–1970s, the offshore spaces of the GFN afford a particularly useful space of flexibility to try to reconcile these objectives. In addition to setting up national champions such as CM via elaborate offshore structures, a major element of this has been, as discussed in chapters 2 and 5, China's promotion of the offshore RMB market as a way of boosting the RMB's international reserve currency status without relaxing capital controls; a policy that has been more or less directly taken (even while being greatly refined and systematized) from the 1960s-era US handbook.

Arguably most interesting, however, are the historical parallels between China's relationship with the GFN since 1978, and the relationships that other socialist states constructed with the GFN a few decades earlier. In fact, the offshore Eurodollar market itself seems to have gotten its start, several years before American firms started to use it, largely as a "capitalist tool in socialist hands"—and specifically in the hands of the Soviet Union. The Soviets had initially gotten off on the wrong foot with the international financial system after the Russian Revolution, when they repudiated the enormous debts that the tsars had taken out in the London and Paris markets. However, the economy of the USSR, even as it became progressively more bureaucratized internally, was from the outset dependent externally on its trading relationships with the capitalist world. Indeed, as described by Sanchez-Sibony (2014, 291) "the Soviet Union had a level of [so-called] 'autarky' comparable to that of Japan" in the decades from WWII to the 1980s, if one judges this by the share of trade in its GDP.

Integration into trade, and in many cases also foreign investment flows, made it necessary for the USSR to also remain integrated into the global financial system. To facilitate this, the tsarist-era connections with London and Paris were maintained: in the case of London by continuing to make use of the existing state-owned Moscow Narodny Bank founded by the tsars, and in the case of Paris by purchasing the Banque Commerciale pour l'Europe du Nord founded (ironically) by wealthy Russian emigrees (CIA 1969). As its political relationship with the US deteriorated after WWII, the USSR found itself confronting a dilemma in relation to the now dollar-dominated international trading and financial system; with the threat looming of a US expropriation or asset freeze of the dollar reserves that the USSR had deposited in American banks. To avert this, its dollar reserves were moved, in the late 1940s, to the Moscow Narodny Bank and Banque Commerciale pour l'Europe du Nord in London and Paris, who in turn did business with various western financial institutions in these cities, and in particular with British merchant banks. There is some debate as to whether the first "true" offshore Eurodollar market loan should be considered to be one made by the Moscow Narodny Bank in London in February 1957, with the assistance of a British merchant bank (see debate on Eurodollar market origins in Burn 1999 and Shaxson 2011). However, the *term* Eurodollar does seem to have been coined in reference to the Soviet Banque Commerciale pour l'Europe du Nord in Paris, whose loans were referred to as "Eurbank dollars," which was eventually shortened to Eurodollars (Dach 1967; Farber 1981).

As Soviet international economic integration deepened, the internationalization of its banks within the GFN also expanded, above all within the major offshore Eurodollar centers. In the 1970s, Moscow Narodny began to jointly underwrite the Eurodollar bond issues of Eastern Bloc governments as part of multinational bank syndicates, beginning with the underwriting with the National Westminster Bank and Morgan Grenfell of a Hungarian Eurobond issue in 1971 (Wilczynski 1976). Meanwhile, Moscow Narodny's Singapore branch became, in the 1970s, a particularly important offshore platform for the bank outside of London. Indeed,

Moscow Narodny actually seems to have played a relatively important role in the initial development of Singapore as a Eurodollar banking center. Some intriguing details of the Soviet Union's financial adventures and misadventures in Southeast Asia are provided by a 1976 *New York Times* special report, which observes that:

> Within two years of its chartering [in Singapore] in 1971 as a "restricted bank" that restricts it only from accepting deposits of less than $100,000, Moscow Narodny has grown to one of the largest banks in Singapore with nearly $600 million in loans.
>
> Most of this capital was funds channeled from Moscow Narodny in London (it is still officially listed as a British Bank by the Monetary Authority of Singapore) and a year later it also had more net loans and advances outstanding than any other Singapore bank, though Citibank, which opened here in 1902, was a close second.
>
> By this time, however, Moscow Narodny was already in trouble both in its Singapore home and in Malaysia and Hong Kong as well.
>
> Shortly after it opened its doors here, Moscow Narodny's new Russian managers went to Singapore's second largest onshore bank, the United Overseas Bank, and lured away its assistant general manager, Mr. Teo. who had previously worked for the Bank of America, and gave him to all outward appearances a virtually unfettered hand in all of its lending operations.
>
> Using its initial capital structure of three million Singapore dollars ($1.2 million in United States currency), Mr. Teo began making a number of loans to his former accounts from United Overseas Bank and a broad range of new enterprises as well—chiefly in the highly speculative areas of property holdings and commodities in Malaysia, Hong Kong and Indonesia.
>
> ...The most spectacular of these was the bank's heavy involvement in the financial troubles of the Mosbert group whose head, Amos Dawe, had now disappeared leaving behind him a string of failing corporations, landholdings and banks.
>
> ...what particularly disturbed the Monetary Authority of Singapore, which is reportedly in the midst of a major investigation of the bank's entire accounting procedures, as well as financial and Government officials in Hong Kong and Kuala Lumpur, was the way in which the bank's funds were channeled through an intricate set of subsidiaries to Mosbert Enterprises in a number of countries—particularly Hong Kong and Malaysia.
>
> Malaysia, it seems, does not allow foreign state-owned banks to operate there, and Hong Kong, with its sensitive proximity to China, was nervous as well...In particular, Malaysia was concerned that in the Mosbert collapse, Moscow Narodny, which had some $60 million in loans outstanding to the $800 million conglomerate, would acquire substantial property in Malaysia.
>
> (Andelman 1976)

260 of STICKY POWER

There are various ways to read this fascinating tale, all of which are relevant to contemporary China. The author of the article, for his part, seems to have assumed that grand strategic machinations permeated every level of Soviet financial operations—even when these plots apparently involved losing large amounts of money. An alternative reading would be that the Soviets were, in this case, perhaps being taken for a ride by their own bank's local Singaporean managers and their associates. Ultimately, however, what really stands out is that the aspiring leader of world communist revolution had somehow managed to stumble into the topsy-turvy position of not only helping to prop up the US dollar as the leading international reserve currency, but also actively helping Britain to reproduce its offshore financial "second empire"—not just in London, but globally across Britain's postcolonial offshore jurisdictional network. Indeed, one could go so far as to say that the international financial relational stage had already been set, by the 1970s, for the vast sponging up of privatized Soviet state wealth by London and its various offshore outposts (Cyprus, etc.) that occurred after the fall of communism in the 1990s—which itself to a large extent just represented the latest reinvention of relationships that predated the USSR. The first tsarist, then Soviet, and then Russian federal state–owned Moscow Narodny Bank itself survived until 2005, when it was absorbed by another Russian state–controlled bank, VTB Bank. This is itself listed, like many other leading post-Soviet Russian business groups, on the London Stock Exchange.

This deep historical continuity in the reproduction of international financial institutions and relationships themselves, even through truly colossal historical political and economic upheavals—including the overthrowing of capitalism itself—is no less evident in the story of China's integration into the GFN, both in relation to China Mobile, and more broadly. As described in chapter 2, this story is not normatively neutral or even primarily economic in nature. It is rather one that arose out of the trauma of 19th-century European invasion. This catalyzed a restructuring of the Chinese political and institutional economic space around the central axis of the treaty ports of Hong Kong and Shanghai, which quickly established themselves as a dominant "onshore–offshore" financial center dyad (with Hong Kong in legal–jurisdictional terms a "more offshore" treaty port than Shanghai; see chapter 2). Importantly, however, the centrality of these European colonial offshore jurisdictions within the Chinese economy was not just something that developed from the "outside-in" from a Chinese standpoint. Rather, these places were themselves progressively colonized by Chinese business and money, which consolidated itself and internationalized around a framework established by the British Empire, and ultimately around even older Chinese regional business networks. Indeed, by the early 20th century, one of the key roles of the Hong Kong–Shanghai axis, centered on the relationship between HSBC and the Shanghai Stock Exchange (both, as noted in chapter 2, technically incorporated in Hong Kong) seems to have become the Chinese financing of businesses elsewhere in the British Empire in

Asia. Of particular importance, in this respect, were HSBC-underwritten Shanghai exchange IPOs by Chinese investor-backed rubber agribusinesses operating in British Malaya; itself located within the sphere of China's commercial relationships for centuries. In 1910, these Shanghai-listed and HSBC-underwritten Sino-British imperial rubber enterprises became the epicenter of what appears to have been China's first stock market bubble—which drew in speculators from various Chinese commercial centers such as Ningbo—as well as a subsequent stock market crash and financial crisis. This seems to have itself been an outgrowth of a slightly earlier London boom in colonial rubber agribusiness IPOs (Thomas 1998).

China's international economic relationships, like Russia's, were severely disrupted in the early and mid-20th century by war and revolution. However, the Chinese government under Mao, like the USSR, seems to have made use of the offshore Eurodollar market for its international banking needs (Burn 1999; Farber 1981). Moreover, the radical Maoist experiment was over relatively quickly, with the period from the beginning of the Great Leap Forward in 1958 to Mao's death in 1976 only spanning eighteen years. This was short enough that many of the same people who had been involved in private business as late as the 1950s were able to play an important role in the restoration of the market economy from the late 1970s. Within the Mainland, the most prominent such figure was the famous "red capitalist" Rong Yiren. Rong had decided to stay in the Mainland and endorse Mao during the postrevolutionary period when most business leaders were fleeing to Taiwan or Hong Kong, and was allowed to maintain effective control of his family business group for a time in the 1950s. After being politically purged during the upheavals of the Great Leap Forward and Cultural Revolution, he was rehabilitated and placed in charge of a newly created state-owned conglomerate, CITIC, by Deng Xiaoping in 1979, and was eventually made vicepresident of China between 1993 and 1998. CITIC, with its mixture of state and private ownership, and its listed arm in Hong Kong and sprawling networks of offshore subsidiaries, was in some respects the prototype for the sort of GFN-oriented state-owned multinationals represented by China Mobile. Aside from acting as a de facto fiefdom of Rong and his family, whom it turned into multibillionaires, CITIC played a key national strategic role in helping local governments in China to tap into global financial markets to support local development; being designated, in 1989, one of the "Big Ten Funding Windows" for borrowing abroad (Clifford and Barnathan 1998; Jun 1999). Ironically, in the context of the CM case study, our interview partners in China sometimes referred to CITIC as China's Goldman Sachs.

Ultimately, then, what appears to be more certain than the implications of China's relationship with the GFN for the trajectory of China's development and place in the world, is the perpetuation of this relationship itself. China will either colonize, or be colonized by the GFN—or more likely both at the same time—but it is exceedingly unlikely to disentangle itself from this system. Importantly, what this also means is that the core institutional and relational structures within the GFN itself are also more likely than not to continue to perpetuate themselves over deep historical timescales, even if inevitably being modified and expanded in various ways by China's entry into them. Regardless of China's success at elevating the RMB to the center of the global monetary system, for example, what one can say is that the way that this strategy has been pursued so far has been centrally mediated though the structures of Britain's offshore "second empire." Measured by total payments, Hong Kong currently takes the lead as an RMB center with a 75% market share, followed by London (6.4% UK share) and Singapore (3.7%; SWIFT 2020). Meanwhile, London itself is by far the most important market for RMB FX spot transactions, wherein the UK holds a 38% worldwide market share—significantly ahead of Mainland China itself, which only has a 15% share of worldwide FX spot transactions in its own currency (rising to 24% if Hong Kong is included; SWIFT 2020).

Looking at China Mobile, China's "national champion"-building has nurtured the global financial centers of London (through Linklaters), and even more so New York (through Goldman Sachs, the New York Stock Exchange, and Sullivan & Cromwell). Shanghai, meanwhile, has been largely cut out of the loop, with the emerging financial axis within China, in this context, running directly from the center of political power in Beijing to the postcolonial financial hub and "midshore" platform of Hong Kong. This in turn acts as the primary go-between linking Mainland China to international financial markets, and Beijing to the NY–LON axis in particular. Beijing as well as Shanghai may in the future more directly challenge Hong Kong's role as a financial center. However, Hong Kong's pervasively entrenched, multidimensional role in structuring the institutional fabric of the Mainland economy itself, will make its conjoined position as not only a financial market center, but also a legal and regulatory hub, very difficult to overturn— if nothing else at the level of path-dependent legacy standards and relationships, even if the parameters of "one country, two systems" are progressively eroded.

To be sure, and as illustrated by current events, Hong Kong's positioning between Beijing and New York–London is risky even while being profitable, as Hong Kong functions above all as a *reputational* intermediary for the Chinese corporate sector, with China's national champions in the lead. At one level, the Hong Kong and New York listings and Hong Kong audits of CM open the company to public oversight, bringing into light, for example, the existence of offshore entities within its structure. Beijing-controlled China Mobile Communications Corporation, however, as well as the functions of CM's BVI and other offshore entities, remain a black box for the public. For the time being, foreign investors may trust the FABS providers involved and Hong Kong, but given the prevailing opacity, the foundations of this trust are fragile. Equally important, moreover, is not simply investor trust, but the international political trust that underpins the internationalization of these firms at a deeper level. This has now, in effect, broken down altogether in the context of the recent US termination of China Mobile's New York listing, in what is likely to be merely a harbinger of additional frictions to come.

Crucially, however, as illustrated by the case of the USSR after WWII, not to mention the dire political relationship between the USA and the UK throughout most of the 19th century, we have in some sense been here before, in a historical sense. Other countries have, in other words, had far worse political falling outs with one another than that between the USA and the China at present, that cut across and disrupt the connections of the GFN, and in many cases lead to outright war (including between the USA and UK), without doing much, if any damage to the organization of the network from the standpoint of a longer historical timescale. Indeed, on such a long-term historical timescale, what most often appears to triumph—not least as exhibited in the USSR—is the power of money itself as a social relation, whose creation, ultimately, is deeply embedded within the institutional and relational framework of the GFN, thus providing the basic source of this network's durable power.

In this respect, we should ask, in particular, about the impact of foreign FABS firms, and engagement with the GFN broadly, on the internal practices of Chinese firms. By equipping the executives of Chinese SOEs with stocks and stock options, for example, they have nurtured a class of more independent managers. By 2008, CM's executives cashed in options worth $1.5bn (McGregor 2010). This was against the recommendation of the Communist Party of China, but it seems that people involved preferred money to promotion in party ranks. This is a reminder that even without significant foreign ownership, financial practices driven by FABS firms, in conjunction with the raging financial "animal spirits" endemic within China itself, may produce results unwelcome to or uncontrollable by the Chinese government. In fact, in 2011, one of China Mobile's top executives was given a suspended death sentence for taking bribes, suggesting that the company has also not escaped the problem of corruption endemic to the Chinese corporate sector (McGregor 2010). While the ongoing anti-corruption drive has clearly created a general climate of fear throughout government agencies that may have reduced such behavior by SOE managers, it is unclear how long such an initiative can be politically sustained. State power, as we have shown throughout this book, is absolutely integral to the whole constitution of global finance. Property itself, however, more or less "wants" to be private, and over the long run it is difficult to not give it what it wants.

9

Asset Management as a Digital Platform Industry

A Global Financial Network Perspective

9.1 Introduction

From the invention of writing, to Nathan Rothschild's apocryphal carrier pigeons, the financial sector has always been a precocious adopter of information and communications technology. In 1837, one French deputy declared that "I have never seen telegraphic lines established by private persons with good intentions"; they serve to "establish a brigandage, so as to rob those who do not have news of the Paris Bourse" (Flichy 1993). However, there is a growing sense of a new era of technological disruption in finance, with two narratives now particularly prominent. The first is disruptive automation; one study suggests that 23% of financial analyst, and 58% of financial adviser jobs may be lost in the near future (Frey and Osborne 2017). The second is disruptive decentralization, with three notable subcomponents. First, at the firm level, incumbent giants are expected to be brought down by swarms of innovative FinTech start-ups (Arner et al., 2016). Meanwhile, geographically, incumbent financial centers (e.g. Wall Street) will be hollowed out by competition with upstart, tech-savvy locales (Tett 2018). Finally, with respect to governance, regulators will be outflanked by the institutions of Web 3.0—e.g. decentralized blockchain ledgers (*Economist* 2018a; Swan 2015).

In general, these narratives are uncannily reminiscent of the utopian (or dystopian) predictions of the early days of the internet; or in the case of automation, more longstanding predictions about the obsolescence of work. As noted by the *Economist* (2018b), the internet has not only failed to bear out early predictions of a decentralized, libertarian "flat world," but has largely led to the opposite outcome, wherein a growing number of industries are controlled by massive monopolistic firms, which are based in a handful of elite locations, serve as agents of unprecedentedly pervasive regimes of state surveillance and control, and have catalyzed an explosion of low paid menial work in the "gig" economy.

At the center of this paradox is a business model dubbed the "digital platform economy" (Evans and Gawer 2016; Kenney and Zysman 2016; Langley and

Sticky Power. Daniel Haberly and Dariusz Wòjcik, Oxford University Press.
© Daniel Haberly and Dariusz Wòjcik (2022). DOI: 10.1093/oso/9780198870982.003.0009

Leyshon 2017). Notably, for all of the analyses of the impact of new technologies in finance, and of the digital platform economy outside of finance, there has not been a systematic evaluation of the impact of the digital platform model on asset management. Here we fill this gap, by (1) building an expanded version of the GFN framework for conceptualizing the organizational and geographic logic of the digital platform economy in finance, and (2) examining the deepening impact of the digital platform model on asset management.

As we will show, asset management is being profoundly disrupted by the rise of what we dub digital asset management platforms—or DAMPs—which encompass a vertically integrated set of services ranging from index fund and ETF provision, to robo-advising, to third-party analytics and trading support. Like other digital platforms, DAMPs do not so much leverage technology to enhance their competitiveness within markets, as to radically restructure the market itself. Moreover, as for other platforms, their rise has been associated with a paradox of centralization through democratization, wherein reductions in customer costs are counterintuitively coupled to oligopoly or monopoly. However, we also show that the peculiar characteristics of the financial sector—and above all, the extent to which it *already resembles* the digital platform economy—have led to differences in the logic and implications of the rise of DAMPs, in comparison to other industries. In particular, DAMPs (1) have tended to asymmetrically disrupt different dimensions of market efficiency,[1] (2) are generally less suited to regulatory arbitrage than other tools already at the disposal of financial firms, and (3) have mostly reinforced rather than challenged the position of incumbent asset management firms and centers.

The remainder of this chapter is divided into eight sections. In section 9.2 we review the digital platform economy, before examining in section 9.3 how its logic interacts with the unique characteristics of the financial sector. From a geographic standpoint, we outline an expanded version of the GFN framework that is tailored toward a problematization of the deepening impact of information technology on finance. Next, in section 9.4, we examine the business models of the most important DAMPs, before demonstrating, in section 9.5, how these have produced a classic digital platform paradox of centralization through democratization. In sections 9.6–9.8, we probe the geographic dimensions of the rise of DAMPs, before concluding with a discussion of the broader implications of this business model for asset management and finance.

9.2 The Digital Platform Economy

There is a growing awareness that the information age economy is dominated by a specific organizational form, dubbed the "digital platform economy" (Evans and Gawer 2016; Kenney and Zysman 2016; Langley and Leyshon 2017). The digital

---

[1] Specifically "information-arbitrage," "fundamental valuation," and "functional" efficiency (Tobin, 1984).

platform economy can be conceptualized as a collection of technology-enabled hub-and-spokes business models, wherein a platform-providing lead firm coordinates the activities of platform users. As noted by Evans and Gawer (2016), there are two basic types of digital platform. The first (e.g. operating systems) establish a core of tools and standards that serve as a foundation for third-party software or content. Meanwhile, the second establishes a marketplace wherein various categories of user transact with one another, and/or the platform provider itself.

The line between these platform types is blurry. Broadly speaking, however, it is the second that has been associated with the disruption of traditionally non-ICT-centered industries, including advertising, taxi service, accommodation, and retail. This disruption generally follows a stereotyped pattern, wherein the cost of a good or service is dramatically reduced through some mixture of both technology-enabled efficiency enhancement, and technology-enabled organizational arbitrage.

First, the disruptive potential of platforms typically stems from their enhancement of market "efficiency," such that incumbent intermediaries or participants are rendered obsolete (Langley and Leyshon 2017).[2] Platforms typically boost multiple dimensions of efficiency in a complementary manner (Edelman and Geradin 2015), with an emphasis on "allocative efficiency"—i.e. setting prices at a market-clearing rate with respect to supply and demand—"informational efficiency"—i.e. the extent to which prices reflect informed assessments and expectations of the past, present, and future—and finally what Tobin (1984) dubs market "functional efficiency"—i.e. the overhead costs of the pricing process compared to the socioeconomic value it provides. At the center of the enhancement of all three, for most platforms, are "big-data"-fed analytics. In online advertising for example, this entails analyzing user data to determine exactly how much a user's clicks/views are worth to whom in any given context, thus ensuring optimal advertising spending allocation. Automation of the whole process drives costs to the lowest possible level. Also important to market efficiency enhancement, for many platforms, is intensified producer competition enabled by reduced market entry barriers. Ride-sharing services, for example, optimize supply–demand matching not only by calculating exactly how much rides should cost in a particular time and place (e.g. "surge pricing"), but by enabling individuals to become drivers (Edelman and Geradin 2015).

Platforms nearly always provide some genuine technology-enabled market "efficiency" enhancement. However, platform competitiveness also typically rests, at least partially, on technology-enabled organizational arbitrage; usually made possible by the control that platform providers gain over markets in the process

---

[2] According to Langley and Leyson (2017), "The underlying intermediary logic of the platform is that it solves coordination problems in market exchange by extending the distance-shrinking networking capacities of the internet."

of enhancing their efficiency (Edelman and Geradin, 2015; Langley and Leyshon 2017). Most importantly, providers are typically able to externalize various costs to users. Often, this is done by harvesting users' "digital labor" (or "digital exhaust") (Fumagalli 2018; Neef 2014). In other cases (e.g. the "gig" economy), platform providers serve as brokers coordinating the delivery of paid services, meaning that customer income cannot simply be pocketed without compensating producers. Even here, however, providers typically externalize the largest possible component of costs—usually by leveraging platform control to blur the boundary between market and hierarchical coordination (e.g. reclassifying employment-like relations as subcontracting). This often entails a business model predicated on arbitraging labor and other regulations, with the spread of digital platforms thus a legally and politically contentious process (Davies et al. 2017; Edelman and Geradin 2015).

Taken as a whole, digital platforms have pushed the information economy in counterintuitive directions—particularly when viewed against the rather utopian predictions of the early internet era. On the one hand, their rise has intensified the paradox noted by Lessig (2006), wherein the very features of cyberspace that make it resistant to state regulatory authority—namely its organizational and geographic slipperiness—have encouraged the emergence of countervailing "sovereigns of everywhere," with an increasingly pervasive and intrusive reach. Meanwhile, even more striking is what can be dubbed the digital platform paradox of centralization through democratization (Acquier et al. 2017; Langley and Leyshon 2017). Platforms are democratizing insofar as they offer reduced costs and increased convenience for customers, and/or lower entry barriers for producers. However, they also create new privately controlled market choke points, with a "winner-take-all" concentration of market share at the level of platform providers typically fostered by powerful interlocking increasing returns (*Economist* 2018c). First are "network effects" wherein new users further enhance platform attractiveness to other users. Second are data-based returns to scale, wherein "More information lets firms develop better services, which attracts more users, which in turn generate more data" (*Economist* 2018d). Third are conventional scale economies stemming from the predominantly fixed cost structure of platforms (itself often a product of how providers can pick and choose which costs to internalize versus externalize to users). Crucially, the paradox of centralization through democratization also operates geographically, with the "superstar effect" in knowledge-driven industries more often exacerbating regional inequalities than creating an ICT-enabled level competitive playing field (Davies et al. 2017; Quah 1996).

9.3 Finance as a Digital Platform Industry: A Global Financial Network Perspective

Our argument is that technological disruption in finance is increasingly converging on the digital platform model. However, finance has unusual characteristics that have caused this to occur in a different manner from other industries. Ironically, these differences stem from the extent to which two key features of the digital platform economy have always been central to finance; namely its informational intensity, and its regulatory and organizational fluidity.

First, harnessing the power of big data to maximize market efficiency is more evolutionary than revolutionary in finance. Indeed, gathering and processing market information has always been the industry's lifeblood (Wójcik 2011a). From the standpoint of digital platform development, what is most important is that the financial sector's massive existing apparatus of information gathering and processing has, as noted by Tobin (1984), long produced a sharply asymmetrical development of different aspects of market efficiency—particularly in the securities market. First, from an informational standpoint, financial markets tend to be characterized by much higher "information arbitrage efficiency" than "fundamental valuation efficiency." "Information arbitrage efficiency" is high in the sense that the market is so overcrowded with investors seeking to identify and exploit opportunities for pricing arbitrage, that it becomes difficult for anyone to consistently outsmart the market consensus. However, this does not mean that the consensus itself is particularly good at anticipating and pricing future events—as evidenced by volatility levels far in excess of changes in underlying fundamentals (Shiller 2003; Tobin 1984). Indeed, the same liquidity that enables "information arbitrage efficiency" may undermine "fundamental valuation efficiency" by facilitating speculative manias and other pathologies.

Also very low, Tobin argues, is the "functional efficiency" of financial markets, as defined by the extent to which their operational costs (salaries, profits, etc.) are justified by the services they perform. From Tobin's standpoint, the key question is value to society. However, finance's "functional efficiency" is arguably also quite low for market participants. Indeed, as for fundamental valuation efficiency, low functional efficiency appears to be a counterintuitive corollary of high information arbitrage efficiency, as the same overcrowding of securities markets that allows for information to be rapidly incorporated into prices undermines the ability of participants to make money (see section 9.4). There is overwhelming evidence that nearly all fund managers underperform market average indices once operational costs are deducted (Malkiel 2013).

Taken as a whole, these disconnects between different aspects of financial market "efficiency" imply that the conventional digital platform pattern of disrupting industries by simultaneously boosting all aspects of market efficiency, in a complementary manner, is unlikely to find much purchase in finance. Rather, platforms are likely to operate asymmetrically on different aspects of efficiency.

Just as striking as the parallels between the informational intensity of the digital platform economy, and finance as traditionally structured, are their parallel organizational and geographic fluidity. The activities of financial firms, like digital platform providers, are enormously consequential for the "real" economy. However, the products directly provided by both are mostly constituted, in a literal sense, of abstract textual and numerical "code." Of primary importance in finance are private contracts (Haberly and Wójcik 2017a; Knuth and Potts 2015; Pistor 2013; 2019). Like software, these contracts can, at least in common law-based systems, be crafted in almost unlimited innovative ways so long as they remain within the bounds of public law and regulation—which are themselves mutable via choice of jurisdictional arena and political lobbying. The result is a deep structural commonality between the dialectics of legal–regulatory innovation/avoidance/mobility, and state regulatory response, in finance and cyberspace (Ferri and Minsky 1992; Lessig 2006)—however a commonality in which Silicon Valley, for all of its recent controversies, is an amateur when compared to Wall Street or the City. The question this raises is whether the emergence of a new financial technological architecture will have any impact at all on the basic logic of this dialectic of regulatory avoidance and reaction in finance, or simply define a new chapter in an old story.

Crucially, none of these questions can be addressed in a geographic vacuum. As financial geographers have long observed, the informational efficiency of financial markets must be generated by the human and material apparatus of financial centers (Cook et al. 2007; Wójcik 2011a; Zook and Grote 2017). The key question is how the "old" human-relational informational geography of finance will interact with its increasingly important "new" virtual informational geography—and just as importantly, the geography of behind-the-scenes technicians who craft its algorithms. Similarly, geographers (e.g. Coe et al. 2014; Haberly and Wójcik 2017a; Knuth and Potts 2016; Roberts 1994) have long emphasized that the abstract legal–regulatory dimension of finance must be structured through real places—even if only law offices housing the documentation of "brass plate" companies. In this respect, the key question is how this "paper" geography of finance will interact with the growing importance of its "virtual" geography.

Addressing these questions requires an analytical framework that conceptualizes the evolution of financial geographies in terms of the intersection between multiple, qualitatively different geographic logics, rather than simply a single overarching logic of financial center agglomeration. The outline of such an approach is provided by the GFN framework, which conceptualizes the geography of finance in terms of a multidimensional logic of financial center specialization across different functional spheres. The basic version of the GFN framework, however, only problematizes two types of financial center—namely offshore jurisdictions and substantive financial centers—whose respective roles have in many respects not fundamentally changed for centuries, and thus do not necessarily capture all of the nuanced geographic impacts of new technologies. In Figure 9.1, we outline an expanded GFN framework for conceptualizing the geographic evolution of FinTech specifically, that problematizes financial geographies in terms of the *four*-pronged interactions between what we dub the "relational," "virtual," "technical," and "paper" geographies of finance. Each sphere has its own logic of centripetal and

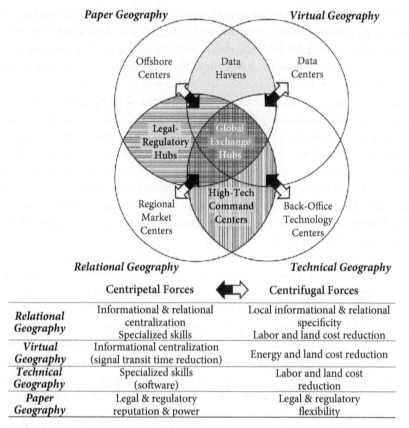

Fig. 9.1 Multiple geographies of financial centers in an expanded GFN framework

Source: authors; adapted from Haberly et al. (2019).

centrifugal processes—both internally and in relation to other spheres—which are seen as combining to condition the role and formation of particular financial centers.

Implicit in this framework is the potential for a technology-enabled centrifugal unbundling of the geography of finance. In the most extreme scenario, incumbent global financial market clearinghouses and command centers might be rendered obsolete by the rise of four-pronged decentralized networks. In these networks, the core market information processing functions of finance would increasingly be performed by computerized data centers located wherever land and energy are cheapest (see Jaeger et al. 2009). Meanwhile, human labor would increasingly be bifurcated between back-office technical and front-office client relational roles. In theory, neither need be located near each other, nor near data centers. Technical jobs might gravitate toward "back-office technology centers," with Silicon

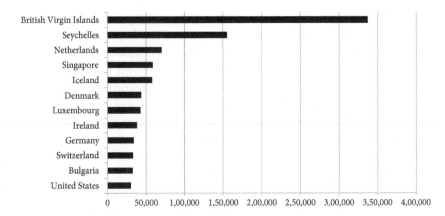

Fig. 9.2 Servers per million inhabitants, 2017
Source: World Bank; adapted from Haberly et al. (2019).

Valley (and its international low-wage offshoots) perhaps eating the bulk of financial industry employment and value. Meanwhile, the remaining relational roles in finance might be dispersed to "regional market centers" embedded within locally specific bodies of knowledge and relationships (see Dixon and Monk 2014).

Finally, the "paper" organization of financial vehicles and contracts need not correspond to any of these three layers, but rather might reside in an offshore network offering maximum legal and regulatory flexibility. As financial activity becomes increasingly "virtual," onshore jurisdictional connecting factors might be severed by financial "data havens"—i.e. offshore jurisdictions which attract electronic transactions and record-keeping (Jaeger et al. 2009). As shown in Figure 9.2, the British Virgin Islands and Seychelles already have far more servers per capita than any other countries/jurisdictions. Several offshore jurisdictions are jostling to become cryptocurrency hubs (Kahn 2015).

Some elements of this scenario of technologically driven financial geographic unbundling are clearly unfolding. However, there is reason to believe that it is unlikely to progress to extremity, due to the operation of countervailing centripetal forces both within and between each of the four functional spheres in Figure 9.1. First, the "virtual" geography of financial market information processing is less unmoored from the traditional "relational" geography of financial centers than might be expected (Wójcik 2011a; Zook and Grote 2017). For trading, the information technology-enabled acceleration of transaction pace has more than canceled out any communications technology-enabled compression of distance, with trader servers clustering near securities exchanges to gain a fleeting advantage in signal travel time. From both a human and machine standpoint, these locations—which we dub "global exchange hubs" in Figure 9.1—remain the leading global financial command centers. For the most part, these are the same places that have long been dominant in this respect (e.g. New York, London). Indeed, as detailed by Wójcik (2011a), technology has overwhelmingly promoted a further concentration of securities market activity—both human and electronic—in already dominant centers. To the extent that spatial diffusion occurs, it appears to be largely within these exchange hubs, with activities sprawling outward from traditional financial districts into ever-larger global financial city-regions (e.g. Mahwah, NJ and Stamford, CT are respectively the centers of exchange/trader servers and hedge fund management for New York).

Meanwhile, as we discussed in chapters 5–7, the space for an unbundling of the "paper" offshore legal–regulatory geography of finance from the "real" geography of financial centers is actually narrowing. Decades of efforts to combat offshore tax and regulatory arbitrage by expanding the extraterritorial jurisdiction of onshore states have increasingly forced offshore centers to operate with one (or both) feet inside of onshore regulatory frameworks (Haberly and Wójcik 2017a; Roberts 1994). In the most extreme case, the Chinese government has, as described in chapters 5 and 8, directly undertaken the construction and operation of offshore state-owned enterprise listing and RMB trading facilities (Hall 2017b; Wójcik and Camilleri 2015). More broadly, for prudential regulation, the Basel framework has, as we discuss in chapters 5 and 6, tackled Euromarket arbitrage by assigning global supervision of multinational banks to the home states where they are headquartered (D'Hulster 2012). Meanwhile, securities regulatory jurisdiction (particularly for the USA) is increasingly defined substantively based on to and by whom and where securities are promoted, traded, and sold, with paper vehicle domicile of decreasing relevance (see chapter 6 and Chang 2003). Finally, political pressure on tax havens has prompted firms to seek plausible deniability by using larger (e.g. OECD) havens (see chapter 7 and *Economist* 2013a). As shown in Figure 9.1, the paper geography of finance thus remains anchored by what can be dubbed "legal–regulatory hubs" located within the dominant traditional financial centers—and above all the leading "global exchange hubs." This is not just a public regulatory issue, but also entangled with the role of these centers as hubs for private contractual law, wherein jurisdictional reputation and accumulated legal precedent are of paramount importance. Indeed, as discussed in chapter 2, the most influential legal frameworks (e.g. New York) provide the basis for global financial law export industries (Knuth and Potts 2015).

Finally, the "technical" and "relational" geographies of finance are entangled with both one another and the "paper" geography of finance. Regardless of whether humans are removed from directly performing activities (e.g. stock-picking), the technical side of finance must be embedded in higher-order sector-specific skills and strategy, responsive to a rapidly changing competitive landscape. It is unclear whether "back-office technology-centers" can, regardless of software expertise, compete with established financial centers in these respects. Particularly notable is that financial innovation must, regardless of technological content, involve "paper" contractual innovation requiring a deep expertise in relevant areas of law and regulation (see Haberly and Wójcik 2017a). This entails not only familiarity with current regulation, but also expertise and investment in the type of sustained political engagement necessary to shape regulation. Notably, most of the largest Silicon Valley firms, including Google and Amazon, have so far been deterred from entering financial services by the unfamiliar and high-risk regulatory complexities this would entail (Willmer and Kumar 2017). While Facebook is now braving these waters with its Libra cryptocurrency project, it appears to be doing a remarkably poor job of navigating their regulatory and political dimensions (see conclusion)—particularly if one compares it to, for example, the political adeptness of Wall Street investment banks at promoting financial innovation prior to the global financial crisis (see chapter 3). Meanwhile, the burgeoning scale of New York's FinTech industry underscores the capacity for the largest financial legal–regulatory and exchange hubs to become centers of finance-specific software expertise (Gach and Gotsch 2016).

In the remainder of this chapter, we put the pieces from the previous two sections together to examine the deepening technological disruption of asset management. As we show, this disruption closely follows the pattern seen in other sectors insofar as it exhibits both (1) a digital platform model of undercutting incumbent cost structures by boosting various aspects of market efficiency, and (2) the associated digital platform economy paradox of centralization through democratization. However, the factors outlined in this section have also resulted in notable divergences of the pattern of technological disruption from that seen in nonfinancial sectors.

9.4 The Rise of Digital Asset Management Platforms (DAMPs)

Asset management is in many respects a natural fit for the digital platform economy insofar as managers do not intermediate funds through their own balance sheets, but rather act as matchmakers between securities issuers and investors. Until recently, however, this commonality with the platform economy model has been overshadowed by a paradigm of asset manager competition that is in other respects the digital platform model's antithesis. Rather than acting as low-cost, transparent conduits between investors and the securities market, this has entailed managers charging high fees to cover high costs—particularly highly paid labor—incurred in an attempt to beat the returns of their peers (Bernstein 2005; Malkiel 2013). Moreover, while investment banks (together with other traditional FABS firms) have in many respects always played a classic market "platform" role — by acting as matchmakers that reduce securities market transaction costs by leveraging their informational and relational centrality — they mostly concentrate and retain the resulting rents in the form of inflated profits and payrolls, rather than returning them to other market participants in the form of reduced overheads and fees (see chapter 3).

The growing computational intensity of asset management has not necessarily challenged the securities industry's traditional cost-gouging business model. "Quant" hedge funds, for example, essentially just substitute high-cost superstar algorithms for high-cost superstar stock-pickers. In terms of the sheer amount of money involved, however, this computerized replication of the traditional high-cost fund management model has increasingly been overshadowed by the rise of what we dub "digital asset management platforms" (DAMPs). Rather than using technology to gain a competitive edge within the securities market, DAMPs fundamentally restructure the market itself, generating enormous cost savings for investors, and radically disrupting incumbent business models.

As shown in Figure 9.3, there are four key types of DAMP. Oldest are index (passive) funds, which are very simple algorithmic funds that minimize investor fees by simply "buying the market." These funds piggyback on the high preexisting information arbitrage efficiency of securities markets to dramatically enhance market functional efficiency. Exchange traded funds (ETFs) are a subset of index funds which further enhance functional efficiency by restructuring the fund management process as a two-sided market platform. Lying between fund managers and the securities market—and blurring the boundary between managers and the market itself—are "asset manager support platforms." These provide services to both active and passive managers including portfolio risk management, trading optimization and execution, and regulatory compliance support. In contrast to the simplicity of index funds, these employ sophisticated data-driven analytics to enhance both the fundamental valuation efficiency and functional efficiency of the

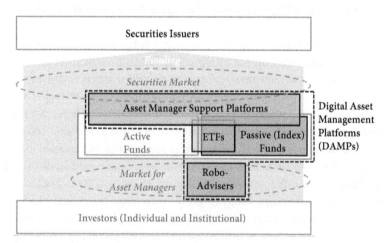

Fig. 9.3 Digital asset management platforms (DAMPs)
Source: authors; adapted from Haberly et al. (2019).

securities market. Finally, the newest DAMPs are robo-advisers, which in practice largely act as ETF distributors. Robo-advisers bear the closest resemblance to digital platforms outside of finance in that they simultaneously boost all aspects of market efficiency, in a complementary manner, in the retail market for fund managers—as opposed to the securities market itself.

Arguably the oldest exemplar of the digital platform model, either in or outside of finance, is the index fund. Index funds were conceived as a thought experiment accompanying the development of the efficient market hypothesis (EMH). By using the first generation of reasonably powerful computers to perform empirical statistical analysis (Bernstein 2005), early EMH researchers identified a conundrum in US securities markets; the same overcrowding of markets with participants that allowed for newly released information to be rapidly incorporated into prices, depleted the actionable arbitrage opportunities on which participants depended to make money (see Fama 1995; Malkiel 2013). The problem was that searching for and exploiting the residual arbitrage opportunities was expensive. Net of costs (research, trading, etc.), Ellis (1975) found that 85% of US fund managers had underperformed the S&P 500 index—i.e. what could be more or less expected from simply buying stocks at random—over the previous decade. In Tobin's (1984) terminology, this implied that market "information arbitrage efficiency" was vastly higher than "functional efficiency."

Early EMH claims regarding securities market efficiency are controversial (Tobin 1984); however, what has been robust is the specific finding that information arbitrage efficiency is, at least in the USA, high enough to translate into very low asset manager functional efficiency (i.e. returns net of costs; Malkiel 2013). It is this practical observation that has driven the rise of index funds, which are very simple algorithmic funds that allow investors to passively buy and hold a cross-section of the entire market—thus eliminating the conventional fund management apparatus of analysts, traders, etc. Rather than chasing gross returns at any cost, index funds compete on price, maximizing net returns by driving down operational overheads to the lowest possible level, while earning a gross return exactly equal to the market average (Bernstein 2005; Malkiel 2013).

By serving as cheap and transparent vehicles for investors to "buy the market," index funds fundamentally transform asset management—above all by radically undercutting industry fees and employment. Unsurprisingly, they were fiercely resisted by the industry when first proposed by academics, and ultimately would not be pioneered in the money centers of the northeast, but rather a triangular network linking the San Francisco Bay area to MIT and the University of Chicago (Bernstein 2005). Playing a key role in establishing this network was an analyst at Smith Barney, John McQuown, who had personal connections to finance researchers at the University of Chicago, and in 1963 began working with an MIT computer scientist to develop algorithmic investing techniques. Their IBM mainframe rentals attracted the attention of "IBM people, who were always on the lookout for anything that might demonstrate to prospective customers the versatility and power of the computer" (Bernstein 2005, 210). Via an IBM executive forum in San Jose, McQuown was invited to implement algorithmic investing at San Francisco–based Wells Fargo. Despite opposition from colleagues alarmed by the "...guys in white smocks with computers whirring" (Bernstein 2005, 213), McQuown's project would, with consultative input from many leading academic finance figures (including Eugene Fama), radically transform the bank's approach to investment management. Ironically, indexing was adopted "by default," as even this simplest algorithmic strategy was "a nightmare" to implement on 1970s-era computers. However, having launched the first indexed products in 1971, the management of Wells Fargo had by the end of the 1970s become so impressed with these that they decided to eliminate conventional active fund management (Bernstein 2005).

The San Francisco–based operation established by Wells Fargo remains the market leader in indexed products—notwithstanding changes in ownership from its reorganization as a joint venture with Nikko Securities in 1990, to its sale to Barclays in 1995, and finally its purchase by BlackRock in 2009. During this time, two additional developments have impacted index investing. The first was the launch of the first index mutual fund—open to small retail investors—by Vanguard in 1975. The second was the development of the exchange traded fund (ETF) in the late 1980s and early 1990s.

Whereas index funds transform the relationship between investors and securities markets, ETFs transform securities markets themselves by allowing market indices to be repackaged and traded as securities on these markets. ETFs are not managed like conventional funds, but are rather structured as two-sided market platforms. On one side, investors buy and sell ETF shares on the secondary market; on the other, arbitrageurs (e.g. investment banks) exchange specified baskets of securities with the ETF for "creation units"—i.e. primary market ETF share issues and repurchases—such that alignment is maintained between (1) the market value of the ETF's portfolio and the market value of its shares, and (2) ETF portfolio composition and the index it tracks. This platform architecture allows ETFs to achieve exceptionally low operational costs. ETF are also more liquid than conventional mutual funds, with intra-day trading possible (Hill et. al. 2015).

Although index funds have grown rapidly since the 1970s, it is only since the global financial crisis that their inflows have become so large as to reduce the total AUM of active funds (Figure 9.4). Since 2007, the indexed share of US equity fund AUM has nearly tripled to 43%, with ETFs accounting for approximately 40% of this (Sushko and Turner 2018). Theoretically, there should be a ceiling on passive fund growth, as it will eventually impair the information arbitrage efficiency of markets, creating new arbitrage opportunities for active investors. However, this has not happened so far. Over 2006 to 2016, 82% of active US equity funds underperformed the S&P index benchmark (S&P Global 2017), essentially the

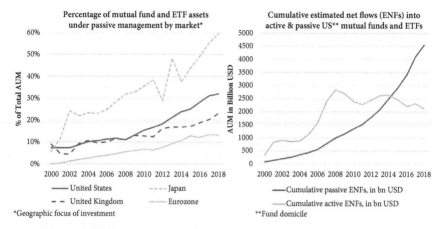

Fig. 9.4 Passive percentage of mutual fund and ETF AUM by market, and net flows into active and passive US mutual funds and ETFs, 2000–2018
Source: Lipper; adapted from Haberly et al. (2019).

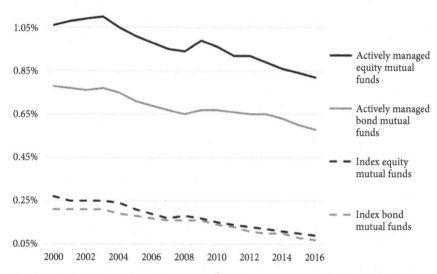

Fig. 9.5 (US) Active and passive mutual fund fees as a percent of AUM, 2000–2016
Source: authors; adapted from Haberly et al. (2019).

same as the 85% found by Ellis (1975). Furthermore, similar shares of international funds have underperformed their respective benchmarks (see S&P 2017), driving a rapid growth of passive investing in major securities markets outside of the US (see Figure 9.4 and Sushko and Turner 2018). As shown in Figure 9.5, the cost advantage of passive over active funds is actually widening in ratio terms. Indeed, the trend is toward a zero-fee model of index funds and ETFs as cross-subsidized multisided markets—with the first zero-fee funds recently launched by

Fidelity—wherein fund investors cease to be paying customers, and rather become a resource enabling the accumulation of liquid securities that can be profitably lent to investment banks and short-sellers (Kaissar 2018).

The early development of index funds, in an era of still-primitive computers, can be attributed to their ability to use extremely simple algorithms to boost the securities market's relatively low level of functional efficiency, by piggybacking on the market's much higher level of information-arbitrage efficiency—in other words, their harnessing of the ready-made "computer" of the market. However, as computing power has increased, new DAMPs have emerged that bear a closer resemblance to the stereotyped digital platform model of employing sophisticated analytics to boost multidimensional market efficiency. Most influential are what can be dubbed "asset manager support platforms" (Figure 9.3), and above all BlackRock's Aladdin. This was developed in the late 1980s as an in-house risk management tool for bond portfolios, and has subsequently expanded into a comprehensive "operating system"—or as CEO Larry Fink describes it, "the Android of finance" (Schatzker 2017)—sold to asset managers as a cloud-based subscription. According to BlackRock (2018), "The Aladdin platform combines sophisticated risk analytics with comprehensive portfolio management, trading and operations tools on a single platform to power informed decision-making, effective risk management, efficient trading and operational scale." Aladdin's scale is staggering; from 2013 to 2017, the value of the assets it guided increased from $11 trillion to $20 trillion (Mooney 2017), and has since increased to the $20–$30 trillion range (Beales 2020, Massa 2020). This is roughly equal to the capitalization of the New York Stock Exchange, and larger than the GDP of the United States. Moreover, Aladdin's importance to asset managers appears to be as deep as it is broad; according to the CEO of New York Life Investors: "Aladdin is like oxygen. Without it we wouldn't be able to function" (Gara 2017).

Aladdin's heart can be described as a data-mining-powered enhancement of securities market "fundamental valuation efficiency." Reflecting its origins, what remain most important are portfolio risk management tools (Betz 2016); as an example of their scope and power, one BlackRock fund manager recounts how Aladdin told him to purchase $400 million in US treasuries to offset geopolitical risk from a North Korean missile test (Gara 2017). In addition, Aladdin offers tools which broadly boost asset management "functional efficiency" in areas from trading optimization and execution (bypassing investment banks) to regulatory filing preparation. As Aladdin's scale, scope and sophistication have grown, it has increasingly blurred a number of boundaries; notably between human and algorithmic management (see section 9.8), between BlackRock and other asset managers, between the internal operations of asset managers and the markets in which they operate, and ultimately, by extension, between BlackRock and the securities market as a whole. With respect to the last, Aladdin's risk management algorithms have become so influential as to raise concerns that they might actually create systemic risks by inducing correlated market participant behavior (*Economist* 2013b).

The newest area of DAMP development is robo-advising. Rather than the securities market, this targets the retail market for fund management products. At the most basic level, robo-advisers serve as online price comparison tools which steer clients into the lowest cost investment products; in practice usually ETFs (Kaya 2017). However, robo-advisers also typically develop tailor-made product portfolios based on client situation and preferences. The sector is still relatively small, with ca. $140 billion AUM at YE-2017; however, it has been growing at 50%–100% per year (Mason 2017). As we detail in section 5, robo-advisers are increasingly becoming virtual "front offices" for sprawling vertically integrated DAMP ecosystems.

9.5 A Democratization of the Capital Market?

A recurrent theme in FinTech discussions is the prediction of industry decentralization, with incumbent giants seen as being threatened by innovative and nimble start-ups. Arner et al. (2016) go so far as to argue that the "new era of FinTech [is]...defined not by the financial products or services delivered but by who delivers them." In practice, however, the rise of DAMPs has produced a classic digital platform paradox of centralization through democratization. On the one hand, ETFs and robo-advisers offer users dramatically reduced costs, which arguably level the playing field in favor of smaller investors. Similarly, Aladdin's tool package provides smaller institutional investors with capabilities that were formerly available only to their larger peers. However, DAMPs also exhibit pronounced increasing returns that are producing a winner-take-all concentration of platform provider market share. Indeed, a remarkably large proportion of the asset management industry has come under the control of just three firms—BlackRock, Vanguard and State Street (see Fichtner et al. 2017; Haberly and Wójcik 2017b). These increasingly act as not only horizontal monopolies/oligopolies within individual DAMP segments, but vertical monopolies which internalize control of all segments.

Figures 9.6 and 9.7 show the pronounced concentration of index fund and ETF management, and how this has driven overall asset management industry concentration. As shown in Figure 9.6, active management remains fragmented, with the 10 largest managers worldwide only having a 27% market share in 2016. However, passive managers, with zero research costs, are able to realize almost unlimited scale economies once fixed costs are underwritten. The result is snowballing growth wherein increasing scale allows the largest providers to further reduce costs/fees, which in-turn attracts additional clients (Haberly and

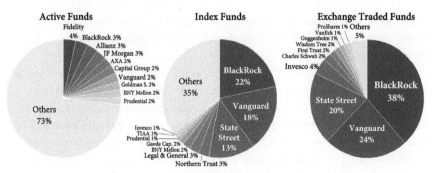

Fig. 9.6 Worldwide market shares of top-ten managers of active, index (passive) and exchange traded funds (ETFs) in 2016

Sources: authors' calculations based on P&I/Willis and Towers Watson; P&I; PWC; adapted from Haberly et al. (2019).

Fig. 9.7 US (top) and worldwide (bottom) asset manager market share change by size category, 2006–2016

Source: authors; adapted from Haberly et al. (2019).

Wójcik 2017b; Malkiel 2013; Sushko and Turner 2018). The "big three" passive managers—BlackRock, Vanguard, and State Street—control more than half of the index fund market, while the top-ten firms control two-thirds. Concentration is even more pronounced in ETFs due to network effects wherein ETF popularity increases liquidity, which in-turn increases popularity. The big-three have an 82% market share. BlackRock—dubbed the "Amazon of Wall Street" (Gara 2017)—has a slightly higher ETF market share, via its iShares products, than Amazon has in online retail (38% vs 37%; *Economist* 2018d).

As shown in Figure 9.7 the rapid growth of index funds and ETFs from 2006 to 2016 produced a marked concentration of the asset management sector as a whole, at both the US and global level. Virtually all market share gains went to the big three passive managers—BlackRock, Vanguard, and State Street—while smaller firms lost market share. Remarkably, Vanguard alone accounted for more than half of the total inflows of the entire global fund management industry in 2016 (*Economist* 2017). Concentration is even more pronounced once ancillary platforms are accounted for; the $20 trillion in assets guided by Aladdin, as of 2017, was three times larger than BlackRock's directly managed funds.

Even robo-advising—whose development was spearheaded by start-ups—has developed a highly concentrated structure, in which robo-advisers act as virtual "front offices" for vertically integrated DAMP ecosystems (Mason 2017). As one analyst puts it, "advice is ultimately a vehicle to unify control over client wealth" (McLaughlin 2016). The second largest index fund and ETF manager, Vanguard, has a 50% greater robo-advising market share than the next nine largest robo-advisers combined (Figure 9.8), with its robo-adviser's recommendations appearing moreover to consist almost exclusively of its own index funds and ETFs (Reklaitis 2015). Its main long-term competitor appears to be BlackRock, which entered robo-advising through the 2015 purchase of FutureAdvisor as part of a push to make Aladdin for Wealth Management available for "every small account" (Schatzker 2018), including "millions of retail investors" (Segal, 2016). In

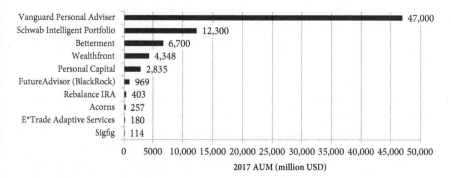

Fig. 9.8 Top-ten US robo-advisers 2017

Source: Crigger (2017); adapted from Haberly et al. (2019).

2017, BlackRock expanded into the European robo-adviser market by purchasing Scalable Capital, "which uses exchange-traded funds from BlackRock and others to build low-cost portfolios for clients" (Jessop and Hunnicutt 2017). In 2018, it extended its virtual front office by investing in "micro-investing" mobile app Acorns, which "allows customers to automatically invest spare change from everyday purchases...in exchange-traded funds from BlackRock and Vanguard" (Rosenbaum 2018).

9.6 The Geography of DAMPs I: Command and Control

Just as technological disruption has been predicted to decentralize firm-level financial industry structure, many have argued that the industry's geographic structure is likely to become more dispersed—or at least shift away from traditionally dominant centers. Tett (2018), for example, argues that managers are cutting costs by moving from New York to lower-cost locations, with this move facilitated by the fact that "the internet makes it possible to trade securities and do research anywhere in the world." Indeed, Alliance Bernstein's 2018 headquarters move from New York to Nashville has led to suggestions that even the command-and-control functions of dominant financial centers are threatened by technology-driven cost-cutting (Clark and Buhayer 2018). More recently, the explosion of home working during the Covid-19 pandemic has raised questions about the basic survival of physical offices as opposed to remote work, with the stakes of this debate being particularly high for the future of leading financial firms and centers (Natarajan 2021). Furthermore, even if decentralization fails to materialize, this need not imply the continued leadership of incumbent centers; rather, as JP Morgan's CEO recently warned, finance might become the latest industry to be eaten by Silicon Valley (Dimon 2014).

In fact, as shown in Figures 9.9 and 9.10 neither of these scenarios was playing out, at least for command and control, on any long-term basis that was visible prior to the disruption of the Covid-19 pandemic. Rather, 2006–2016 witnessed a clear tendency toward winner-take-all market share consolidation among US asset management centers (Figure 9.9a). Combined with a transatlantic shift of industry dominance from Europe to the US (see section 7), this produced a global winner-take-all city-level concentration trend (Figure 9.9b), with the single largest center, New York, consuming 36% of worldwide market share gains (increasing its market share by 66% in ratio terms). The growth of the "big-three" DAMPs has been the largest driver of this winner-take-all concentration, with their direct contribution shown by the difference between black and gray bars in Figure 9.9. BlackRock is headquartered in New York, while State Street and Vanguard are headquartered in the second and third largest US asset management centers, Boston and Philadelphia. The last has enjoyed exceptionally rapid growth attributable to Vanguard

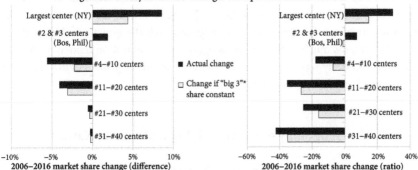

Figure 9a. US city-level asset manager headquarters concentration

Each category compares the correspondingly ranked cities from 2006 and 2016. New York, Boston, and Philadelphia held the top-3 spots (respectively) in both 2006 and 2016.
*"Big three" refers to BlackRock, Vanguard, and State Street (headquartered in New York, Philadelphia, and Boston respectively)

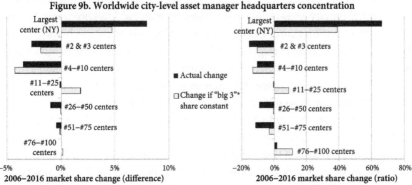

Figure 9b. Worldwide city-level asset manager headquarters concentration

Each category compares the correspondingly ranked cities from 2006 and 2016. New York, held the top spot in both years
*"Big three" refers to BlackRock, Vanguard, and State Street (headquartered in New York, Philadelphia, and Boston respectively)

Fig. 9.9 US (top) and worldwide (bottom) city-level asset manager headquarters concentration (with and without "big-three" passive manager growth)

Source: authors; adapted from Haberly et al. (2019).

*% of AUM of top-500 AM firms worldwide, accounted for by firms with HQ in metro area

Fig. 9.10 Change in worldwide asset manager market share by headquarters city, 2006–2016

Sources: authors' calculations based on Willis and Towers Watson; Bloomberg.com; adapted from Haberly et al. (2019).

(Figure 9.10); a particularly interesting case which underscores that costs can be reduced by simply moving to the suburbs (Malvern, PA), while remaining within a leading financial agglomeration. Notably, although the growth of the big three DAMPs explains much of the overall geographic concentration tendency, there is still a large underlying concentration trend even when the growth of the big-three is removed (gray bars in Figure 9.9).

9.7 The Geography of DAMPs II: Regulation and Nationality

Intriguingly, these results suggest that technological disruption is mostly reinforcing rather than challenging the status quo geography of asset management. However, the analysis in section 9.6 has two limitations. First, it does not account for the potential for city-level trends to be driven by national-level processes. Second, it does not account for intra-firm organizational trends; particularly the possibility that incumbent centers might be hollowed out functionally (e.g. in tech-related employment) even while consolidating their position as command-and-control centers. In this and the following section we address these two issues.

Notably, in contrast to digital platforms outside of finance—wherein competitiveness is often directly linked to technologically enabled regulatory arbitrage—DAMP business models do not seem to be premised on undercutting regulation. To be fair, many have run into regulatory barriers; when ETFs were first proposed they were incompatible with the Investment Company Act, and could not be implemented until lobbying convinced the SEC to change the relevant rules (Hill et al. 2015). However, where regulatory avoidance itself is the objective, financial firms have always had more attractive tools at their disposal (e.g. pre-crisis shadow banking). In fact, in the context of postcrisis regulatory tightening, index funds seem to have gained competitive advantage not from their ability to circumvent tightened regulation, but rather their ability to leverage economies of scale to comply with it at a lower unit cost (per-AUM) than active funds.

This does not mean that post-crisis regulatory restructuring has not impacted asset management, but rather that these impacts have (with the exception of the point above) been more or less the same for DAMPs and traditional asset managers. As shown in Figures 9.11–9.12, the most important trend has been a shift from the pre-crisis dominance of European banks, to the post-crisis dominance of American independent fund managers. Ironically, the rapid pre-crisis growth of European bank securities activities appears to have been, as discussed in chapter 5, partly a product of the paradigm of consolidated supervision established by Basel, which shifted regulatory primacy to bank home states. Following Glass–Steagall's repeal, this encouraged the acquisition of American securities firms by European banking conglomerates with even weaker home capital supervision than American banks—and above all by British and Swiss midshore national banks (see chapter 5).

*Group defined as a "bank" for regulatory purposes if it includes a banking subsidiary.
Allianz classified as bank in 2006 due to ownership of Dresdner Bank (sold to Commerzbank in 2008)

Fig. 9.11 Top-five world asset managers in 2006 and 2016
Source: authors' calculations based on Towers Watson; adapted from Haberly et al. (2019).

As shown in Figure 9.11, four of the world's top-five asset managers in 2006 were European banks; albeit with their actual fund management operations largely concentrated in New York and London. Largest was Switzerland's UBS, which owned three of what had been the top-twenty American investment banks in the 1980s (see chapter 5); #2 was Barclays, which owed its size to its ownership of Wells Fargo's former index fund division.

Since the crisis, this pattern has been reversed, with independent US fund managers holding four of the top-five asset manager spots in 2016, and banks disappearing entirely from the top five (Figures 9.11–9.12). As discussed in chapter 5, sprawling European national champion banks were ultimately too large relative to their home economies to be decisively recapitalized by home governments in the wake of the crisis. Consequently, they were forced to restore themselves to health through asset sales—including of asset management arms—with the particularly overextended midshore national British and Swiss banks undergoing the largest downsizing (Figures 9.10–9.11). Basel III's supplementary capital requirements for "systemically important financial institutions" (SIFIs) have accelerated bank divestments of noncore operations, including asset management arms. Notably, assets under management, as opposed to an institution's own balance sheet, are excluded from SIFI criteria—with lobbying by BlackRock reportedly playing a role in this exclusion (Tracy and Krouse 2016)—allowing independent asset managers to retain a relatively lean regulatory footprint compared to other large financial firms.

In practice, most divested bank assets have been purchased by American independent fund managers (Figure 9.12)—mostly as a path-dependent result of there being more American than European independent fund managers to begin with (due the historical dominance of universal banks in Europe). Banks have also spun-off asset management divisions as standalone managers, with BlackRock as it currently exists emerging out of both trajectories of restructuring. From 1995, BlackRock operated as a subsidiary of PNC Financial, before becoming jointly owned by PNC and Merrill Lynch following its purchase of Merrill Lynch's asset management arm. In 2009, BlackRock became the world's largest fund manager

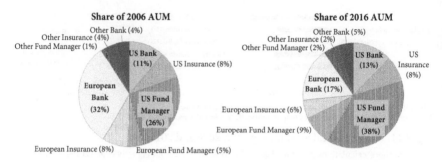

Fig. 9.12 Asset management market shares by manager type, 2006 and 2016

Sources: Authors' calculations based on Willis and Towers Watson; Bloomerg.com; adapted from Haberly et al. (2019).

when a distressed Barclays sold it its index fund and ETF operation (taking a stake in BlackRock in the process). Ultimately, all of these bank stakes in BlackRock were divested (apart from a minority PNC stake), leaving it as an independent manager.

9.8 The Geography of DAMPs III: Functional Specialization and Diversification in the Global Financial Network—the Case of BlackRock

What is intriguing about this musical chairs of asset manager parentage is that it has little bearing on the functional structure of DAMPs—the original San Francisco–based index fund operation that McQuown established at Wells Fargo in the 1970s, for example, has remained the market leader whether owned by Barclays or BlackRock. Like the finding that the rise of DAMPs has consolidated rather than challenged the position of the largest incumbent financial centers, the paramount importance of regulation in pre/postcrisis asset manager parentage shifts suggests that the geography of DAMP *command and control* overwhelmingly reflects their identity as financial firms, rather than their identity as technology firms. However, this raises the question of how the latter identity is reflected in their geography. In the remainder of the paper, we shed light on this by mapping the world's largest fund manager, BlackRock, through the lens of the Global Financial Network framework outlined in section 9.3.

In theory, a financial firm could keep one foot in a headquarters location for regulatory and other reasons, even while (as detailed in section 9.3) redistributing the bulk of its activities centrifugally to specialized "paper" offshore centers, "virtual" data centers, "back-office technology centers," and front-office "regional market centers." As we will show, BlackRock's organization partially reflects such a logic; however, there are also powerful agglomerative effects within and between

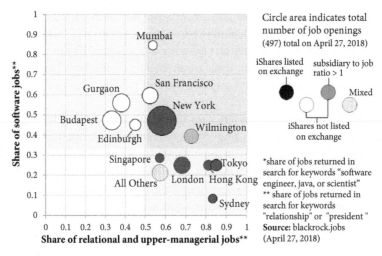

Fig. 9.13 BlackRock job openings by city and type, April 2018

Source: authors' calculations based on blackrock.jobs (April 27, 2018); adapted from Haberly et al. (2019).

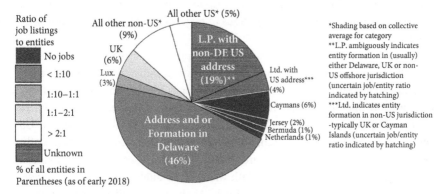

Fig. 9.14 BlackRock internal structure by jurisdiction (entity counts), early 2018

Source: authors' calculations based on Orbis; OpenCorporates; adapted from Haberly et al. (2019).

the different functional spheres in Figure 9.1, that keep centrifugal unbundling tendencies in check.

Figure 9.13 provides an overview of BlackRock's geography based on keyword analysis of all 497 job openings on BlackRock's website on April 27 2018, the domiciles of all BlackRock entities recorded in Orbis (also see Figure 9.14), and the listing exchanges of BlackRock's iShares family of ETFs. City circle areas represent total job openings, while X- and Y-axis positioning shows job role mixture.[3] Y-axis positioning shows the percentage of jobs associated with software-linked keywords

---

[3] Keyword search lists were refined experimentally to avoid false positives.

(software, engineer, scientist, or java); X-axis position shows the percentage of jobs associated with relational and upper-managerial keywords ("relationship" or "president"). Circle shading indicates whether any iShares ETFs are listed on a city's exchanges (black), whether there are anomalously numerous BlackRock entities compared to employment (gray), or whether neither of these conditions is met (white).

BlackRock's employment underscores that it is as much a technology as a financial firm, with 42% of job listings software-related. Furthermore, aspects of its organization clearly reflect a technology-enabled logic of centrifugal geographic specialization and dispersion. Two back-office technology centers—Budapest in Hungary, and Gurgaon in India—account for 26% of software job listings. Edinburgh (with lower costs than London) also appears to serve as a back-office technology center. This pattern supports Tett's (2018) argument that US asset managers are cutting costs by moving jobs to low-cost locales, even while questioning the assumption that these must be US locales. Furthermore, BlackRock's "brain," Aladdin, is not housed in a stock exchange co-location center, but rather a server farm in Wenatchee, Washington, between two hydroelectric dams. Finally, BlackRock's "paper" geography corresponds tenuously to employment, with Delaware and other offshore jurisdictions of hugely disproportionate importance (Figure 9.14).

However, BlackRock also shows countervailing tendencies toward geographic centralization, as well as functional diversification at individual geographic sites. BlackRock's largest high-tech employment center is Manhattan, which has more software job openings than Gurgaon and Budapest combined, and is where BlackRock Solutions, which includes Aladdin, is based. BlackRock's largest US offices—New York, San Francisco, and Wilmington, Delaware—also have strikingly diversified mixtures of software-intensive and more conventional financial center functions. This is congruent with what can be dubbed the "cyborg" investment management approach of BlackRock. As the head of BlackRock Solutions puts it: "'human plus computer' will always lead to a better result than computer alone or a human alone" (Segal 2016). This philosophy is most important in active management, in which—notwithstanding its much larger passive AUM—BlackRock has the world's second largest market share (Figure 9.6). As CEO Larry Fink described a recent equities team reorganization:

> This wasn't about machines replacing human beings. Some of our large-cap products, our core alpha products, were underperforming, but our quant equity teams were doing quite well...They were looking at different insights. We wanted a much more holistic platform where the fundamental teams can work with the model people. They see things that the model people do not see, and more importantly we wanted to have the output of the models going to some of the fundamental people. Cross-fertilization, no different from what we do in fixed

income...We have a venture...in AI, a whole group of people working on developing computer-based investing. And that's truly a computer saying, "Buy this.
Sell that." [But] We're not there yet...there's no true AI yet in investing.

(Schatzker 2017)

Particularly intriguing is the apparent functional convergence between Black-
Rock's New York and San Francisco offices (the latter built around Wells Fargo's
pioneering index fund operation acquired via Barclays). Beyond the technological intensity of operations in New York, this entails a growing importance of
San Francisco–based relational functions. Both BlackRock's corporate governance
office and its regional head for the Americas are based in San Francisco. Interestingly, this appears to largely reflect the extent to which the regional growth of
both tech firms, and reservoirs of investible capital (including the two largest US
pension funds in Sacramento), are driving conventional relational financial center
agglomeration. According to CEO Larry Fink, the head of Americas' move to San
Francisco was motivated by both the "critical importance to BlackRock of tapping
into innovation on the west coast," and the fact that "the region is home to many
of our largest clients" (Smith 2017).

Notwithstanding this convergence, however, the New York securities market
poses a daunting barrier to any pretensions of San Francisco to become the US
financial capital. As detailed by Wójcik (2011a), exchange platform virtualization has overwhelmingly promoted a concentration rather than diffusion of both
the technical and human geographies of the securities market. In the US, nearly
all regional exchanges have been absorbed by New York, with most of the US
securities market now located, in a literal sense, in the NYSE Liquidity Center
in the New York suburb of Mahwah, NJ. Notably, this contains what remains
of the formerly San Francisco–based Pacific Stock Exchange, which pioneered
many areas of online exchange platform development. This is consolidated into the
NYSE Arca platform, on which most US ETFs (including BlackRock's) are listed.
BlackRock's international employment is also, with the exception of technology-
oriented back offices, concentrated in dominant regional exchange hubs—most
importantly London, Tokyo, Hong Kong, Singapore, and Sydney. The distribution
of employment among these sites is itself extremely polarized, with London accounting for 42% of the total. London accounts for 77% of BlackRock's European
job openings outside of the back-office technology centers of Budapest and Edinburgh, suggesting that virtually all of its European relational and trading activities
are concentrated there.

Another parallel between BlackRock's US and international organization is the
entanglement of "paper" and "real" operational geographies. A securities market is
not simply an informational, but also a contractual and regulatory nexus—as such,
the distribution of entities in Figure 9.14 does not fully capture the importance

of the major exchange hubs to BlackRock's "paper" geography. London, Singapore, and Hong Kong, in particular, have, as discussed in earlier chapters, built their positions as financial centers on legal–regulatory foundations, particularly by bridging the divide between "onshore" institutional reputation and "offshore" institutional flexibility. Notably, BlackRock's largest incorporation hub, Delaware, appears to be following a similar developmental trajectory. Wilmington, Delaware is BlackRock's third largest US hiring site, with a diversified mix of technical and relational–managerial jobs.

9.9 Conclusion

On August 2, 2018, asset manager shares plunged following an announcement by the world's largest active fund manager—Boston-based Fidelity—that it would be one-upping the traditional low-cost passive leaders by offering the first zero-fee index funds. Even while "taking the democratization of investing to a whole new level" (Bernard, 2018), this final evolution of asset management into a free service, provided through cross-subsidized platforms, is expected to intensify an already ongoing industry shake-out and consolidation (Kaissar 2018).

The evidence in this chapter underscores the scale of this technology-driven upheaval; however, it also suggests that the identity and geography of digital asset management platform providers has remained, to a rather counterintuitive extent, aligned with their identity as financial firms rather than as technology firms. Indeed, by focusing on the potential for finance to be disrupted from the outside by tech startups, many contemporary commentaries appear to have underestimated the extent to which the industry is already being transformed from within. Notably, the San Francisco Bay Area has been a key locus of technological innovation in asset management for decades, from the development of index funds in the 1970s, to the expansion of ETFs in the 1990s; however, the most important actors in this innovation have been major multinational banks and fund managers. Furthermore, while Bay Area startups have recently spearheaded the development of robo-advising, these pioneers are increasingly being either outcompeted or purchased by established financial giants. Perhaps most strikingly, from a geographic standpoint it is the leading incumbent asset management centers of the US Northeast—and above all New York—which have been the largest beneficiaries of the tendency toward technology-enabled winner-take-all industry consolidation.

To a large extent, this continuity appears to reflect the fact that both the informational intensity, and regulatory and organizational fluidity of the digital platform model are more evolutionary than revolutionary in finance. What appears to be particularly important, is that financial innovation has always been entangled in a labyrinth of "paper" legal, regulatory, and, broadly speaking, political dimensions. Notwithstanding their unflappable willingness to spearhead not only technological, but also regulatory disruption in other industries, the major Silicon Valley tech giants themselves appear to be rather out of their depth in this context. Indeed, with the exception of payments, these firms have mostly been too intimidated by the regulatory complexities of finance to attempt to enter the sector. Facebook may now be breaking with this pattern with its foray into cryptocurrencies. However, its ham-handed approach to dealing with regulators—despite needing to navigate a minefield of digital privacy and financial regulatory issues spanning numerous countries (Kharif 2019)—suggests that the very culture of disruption that underpins the success of Silicon Valley tech firms may paradoxically hinder their ability to disrupt financial services. This makes them poorly placed to compete with financial firms who have no such problems adopting technological innovations, including by directly internalizing control over Silicon Valley offices and start-ups. As one partner at venture capital firm Sequoia Capital described FinTech broadly, "companies that move fast and break things are not going to work in this regulated environment" (Levine 2021d).

For a time, it seemed that the apparent ability of Chinese information technology giants (e.g. Alibaba) to carve out a rapidly growing role in financial services might be an exception to the general struggles of tech firms to deal with the political and regulatory issues this entails (Jia and Kenney 2016; Töpfer 2018). However, even this apparent anomaly was largely eliminated in late 2020, when the government of China suddenly initiated a full-scale regulatory assault on prominent FinTech firms; launched to dramatic effect by interrupting at the last minute Alibaba's planned IPO of its Ant Financial division, which would have made the latter one of the world's largest financial services firms by market capitalization. What is particularly striking about this incident is the extent to which it seems to have been precipitated by the same attitude of apparently congenital tech sector regulatory and political arrogance that has sabotaged the efforts of Silicon Valley tech firms to enter financial services. Indeed one of the immediate triggers for the government's crackdown appears to have been a widely publicized speech made by Alibaba's founder Jack Ma shortly before Ant's planned IPO, in which he compared traditional banks to "pawn shops," and implied that China's approach to financial regulation was "outdated" (Bloomberg 2020).

Entry into finance, it seems, threatens to exacerbate the already severe tension between the traditional culture of innovation of tech firms, and the growing political pressure on digital platform providers to evolve into a role with which financial firms have long been familiar; i.e. that of state-supervised utilities who can at most use subtle and roundabout strategies to subvert this supervision. In fact, the most successful digital asset management platform providers have an even more utility-like character than most financial firms; as reflected in their shallow depth of value extraction compared to breadth of financial market footprint,[4] lack of aggressive regulatory arbitrage, and corporate identities that openly promote "boringness" (see Wee 2012). Indeed, BlackRock's role in the TARP program entailed it acting as more or less an extension of the Federal Reserve (Lipton and Merced 2009).

Most notably, the geography of the world's leading financial centers has, for centuries, been perhaps the single most stable and slowly changing layer of the world's economic geography (Arrighi 1994). Given the tremendous technological upheavals that have already occurred over this period, there is reason to expect that this geographic stability will persist.

[4] BlackRock only has one-fifth of JP Morgan's and one-twelfth of Google's market capitalization. Vanguard, meanwhile, has a mutual ownership structure that effectively makes it an investor cooperative.

10
A Great Transformation?

Money is a very strange sort of product. Polanyi (2001) called it a "fictitious commodity," which can be rendered tradable on and regulated by markets, but at the same time remains fundamentally a human social relation that is inextricably embedded within the broader fabric of society. This social embeddedness of money, and of finance as a system for producing money, is nowhere so clearly underscored than in their historical entanglement with organized religion. According to Graeber (2011, 59), "from Sumer to Classical Greece, silver and gold were dedicated as offerings in temples. Everywhere money seems to have emerged from the thing most appropriate for giving to the gods." Notably, in the earliest civilizations, these precious metals did not actually circulate as currency—indeed coinage was not even invented until around 600 BC. Rather, they mostly just accumulated in the treasuries of temple and palace complexes, which from the very beginning of civilization in Sumer seem to have become the central anchors in abstract credit-based monetary systems. This was not, moreover, just a pattern observed in ancient Mesopotamia. One also sees, for example, Buddhist temples in medieval India and Tang dynasty China essentially developing into banks, with a capital base consisting of the "inexhaustible treasuries" built up through believer donations. Even in medieval Europe, which was exceptionally intolerant on religious grounds of not just usury, but commercialized profit-making generally, one sees the religious order of the Knights Templar emerging as one of the central players in the credit system during the Crusades (Graeber 2011).

Seen from a modern perspective, this fusion of religious institutions with the credit system might seem fundamentally bizarre, corrupt, and in many contexts more than slightly hypocritical. However, it actually cuts straight to the heart of the basic nature of finance and money, namely that these institutions, at the end of the day, are built on nothing more than an act of collective faith. Indeed, of the latest brand of money, Weisenthal (2021) observes how:

Bitcoin was developed by a mystical figure, with no known corporeal presence, called Satoshi Nakamoto. His true name is unknown. At some point, Nakamoto stopped posting online altogether, departing the earthly plane. He's never once sold a coin, either, creating this thing of massive value with no clear indication of having cashed in. A selfless figure.

Sticky Power. Daniel Haberly and Dariusz Wòjcik, Oxford University Press.
© Daniel Haberly and Dariusz Wòjcik (2022). DOI: 10.1093/oso/9780198870982.003.0010

Nakamoto's writings are sacred texts. There's the Bitcoin white paper and his early message board postings at Bitcointalk.com, where he corresponded with fellow cypherpunks interested in creating digital money. Those early correspondees are the Bitcoin saints.

Bitcoin's worldview has other religious features. There are devils (bankers and central bankers), implicit promises of riches for the true believers who HODL (hold without selling), and damnation for the no-coiners who reject the way.

The inevitable equal and opposite reaction to the vesting of faith or trust in these types of abstract forces or constructs is the impulse to ground them in some sort of substantive and durable architecture. The purpose of the GFN is, in essence, to provide such an architectural backbone to finance, to allow for the credible production of money as a social relation. The production of this social relation involves multiple discrete informational, legal, accounting, and political elements, each of which operates and is organized according to a distinct logic. Ultimately, however, the logic of monetary production—or, more precisely, of *high-quality, credible* monetary production—is fundamentally centripetal rather than centrifugal, with the power of the GFN stemming from the way that it integrates all of the various elements of monetary production together in a centralized manner.

The basic logic of this integration process can be described as one of *centralized specialization*. In other words, it involves a logic of monetary production whose various functional elements can become partially dissociated from one another geographically, even while each of these elements tends to both experience a process of geographic centralization internally, and to be integrated into an overarching cross-functional relational centralization with one another. The latter tends to concentrate power in the hands of a small number of leading financial centers, private financial gatekeepers, and public authorities; who are in the position to integrate, coordinate, and backstop financial information flows, relationships, and activities across the various specialized nodes in the GFN, and between these nodes and the "hinterlands" of the broader economy.

Crucially, most of what have often been described as decentralizing or footloose tendencies in finance are actually, on close analysis, just optical illusions produced by the logic of functional geographic *specialization* that occurs within this overarching logic of GFN *centralization*. To summarize such "centrifugal" interpretations of global finance: the offshore system is usually interpreted as the penultimate expression of and vehicle for an international fiscal and regulatory "race to the bottom" mediated through the mobility of private capital, which is seen as hollowing out the territorially imprisoned authority of the state, and presenting a threat to the established position of any given financial center. To the extent that the hollowing out of the state by global markets is defied, this is seen to be mostly linked to either a right-wing nationalist populist retreat from globalization, or the rise of a new authoritarian state capitalist economic model led by China. The latter is presented as a sort of diametrically opposed other to the purportedly free market economies of the West, constructing a new architecture of globally projected state economic control. Technology, meanwhile, is widely conceptualized as intensifying the (China excepted) general underlying centrifugal logic of global financial mobility and decentralization; not just geographically, but also organizationally, with increasingly fluid, anonymized, and "democratized" markets seen as potentially rendering obsolete the whole architecture of established financial centers and gatekeepers. Put together, Bitcoin's trillion-dollar-and-climbing market value, the emptying of financial centers by Covid-19, and the overpowering of hedge fund short sellers by Reddit-coordinated Robinhood "stonk" traders—who like the hedge fund traders are now sitting at home in their pajamas—are just the final nails in the coffin of the old world of concentrated geographic, institutional, and political power in finance.

What we have shown in this book is that these types of arguments are almost entirely wrong, or at least highly misleading. The basic logic of offshore finance, for example, actually revolves around the *centralization* of the legal–geographic footprint of global financial production within a tightly knit network of functionally specialized and complementary jurisdictions. Notable examples include the leading role of the Cayman Islands in securitizations and hedge funds, Ireland and Luxembourg in European market-oriented fund management and certain types of corporate profit-shifting, the City of London in the Eurodollar market, the Netherlands in offshore corporate holding companies, and Delaware in the legal domiciliation of finance and business within the USA in general. This logic of centralized offshore legal–geographic functional specialization, moreover, does not steal business away from the leading financial centers such as Wall Street or London, but rather directly expands their reach and competitiveness. The roots of the offshore system and its relationship with leading financial centers, both in terms of general function and the roles of specific jurisdictions in it, are furthermore deeply historical, essentially stretching back to the emergence of western capitalism itself out of the Middle Ages. The offshore system is not some novel product of post–WWII developments in information technology or financial innovation; it is rather in many respects the oldest and most durable part of the GFN, which houses and protects much of its core legal–institutional DNA.

Furthermore, the idea that financial globalization can in any way hollow-out state authority is conceptually nonsensical, given that finance is both fundamentally dependent on, and intrinsically vulnerable to, the "protection racket" of the state. What the integration of the GFN rather does is take power away from the majority of states in the world, and transfer it to the strongest imperial states or "world governments," who in conjunction with non-state multilateral organizations (and a few sovereign wealth-rich states), possess the capabilities to extend their legal, regulatory, and fiscal reach to all corners of the globe. The USA, above all, plays such an imperial role within the contemporary GFN. Indeed, the US capacity to project its surveillance, regulatory, and taxation capabilities throughout the GFN has become progressively stronger rather than weaker over time, particularly over the past twenty to thirty years.

It may very well be that the Trump administration's erratic behavior has cut away at the basic foundations of US global leadership in ways that will have serious long-term ramifications. However, there is, as of the writing of the book, no evidence that the basic elements of US global financial and monetary power have so far, at least, really weakened at all, with the offshore world continuing to serve as a particularly important lynchpin of this system of power. The global tax haven system, for example, from a US standpoint basically steals tax revenues from weaker states, and places them within the global fiscal dragnet of the US Internal Revenue Service. In 2016, for example, an EU state aid ruling ordered Apple to pay billions of dollars in back taxes to Ireland, where it had been aggressively sheltering profits. This prompted bipartisan apoplexy in Washington at the fact that the EU had just stolen offshore funds (deferred taxes) *belonging to the IRS*. Democratic Senator Chuck Schumer, for example, called it "a cheap money grab by the European Commission, targeting US businesses and the US tax base" (Donnan 2016). Meanwhile, the offshore Eurodollar market essentially converts the savings of the world into a bottomless US federal credit line. This credit line is deliberately kept open by the 1984 Portfolio Interest Exemption, which was implemented to "provide the United States Treasury, as well as domestic corporate borrowers, direct access to cheaper capital available on the Eurobond market" (Dilworth 1985). As Avi-Yonah (2013) puts it, "the result was astonishing: Over $300 billion were invested in the USA from Latin America alone—a sum exceeding all of the official aid received by Latin American countries during the entire 1980s," while "since 1984 no developed country has been able to collect withholding tax on interest paid to non-residents, because if it tried to do so the funds would be shifted to the US."

The offshore world has indeed to a large extent become, particularly since the 2010 passage of FATCA, an increasingly transparent global financial bell jar and playground from the standpoint of the US federal government, even while appearing to be an opaque and unreachable realm for most other governments. In fact, certain US states have increasingly become the most opaque parts of the global offshore system, due to the failure of the USA to sign onto reciprocal automatic tax information exchange agreements of the type it imposes on other countries' financial institutions (Bullough 2019). The US dollar, meanwhile, is not only something that allows the US Federal Reserve to play the role of an indispensable global financial "protector" in the event of crises—most recently in response to the early 2020 Covid-19 crash (Wójcik and Ioannou 2020)—but that has been weaponized to allow the USA to unilaterally pursue virtually any extraterritorial political, regulatory, or fiscal agenda that it chooses, no matter how little political support it has abroad (e.g. enforcing sanctions on Iran; *Economist* 2020a; Emmenegger 2015).

The hegemony of the dollar still remains unchallenged outside of the realm of pure future speculation. Despite China, for example, having surpassed the USA as the world's leading trading economy, 87% of global trade credit continues to be dollar denominated, compared to the RMB's 2% share (SWIFT 2020).

Clearly the geopolitical and economic challenge posed by China to US global leadership is real. However, the purportedly Manichean divide between China's "state capitalist" model and the so-called free market model of the USA is in reality extremely blurry from an institutional and political, as well as a geographic stand-point. For starters, the United States is, and since the days of Alexander Hamilton always has been, in many respects just as much a state capitalist as China. This US state capitalism operates via the vast balance sheets of the Federal Reserve ($7.6 trillion), the indirect nationalization of the US home mortgage market via Fannie Mae ($4 trillion) and Freddie Mac ($2.6 trillion), and a $1.6 trillion federal stu-dent loan portfolio—adding up to (even without Social Security's $2.9 trillion) a combined financial *asset side* of the US federal balance sheet of nearly $16 trillion, or 75% of US GDP (Department of Education 2021; Fannie Mae 2021; Federal Reserve 2021; Freddie Mac 2021). Indeed, the global financial system could not really operate at all without the state capitalism of the Federal Reserve, or the role of US government debt as an indispensable universal collateral. On top of this, the USA operates a globalized de facto state venture capitalism via the largely military–industrial subsidization of, and often direct investment in (e.g. the Department of Energy's half billion dollar 2010 loan to Tesla) technology company R&D on the one hand, and the extraction of a return from the offshore IP rents generated by US technology firms via the US global extraterritorial tax system on the other (now tightened in relation to offshore IP by the 2017 TCJA tax reform; Davis 2019). One also needs to take into account the huge mass of state and local pension funds in the USA; the state of Wisconsin alone, for example, with its 5.8 million inhabi-tants, manages 129 billion dollars, roughly the same AUM as the Korean national sovereign wealth fund (ETF 2021).

Meanwhile, "Chinese" state capitalism (or market socialism) is actually in many respects almost as much American or British as Chinese in character. As we showed in chapter 8, the leading Chinese SOEs themselves are often largely prod-ucts of the organizational and marketing efforts of American investment banks, as oriented simultaneously toward the New York and Hong Kong capital markets, and from a jurisdictional standpoint largely domiciled within current and former UK overseas territories. Even in the midst of the deteriorating political relationship between the USA and China, the financial entanglement between them remains profound, and is sometimes manifested in surprising ways. Hong Kong Chief Ex-ecutive Carrie Lam, for example, has recently complained that she cannot even open a bank account within Hong Kong itself, due to being placed under US sanc-tions, and is thus forced to keep, as she puts it, "piles of cash at home" (Brooker 2020).

Technology, moreover, far from reversing or undermining the interconnected processes of GFN centralization, for the most part directly intensifies them. From a political standpoint, as observed by Lessig (2006), the rise of information technology, in finance as in other sectors, accelerates the emergence of free-range global extraterritorial "sovereigns of everywhere." The USA and China, in particular, each now possesses a stable of global technology and technology-enabled financial giants who act as extensions of their respective national regulatory and surveillance apparatuses. In the case of the USA, most of the world's foreign financial firms of any significance have now been pressed, via FATCA, into this global extraterritorial apparatus, even without taking into account the global surveillance capabilities that the US national security state derives via Silicon Valley tech firms. Meanwhile, technology further intensifies the centripetal "platform"-centralization logic that pervades financial markets themselves, both geographically and organizationally. Geographically, the world's already leading financial center, New York, seems to be the single biggest winner so far of the FinTech revolution, both by virtue of its ability to tap into the capabilities of other tech centers such as Silicon Valley, and its ability to cultivate finance-specific tech expertise internally. Meanwhile, far from decentralizing the distribution of power within financial markets, FinTech has simply opened the door within finance to the rise of the singularity-like monopolies that characterize the digital platform economy more broadly, albeit with regulation and politics-savvy Wall Street financial firms such as BlackRock, more than Silicon Valley tech firms, carving out the apex position. Even Goldman Sachs is now getting on the low-fee mass market online retail banking and robo-advising train, with its new Marcus platform, which is also linked to a new Apple-branded credit card (Levine 2021e). Meanwhile, Facebook's, and even Alibaba's financial ventures are floundering due to their inability to navigate the hard reality of entrenched political and institutional soft power in finance. They have tried to bring an app to what is still largely a lawyer and lobbyist fight, and the outcome has been predictably poor.

Above all, what is striking about the GFN is its historical durability; both in an overall functional sense, and in terms of the role within it of specific leading financial centers, and even specific leading FABS firms. A century ago, the most important bank in America, at the center of the Money Trust, was JP Morgan; today, the largest bank in America is JP Morgan. Morgan may very well still be the largest bank in America a hundred years from now. In a system that revolves, above all, around relational capital and centrality, and the accumulated architecture of interconnected legal and institutional legacy standards, the dominant financial centers, actors, and relationships will inherently tend to reproduce their own dominance over time. This is not to say that the financial system does not change. However, it changes slowly, and it mostly changes through the addition rather than the subtraction of elements.

Even an institution as superficially disruptive as Bitcoin, which in theory appears to circumvent the whole established institutional and relational structure of finance, cannot escape from the logic of how this structure reproduces its power historically. Indeed, the whole idea of trying escape from this power presents a logical paradox; as Levine (2021f) puts it:

> What makes Bitcoin worth $47,000 is not that its code is somehow worth that amount; what makes it worth $47,000 is that people are willing to buy it for that price. And the reason that they're willing to buy it for that price is—in part, in increasingly important part—that it fits in with the rest of the financial system, that the *traditional* systems of *trust* that make up the mainstream financial system have accepted and incorporated Bitcoin...Nothing can really be a reliable store of value until you can custody it at BoNY Mellon. Now you can.

Certain political shocks can leave a lasting imprint on this network-relational architecture of financial power; with disruptions to the international market connections that are the very lifeblood of financial centers being particularly damaging. Amsterdam, for example, while still a key node in international finance today, never entirely recovered as a financial center from the Napoleonic occupation, annexation, and Continental System blockade of its relationship with the UK/London—with a great deal of its financial activity, and a number of its leading financial actors (including its leading merchant bank Hope & Co.), directly fleeing to London. Brexit could theoretically have similar long-term impacts on London's relative standing. Indeed, as discussed in chapter 4, a great deal of London's share trading activity now seems to be, after 200 years, fleeing back to Amsterdam, to escape the Continental System–style blockade that the UK has now inexplicably imposed on itself.

By and large, however, the global financial network shows extraordinary historical resilience in the face of the changing winds of international politics, and it is this political resilience, as much as anything, which underpins its broader historical durability. Indeed, the impacts of Brexit itself, including the current resurgence of Amsterdam and its link with London—which simultaneously represents the reproduction of centuries-old relationships between these two financial centers, and the desire of London-based financial firms to, as much as possible, avoid actually shifting employment by making use of Dutch trading platforms shells (e.g. as set up by the LSE)—have actually underscored this durability on multiple levels. Brexit is, in effect, a sort of natural experiment to see just how easy or hard it is to destroy an international financial center, and as it turns out, this is in fact very, very hard; much harder, in fact, than the destruction of the rest of the British economy.

Various politically and economically hegemonic *powers* come and go, and in various capacities and to varying degrees both influence and make use of the GFN, and yet the basic structure of the network remains—growing by accretion without really losing its older elements. Even more importantly, the GFN shows a powerful capacity to adapt itself to a continuously changing international regulatory and political *environment*, even while preserving most its basic character and structure through successive adaptive reconfigurations.

The tremendously resilient adaptive and co-optive capacity of the GFN raises incredibly difficult, and indeed rather uncomfortable questions in relation to the proposal of policy recommendations for reforming finance. Perhaps most troubling, is the manner in which the most sweeping and ambitious reform programs tend to end up being dismantled by the same governments implementing them— often inadvertently at the very same time that they are being implemented. After WWII, for example, the USA and the UK were presented with an opportunity unprecedented in the entire course of human history to draw up a comprehensive blueprint, basically from scratch, for the governance of the global financial and monetary system. As if this weren't already an amazing enough opportunity, the greatest economist of the 20th century, who had literally written the book on monetary and financial governance, was recruited to directly lead the British delegation in this effort.

Ultimately, the system that was constructed ended up lasting around twenty-six years, if measured from the end of WWII to Nixon's closing of the gold window in 1971—in other words, roughly the same length of time that has now elapsed since the beginning of the dot com bubble. Obviously Keynes's advice was not entirely followed in the construction of this system, and if he had been more closely listened to—particularly in relation to his blueprint for a Global Clearing Union, wherein central banks would have had access to enormous mutual overdraft facilities in a neutral global reserve currency (as opposed to the US dollar)—the problems that developed may have been less acute. However, it is not clear that even this would have fundamentally resolved the basic nature of the political dilemmas at play. Specifically, as discussed in chapter 5, the same powerful states that were putting in place national and international regulatory and governance frameworks to advance some of their political and economic objectives—and above all the USA and the UK—invariably found that these frameworks created various rigidities and problems from the standpoint of other policy objectives. To deal with this, these states (and agencies within them) thus actively sought out the help of, and helped to reconsolidate the power of, elements of the GFN that afforded them short-term flexibility to sidestep specific dilemmas; but ultimately destabilized the whole regulatory architecture they were trying to protect.

Even more striking cases of the largely inadvertent rechanneling of even the most sweeping systemic reform agendas, such that they effectively become turned back upon themselves and ultimately implode, can be found throughout the socialist world. As discussed in chapter 8, the depth of the socialist world's relationship with the GFN—from the USSR to contemporary China—is something that has always transcended any ostensible ideological goals or proclivities. Whether China's apparent bid to "steal" the British postcolonial offshore network from the active imperial leadership of the USA will eventually be successful, remains to be seen. Clearly Carrie Lam would prefer being able to open a bank account in Hong Kong for her "piles of cash at home." However, as far as the historical reproduction of the power structures of the GFN itself are concerned (even if not necessarily its inhabitants), it is not clear that it actually matters who comes out on top in this struggle. Even the most radical projects of systemic reform—including the overthrowing of capitalism itself—at the end of the day seem to end up largely reinforcing the power of, even if also in various ways modifying and expanding, the inherited structures of the GFN.

Crucially, though, this does not mean that there is no such thing as durable historical agency in the shaping of the GFN. However, where this durable agency seems to be mostly manifested is not really though any sort of regulatory, or even broadly speaking "governance" framework, but rather through the construction of innovative financial *institutions*—both private and public—that are able to in some way render themselves indispensable to many different actors and constituencies. The construction of central banks, for example, could clearly be placed in such a category: with these institutions being both essential for the effective operation of financial markets, and clearly welfare improving when viewed at a very broad level. Even if the particular nature of central bank intervention is always fraught politically, and may more or less work to the benefit of particular groups or places as opposed to others, it is difficult to imagine how anyone's life would be improved by deconstructing these institutions. Indeed, as argued by Polanyi (2001), central banks seem to have an unusually strong tendency, as institutions go, to evolve into a sort of central nexus for cross-class political–economic cohesion and state-building—a tendency that we argue, below, should be very actively exploited and built upon.

With this in mind, we would thus argue that the basic guiding principle behind financial reform, broadly, needs to be an overriding emphasis on proactively building up and stewarding the financial system that we *do* want, rather than simply trying to reactively stamp out and rein in the financial system that we do not want. Moreover, in pursuing this positive focus on financial institution-building, it is crucial that we maintain an emphasis not only on pursuing various socioeconomic goals, but also simultaneously making the financial system in some sense "work better" from an efficiency standpoint on its own terms. If the financial institutions that you build do not actually function effectively as financial institutions, they will quickly end up being circumvented and/or dismantled, ultimately taking your socioeconomic goals with them. Conversely, though, if they do work well on a basic efficiency level, the achievement of these goals will be much more difficult to overturn.

The general importance of maintaining a positive focus on financial institution-building, as opposed to just a negative focus on regulation, is underscored by the wildly successful "developmental states" of East Asia, including contemporary China, as well as Japan and South Korea historically. The implementation of negatively defined financial regulation in developmental states is, generally speaking, a mess. In boom-era Japan, the banks were literally in bed with the regulators (Horvat 1998), and in contemporary China, it is mostly the various discombobulated parts of the state itself that have played the leading role in subverting the state's own financial regulations (via instruments such as local government finance vehicles, etc.; Walter and Howie 2011). If one is to judge by economic growth, however, these same developmental states nevertheless excel at positive financial institution-building, which is indeed in many respects the very foundation of their economic dynamism. This is powered, in effect, by a sort of a perpetual credit-fueled investment bubble that is set in motion, sustained and channeled by the state in a semi-controlled manner, and can catapult economies from low to high income status within a few decades (Ozawa 2001; Wade and Veneroso 1998).

This is not to say that every place on earth should try to import off-the-shelf financial institutional templates modeled on these developmental states; the developmental state model is basically the financial equivalent of nuclear power, generating massive amounts of energy, but constantly threatening to melt down (as eventually happened in both Japan and South Korea), and ultimately having an inherently limited shelf-life (see Ozawa 2001). Rather, the point is to underscore the importance of viewing finance as a powerful and indispensable social *technology*—whose institutional development needs to be proactively prioritized in order to be channeled in particular desired directions, not simply to enable, but actually as a precondition of socioeconomic progress—rather than treating finance as some sort of evil unclean force that gets in the way of and distorts the operation of the "real" economy, and which simply needs to be constantly boxed in and suppressed at every turn. A wise approach to managing finance does not just allow the private sector to lead financial innovation, while the government behaves in an entirely reactive way by constantly scrambling to put in place ad hoc and ultimately futile barriers to this innovation. Rather, the focus needs to be on leading and channeling the process of financial innovation and institutional development itself in the direction that you want it to go. In pursuing such a focus, it is important to remember that future political shifts are likely to twist and distort, and possibly try to tear down, the innovations that you put in place today. At the same time, however, thanks to the inherent "sticky power" of finance itself, well-designed financial institutional systems are, broadly speaking, fairly likely to endure, even if they will invariably be repurposed in various ways.

What exactly is it that we want to achieve through such reforms? Clearly there are many possible answers to this. However, the analysis in this book points toward a general objective: namely to construct a financial system that fosters a broad-based geographic and socioeconomic distribution of access to financial resources,

on attractive, equitable, and sustainable terms—which can provide a foundation for broad-based socioeconomic opportunity and prosperity generally—as
opposed to a system that fosters the progressive concentration of an ever-greater
proportion of the world's wealth and power in a tiny number of hands, in a handful
of leading financial centers.

To think about how to go about constructing such a financial system, it is important to build upward axiomatically from the basic conceptualization of what the
monetary instruments manufactured by the financial system actually *are*; namely
nothing more than a formalized representation of social trust. Likewise, the inherent tendency for the GFN to concentrate wealth and power in a small number of
hands and places, is a product of relational and informational bottlenecks within
the matrix of socioeconomic trust, which by default tend to be resolved via relatively centralized mechanisms. Perhaps the most extreme example of this logic,
ironically, is provided by the Soviet Union, which basically stamped out its domestic matrix of socioeconomic trust almost entirely—both in a monetary and
financial institutional sense specifically, and in a more general sociological sense—
and at the end of day, arguably as a direct result, ended up transferring the larger
part of its collective wealth to external hubs of financial power such as London.

Conversely, as this case suggests, if we are to produce a financial system that
is geared towards the provision of widely available, equitable, sustainable, and attractive conditions of financial access for both households and firms, with the goal
of promoting broad prosperity, the basic task would seem to be one of breaking or restructuring the informational and relational bottlenecks within finance
that tend to intrinsically promote the concentration of wealth and power. Directly
tackling the monopolistic or oligopolistic position of the existing gatekeepers that
control these bottlenecks, by either breaking them up into more competitive units
or enrolling them more directly as closely supervised utilities, is potentially part of
what this entails. However, we would argue that the gains from this are likely to be
secondary, and indeed inherently unsatisfactory and unstable, without also paying positive attention to building up a matrix of alternative institutional channels
around the dominant financial gatekeepers and centers; or in other words, constructing what could be described as pervasive financial "institutional thickness"
(Amin and Thrift 1994).

Perhaps most importantly, in the context of such a project, it is critical that we
escape from the conceptual bugbear of trying to analyze finance entirely or even
primarily in terms of the provision or investment of "capital." What we are really
talking about in finance is, in a concrete sense, actually the completion of interlocking circuits of relationships that allow people to flexibly and elastically draw
on resources from one another; with these relationships often linking people who
are literally neighbors, but end up having to mediate their interactions through
some distant financial center. What matters in this context is not really how much

you "own," as represented by capital, but rather how much and how sustainably you are able to spend; in other words, your ability to maintain *liquidity*.

The old European nobility, for example, were usually massively in debt, and probably could have been considered technically insolvent much of the time, but this never stopped them from continuing to live lavish credit-fueled lifestyles buttressed by a matrix of political and legal privileges. Whether they had a technically positive or negative net "capital" at any given moment was irrelevant; all that mattered was that they were able to find ways to remain liquid, and to avoid any serious consequences at moments when they might have been relatively illiquid (Pistor 2019). In imperial Russia, for example, the tsars originally set up banks to continuously refinance and bail out the nobility (Garvy 1972), and the first mortgage securitization-based lending institution was founded by Fredrick the Great in 18th-century Prussia for the same purpose; as he put it "saving four hundred of Silesia's 'best families' from ruin" (Pistor 2019, 94). Similarly, when the English aristocracy experienced a severe debt crisis in the 17th century, they were mostly able to avoid having to sell off land by simply taking out new mortgage debts on more favorable terms—which was itself predicated on creative reinterpretations, affirmed by the court system, of legal constraints imposed by their own intergenerational estate preservation trusts (Ward 1991). Even today, as exhibited by, for example, many large Japanese business groups since the 1990s, solvency (i.e. having a substantively net positive capital) is hardly a universal precondition for success or survival, even in a capitalist system, as long as you can remain liquid. The Trump family business empire, with its perennially intractable debts and endless shell games of bankruptcies and tax-deductible losses, more or less illustrates the same principle. Indeed, in a world where perhaps 80% or more of S&P 500 market capitalization is backed by intangibles (Ponemon Institute 2019), capital and solvency are really just a matter of subjective opinion; all that actually matters is whether you can remain liquid.

This condition of liquidity is ultimately determined, above all, by your relational access to the gatekeepers of monetary social power—or as the officials of the Bank of England put it in the 19th century, whether you have a "name of sufficient standing" from the perspective of these gatekeepers (Chapman 1979). Such a "name of sufficient standing" on the world stage in a broad sense, and all the attendant raw monetary social power that it commands, is really what China Mobile, for example, which hails from a country that is already dripping with capital, was trying to gain by going through the otherwise apparently pointless rigmarole of a New York listing. China has absolutely no need to import capital—in 1997, when China Mobile launched its New York IPO, China ran a current account surplus of 3.8% of GDP (World Bank 2020)—and a large state-owned enterprise such as China Mobile is one of the last firms that would ever need to obtain capital from abroad to compensate for an inability to obtain it from financial institutions at home. Rather, by such measures, and others such as the internationalization of the

RMB, the Communist Party is essentially trying to gain entry at the highest global level into what Graeber (2011) dubs the easygoing "communism of the rich." This is an incomparably more valuable prize than mere capital, as it effectively implies an ability to conjure control over resources and people worldwide out of thin air, as needed, in a way that becomes more or less automatically self-perpetuating once it is established. A globally respected and highly valued international stock market listing in the case of a corporation, or international reserve currency issuer status in the case of a government, are two of the ultimate expressions of such power, which both effectively amount to an enormous blank check written by the world at large.

Ironically, critical Marxian approaches to conceptualizing finance and financialization are actually quite poorly suited to understanding the nature of this form of social power, as their focus on *capital* more or less reifies the self-serving mythologies promoted by the financial sector itself regarding its role in the economy and society. Nothing would suit Goldman Sachs better than watching its critics spinning their wheels trying to figure out how it fits into the "circuits of capital" of finance capitalism. Capital barely enters into the picture for such a firm, apart from as a nuisance on its balance sheet to be minimized; as leading early 19th-century New York financier Arthur Bronson described banking: "The possession of capital was of no use except to inspire confidence. This being more fully established...the latter was found a great inconvenience—a source of real annoyance" (Haeger 1979, 260). Companies such as Goldman Sachs are rather, in effect, the priests sitting at the top of the Ziggurat of global finance, who control and exploit access to the various codes, mysteries, and myths of this system, and are to a large extent able to shape the parameters of reality itself within it. They are able to essentially just pull wealth out of the ether for themselves and their elite clientele by leveraging their name, connections, and expertise, without having to worry in the slightest about the consequences of bad decisions. Perhaps most ironically, by conflating class with an inanimate object (capital), a Marxian framework of analysis actually hugely understates the importance of class in a true human social sense in this context.

Indeed, capitalism itself isn't really about capital, it's all about the money, and insofar as money is nothing more than credit, ultimately needs to be understood as a system that above all strives toward the endless expansion of the social relations of credit. What is called "capital" in capitalism is really just a type of collateral, which is granted a relatively privileged position compared to what it enjoys within noncapitalist social systems, but even within capitalism actually remains relatively weak in comparison to other forms of social collateral. Perhaps most importantly, the superficially fundamental distinction between what you *owe* and what you *own* in capitalism is in reality extremely ambiguous, insofar as both ultimately just represent mechanisms for accessing (or creating) credit money. The devil is rather always in the details of the terms on which money is accessed/created, whether via operations on the asset or the liability side of your balance sheet (which are ultimately the same thing from a collective societal perspective). Debt is power, provided that you can control the terms on which it is structured. The whole wealth of the American white suburban middle class is built on mortgage debt, provided via a state-sponsored mechanism that is almost identical to that established by Fredrick the Great to preserve the power of the Prussian nobility. Nobody in capitalism is more heavily indebted than banks, and it is this very indebtedness that is the source of their unparalleled wealth.

Money, in other words, isn't a veil for or a phase in the accumulation or capital, and is most definitely never something that can be considered to be a "fictitious" representation of or form of capital. On the contrary, it is more accurate to say that the whole concept of capital within capitalism is just a veil for the social power of money. The power of Marx's M-C-M' and M-M' are both equally insignificant in the face of the power to manufacture money itself: or in other words, the power of … -M. This isn't just a question of the internal operation of the financial sector itself. Right now the two richest men in the world, for example, are Jeff Bezos and Elon Musk, whose wealth is only vaguely related to the underlying profits generated by the enterprises they control, being rather a socially constructed representation of expected future potential. Amazon only has the 16th largest profits of any company in the world (earning only half the profits of Google/Alphabet, and less than any of China's big-four state-owned banks), despite being as of April 2021 #4 worldwide by market cap (larger than Google/Alphabet, and more than twice the total combined value of China's big-four banks; *Forbes* 2021). Meanwhile, Tesla's April 2021 market cap of just under $700 billion (roughly the GDP of Saudi Arabia, compared to Amazon's South Korea–sized market cap) is built on a bit over $20 billion in capital raised, plus less than a billion dollars of total cumulative profits (Hull 2020). Most of this capital raised is actually still sitting, in a net sense, on Tesla's balance sheet as just under $20 billion in cash (including a couple of billion dollars in Bitcoins).

Bezos and Musk—who now holds the title of "Technoking of Tesla" according to the firm's latest 8-K filing—have each essentially just converted a compelling story directly into an almost incomprehensible sum of money, in the form of liquid market capitalization, by running these stories through Wall Street. This money does not really come from anywhere, it is mostly just a systemic product of credit creation bidding up the value of instruments packaged as prophecies; with the power of finance being its ability to make these prophesies self-fulfilling, thus rewriting the fabric of reality itself in the image of imagination. What is called a "bubble" is really just part of this process of overwriting reality. Bubbles burst, but by this point they have already transformed the world. Insofar as their stories (and money instruments, e.g. publicly traded stock) are relatively accessible and straightforward, moreover, Bezos and Musk are in some sense both amateurs at this game. Broadly speaking, the more convoluted and esoteric that money becomes, from bills of exchange, to collateralized debt obligations, to FOMO ETF shares, the greater the power that accrues to those who control and are privy to the mysteries of its manufacture.

The power wielded by the GFN at the heart of capitalism thus does not really stem from its provision or control of capital, but rather its control of the much more fundamental relationships and institutions within which money is embedded as a social relation—and it is on this that we need to focus our attention in relation to the construction of broad-based financial "institutional thickness" as the centerpiece of a project of systematic reform. From the standpoint of *function*, such a reform agenda needs to above all be oriented toward what can be described as the *democratization of liquidity*; or, in other words, allowing households, firms, and governments (at various levels) to elastically access money whenever they need it without resorting to borrowing on usurious terms. Indeed, the basic distinction between "capitalism" and "socialism," from the standpoint of substantive social relations and outcomes, to a large extent hinges on the details of how liquidity access is structured in society. Both the "baseline communism" of the tribe or village, and the easygoing "communism of the rich," are above all mediated through the continual and largely unconditional mutual extension of credit on easy terms; or put more simply, the mutual granting of favors without any expectation of immediate reciprocation (Graeber 2011). Liquidity is everything in finance. Market liquidity is what allows the wealth of Musk and Bezos to exist as more than just a hypothetical abstraction. Liquidity management is what breaks down, at the systemic level, to create financial crises, and what allows private financial institutions to hold society hostage when these crises erupt. Speculative bubbles can form and dissipate without having any effect at all on financial stability, until they are plugged into short-term liquid funding mechanisms which simultaneously operate as part of the payments system.

Importantly, apart from simply providing short-term credit, institutional mechanisms also need to be created to make long-term funds widely available to households, firms, and governments to make worthwhile investments—with the structuring of these funds in terms of maturity, flexibility of repayment, etc., being commensurate with the level and nature of risks entailed by these investments. However, this is itself something that is in many respects more usefully analyzed from the standpoint of liquidity than capital provision; what you need when you are starting a business is not really capital in some mystical sense, but rather just plain old money that you can access to spend now, without being crippled by the usurious extraction of interest payments later. Notably, for an institutional system of long-term funding provision to work effectively, it also needs to have some mechanism for disposing of the financial "pollution" produced by failed investments, that does not discourage productive risk-taking by ruining the lives of those engaged in it, or allow this financial pollution to throw into havoc or weigh down the operation of the financial system or economy. In other words, what is simplistically derided as moral hazard should be treated as more of a feature to be managed and deployed, than a bug to be stamped out, within the system of short and long-term liquidity provision. Ultimately, the key question is who should have access to moral hazard and to what ends? The best answer to this, we would suggest, is, basically, everybody, for any socially useful purpose.

Relatedly, a well-built financial institutional framework needs to incorporate various short and long-term risk insurance mechanisms for firms and households, including in relation to the funding of retirement. These are all, in effect, just ways of socializing the management of liquidity via mechanisms other than conventional borrowing and lending, wherein the repayment of the loans drawn on society by households occurs, in effect, before the loans are actually taken out in a statistical average sense. Indeed, the boundary between insurance and credit-based liquidity management is in many respects ambiguous, and they may in certain contexts be considered partially interchangeable. A credit line can effectively function as insurance if it is generous enough.

In terms of the approach to designing the *form* of financial institutions, there are clearly numerous solutions that could be devised to achieve these various goals. Broadly speaking, however, the GFN framework suggests some general key points and pitfalls to problematize. Particularly important is the recognition of the counterintuitive way that markets, despite being at one level decentralized institutions, will almost inexorably develop—and to a large extent actually require for their operation—centralized institutional platforms. This platform paradox is almost certainly being strengthened rather than weakened by the ongoing development of technology, and thus needs to receive even greater attention than was already the case in the past. Notably, from an institutional design standpoint, this paradox implies two possible approaches to the achievement of financial "institutional thickness." The first can be described as a monopoly "utility" market platform model, that seeks to actually realize the financial mass democratization potential of FinTech; thus achieving pervasive financial institutional thickness via relatively centralized mechanisms. Meanwhile, the second can be described as the "frontier finance" model (see Dixon and Monk 2014; Urban 2018), which effectively seeks to circumvent markets and gatekeepers in finance altogether; achieving pervasive financial institutional thickness by establishing decentralized local and translocal networks of relationships between public and private financial and nonfinancial actors.

We would suggest that these two approaches to financial institutional thickness-building are probably best conceptualized as being complementary with one another; with a promising guiding focus to the financial institutional design process being the question of how to simultaneously implement and put them together. With respect to the centralized market platform "utility"-building aspect of this project, we would suggest that the task is simplified by the fact that the most important such platforms already exist; namely the central banks that act as the central anchors and market-makers in the most important financial market of all, namely for high-powered *liquidity*. Currently, with the exception of physical legal tender, direct access to this central wellhead of socialized monetary power is limited (with a few exceptions) to the governments that control central banks, and the financial institutions that operate under their umbrella of protection. There is, however, a growing push to create universal access to central banks via central bank digital currencies (CBDCs). Currently being piloted in China (with a wider launch planned), these would, in effect, allow everyone to conduct their electronic checking and payments more or less directly at the central bank.

Such a system has an enormous amount to recommend it, being intrinsically pervasive, cheap, and if properly structured, more or less completely immune to runs or financial crises. Indeed, it could very easily render obsolete, in one fell swoop, the whole rent-extracting and unstable system of privatized fractional reserve banking (along with most brands of "shadow banking"). As the *Economist* (2020b) puts it, "the real risk of CBDCs to the financial system may be that they eventually precipitate a new type of bank run: on the idea that banks need to exist at all." Crucially, however, there is also tremendous scope to get CBDC systems wrong. In particular, they have the potential to lead to a system of rigid, commodity-like token money, which would in effect represent a step backward from a more flexible credit-based system.

Avoiding this step backward requires not just creating a new system of digital cash, but also using it to open up to the general public the full range of credit facilities provided by central banks. In other words, everyone needs to be allowed to conduct their own banking through the same privileged channels that only banks themselves are currently allowed to use. What this means is that the digital wallet provided to everyone by the central bank also needs to be combined with, in effect, a digital credit card—and more specifically one that offers the deepest and cheapest possible credit facilities, with the most generous and flexible terms of both access and repayment (in terms of uses of funds, interest rates, maximum monthly payments in relation to current income, conditions for full or partial debt write-off, etc.). Potentially making the system even more powerful, might be its additional combination with some form of universal basic income; which would, in this context, provide a universal foundational collateral that could be directly matched to and used to anchor pervasive liquidity provision via the "universal basic credit line."

Socially, the consequences of these arrangements would in many respects be revolutionary, extending, in effect, the umbrella of de facto socialism within which banks already operate to the public at large. However, such an arrangement would also render large swaths of the current private financial system obsolete on *efficiency* grounds, as banks could never compete with the scale of its social pooling and automatic neutralization of credit risks; not just on the deposit-taking and payments side, but also on the lending side. The central bank could always offer cheaper money than, as well as a higher risk-adjusted (i.e. in absolute terms still low) rate of return on its deposits, than any private financial institution (including shadow banks). Indeed, a key focus of the central bank's management of this system should arguably be to systematically outcompete the latter for short-term funding, to ensure that private financial institutions can only access short-term funds via the central bank itself (see below). This should make it effectively impossible for financial crises to occur, via the structure of basic institutional design, as opposed to trying to prevent crises by waging an endless Sisyphean regulatory battle. The new public institutional framework of liquidity management, moreover, once established, would likely be exceedingly difficult to undo—indeed likely as impractical to abolish as central banks themselves. Both politics and the logic of market competition would tend to hold this system together, rather than constantly trying to fling it apart.

What is particularly interesting is the impact that this arrangement could have on longer-term financial operations outside of liquidity management. The central bank would have to, in effect, either replace the entire banking system by engaging in long-term direct lending itself on a massive scale, or become a sort of universal deposit base for the rest of the banking system, by throwing open its discount window as widely as possible to fund the bulk of the lending operations of all other banks. We would suggest that the former probably represents the concentration of far too much centralized power in a single agency. The latter, however, actually opens the door to a tremendous *potential* decentralization of power in finance, and in the economy more broadly.

In essence, with high-powered money liquidity not only cheap but also ubiquitously available, information would become the sole remaining "currency" of value in finance—far more so than it already is. Profits would accrue more or less automatically to any actor who could link now ubiquitous access to the centralized pool of liquid funding available from the central bank discount window, to information and relationships that would allow these funds to be put to use as investment. Much of the established securities industry, including investment banks and fund managers, would probably not do badly in this system, assuming that the architecture of the securities market was not massively modified (and indeed there does not seem to be any particular need to radically overhaul the stock market or long-term bond market). However, the potential for these (and other) private actors and institutions to act as exploitative gatekeepers for resource access by other actors and places would in theory be radically disrupted, as anyone else would have the ability to directly tap into the same wellhead of high-powered liquid funding.

What would likely benefit, in particular, would be local financial institutional ecologies. Crucially, the elite gatekeepers of the securities markets in leading financial centers, for all of their privileged access to and control over information within their home turf of these apex markets, are in many respects actually fairly disconnected from "substantive" information about how the economy, and world more broadly, is operating around them. Indeed, the passive funds that increasingly dominate securities markets do not even bother trying to figure out what is going on in either the markets or the world more broadly. Underlying actionable information in an economy is rather distributed throughout the economy in a largely decentralized and localized manner. Currently, the ability of this localized information to be connected to money, to generate local investment and growth, is hindered by the centralized gatekeeping structures of the financial system itself (including preferential access by the largest firms to backstops); with the result being that local financial institutions, in general, have a higher cost of funding than their larger peers, and have to moreover be fairly risk averse in their local lending. However, plugging local finance institutions directly into a centralized low-cost stable funding source, that could be accessed more or less automatically on a very large-scale and long-term (i.e. continuously rolled over) basis, should in theory address these issues.

The universal liquid funding base created by the central bank should thus, if properly designed, foster broad-based local financial institutional capacity-building throughout the economy; whether in the form of public, private, or cooperative institutions (or some mix of all three). This would directly build the institutional critical mass that Dixon and Monk (2014) describe as being essential to decentralized regimes of long-term-oriented "frontier finance" (also centered, depending on the context, on various types of pension funds, savings banks, development banks and sovereign development funds, etc.). Crucially, the idea of building up this institutional capacity would ultimately be to increase, in a Keynesian sense, the *demand* for local investment at the microeconomic level; thus ensuring, in conjunction with Keynesian macroeconomic management, that the new system of pervasively available public liquidity does not find itself "pushing on a string." Notably, such a system, with the CBDC liquidity pool at its center, could also be deployed to promote all sorts of economic, social, and environmental objectives in a *centralized* manner, simply (as has historically been done by East Asian developmental states) via central bank "window guidance." Indeed, China clearly plans to use its CBDC as a mechanism to further tighten central government control over the financial system in general (Kynge and Yu 2021). However, we would suggest a need for great caution in trying to attach too many ancillary political goals (and thus conflicts) to this institution's basic social mission of democratizing liquidity itself. What we are trying to do here is establish a basic architecture that will endure through future historical time.

Effective financial institution-building at the supranational level presents greater challenges. Notably, though, one important consequence of the general deprioritization of regulation, within the positive approach to financial institution-building proposed here, is that it should partially neutralize some of the dilemmas surrounding the governance of the global offshore system. Beyond potentially making prudential regulation of private financial firms largely unnecessary, a CBDC system also has the potential to dramatically roll back financial secrecy at a structural level, as it (for better or worse) "enables the central bank to track all transactions at the individual level in real time" (Kynge and Yu 2021). The actual use of offshore jurisdictions is clearly never going to go away; the costs of making use of them are so low, for deep-pocketed actors, that they will continue to be used even if the private economic benefits that accrue are extremely thin. What matters is rather the potential to narrow the scope that they have to cause harm, and in this respect reform can achieve quite a lot.

This is not to say that the potential for the offshore system to cause harm would or even could ever be fully eliminated by narrowing the scope for particular off-shore arbitrage strategies; as the privatized paradigm of rulemaking mediated through offshore could in principle always find a previously unanticipated direction from which subvert any new public policy. As described by Nougayrede (2019), these deeper dilemmas could potentially themselves be tackled, to some extent, by going directly after the *private law* foundations of the institutions, such as shell companies, that comprise the offshore institutional "toolbox"; by addressing basic issues related to, for example, geographic definitions (e.g. corporate "real seat"), and the scope of director liability and corporate veil perceiving (i.e. circumstances when entity limited liability is overridden). Even this, however, would arguably be more of a speed bump for the processes at work here, than an end to them.

The treatment of the offshore realm is also complicated by, and indeed goes to the heart of, the uneven landscape of international political power, centered on the leading world governments such as the United States, and to some extent increasingly (albeit still more potentially) China. There is no easy resolution to the issues raised by this uneven international power landscape, and indeed they may be at some level fundamentally irresolvable. However, there are strategies through which they can be tackled. Perhaps most potentially important, in this respect, is to prioritize the development of multilateral mechanisms for collectively pooling and redrawing the borders of state sovereignty in such a way that the leading world governments cease to monopolize the levers of *extraterritorial* authority. Notably, both the Basel framework of predominantly home state-based extraterritorial prudential supervision, and the increasingly sophisticated OECD/G20 frameworks of coordinated global corporate tax governance and taxpayer information exchange, can basically be seen as existing (even if imperfect) examples of such an approach. These could in theory be deepened, extended, and reformed—to reduce, for example the persistent structural bias in favor of developed as opposed to developing countries in the evolving international tax governance framework (see Hearson 2018). Nougayrede (2019), notably, also suggests that such an international framework approach (coordinated by some international body) could also be extended to the area of law. Such frameworks do not necessarily need to intrude upon national policy prerogative at the state level; rather they can directly bolster it. Within the United States, for example, the ability of states to function as corporate tax havens in relation to other states is limited by the prevalence of formulary-apportionment systems of state corporate taxation, which are designed and implemented on a unilateral basis by each state individually (Clausing 2016). This approach could be more or less transposed, with some modifications, to corporate tax governance at the global scale, with some coordinating assistance from the OECD (Picciotto 2016).

What these tax and regulatory approaches would have in common (and to some increasing extent have already started to achieve) is a leveling of the international playing field of state extraterritorial sovereignty between the great world governments such as the United States, and increasingly China, and other weaker states. Particularly important to ensuring that such institutions actually play this role, is a coordinated alliance-building between relatively weak states (and potentially also non-state actors) to, as necessary, place pressure on the leading world government states to ensure their cooperation. Notably, as of the writing of this book, it seems that the mounting international pressure on US multinational corporate tax avoidance, from both European and developing countries, has ultimately convinced the USA (or at any rate the Biden administration) that its own interests are best served by taking the lead in global corporate tax reform—with the USA now pushing hard for a global minimum tax rate standard. Such a coordinated alliance-of-the-weak approach, crucially, could in theory also be applied to try to induce the participation of the most powerful reserve currency issuers, such as the USA, in some revised version of Keynes's International Clearing Union plan. In fact, some such mechanism would likely tend to be in the national *domestic* economic and social interests of the most powerful world governments anyway, by allowing them to give up some of the problems and burdens (accelerated deindustrialization, etc.) associated with leading reserve currency issuer status, even while sacrificing some of the power accruing from their global monetary "protection rackets."

The type of CBDC-based public liquidity management systems that we propose may actually make the dilemmas surrounding the current use of particular national currencies as global reserve currencies—and thus the need to directly address these dilemmas—more acute than ever; as these new electronic currencies have the potential to suck an even greater proportion of world savings into the hands of the leading reserve currency issuing governments. Indeed, this tendency would be even more pronounced if central banks, as we suggest here, aggressively compete with private institutions to soak up short-term funds in the money market, as part of a strategy to make financial crises structurally impossible. It is possible that China is actually counting on this sort of global suction effect in pushing ahead aggressively, before any other major government, to establish its Digital Currency Electronic Payment (DCEP) currency; which could in theory outflank and render obsolete much of the basic infrastructure of global US dollar dominance, boosting China's own global reserve currency bid. There may thus actually be a Darwinian institutional evolutionary logic, at the global level, that will tend to implement a novel CBDC-centered monetary institutional framework one way or another; and it would seem best that the world's various authorities go about doing this in an at least semi-coordinated and cooperative manner, that won't simply create new and equally hierarchical (and potentially abusive) international power structures.

Notably, the current moment may be as good as any to go about implementing fairly sweeping national and global financial reform projects; whether along the lines suggested here, or along some other lines. The world has just passed through a pandemic-induced economic meltdown that has no precedent in living memory, which has dramatically disrupted both global economic relationships, and established political dogmas regarding the proper scope of state economic intervention. What is also notable, moreover, is that the United States and China each now faces a rather symmetrical landscape of uncertainty regarding its future role in the world, wherein each could just as conceivably find itself dominated as dominant. What this means is that that each now has, in theory, a strong incentive to limit its own future political downside risk by making common cause with weaker states, to put in place relatively fair global institutional and governance mechanisms now.

The emphasis on historical agency, in such reform agendas, is critical. Capitalism is, despite rumors to the contrary, not in crisis in any historical systemic sense, when it is viewed as a system wherein wealth and power flow directly at the highest level from control of the social relation of money itself. This system is rather in rude health. Falling yields are a non-issue when they are the flip side of skyrocketing capital gains, and when the funds that are invested are simply conjured out of the void to begin with. The climate crisis, and attempts to address it, could easily precipitate a wholesale private enclosure, mediated through new financial instruments and markets, of the global ecological and atmospheric commons. To the extent that extreme forms of AI and robotics-enabled automation render various types of goods and services effectively ubiquitous, this will only further enhance the premium attached to more abstract forms of social power, and likely above all financial power. Opportunities abound for the further expansion and consolidation of capitalism. The development of the space economy, for example, if left to its own devices, is likely to represent the final frontier in offshore arbitrage across all legal, regulatory, and fiscal domains. Luxembourg is already positioning itself to take advantage of the limitless potentialities afforded by this economic new geography of nowhere for legal–jurisdictional game-playing on earth — which no doubt have also not failed to escape the US West Coast tech community leading the development of the space economy, given that this same community has already spearheaded a massive expansion of the tax haven system on earth.

In short, the only real potential challenge to the endless historical self-perpetuation of the most abusive elements of power within capitalism, is likely to come from a conscious and proactive institutional restructuring of the financial and monetary system that lies at the heart of capitalism. In designing and implementing these restructuring efforts, it is crucial to recognize that history is most definitely not on our side, and it is not coming to save us. Ultimately, moreover, no approach to financial regulation or institutional design will ever constitute a stable permanent fix for the basic underlying dilemmas discussed here—nor will the inherent tendency for wealth and power to inexorably collapse into the hands of the elite nodes and gatekeepers of finance likely ever disappear. Even if only as a latent potentiality, this is rather an issue that is likely to remain lurking in the background, probably in perpetuity, within any future global socioeconomic order, no matter how progressive or egalitarian in architecture, and regardless of its "socialist" as opposed to "capitalist" appellation. Even if we tried to abolish money altogether, we would just end up calling it something else due the basic logical imperative of maintaining a shared social reference frame of value. None of this is to be pessimistic or fatalistic; rather, it is precisely through the recognition of such deep-seated dilemmas and pitfalls, that we will be best placed to deal with them.

References

Aalbers, M. 2009a. "The globalization and Europeanization of mortgage markets." *International Journal of Urban and Regional Research 33* (2): 389–410.

Aalbers, M. 2009b. "Geographies of the financial crisis." *Area* 41(1): 34–42.

Abraham, J. P. and Van Dicke, P. 2002. "European financial cross-border consolidation: At the crossroads in Europe?" *SUERF Studies 22*, 1–112.

Acharya, V. and Schnabl, P. 2010. "Do global banks spread global imbalances? Asset-backed commercial paper during the financial crisis of 2007–09." *IMF Economic Review 58*: 37.

Acharya, V., Schnabl, P., and Suarez, G. 2013. "Securitization without risk transfer." *Journal of Financial Economics 107*(3): 515.

Acquier, A., Daudigeos, T., and Pinske, J. 2017. "Promises and paradoxes of the sharing economy: An organizing framework." *Technological Forecasting and Social Change 125*: 1–10.

Agence des Participations de Letta (APE) 2013. "The French state as a shareholder." *APE 2013 Report.* http://www.economie.gouv.fr/files/files/directions_services/agence-participations-etat/Documents/Rapports-de-l-Etat-actionnaire/2013/Overview_2013.pdf.

Aizenman, J. 2007. "Large hoarding of international reserves and the emerging global economic architecture." NBER Working Paper No. 13277. http://www.nber.org/papers/w13277.

Aizenman, J. and Lee, J. 2007. "International reserves: Precautionary versus mercantilist views, theory and evidence." *Open Economies Review 18*: 181–214.

Akerloff, G. A. and Shiller, R. J. 2009. *Animal Spirits: How Human Psychology Drives the Economy, and Why It Matters for Global Capitalism.* Princeton, NJ: Princeton University Press.

Aliber, R. Z. and Zoega, G. (eds) 2011. *Preludes to the Icelandic Banking Crisis.* New York: Palgrave Macmillan.

Allen, J. 2009. "Three spaces of power: Territory, networks, plus a topological twist in the tale of domination and authority." *Journal of Power 2*: 197–212.

Allen, J. 2010. "Powerful city networks: More than connections less than domination and control." *Urban Studies 47* (13): 2895–2911.

Allen, J. and Pryke, M. 1994. "The production of service space." *Environment and Planning D, 12*, 453–475.

Allen, J. and Pryke, M. 1999. "Money cultures after Georg Simmel: Mobility, movement, and identity." *Environment and Planning D 17*, 51–68.

Alon, I. and McIntyre, J. R. (eds) 2008. *Globalizing Chinese Enterprises.* New York: Palgrave Macmillan.

Amin, A. and Thrift, N. 1992. "Neo-Marshallian nodes in global networks." *International Journal of Urban and Regional Research 22*, 571–587.

Amin, A. and Thrift, N. 1994. *Globalization, Institutions, and Regional Development in Europe.* Oxford: Oxford University Press.

Amsden, A. H. 1989. *Asia's Next Giant: South Korea and Late Industrialization.* New York: Oxford University Press.

Andelman, D. A. 1976. "Moscow Narodny Bank stirs Singapore trouble." *New York Times* (June 26). https://www.nytimes.com/1976/06/26/archives/moscow-narodny-bank-stirs-singapore-trouble-moscows-narodny-bank.html [accessed March 2, 2021].

Aoki, M., Jackson, G., and Miyajima, H. 2007. *Corporate Governance in Japan: Institutional Change and Organizational Diversity*. Oxford: Oxford University Press.

Aoyama, Y., Benner, C., Berndt, C. et al. 2011. "Emerging themes in economic geography: Outcomes of the Economic Geography 2010 workshop." *Economic Geography 87*: 111–126.

Appadurai, A. 1990. "Disjuncture and difference in the global cultural economy." *Theory, Culture & Society 7* (2–3): 295–310.

Appel, I., Gormley, T. A., Keim, D. B. 2016. "Passive investors, not passive owners." *Journal of Financial Economics 121*: 111–141.

Armitstead, L. 2012. "BlackRock's Michelle Edkins behind wave of shareholder revolts." *The Telegraph* (May 4). http://www.telegraph.co.uk/finance/newsbysector/banksandfinance/9247055/BlackRocks-Michelle-Edkins-behind-wave-of-shareholder-revolts.html.

Arner, D. W., Barberis, J., and Buckley, R. P. 2016. "The evolution of fintech: A new post-crisis paradigm?" *Georgetown Journal of International Law 47*(4): 1345–1393.

Arrighi, G. 1994. *The Long Twentieth Century: Money, Power, and the Origins of our Times*. London: Verso.

Arrighi, G. and Silver, B. 2001. "Capitalism and world (dis)order." *Review of International Studies 27*: 257–279

Arsht, S. S. 1976. "A history of Delaware corporation law." *Delaware Journal of Corporate Law 1*(1): 1–22.

Arteta, C., Carey, M., Correa, R., and Kottor, J. 2013. "Revenge of the steamroller: ABCP as a window on risk choices." *Board of Governors of the Federal Reserve System 1076*. https://www.federalreserve.gov/pubs/ifdp/2013/1076/ifdp1076.pdf [accessed November 9, 2016].

Ashman, I., Bestwick, H. 2003. *Securitisation in the Cayman Islands*. Walkers Attorneys at Law Memo.

Avei, S. B., Schipani, C. A., and Seyhun, H. N. 2018. "Eliminating conflicts of interests in banks: The significance of the Volker Rule." *Yale Journal on Regulation 35*(2): 343–381.

Avi-Yonah, R. S. 2013. "What goes around comes around: Why the US is responsible for capital flight (and what it can do about it)." University of Michigan Law School Public Law and Legal Theory Research Paper Series. Available on SSRN.

Azar, J., Schmalz, M. C., and Tecu, I. 2016. "Anti-competitive effects of common ownership." Ross School of Business Paper No. 1235. http://papers.ssrn.com/sol3/papers.cfm?abstract_id=2427345.

Baker, J. H. 1979. "The Law Merchant and the common law before 1700." *Cambridge Law Journal 38* (2): 295–322.

Baker, R. W. 2005. *Capitalism's Achilles Heel: Dirty Money and How to Renew the Free-Market System*. London: Wiley.

Baker, W. E. 1990. "Market networks and corporate behavior." *American Journal of Sociology 96* (3): 589–625.

Baldursson, F. M. Richard. 2014. "Gambling for resurrection in Iceland: The rise and fall of the banks." CEPR Working Paper. http://cepr.org/sites/default/files/events/papers/1822_BALDURSSON%20-%20Gmabling%20for%20resurrection%20in%20Iceland.pdf.

Barford, V. and Holt, G. 2013. "The rise of 'tax shaming.'" *BBC News* (May 21). http://www.bbc.co.uk/news/magazine-20560359.

Barry, F. 2019. "Aggressive tax planning practices and inward-FDI implications for Ireland of the new US corporate tax regime." *Economic and Social Review* 50(2): 325–340.

Bartlett, R. 2010. "Inefficiencies in the information thicket: A case study of derivative disclosures during the financial crisis." *Journal of Corporate Law* 36(1).

Basel Committee on Banking Supervision (BCBS). 2009. *The Joint Forum Report on Special Purpose Entities*. Basel: Bank for International Settlements.

Bassens, D., Engelen, E., Derudder, B., and Witlox, F. 2013. "Securitization across borders: Organizational mimicry in Islamic finance." *Journal of Economic Geography* 13: 85–106.

Bassens, D. and Van Meetern, M. 2015. "World cities under conditions of financialized globalization: Towards an augmented world city hypothesis." *Progress in Human* Geography 39(6): 752–775.

Baud, C. and Durand, C. 2012. "Financialization, globalization and the making of profits by leading retailers." *Socio-Economic Review* 10: 241–266.

Bayer, K. M. and Bräutigam, L. 2015. "Shadow banking and the offshore nexus—Some considerations on the systemic linkages of two important economic phenomena." ICAE Working Paper Series 40.

BBC. 2020. "Goldman Sachs to pay $3bn over 1MDB corruption scandal." *BBC News* (October 22). https://www.bbc.co.uk/news/business-54597256 [accessed April 3, 2020].

BBC. 2017. *Man of Steel: Sanjeev Gupta*. BBC documentary.

Beales, R. 2020. "BlackRock is becoming the new, old Goldman Sachs." *Reuters* (June 4). https://www.reuters.com/article/us-blackrock-goldman-sachs-breakingviews-idUSKBN23B36U [accessed April 12, 2021].

Bean, B. and Wright, A. L. 2015. "The U.S. Foreign Account Tax Compliance Act: American legal imperialism?" *Journal of International & Comparative Law* 21(2): 333–368.

Beardsworth, T. 2019. "Vodafone invests in fund making money off its own late payments." *Bloomberg* (March 18). https://www.bloomberg.com/news/articles/2019-03-18/vodafone-finds-a-novel-investment-to-make-money-off-its-suppliers?sref=45uaXh1D [accessed April 11, 2020].

Beaverstock, J. V., Hoyler, M., Pain, K., and Taylor, P. J. 2001. *Comparing London and Frankfurt as World Cities: A Relational Study of Contemporary Urban Change*. London: Anglo-German Foundation for the Study of Industrial Society.

Beaverstock, J. V., Hoyler, M., Pain, K., and Taylor, P. J. 2005. "Demystifying the euro in European financial centre relations: London and Frankfurt, 2000–2001." *Journal of Contemporary European Studies* 13(2): 143–157.

Beaverstock, J. V., Smith, R. G., and Taylor, P. J. 2000. "World city network: A new metageography." *Annals of the Association of American Geographers* 90(1): 123–134.

Bell, S. 2001. "The role of the state and the hierarchy of money." *Cambridge Journal of Economics* 25: 149–163.

Beltran, D. O., Cordell, L., and Thomas, C. P. 2013. "Asymmetric information and the death of ABS CDOs. Board of Governors of the Federal Reserve System International Finance." Discussion Papers Number 1075. https://www.federalreserve.gov/pubs/ifdp/2013/1075/ifdp1075.pdf.

Benediktsdottir, S., Danielsson, J., and Zoega, G. 2011. "Lessons from a collapse of a financial system." *Economic Policy* 26: 183–235.

Berle, A. and Means, G. 1932. *The Modern Corporation and Private Property*. New York: Macmillan.

Berle, A. and Means, G. 1999. *The Modern Corporation and Private Property*, 2nd edn. Piscataway: Transaction.

Bernard, T. S. 2018. "Fidelity tries luring investors with two new no-fee funds: So what's the catch?" *New York Times* (August 10). https://www.nytimes.com/2018/08/10/business/fidelity-mutual-funds-fees.html.

Bernstein, P. L. 2005. *Capital Ideas: The Improbable Origins of Modern Wall Street*. Hoboken, NJ: Wiley.

Bernstein, P. L. 2007. *Capital Ideas Evolving*. Hoboken, NJ: Wiley.

Betz, F. 2016. *Models of Financial Markets*. Asian Business Research 1(2): 30–45.

Bhagwati, J. 1998. "The capital myth: The difference between trade in widgets and dollars." *Foreign Affairs 77*(7–12).

Bickers, R. and Jackson, I. 2016. "Introduction: Land, law and power: Treaty ports and concessions in modern China." In *Treaty Ports in Modern China: Law Land and Power* edited by R. Bickers and I. Jackson. New York: Routledge, 1–22.

Black, L. S. 1977. "The Delaware tender offer law." *New York Law School Law Review 23*(3): 461–478.

BlackRock 2015. "BlackRock: Worldwide leader in asset and risk management." White Paper. http://www.blackrock.com/corporate/en-gb/literature/whitepaper/viewpoint-blackrock-worldwide-leader-in-asset-management.pdf.

BlackRock. 2018. *Aladdin Platform Overview*. https://www.blackrock.com/aladdin/offerings/aladdin-overview [accessed August 14, 2018].

Blonigen, B. A. and Davies, R. B. 2004. "The effects of bilateral tax treaties on U.S. FDI activity." *International Tax and Public Finance 11*: 601–622.

Bloomberg. 2017. *Tracking Tax Runaways* [database]. https://www.bloomberg.com/graphics/tax-inversion-tracker/

Bloomberg. 2020. "Why China change the rules on Jack Ma's Ant Group." *Bloomberg News* (November 5). https://www.bloomberg.com/news/articles/2020-11-05/why-china-changed-the-rules-on-jack-ma-s-ant-group-quicktake?sref=45uaXh1D [accessed January 8, 2021].

Bloomberg Businessweek. 2011. "Big banks go after 401k trillions." Available: http://www.businessweek.com/magazine/content/11_15/b4223053701239.htm.

Boerner, L. and Hatfield, J. W. 2017. "The design of debt clearing markets: Clearinghouse mechanisms in pre-industrial Europe." *Journal of Political Economy 125*(6): 1991–2037.

Bordo, M. D. 1990. "The lender of last resort: Alternative views and historical experience." *Economic Review* (January/February): 18–29.

Boyer-Xambeau, M. T., Deleplace, G., and Gillard, L. 1994. *Private Money and Public Currencies: The Sixteenth Century Challenge*. London: Routledge.

Braithwaite, J. and Drahos, P. 2000. *Global Business Regulation*. Cambridge, UK: Cambridge University Press.

Braudel, F. 1985. *Civilization and Capitalism, 15–18th Century, Volume II: The Wheels of Commerce*. London: Fontana Press.

Braudel, F. 1992. *Civilization and Capitalism, 15–18th Century, Volume III: The Perspective of the World*. Berkeley and Los Angeles: University of California Press.

Braudel, F. 2019. *Out of Italy: Two Centuries of World Domination and Demise*. London: Europa.

Brenner, N., Peck, J., and Theodore, N. 2010. "Variegated neoliberalism: Geographies, modalities, pathways." *Global Networks 10*: 182–222.

Brezis, E. S. 1995. "Foreign capital flows in the century of Britain's industrial revolution: New estimates, controlled conjectures." *Economic History Review 48*(1): 46–67.

Brooker, M. 2020. "The rich irony of Hong Kong's leader Carrie Lam." *Bloomberg* (November 30). https://www.bloomberg.com/opinion/articles/2020-11-30/carrie-lam-s-piles-of-cash-show-u-s-sanctions-may-indeed-work?sref=45uaXh1D [accessed February 27].

Brovkin, V. 2001. "Moving money, making money, and parking money overseas: Front companies in offshore jurisdictions." *Demokratizatsiya* 9: 150–166.

Brownstein, A. R., Katz, Rosenblum, S. A., Katz, D. A., and Niles, S. V. 2015. "Some lessons from DuPont-Trian." *Harvard Law School Forum on Corporate Governance and Financial Regulation*, May 18. https://corpgov.law.harvard.edu/2015/05/18/winning-a-proxy-fight-lessons-from-the-dupont-trian-vote/.

Bruck, C. 1988. *The Predators' Ball: The Inside Story of Drexel Burnham and the Rise of the Junk Bond Raiders*. New York: Simon & Schuster.

Bryan, D., Rafferty, M., and Wigan, D. 2017. "Capital unchained: Finance, intangible assets and the double life of capital in the offshore world." *Review of International Political Economy* 24(1): 56–86.

Buckley, P J., Clegg, L J., Cross, A R., Liu, X., Voss, H., and Zheng, P. 2007. "The determinants of Chinese outward foreign direct investment" *Journal of International Business Studies* 38: 499–518

Buiter W. H. and Rahbari, E. 2012. "The European Central Bank as a lender of last resort for sovereigns in the Eurozone." *Journal of Common Market Studies* 50: 6–35.

Buiter, W. H. and Sibert, A. C. 2011. "The Icelandic banking crisis and what to do about it: The lender of last resort theory of optimal currency areas." In *Preludes to the Icelandic Banking Crisis*, edited by R. Z. Aliber and G. Zoega. New York: Palgrave Macmillan, 241–275.

Bullough, O. 2019. "The great American tax haven: Why the super-rich love South Dakota." *The Guardian* (November 14). Via https://www.theguardian.com/world/2019/nov/14/thegreat-american-tax-haven-why-the-super-rich-love-south-dakota-trust-laws [accessed January 10, 2020].

Bunge, J. 2015. "DuPont CEO Ellen Kullman steps down." *Wall Street Journal* (October 5). http://www.wsj.com/articles/dupont-ceo-kullman-steps-down-1444077244.

Bureau of Economic Analysis (BEA). 2013. *US direct investment abroad on a historical cost basis*. http://www.bea.gov/international/di1usdbal.htm.

Bureau of Economic Analysis (BEA). 2021. *GDP by state*. https://www.bea.gov/data/gdp/gdp-state.

Burell, T. H. 2011. "A story of privileges and immunities: From medieval concept to the colonies and United States Constitution." *Campbell Law Review* 34(1): 7–114.

Burn, G. 1999. "The state, the City and the Euromarkets." *International Political Economy* 6(2): 225–261.

Burrough, B. and Helyar, J. 1990. *Barbarians at the Gate: The Fall of RJR Nabisco*. New York: Random House.

Burrows, E. G. and Wallace, M. 1998. *Gotham: A History of New York City to 1898*. Oxford: Oxford University Press.

Büthe, T. and Mattli, W. 2011. *The New Global Rulers: The Privatization of Regulation in the World Economy*. Princeton, NJ: Princeton University Press.

Carden, D., Nasser, Z. 2007. "US tax guidelines for CDO transactions." In *Global Securitization and Structured Finance*. Deutsche Bank, 120–127. http://www.globalsecuritisation.com/07_americas/DB07_120_127_US_CC.pdf [accessed November 29, 2021].

Carlos, A. M. and Neal, L. 2011. "Amsterdam and London as financial centers in the eighteenth century." *Financial History Review* 18(1): 21–46.

Carosso, V. 1979. *More than a Century of Investment Banking: The Kidder, Peabody & Co. Story*. New York: McGraw Hill.

Carosso, V. 1987. *The Morgans: Private International Bankers*. Cambridge, MA: Harvard University Press.

Casella, B. 2019. "Looking through conduit FDI in search of ultimate investors—A probabilistic approach." *Transnational Corporations 26*(1): 109–146.

Cassis, Y. 2006. *Capitals of Capital: A History of International Financial Centres, 1780–2005*. Cambridge, UK: Cambridge University Press.

Cassis, Y. and Wójcik, D. (eds) 2018. *International Financial Centres after the Global Financial Crisis and Brexit*. Oxford: Oxford University Press.

Castells, M. 1996. *The Rise of the Network Society*. Oxford: Blackwell.

Castells, M. 2010. "Globalisation, networking, urbanisation: Reflections on the spatial dynamics of the information age." *Urban Studies 47*(13): 2737–2745.

Cattani, G. and Tschoegl, A. E. 2002. "An evolutionary view of internationalization: Chase Manhattan Bank, 1917 to 1996." Wharton Financial Institutions Working Paper 02–37. https://core.ac.uk/download/pdf/6649809.pdf [accessed Dec. 26 2020].

Chambers, D., Sarkissian, S., and Schill, M. J. 2018. "Market and regional segmentation and risk premia in the first era of financial globalization." *Review of Financial Studies 31*(10): 4063–4098.

Chang, H. J. 2002. *Kicking Away the Ladder: Development Strategy in Historical Perspective*. London: Anthem.

Chang, K. 2003. "Multinational enforcement of US securities laws: The need for the clear and restrained scope of extraterritorial subject-matter jurisdiction." *Fordham Journal of Corporate & Financial Law 9*(1): 89–125

Chapman, S. D. 1979. "Financial restraints on the growth of firms in the cotton industry, 1790–1850." *Economic History Review 32*(1): 50–69.

Charan, R. and Colvin, G. 2015. "Why Vanguard and BlackRock could beat Peltz and Icahn." *Fortune* (June 11). http://fortune.com/2015/06/11/vanguard-blackrock-could-beat-peltz-icahn/.

China Mobile. 2014. *Form 20-F submitted to the United States Securities and Exchange Commission* http://www.chinamobileltd.com/en/ir/reports.php.

China Mobile. 2020. *Investor Relations: Monthly Customer Data*. https://www.chinamobileltd.com/en/ir/operation_m.php [accessed March 7, 2021].

China Telecom (Hong Kong) Limited. 1997. *Prospectus offering American Depositary Shares*. Washington, DC: Securities and Exchange Commission.

Choi, S.-R., Park, D. and Tschoegl, A. E. 2003. "Banks and the world's major banking centres, 2000." *Review of World Economics 139*(3): 550–568.

Choi, S.-R., Tschoegl, A. E., and Yu, C.-M. (1986) "Banks and world's major financial centres, 1970–1980." *Review of World Economics 123*(4): 48–64.

Christensen, J. and Hampton, M. P. 1999. "A legislature for hire: The capture of the state in Jersey's offshore finance centre." In *Offshore Finance Centers and Tax Havens: The Rise of Global Capital*, edited by M. P. Hampton and J. P. Abbott. West Lafayette: Purdue University Press, 166–191.

Christensen, J., Shaxson, N., and Wigan, D. 2016. "The finance curse: Britain in the world economy." *British Journal of International Relations 18*: 255–269

Christophers, B. 2009. "Complexity, finance, and progress in human geography." *Progress in Human Geography 33*: 807–824.

CIA. 1969. *Intelligence Report: Soviet-Owned Banks in the West*. ER 69-28 October 1969. https://www.cia.gov/readingroom/docs/DOC_0000233857.pdf [accessed April 13, 2021].

Clark, G. L. 2002. "London in the European financial services industry: Locational advantages and product complementarities." *Journal of Economic Geography* 2(4): 433–454.

Clark, G. L., Dixon, A., and Monk, A. H. B. 2013. *Sovereign Wealth Funds: Legitimacy, Governance, and Global Power*. Princeton, NJ: Princeton University Press.

Clark, G. L., Gertler, M. S., Feldman, M., and Wójcik, D. (eds) 2018 *The New Oxford Handbook of Economic Geography*. Oxford: Oxford University Press.

Clark, G. L. and Monk, A. 2010a. "Government of Singapore Investment Corporation (GIC): Insurer of last resort and bulwark of nation-state legitimacy." *Pacific Review* 23: 429–451.

Clark, G. L. and Monk, A. 2010b. "The legitimacy and governance of Norway's sovereign wealth fund: The ethics of global investment." *Environment and Planning A* 42: 1723–1738.

Clark, G. L., Monk, A., Dixon, A., Pauly, L. W., Faulconbridge, J., Yeung, J. W., and Behrendt, S. 2010. "Symposium: Sovereign fund capitalism." *Environment and Planning A* 42: 2271–2291.

Clark, G. L. and O'Connor, K. 1997. "The informational content of financial products and the spatial structure of the global finance industry." In *Spaces of Globalization: Reasserting the Power of the Local*, edited by K. R. Cox. New York: Guilford Press, 89–114.

Clark, G. L. and Wójcik, D. 2001. "The city of London in the Asian crisis." *Journal of Economic Geography* 1(1): 107–130.

Clark, G. L. and Wójcik, D. 2007. *The Geography of Finance: Corporate Governance in a Global Marketplace*. Oxford: Oxford University Press.

Clark, P. and Buhayar, M. 2018. "Wall Street slaps down NYC again with Alliance-Bernstein's move to Nashville." *Bloomberg* (May 2). https://www.bloomberg.com/news/articles/2018-05-02/alliancebernstein-chooses-nashville-in-wall-street-rebuke-of-nyc.

Clausing, K. 2016. "The U.S. state experience under formulary apportionment: Are there lessons for international reform?" *National Tax Journal* 69(2): 353–386.

Clifford, M. L. and Barnathan. J. 1998. "The perils of red capitalism." *Bloomberg* (October 26). https://www.bloomberg.com/news/articles/1998-10-25/the-perils-of-red-capitalism?sref=45uaXh1D [accessed March 2, 2021].

Coates, N. and Rafferty, M. 2007. "Offshore financial centres, hot money and hedge funds: A network analysis of international capital flows." In *Global Finance in the New Century: Beyond Deregulation*, edited by L. Assassi, A. Nesvetailova, and D. Wigan. Houndmills, UK: Palgrave Macmillan, 38–54.

Cobb, S. C. 1998. "Global finance and the growth of offshore financial centers: The Manx experience." *Geoforum 29*: 7–21.

Cobham, A. and Janský, P. 2018. "Global distribution of revenue loss from corporate tax avoidance: Re-estimation and country results." *Journal of International Development* 30(2): 206–232.

Cobham, A., Janský, P., and Meinzer, M. 2015. "The Financial Secrecy Index: Shedding new light on the geography of secrecy." *Economic Geography* 91: 281–303.

Coe, N. M., Hess, M., Yeung, H. W. C., Dicken, P., and Henderson, J. 2004. "'Globalizing' regional development: A global production networks perspective." *Transactions of the Institute of British Geographers* 29(4): 468–484.

Coe, N. M., Lai, K. P. Y., and Wójcik, D. 2014. "Integrating finance into global production networks" *Regional Studies* 48: 761–777.

Coffee, J. C. 2001. "The rise of dispersed ownership: The roles of law and the state in the separation of ownership and control." *Yale Law Journal* 111(1): 1–82.

Coffee, J. C. 2015. "Lessons of DuPont: Corporate governance for dummies." *New York Law Journal* (May 28). http://www.newyorklawjournal.com/id=1202727540430/Lessons-of-DuPont-Corporate-Governance-for-Dummies?slreturn=20150824121901.

Cohen, B. J. 1998. *The Geography of Money*. Ithaca, NY: Cornell University Press.

Collins, W. D. 2013. "Trusts and the origins of anti-trust legislation." *Fordham Law Review* 31(5): 2279–2348.

Committee on Ways and Means. 1961. President's 1961 Tax Recommendations: Hearings before the Committee on Ways and Means, *House of Representatives*. Washington, DC: US Congress.

Connor, G., Flavin, T., and Kelly, B. 2012. "The U.S. and Irish credit crises: Their distinctive differences and common features." *Journal of International Money and Finance 31*: 60–79.

Cook, G. S., Pandit N. R., Beaverstock J. V., Taylor P. J., and Pain K. 2007. "The role of location in knowledge creation and diffusion: Evidence of centripetal and centrifugal forces in the City of London financial services agglomeration." *Environment and Planning A 39*(6): 1325–1345.

Cook, T. Q. and Duffield, J. G. 1979. "Money market mutual funds: A reaction to government regulations or a lasting financial innovation?" *Federal Reserve Bank of Richmond Economic Review* (July/August): 15–31.

Cooper, R. 1982. "William Pitt, taxation, and the needs of war." *Journal of British Studies 22*(1): 94–103.

Copland, J. R., Larcker, D. F., and Tayan, B. 2018. "Big thumb on the scale: An overview of the proxy advisory industry." *Stanford Closer Look Series—CGRP72*.

Corbett, J. and Jenkinson, T. 1996. "The financing of industry, 1970–1989: An international comparison." *Journal of the Japanese and International Economies 10*(1): 71–96.

Cottrell, P. L. 1975. "Railway finance and the crisis of 1866: Contractors' bills of exchange, and the finance companies." *Journal of Transport History 3*(1): 20–40.

Covitz, D., Liang, N., and Suarez, G. 2013. "The evolution of a financial crisis: Collapse of the asset-backed commercial paper market." *Journal of Finance 1*(68): 815.

CPFF (Commercial Paper Funding Facility). 2017. Federal Reserve. https://www.federalreserve.gov/regreform/reform-cpff.htm [accessed June 27, 2017].

Craig, S. 2013. "The giant of shareholders, quietly stirring." *New York Times* (May 18). http://www.nytimes.com/2013/05/19/business/blackrock-a-shareholding-giant-is-quietly-stirring.html?_r=0.

Crigger, L. 2017. "A tour of the top 10 robos." ETF.com (January 24). http://www.etf.com/publications/etfr/tour-top-10-robos?nopaging=1 [accessed August 14, 2018].

Croke, J. 2007. "New developments in asset-backed commercial paper." *Orrick, Herrington & Sutcliffe LLP Report*, 3–54.

Crooks, E. 2015. "Dow and DuPont aim to pre-empt activists with megadeal." *Financial Times* (December 9). https://next.ft.com/content/7f43a318-9e51-11e5-8ce1-f6219b685d74.

Crotty, J. 2009. 'Structural causes of the global financial crisis: A critical assessment of the 'New Financial Architecture.'" *Cambridge Journal of Economics 33*: 563–580.

Currier, C. 2007. "Success may be downfall of perfectly good fund." *Bloomberg* (May 15). http://www.bloomberg.com/apps/news?pid=newsarchive&sid=aSw20LBKZpGs.

Curry, T. 1997. "The LDC debt crisis." In *History of the Eighties: Lessons for the Future. Vol. 1, An Examination of the Banking Crises of the 1980s and Early 1990s*, edited by Federal Deposit Insurance Corporation (FDIC). Washington, DC: FDIC, 235–257.

Dach, J. 1967. "The Eurodollar and the risk of currency restrictions." *International Lawyer 1*(3): 392–399.

Dale, E. 1956. "Contributions to administration by Alfred P. Sloan Jr, and GM." *Administrative Science Quarterly 1*(1): 30–62.

Damgaard, J., Elkjaer, T., and Johannesen, N. 2019. "What is real and what is not in the Global FDI network?" *IMF* WP/19/274. file:///C:/Users/Dan/Downloads/wpiea2019274-print-pdf%20(6).pdf [accessed March 7, 2021].

Daniels, P. W. 2012. (ed.) *Producer Services in China: Economic and Urban Development.* Routledge: London, 29–51.

Davies, A. R., Donald, B., Gray, M., and Knox-Hayes, J. 2017. "Sharing economies: Moving beyond binaries in a digital age." *Cambridge Journal of Regions, Economy and Society* 10(2): 209–230.

Davies, M. 2012. "Crown, city and guild in late medieval London." In *London and Beyond: Essays in Honour of Derek Keene,* edited by M. Davies and J. A. Galloway. London: Institute of Historical Research, 247–268.

Davis, C. A. 2019. "Is the tax cuts and jobs act GILTI of anti-simplification?" *Virginia Tax Review* 38(3): 315–396.

Davis, G. F. and Mizruchi, M. S. 1999. "The money center cannot hold: Commercial banks in the U.S. system of corporate governance." *Administrative Science Quarterly* 44(2): 215–239.

Davis, L., Neal, L., and White, E. N. 2003. "How it all began: The rise of listing requirements on the London, Berlin, Paris, and New York stock exchanges." *International Journal of Accounting* 38(2): 117–143.

Davison, D. and Litvinoff, S. 2013. "Update: Tourre extends SEC's reach for foreign transactions involving domestic offerings." *Securities Regulation & Law Report* 45.

Davison, L. 1997. "Continental Illinois and 'too big to fail.'" In *History of the Eighties: Lessons for the Future. Vol. 1, An Examination of the Banking Crises of the 1980s and Early 1990s,* edited by Federal Deposit Insurance Corporation (FDIC). Washington, DC: FDIC, 235–257.

Dawley, S., Marshall, N., Pike, A., Pollard, J., and Tomaney, J. (2011) "The labour market impact of the run on Northern Rock: Continuity and evolution in an old industrial region." Papers in Evolutionary Economic Geography No. 11.09, Utrecht University.

Deacon, J. 2004. *Global Securitisation and CDOs.* London: Wiley.

De Grauwe, P. and Ji, Y. 2013. "Self-fulfilling crises in the Eurozone: An empirical test." *Journal of International Money and Finance* 34: 15–36.

De Jong, D. 2016. "Being Swedish proving too costly for biggest Nordic bank." *Bloomberg* (October 13). https://www.bloomberg.com/news/articles/2016-10-07/being-swedish-proving-too-costly-for-biggest-nordic-bank.

De Long, B. 1991. "Did J.P. Morgan's money men add value? An economist's perspective on financial capitalism." In *Inside the Business Enterprise: Historical Perspectives on the Use of Information,* edited by P. Temin. Chicago: University of Chicago Press, 205–250.

De Long, B. 1992. "J.P. Morgan and his Money Trust." *Wilson Quarterly* 16(4): 16–30.

Department of Education. 2021. *Federal Student Loan Portfolio.* https://studentaid.gov/data-center/student/portfolio [accessed February 27, 2021].

De Roover, R. 1946. "The Medici bank organization and management." *Journal of Economic History* 6(1): 24–52.

De Roover, R. 1963. *The Rise and Decline of the Medici Bank 1397–1494.* Cambridge, MA: Harvard University Press.

Derudder, B., Hoyler, M. and Taylor, P. (2011) "Goodbye Reykjavik: International banking centres and the global financial crisis." *Area* 43(2): 173–182.

Desai, M. A., Foley, C. F., and Hines, J. R. 2004. "Economic effects of regional tax havens." NBER Working Paper 10806. Cambridge, MA: National Bureau of Economic Research. http://www.nber.org/papers/w10806.pdf?new_window=1.

DeYoung, R., Evanoff, D. D., and Molyneux, P. 2009. "Mergers and acquisitions of financial institutions: A review of the post-2000 literature." *Journal of Financial Services Research* 36: 87–110

Dharmapala, D. 2008. "What problems and opportunities are created by tax havens?" *Oxford Review of Economic Policy* 24: 661–679.

D'Hulster, K. 2012. "Cross border banking supervision: Incentive conflicts in supervisory information sharing between home and host supervisors." *Journal of Banking Regulation* 13: 300–319.

Dicken, P. and Lloyd, P. E. 1990. *Location in Space: Theoretical Perspectives in Economic Geography*. New York: HarperCollins.

Dicken, P. J. 2011. *Global Shift: Mapping the Changing Contours of the World Economy*, 6th edn. London: Sage.

Dilworth, L. C. 1985. "Tax Reform Act of 1985—Netherlands Antilles—Effect of the repeal of the 30% withholding tax on portfolio interest payments to foreign investors." *Georgia Journal of International and Comparative Law* 15(1): 111–123.

Dimon, J. 2014. *Chairman and CEO Letter to Shareholders* (JP Morgan Chase & Co. 2014 Annual Report). https://www.jpmorganchase.com/corporate/annual-report/2014/ar-introduction.htm.

Ding, X. L. 2000. "Informal privatization through internationalization: The rise of Nomenklatura capitalism in China's offshore businesses." *British Journal of Political Science 30*: 121–146.

Dixon, A. 2011. "Variegated capitalism and the geography of finance: Towards a common agenda." *Progress in Human Geography 35*: 193–210.

Dixon, A. and Monk, A. H. B. 2014. "Frontier finance." *Annals of the Association of American Geographers 104*: 852–868.

Dixon, A. D. 2012. "Form before function: Macro-institutional comparison and the geography of finance." *Journal of Economic Geography 12*(3): 579–600.

Donnan, S. 2016. "Apple ruling sparks angry reaction in US." *Financial Times* (August 30).

Donovan, D. and Murphy, A. E. 2013. *The Fall of the Celtic Tiger: Ireland and the Euro Debt Crisis*. Oxford: Oxford University Press.

Dooley, P. C. 1969. "The interlocking directorate." *American Economic Review 59*(3): 314–323.

Dorfman, J. 1951. "A Note on the interpenetration of Anglo-American finance, 1837–1841." *Journal of Economic History 11*(2): 140–147.

Dörry, S. 2014. "Strategic nodes in investment fund global production networks: The example of the financial center Luxembourg." *Journal of Economic Geography 15*: 797–814.

Downs, J. M. 1968. "American merchants and the China Opium Trade, 1800–1840." *Business History Review 42*(4): 418–442.

Drucker, P. F. 1976. *The Unseen Revolution: How Pension Fund Socialism Came to America*. Oxford: Butterworth-Heinemann.

Dübel, H. 2013. "The capital structure of banks and the practice of bank restructuring." *CFS 2013* (04).

Dunlavy, C. A. 2004. "From citizens to plutocrats: Nineteenth century shareholder voting rights and theories of the corporation." In *Constructing Corporate America: History, Politics, Culture*, edited by K. Lipartito and D. B. Sicilia. Oxford: Oxford University Press, 66–93.

Dunning, J. H. and Narula, R. (eds) 1996. *Foreign Direct Investment and Governments: Catalysts for Economic Restructuring*. London and New York: Routledge.

Economist. 2009. "Reykjavík-on-Thames." January 29.

Economist. 2012. "Rival versions of capitalism: The endangered public corporation." May 19. http://www.economist.com/node/21555562.

Economist. 2013a. "The new American capitalism: Rise of the distorporation." October 26. http://www.economist.com/news/briefing/21588379-mutation-way-companies-are-financed-and-managed-will-change-distribution.

Economist. 2013b. "The rise of BlackRock." December 7. http://www.economist.com/news/leaders/21591174-25-years-blackrock-has-become-worlds-biggest-investor-its-dominance-problem.

Economist. 2013c. "Onshore financial centers: Not a palm tree in sight." February 16. https://www.economist.com/special-report/2013/02/16/not-a-palm-tree-in-sight.

Economist. 2013d. "The Monolith and the Markets." December 7. https://www.economist.com/briefing/2013/12/07/the-monolith-and-the-markets

Economist. 2014. "Fund management: Will invest for food." May 3. http://www.economist.com/news/briefing/21601500-books-and-music-investment-industry-being-squeezed-will-invest-food.

Economist. 2015a. "Activist funds: An investor calls." February 7. http://www.economist.com/news/briefing/21642175-sometimes-ill-mannered-speculative-and-wrong-activists-are-rampant-they-will-change-american.

Economist. 2015b. "Mutual funds and airline competition: Who really owns the skies?" June 11. http://www.economist.com/blogs/freeexchange/2015/06/mutual-funds-and-airline-competition.

Economist. 2016. "HSBC: London v Hong Kong: East is Eden." February 6. https://www.economist.com/news/finance-and-economics/21690101-bankings-longest-and-most-successful-identity-crisis-east-eden.

Economist. 2017. "The investment-management industry faces a big squeeze." May 11. https://www.economist.com/finance-and-economics/2017/05/11/the-investment-management-industry-faces-a-big-squeeze.

Economist. 2017. "A legal vulnerability at the heart of China's big internet firms." September 16. https://www.economist.com/business/2017/09/16/a-legal-vulnerability-at-the-heart-of-chinas-big-internet-firms.

Economist. 2018a. "Raiders of the killer app." June 30.

Economist. 2018b. "Special report: Fixing the internet." June 30.

Economist. 2018c. "More knock-on than network." June 30.

Economist. 2018d. "A new school in Chicago." June 30.

Economist. 2020a. "American economic power: Spooked by sanctions." January 18–24.

Economist. 2020b. "The disintermediation dilemma." December 5–11.

Economist. 2021. "Corporate China: A chill descends." January 16–22.

Edelman, B. G. and Geradin, D. 2015. "Efficiencies and regulatory shortcuts: How should we regulate companies like AirBNB and Uber?" *Stanford Technology Law Review* 19(2): 293.

Eden, L. and Kudrle, R. 2005. "Tax havens: Renegade states in the international tax regime?" *Law & Policy 21*(1): 100–127.

Edwards, J. and Ogilvie, S. 2012. "What lessons for economic development can we draw from the Champagne fairs?" *Explorations in Economic History 49*(2): 131–148.

Eichengreen, B. 1995. "Financing infrastructure in developing countries: Lessons from the railway age." *World Bank Research Observer 10*(1): 75–91.

Eisenberg, T. and Miller, G. 2006. "Ex ante choices of law and forum: An empirical analysis of corporate merger agreements." *Vanderbilt Law Review 59*(6): 1975–2013.

Elliot, M. 2008. "A tale of three cities." *Time* (January 17).

Ellis, C. D. 1975. "The loser's game." *Financial Analysts Journal* (July/August): 19–26.

Eltis, W. 2001. "Lord Overstone and the establishment of nineteenth-century monetary orthodoxy." *University of Oxford Discussion Papers in Economic and Social History No. 42.* https://www.nuff.ox.ac.uk/Economics/History/paper42/42eltis.pdf [accessed December 19, 2020].

Emmenegger, P. 2015. "The long arm of US justice: US structural power and international banking." *Business and Politics 17*(3): 473–493.

Engel, K. 2001. "Tax neutrality to the left, international competitiveness to the right, stuck in the middle with Subpart-F." *Texas Law Review 79*(6): 1525–1607.

Engelen, E. 2011. "'Cognitive closure' in the Netherlands: Mortgage securitization in a hybrid European political economy." *Environment and Planning A 43*: 1779–1795.

Engelen, E., Erturk, I., Froud, J. et al. 2011. *After the Great Complacence: Financial Crisis and the Politics of Reform.* Oxford: Oxford University Press.

Epstein, G., ed. 2005. *Financialization and the World Economy.* Cheltenham, UK: Edward Elgar.

Epstein, R. A. and Rhodes, M. 2016. "International in life, national in death? Banking nationalism on the road to banking union." In *Political and Economic Dynamics of the Eurozone Crisis,* edited by J. A. Capraso and M. Rhodes. Oxford: Oxford University Press, 200–232.

Errico, L. and Musalem, A. 1999. "Offshore banking: An analysis of micro- and macroprudential issues." IMF Working Paper 99/5. https://www.imf.org/external/pubs/ft/wp/1999/wp9905.pdf.

Essletzbichler, J. and Rigby, D. L. 2007. "Exploring evolutionary economic geographies." *Journal of Economic Geography 7*: 549–571.

Esteban, J. C. 2001. "The British balance of payments, 1772–1820: India transfers and war finance." *Economic History Review 54*(1): 58–86.

ETF (Wisconsin Department of Employee Trust Funds). 2021. *Latest Investment Performance.* https://etf.wi.gov/wrs-performance/latest-investment-performance [accessed February 27, 2021].

European Commission. 2015. "Study on structures of aggressive tax planning and indicators: Final report. EC taxation papers." Working Paper 61—2015. https://ec.europa.eu/taxation_customs/sites/taxation/files/resources/documents/taxation/gen_info/economic_analysis/tax_papers/taxation_paper_61.pdf [accessed October 31, 2018].

Evans, P. C. and Gawer, A. 2016. "The rise of the platform enterprise: a global survey." *Center for Global Enterprise, Emerging Global Platform Series* (January).

Faith, N. and Macleod, A. 1979. "The mysterious private banks of Geneva." *Euromoney* (November 1). https://www.euromoney.com/article/b1d06hwcxgbq9y/the-mysterious-private-banks-of-geneva?copyrightInfo=true [accessed January 10, 2020].

Fama, E. F. 1995. "Random walks in stock market prices." *Financial Analysts Journal 51*(1): 75–80.

Fan, W. 2010. "Construction methods for the Shanghai Stock Exchange indices: 1870–1940." Shanghai Stock Exchange Project, Yale School of Management. https://som.yale.edu/sites/default/files/files/SSE-CC.pdf [accessed December 30, 2020].

Fannie Mae (Federal National Mortgage Association). 2021. *Fannie Mae 2020 Form 10-K.*

Farber, B. M. 1981. "International Banking Facilities: Defining a greater U.S. presence in the Eurodollar market." *Law and Policy in International Business 13*(4): 997–1046

Farhi, E. and Tirole, J. 2012. "Collective moral hazard, maturity mismatch, and systemic bailouts." *American Economic Review 102*(1): 60–93

Faulconbridge, J. R. 2004. "London and Frankfurt in Europe's evolving financial centre network." *Area 36*(3): 235–244.

Federal Reserve. 2012. "Assets and liabilities of U.S. branches and agencies of foreign banks." June 30. http://www.federalreserve.gov/econresdata/releases/assetliab/
assetsliab20120930.htm [accessed October 8, 2014].

Federal Reserve. 2013. "Usage of Federal Reserve credit and liquidity facilities" [last updated
December 9, 2013]. http://www.federalreserve.gov/newsevents/reform_transaction.htm
[accessed October 8, 2014].

Federal Reserve. 2014. "Factors affecting reserve balances." http://www.federalreserve.gov/
releases/h41/ [accessed October 8, 2014].

Federal Reserve. 2021. *Credit and Liquidity Programs and the Balance Sheet.* https://www.
federalreserve.gov/monetarypolicy/bst_recenttrends.htm [accessed February 27, 2021].

Felipe, J. 1999. "Total factor productivity growth in East Asia: A critical survey." *Journal of
Development Studies* 35(4): 1–41.

Ferguson, N. 1998. *The House of Rothschild: Money's Prophets 1798–1848.* New York:
Penguin.

Ferguson, N. 2009. *The Ascent of Money: A Financial History of the World.* London: Penguin.

Fernandes, N. and Giannetti, M. 2014. "On the fortunes of stock exchanges and their
reversals: Evidence from foreign listings." *Journal of Financial Intermediation* 23(2):
157–176.

Ferran, E., Moloney, N., Hill, J., and Coffee J. 2012. *The Regulatory Aftermath of the Global
Financial Crisis.* Cambridge: Cambridge University Press.

Ferri, P. and Minksy, H. P. 1992. "Market processes and thwarting systems." *Structural
Change and Economic Dynamics* 3(1): 79–91.

Fichtner, J., Heemskerk, E. M., and Garcia-Bernardo, J. 2017. "Hidden power of the big
three? Passive index funds, re-concentration of corporate ownership, and new financial
risk." *Business and Politics* 19(2): 298–326.

Financial Crisis Inquiry Commission (FCIC) 2011. *The Financial Crisis Inquiry Report:
Final Report of the National Commission on the Causes of the Financial and Economic
Crisis in the United States.* Washington, DC: US Government Printing Office.

Financial Services Authority (FSA). 2011. "The failure of the Royal Bank of Scotland."
Financial Services Authority Board Report. https://www.fca.org.uk/publication/
corporate/fsa-rbs.pdf.

Findley, M., Nielson, D., and Sharman, J. 2012. "Global Shell games: Testing money launder-
ers' and terrorists' access to shell companies." *Griffith University Centre for Governance
and Public Policy Research Report*

Fink, L. 2015. "Our gambling culture: Letter to US CEOs." Reprinted in *Perspectives on the
Long Term: Building a Stronger Foundation for Tomorrow.* Canada Pension Investment
Board and McKinsey and Company. http://viewer.zmags.com/publication/a1b195ee#/
a1b195ee/4.

FINMA. 2009. "Financial market crisis and financial market supervision." *Swiss Financial
Market Supervisory Authority (FINMA) report.* https://www.finma.ch/en/news/2009/09/
mm-bericht-finanzmarktkrise-20090914/.

Fishlow, A. 1985. "Lessons from the past: Capital markets during the 19th century and the
interwar period." *International Organization* 39(3): 383–439.

Flichy, P. 1993. "The birth of long distance communication: Semaphore telegraphs in Europe
(1790–1840)." *Réseaux: The French Journal of Communication* 1(1): 81–101.

Flood, J. 2007. "Lawyers as sanctifiers: The role of elite law firms in international business
transactions." *Indiana Journal of Global Legal Studies* 14(1): 35–66.

Florida, R. and Hathaway, I. 2018. "Rise of the global startup city: The new map of en-trepreneurship and venture capital." *Center for American Entrepreneurship report*. http://startupsusa.org/global-startup-cities/report.pdf [accessed December 30, 2020].

Focarellia, D. and Pozzolo, A. F. 2008. "Cross-border M&As in the financial sector: Is banking different from insurance?" *Journal of Banking & Finance 32*: 15–29.

Forbes 2021. Forbes Global 2000 List, 2021. https://www.forbes.com/lists/global2000/#6b4c37e5ac04 [accessed November 26, 2021].

Foster, W. T. 1922. The circuit flow of money. *American Economic Review 12*(3): 460–473.

Fratianni, M. 2006. "Government debt, reputation and creditors' protections: The tale of San Giorgio." *Review of Finance 10*(4): 487–506.

Fratianni, M. 2009. "The evolutionary chain of international financial centers." In *The Changing Geography of Banking and Finance*, edited by A. Zazzaro, M. Fratianni, and P. Alessandrini. Boston: Springer, 251–276.

Freddie Mac (Federal Home Loan Mortgage Corporation). 2021. *Freddie Mac 2020 Form 10-K*.

Freeland, R. F. (author) and Granovetter, M. (ed.) 2001. *The Struggle for Control of the Modern Corporation: Organizational Change at General Motors, 1924–1970*. Cambridge, UK: Cambridge University Press.

French, S., Leyshon, A., and Thrift, N. 2009. "A very geographical crisis: The making and breaking of the 2007–2008 financial crisis." *Cambridge Journal of Regions, Economy, and Society 2*: 287–302.

French, S., Leyshon, A. and Wainwright, T. 2011. "Financializing Space, Spacing Financial-ization." *Progress in Human Geography 35*: 789–819.

Freund, J., Curry, T., Hirsch, P., and Kelly, T. 1997. "Commercial real estate and the banking crisis of the 1980s and early 1990s." In *History of the Eighties: Lessons for the Future. Vol. 1, An Examination of the Banking Crises of the 1980s and Early 1990s*, edited by Federal Deposit Insurance Corporation (FDIC). Washington, DC: FDIC, 235–257.

Frey, C. B. and Osborne, M. A. 2017. "The future of employment: how susceptible are jobs to computerisation?" *Technological Forecasting and Social Change 114*: 254–280.

Fried, B. 2011. "Mandela's lessons in truth for City high-fliers." *Financial Times* (April 7).

Frieden, J. 1988. "Sectoral Conflict and Foreign Economic Policy, 1914–1940." *International Organization: 42*(1): 59–90.

Friedmann, J. 1986. "The world city hypothesis." *Development and Change 17*: 69–83.

Froud, J., Johal, S., Leaver, A. and Williams, K. 2006. *Financialization and Strategy: Narrative and Numbers*. London: Routledge

Froud, J. Haslam, C., Johal, S., and Williams, K. 2000. "Shareholder value and Finan-cialization: Consultancy promises, management moves." *Economy and Society 29*(1): 80–110.

Fumagalli, A., Lucarelli, S., Musolino, E., and Rocchi, G. 2018. "Digital labour in the platform economy: The case of Facebook." *Sustainability 10*(6): 1757.

Gach, R. and Gotsch, M. 2016. "Fintech's golden age." *Fintech Innovation Lab Report*. http://pfnyc.org/wp-content/uploads/2017/04/Fintech-Golden-Age_2016-06.pdf.

Galanter, M. and Roberts, S. 2008. "From kinship to magic circle: The London commercial law firm in the twentieth century." *International Journal of the Legal Profession 15*(3): 143–178.

Galbraith, J.K. 1975. *Money: Whence it Came, Where It Went*. London: Penguin.

Gaponomics. 2011. "Regional income inequality has risen in many countries: What should be done about it?" *The Economist* (March 10).

Gapper, J. 2008. "Whatever is good for Goldman…" *Financial Times* (September 24).

Gara, A. 2017. "BlackRock's edge: Why technology is creating the Amazon of Wall Street." *Forbes* (December 26). https://www.forbes.com/sites/antoinegara/2017/12/19/black rocks-edge-why-technology-is-creating-a-6-trillion-amazon-of-wall-street/#5881b6c2 561b.

Garcia-Bernardo, J., Fichtner, J., Takes, F. W., and Heemskerk, E. M. 2017. "Uncovering off-shore financial centers: Conduits and sinks in the global corporate ownership network." *Scientific Reports 7*: 1–10.

Garvy, G. 1972. "Banking under the tsars and the Soviets." *Journal of Economic History 32*(4): 869–893.

Geisst, C. R. 1997. *Wall Street: A History*. Oxford: Oxford University Press.

Gelderblom. O. and Jonker, J. 2004. "Completing a financial revolution: The finance of the Dutch East India trade and the rise of the Amsterdam capital market, 1595–1612." *Journal of Economic History 64*(3): 641–672.

Gennaioli, N., Schleifer, A., and Vishny, R. 2015. "Money doctors." *Journal of Finance 70*(1): 91–114.

Gerschenkron, A. 1962. *Economic Backwardness in Historical Perspective: A Book of Essays*. Cambridge, Massachusetts: Belknap Press of Harvard University Press.

Gibbons, W. J. 1956. "Tax effects of basing international business abroad." *Harvard Law Review 69*(7): 1209–1249.

Goetzmann, W. N. 2016. *Money Changes Everything: How Finance Made Civilization Possible*. Princeton: Princeton University Press.

Gorton, B. and Souleles, N. 2007. "Special purpose vehicles and securitization." In *The Risks of Financial Institutions*, edited by M. Carey and R. M. Stulz. Chicago: Chicago University Press, 456–602.

Gorton, G and Metrick, A. 2010. "Regulating the shadow banking system." *Brookings Papers on Economic Activity 41*(2): 261

Gorton, G. and Metrick, A. 2012. "Securitized banking and the run on repo." *Journal of Financial Economics 104*(3): 425–451.

Gowa, J. 1985. "Subsidizing American corporate expansion abroad: Pitfalls in the analysis of public and private power." *World Politics 37*(2): 180–203.

Gowan, P. 2009. "Crisis in the heartland: Consequences of the new Wall Street system." *New Left Review 55*: 5–29.

Graeber, D. 2011. *Debt: The First 5000 Years*. New York: First Melville House Printing.

Gregory, F. W. 1983. "A tale of three cities: The struggle for banking stability in Boston, New York, and Philadelphia, 1839–1841." *New England Quarterly 56*(1): 3–38.

Griffin, D. and Browning, J. 2021. "Greensill downfall spurred by Sydney Insurance manager's firing." *Bloomberg* (March 5). https://www.bloomberg.com/news/articles /2021-03-05/greensill-downfall-spurred-by-firing-of-sydney-insurance-manager?sref= 45uaXh1D [accessed April 13, 2021].

Grind, K. and Lublin, J. S. 2015. "Vanguard and BlackRock plan to get more assertive with their investments." *Wall Street Journal* (March 4). http://www.wsj.com/articles/vanguard-and-blackrock-plan-to-get-more-assertive-with-their-investments-1425445200.

Grossman, S. J. and Stiglitz, J. E. 1980. "On the impossibility of informationally efficient markets." *American Economic Review 70*: 393–408.

Grote, M. H. 2009. "Financial centers between centralization and virtualization." In *The Changing Geography of Banking and Finance*, edited by A. Zazzaro, M. Fratianni, and P. Alessandrini. Boston: Springer, 277–294.

Gruin, J. and Knaack, P. 2020. "Not just another shadow bank: Chinese authoritarian capitalism and the 'developmental' promise of digital financial innovation." *New Political Economy 25*(3): 370–387.

Guex, S. 2000. "The origins of the Swiss banking law and its repercussions for Swiss federal policy." *Business History Review* 74: 237–266.

Guillen, M. F. and Tschoegel, A. E. 2000. "The internationalization of retail banking: The case of the Spanish banks in Latin America." *Transnational Corporations* 9: 63–98.

Guthrie, J. 2011. "Stability talks would stem bank diaspora backchat." *Financial Times* (March 31), 20.

Haberly, D. 2011. "Strategic sovereign wealth fund investment and the new alliance capitalism: A network mapping investigation." *Environment and Planning A* 43(8): 1833–1852.

Haberly, D. 2014. "White knights from the Gulf: Sovereign wealth fund investment and the evolution of German industrial finance." *Economic Geography* 90(3): 293–320.

Haberly, D. 2021. "Offshore and the political and legal geography of finance: 1066–2020 AD." In *The Routledge Handbook of Financial Geography*, edited by J. Knox-Hayes and D. Wójcik. New York: Routledge, 552–584.

Haberly, D., MacDonald-Korth, Urban, M., and Wójcik, D. 2019. "Asset management as a digital platform industry: A global financial network perspective." *Geoforum* 106: 167–181.

Haberly, D. and Wójcik, D. 2015a. "Regional blocks and imperial legacies: Mapping the global offshore FDI network." *Economic Geography* 91(3): 251–280.

Haberly, D. and Wójcik, D. 2015b. "Tax havens and the production of offshore FDI: An empirical analysis." *Journal of Economic Geography* 15(1): 75–101.

Haberly, D. and Wójcik, D. 2017a. "Culprits or bystanders? Offshore jurisdictions and the global financial crisis." *Journal of Financial Regulation* 2(1): 233–261.

Haberly, D. and Wójcik, D. 2017b. "Earth incorporated: Centralization and variegation in the global company network." *Economic Geography* 93(3): 241–266.

Haberly, D. and Wójcik, D. 2020. "The end of the great Inversion: Offshore national champion banks and the global financial crisis." *Journal of Economic Geography* 20(6): 1263–1292.

Hablutzel, P. N. 1992. "British banks' role in UK capital markets since the big-bang." *Chicago-Kent Dedication Symposium* 1(68): 365–376.

Haeger, J. D. 1979. "Eastern financiers and institutional change: The origins of the New York Life Insurance and Trust Company and the Ohio Life Insurance and Trust Company." *Journal of Economic History* 39(1): 259–273.

Hall, P. 2003. "Londra, metropolis riluttante" *Urbanistica* (May/August): 21–31.

Hall, P. A. and Soskice, D. 2001. *Varieties of Capitalism: The Institutional Foundations of Comparative Advantage*. Oxford: Oxford University Press.

Hall, P. A. and Thelen, K. 2009. "Institutional change in varieties of capitalism." *Socio-Economic Review* 7: 7–34.

Hall, S. 2010. "Geographies of money and finance I: Cultural economy, politics and place." *Progress in Human* Geography 35(2): 234–245.

Hall, S. 2017a. "Regulating the geographies of market making: Offshore renminbi markets in London's international financial district." *Economic Geography* 94(3): 259–278.

Hall, S. 2017b. "Rethinking international financial centres through the politics of territory: Renminbi internationalisation in London's financial district." *Transactions of the Institute of British Geographers* 42(4): 489–502.

Hall, S. 2018. *Global Finance*. London: Sage.

Hamilton, A. 1790. *Report Relative to a Provision for the Support of Public Credit*. Treasury Department Report to the Speaker of the House of Representatives.

Hampton, M.P. 1996. *The Offshore Interface: Tax Havens in the Global Economy*. London: Macmillan.

Hannah, L. 2007. "What did Morgan's men really do?" *CIRJE Discussion Paper*. http://www.cirje.e.u-tokyo.ac.jp/research/dp/2007/2007cf465.pdf [accessed December 19, 2020].

Hannah, L. 2011. J.P. "Morgan in London and New York before 1914." *Business History Review* 85(1): 113–150.

Hansmann, H. 2006. "Corporation and contract." *American Law and Economics Review* 8(1): 1–19.

Harris, L. 2003. *Trading and Exchanges: Market Microstructure for Practitioners*. Oxford: Oxford University Press.

Hartford, T. 2017. "How the world's first accountants counted on cuneiform." BBC https://www.bbc.co.uk/news/business-39870485 (accessed April 14, 2021).

Harvey, D. 1973. *Social Justice and the City*. London: Edward Arnold.

Harvey, D. 1982. *The Limits to Capital*. Oxford: Blackwell.

Harvey, D. 2011. "Roepke lecture in economic geography—Crises, geographic disruptions and the uneven development of political responses." *Economic Geography* 87: 1–22.

Harwit, E. 2008. *China's Telecommunications Revolution*. Oxford: Oxford University Press.

Hatton, K. and Pistor, K. 2011. "Maximizing autonomy in the shadow of great powers: The political economy of sovereign wealth fund investment." *Columbia Journal of Transnational Law 50*: 1.

Hawley, J. P. and Williams, A. T. 2000. *The Rise of Fiduciary Capitalism: How Institutional Investors Can Make Corporate America More Democratic*. Philadelphia: University of Pennsylvania Press.

Hayton, J. C., Allen, D. G., and Scarpello, V. 2004. "Factor retention decisions in exploratory factor analysis: A tutorial on parallel analysis." *Organizational Research Methods 7*: 191–205.

Hearson, M. 2016. "Measuring tax treaty negotiation outcomes: The Actionaid tax treaties dataset." International Centre for Tax and Development Working Paper 47. https://opendocs.ids.ac.uk/opendocs/bitstream/handle/20.500.12413/11206/ICTD_WP47.pdf [accessed March 7, 2021].

Hearson, M. 2018. "The challenges for developing countries in international tax justice." *Journal of Development Studies* 54(10): 1932–1938.

Helleiner, E. 1994. *States and the Emergence of Global Finance: From Bretton Woods to the 1990s*. Ithaca, NY: Cornell University Press.

Helleiner, E. 1995. "Explaining the globalization of financial markets: Bringing states back in." *Review of International Political Economy* 2(2): 315–341.

Helleiner, E. 2014. *The Status Quo Crisis: Global Financial Governance After the 2008 Meltdown*. Oxford: Oxford University Press.

Henry, J. S. 2012a. "Revised estimates of private banking assets under management and total client assets—Top-50 global private banks, 2005–2010." *Tax Justice Network research report*. http://taxjustice.blogspot.ch/2012/07/the-price-of-offshore-revisited-and.html.

Henry, J. S. 2012b. "The price of offshore revisited: New estimates for missing global private wealth, income, inequality, and lost taxes." *Tax Justice Network Research Report*. http://www.taxjustice.net/cms/upload/pdf/Price_of_Offshore_Revisited_120722.pdf.

Herring, R. 2007. "Conflicts between home and host country prudential supervisors." In *International Financial Instability: Global Banking and National Regulation*, edited by D. Evanoff, J. LaBrosse, and G. Kaufman. Singapore: World Scientific Publishing, 201–219.

Hidy, R. W. 1941. "The organization and functions of Anglo-American merchant bankers, 1815–1860." *Journal of Economic History 1*: 53–66.

Hidy, R. W. 1944. "The House of Baring and the Second Bank of the United States, 1826–1836." *Pennsylvania Magazine of History and Biography* 38(3): 269–285.

Hilferding, R. 1981. *Finance Capital: A Study of the Latest Phase of Capitalist Development*, edited by Tom Bottomore. London: Routledge & Kegan Paul.

Hill, J. M., Nadig, D., and Hougan, M. 2015. "A comprehensive guide to exchange traded funds (ETFs)." *CFA Institute Research Foundation*. http://www.cetfa.ca/files/1433184781_CFA%20-%20ETF%20Report.pdf.

Hirschman, A. O. 1958. *The Strategy of Economic Development*. New Haven, CT: Yale University Press.

Ho, K. 2009. *Liquidated: An Ethnography of Wall Street*. Durham, NC: Duke University Press.

Hodgson, G. M. 2008. "How Veblen generalized Darwinism." *Journal of Economic Issues 42*: 399–405.

Holden, R. T. 2005. "The original management incentive schemes." *Journal of Economic Perspectives 19*(4): 135–144.

Hong, Q. and Smart, M. 2010. "In praise of tax havens: International tax planning and foreign direct investment." *European Economic Review 54*: 82–95.

Höpner, M. and Krempel, L. 2004. "The politics of the German company network." *Competition & Change 8*: 339–356.

Horvat, A. 1998. "MoF fries in 'no pan shabu shabu." *Euromoney* (March). https://www.euromoney.com/article/b1320fdq16wkw9/mof-fries-in-no-pan-shabu-shabu [accessed March 2, 2021].

Hudson, A. 2000. "Offshoreness, globalization and sovereignty: A postmodern geo-political economy?" *Transactions of the Institutions of British Geographers 25*: 269–283.

Hull, D. 2020. "Tesla raising up to $5 billion in third share sale this year." *Bloomberg* (December 8). https://www.bloomberg.com/news/articles/2020-12-08/tesla-raising-up-to-5-billion-in-third-capital-raise-this-year?sref=45uaXh1D [accessed March 15, 2021].

Hulten, C. R. 2001. "Total factor productivity: A short biography." In *New Developments in Productivity Analysis*, edited by C. R. Hulten, E. R. Dean, and M. J. Harper. Chicago: University of Chicago Press, 1–53.

Hunt, N. 2013. "Contraband, free ports, and British merchants in the Caribbean world, 1739–1772." *Diacronie Studi di Storia Contemporanea 13*(1): 1–12.

Hurley, E. W. 1977. "The commercial paper market." *Federal Reserve Bulletin 63*(6): 525–536.

ICB (Independent Commission on Banking) 2011. "Interim report: Consultation on reform options." *ICB*, London, April.

IMF (International Monetary Fund) 2010. "Global financial stability report: sovereigns, funding, and systemic liquidity." *IMF*, Washington, DC, October.

Ingham, G. 1996. "Money is a social relation." *Review of Social Economy 54*(4): 507–529.

Ingham, G. 1998. 'On the underdevelopment of the 'sociology of money." *Acta Sociologica*, 41(1): 3–18.

Innes, M. A. 1914. "The credit theory of money." *Banking Law Journal 31*(2): 151–168.

Innes, W. C. 1983. *Social Concern in Calvin's Geneva*. Eugene: Pickwick Publications.

Jacobs, J. B. 2011. "'Patient capital': Can Delaware company law help to revive it?" *Washington and Lee Law Review 68*(4): 1646–1664.

Jaeger, P. T., Lin, J., Grimes, J. M., and Simmons, S. N. 2009. "Where is the cloud? Geography, economics, environment, and jurisdiction in cloud computing." *First Monday 14*(5).

Jenks, L. H. 1951. "Capital movement and transportation: Britain and American railway development." *Journal of Economic History 11*(4): 375–388.

Jensen, M. C. and Meckling, W. H. 1976. "Theory of the firm: Managerial behavior, agency costs and ownership structure." *Journal of Financial Economics 3*: 305–360.

Jeremy, D. I. 1977. "Damming the flood: British government efforts to check the outflow of technicians and machinery, 1780–1843." *Business History Review 51*(1): 1–34.

Jessop, S. and Hunnicutt, T. 2017. "BlackRock takes scalable capital stake in Europe 'Robo-Advisor' push." *Reuters* (June 20). https://www.reuters.com/article/us-blackrock-scalablecapital/blackrock-takes-scalable-capital-stake-in-europe-robo-advisor-push-idUSKBN19A322

Jessop, S. and Kumar, N. 2014. "Passive funds an active threat for Europe's fund managers." *Reuters* (August 31). http://uk.reuters.com/article/2014/08/31/uk-investment-funds-passive-insight-idUKKBN0GV0F020140831.

Jia, K., Kenney, M. 2016. "Mobile internet business models in China: Vertical hierarchies, horizontal conglomerates, or business groups?" BRIE Working Paper 2016-6. http://www.brie.berkeley.edu/wp-content/uploads/2015/02/Working-Paper-2016-6.JiaKenney.pdf [accessed December 18, 2020].

Johnson, C. 1982. *MITI and the Japanese Miracle: The Growth of Industrial Policy, 1925–1975*. Stanford: Stanford University Press.

Johnson, S. and Kwak, J. 2010. *13 Bankers: Wall Street Takeover and the next Financial Meltdown*. New York: Pantheon.

Jones, A. 2002. "The 'global city' misconceived: The myth of 'global management' in transnational service firms." *Geoforum 33*: 335–350.

Jones, A. 2003. *Management Consultancy and Banking in an Era of Globalization*. Basingstoke: Palgrave Macmillan.

Jun, Z. 1999. "Closure of Financial Institutions in China." *BIS Report*. https://www.bis.org/publ/plcy07u.pdf [accessed March 2, 2021].

Kadens, E. 2004. "Order within law, variety within custom: The character of the medieval merchant law." *Chicago Journal of International Law 5*(1): 39–66.

Kadens, E. 2015. "The medieval Law Merchant: The tyranny of a construct." *Journal of Legal Analysis 7*(2): 251–289.

Kahn, J. 2015. "Greeting from Bitcoin Island." *Bloomberg* (September 8). https://www.bloomberg.com/news/features/2015-09-07/isle-of-man-tax-haven-with-tailless-cats-becomes-bitcoin-hub.

Kaissar, N. 2018. "Fidelity's no-fee funds unleash the power of free." *Bloomberg* (August 2). https://www.bloomberg.com/view/articles/2018-08-02/fidelity-s-no-fee-funds-unleash-the-power-of-free.

Kamin, D., Gamage, D., Glogower, A., et al. 2019. "The games they will play: Tax games, roadblocks, and glitches under the 2017 tax legislation." *Minnesota Law Review 103*(3): 1439–1522.

Kandel, E., Kosenko, K., Morck, R., and Yafeh, Y. 2019. "The great pyramids of America: A revised history of U.S. business groups, corporate ownership, and regulation, 1926–1950." *Strategic Management Journal 40*(5): 781–808.

Kapstein, E. B. 1991. "Supervising international banks: Origins and implications of the Basel Accord." *Essays in International Finance No. 185* (December). International Finance Section, Department of Economics, Princeton University. https://www.princeton.edu/~ies/IES_Essays/E185.pdf.

Kapstein, E. B. 1994. *Governing the Global Economy: International Finance and the State*. Cambridge, MA: Harvard University Press.

Kar, D. and Freitas, S. 2012. "Illicit financial flows from developing countries: 2001–2010." *Global Financial Integrity Research Report*. http://www.gfintegrity.org/report/illicit-financial-flows-from-developing-countries-2001-2010/.

Karreman, B and Van Der Knaap, B. 2012. "The geography of equity listing and financial centre competition in mainland China and Hong Kong." *Journal of Economic Geography* 12: 899–922.

Kaya, O. 2017. "Robo-advice—A true innovation in asset management. EU Monitor Global Financial Markets." *Deutsche Bank Research.* https://www.dbresearch.com/PROD/RPS_ EN-PROD/PROD0000000000449125/Robo-advice_%E2%80%93_a_true_innovation_ in_asset_managemen.pdf.

Kenney, M. and Zysman, J. 2016. "The rise of the platform economy." *Issues in Science and Technology* 32(2): 61–69.

Keynes, J. 1936. *The General Theory of Employment, Interest and Money.* Cambridge: Cambridge University Press.

Kharif, O. 2019. "Why (almost) everyone hates Facebook's cryptocurrency Libra." *Bloomberg.* July 16. https://www.bloomberg.com/news/articles/2019-07-16/why-every-body-almost-hates-facebook-s-digital-coin-quicktake.

Kindleberger, C. P. 1973. "The formation of financial centers: A study in a comparative economic theory." Massachusetts Institute of Technology (MIT), Department of Economics Working Paper No. 114.

Kindleberger, C. P. 1984. *A Financial History of Western Europe.* New York: Oxford University Press.

Kindleberger, C. P. 1986. *The World in Depression: 1929–1939, Revised and Enlarged Edition.* Berkeley: University of California Press.

Kindleberger, C. P. and Aliber, R. Z. 2005. *Manias, Panics and Crashes: A History of Financial Crises.* Basingstoke: Palgrave.

Klagge, B. and Martin, Ron. 2005. "Decentralized versus centralized financial systems: Is there a case for local capital markets?" *Journal of Economic Geography* 5: 387–422.

Knafo, S. 2008. "The state and the rise of speculative finance in England." *Economy and Society* 37(2): 172–192.

Knox-Hayes, J. 2016. *The Culture of Markets: The Political Economy of Climate Governance.* Oxford: Oxford University Press.

Knuth, S., Potts, S. 2016. "Legal geographies of finance: Editors' introduction." *Environment and Planning A* 48(3): 458–464.

Kohn, M. 1999a. "Bills of exchange and the money market to 1600." Dartmouth College Department of Economics Working Paper 99-04. Available on SSRN.

Kohn, M. 1999b. "The capital market before 1600." Dartmouth College Department of Economics Working Paper 99-06. Available on SSRN.

Kohn, M. 1999c. "Early deposit banking." Dartmouth College Department of Economics Working Paper 99-03. Available on SSRN.

Koo, R. 2008. *The Holy Grail of Macroeconomics: Lessons from Japan's Great Recession.* Singapore: Wiley.

Kothari, V. 2006. *Securitization: The Financial Instrument of the Future.* Hoboken, NJ: Wiley.

Kotz, D. M. 1979. "The significance of bank control over large corporations." *Journal of Economic Issues* 13 (2): 407–426.

Kovacic, W. E. and Shapiro, C. 2000. "Antitrust policy: A century of economic and legal thinking." *Journal of Economic Perspectives* 14(1): 43–60.

KPMG. 2018. *Global Tax Rates Table.* https://home.kpmg.com/xx/en/home/services/ tax/tax-tools-and-resources/tax-rates-online/corporate-tax-rates-table.html [accessed October 31, 2018].

Krippner, G. R. 2005. "The financialization of the American economy." *Socio-Economic Review* 3: 173–208.

Kynge, J. and Yu, S. 2021. "Virtual control: The agenda behind China's new digital currency." *Financial Times* (February 17). https://www.ft.com/content/7511809e-827e-4526-81ad-ae83f405f623 [accessed March 14, 2021].

LaFranco, R. and Sazanov, A. 2013. "How Russia's 20 biggest billionaires hide their fortunes from the government." *Bloomberg News* (May 1). http://business.financialpost.com/2013/05/01/how-russias-20-biggest-billionaires-hide-their-fortunes-from-the-government/.

Lai, K. P. Y. 2012. "Differentiated markets: Shanghai, Beijing and Hong Kong in China's financial centre network." *Urban Studies* 49: 1275–1296

Landgraf, R. 2016. "A wake-up call to Europe's CEOs." *Handelsblatt* (February 4). https://global.handelsblatt.com/edition/361/ressort/finance/article/a-wake-up-call-to-europe.

Langley, P. 2008. *The Everyday Life of Global Finance*. Oxford: Oxford University Press.

Langley, P. and Leyshon, A. 2017. "Platform capitalism: the intermediation and capitalisation of digital economic circulation." *Finance and Society* 3(1): 11–31.

La Porta, R., Lopez-de-silanes, F., and Shleifer, A. 1999. "Corporate ownership around the world." *Journal of Finance* 54(2): 471–517.

Lardy, N R. 2012. *Sustaining China's Economic Growth After the Global Financial Crisis*. Washington, DC: Peterson Institute for International Economics.

Larson, M. J., Schnyder, G., Westerhuis, G., and Wilson, J. 2011. "Strategic responses to global challenges: The case of European banking, 1973–2000." *Business History* 53: 40–62.

Lash, S. and Urry, J. 1987. *The End of Organized Capitalism*. Madison: University of Wisconsin Press.

Lazonick, W. 1990. "Organizational capabilities in American business: The rise and decline of managerial capitalism." *Business and Economic History* 19: 35–54.

Lazonick, W. and Tulum, O. 2011. "US biopharmaceutical finance and the sustainability of the biotech business model." *Research Policy Journal* 40: 1170–1187.

Ledyaeva, S., Karhunen, P., and Whalley, J. 2013. "If foreign investment is not foreign: Round-trip vs. genuine foreign investment in Russia." *Working Paper*. https://tippie.uiowa.edu/economics/tow/papers/ledyaeva-spring2013.pdf.

Lee, R., Clark, G. L., Pollard, J., and Leyshon, A. 2009. "The remit of financial geography—Before and after the crisis." *Journal of Economic Geography* 9: 723–747.

Le Marchant, C. M. 1999. "Financial regulation and supervision offshore: Guernsey, a case study." In *Offshore Finance Centers and Tax Havens: The Rise of Global Capital*, edited by M. P. Hampton and J. P. Abbott. West Lafayette: Purdue University Press, 212–229.

Lessig, L. 2006. *Code, Version 2.0*. New York: Basic Books.

Levine, J. H. 1972. "The sphere of influence." *American Sociological Review* 37(1): 14–27.

Levine, M. 2021a. "Greensill didn't just finance supply chains." *Bloomberg* (March 17). https://www.bloomberg.com/opinion/articles/2021-03-17/greensill-didn-t-just-finance-bluestone-s-supply-chain?sref=45uaXh1D [accessed April 11, 2021].

Levine, M. 2021b. "Facebook's Supreme Court takes a case: Also SPACs, hacks, ACH and stats." *Bloomberg* (January 22). https://www.bloomberg.com/opinion/articles/2021-01-22/facebook-s-supreme-court-takes-a-case?sref=45uaXh1D [accessed February 27, 2021].

Levine, M. 2021c. "Goldman CEO wants his bankers back at work." *Bloomberg* (March 15). https://www.bloomberg.com/opinion/articles/2021-03-15/goldman-sachs-ceo-david-solomon-wants-his-bankers-back-at-the-office?sref=45uaXh1D [accessed March 15, 2021].

Levine, M. 2021d. "Gamestop hearing featured no cats." *Bloomberg* (February 19). https://www.bloomberg.com/opinion/articles/2021-02-19/gamestop-hearing-featured-no-cats [accessed February 22, 2021].

Levine, M. 2021e. "Goldman has an investing robot." *Bloomberg* (February 16). https://www.bloomberg.com/opinion/articles/2021-02-16/goldman-adds-robo-adviser-to-marcus-consumer-brand?sref=45uaXh1D [accessed March 8, 2021].

Levine, M. 2021f. "GameStop missed all the fun: Also buybacks, Bitcoins and Elon Musk proximity pricing." *Bloomberg* (February 11). https://www.bloomberg.com/opinion/articles/2021-02-11/why-gamestop-didn-t-sell-any-stock-during-the-reddit-rally?sref=45uaXh1D [accessed March 8, 2021].

Levy, J. D. 2011. "The return of the state? French economic policy under Nicholas Sarkozy." Working Paper. http://www.euce.org/eusa/2011/papers/5e_levy.pdf.

Lewellen, K. and Robinson, L. 2013. "Internal ownership structures of U.S. multinational firms." Working Paper. http://faculty.tuck.dartmouth.edu/images/uploads/faculty/leslie-robinson/LewellenRobinson.pdf.

Lewis, M. 2010. *The Big Short: Inside the Doomsday Machine.* London: Penguin.

Lewis, M. 2011. *Boomerang: The Biggest Bust.* London: Penguin.

Lewis, M. K. 1999. "International banking and offshore finance: London and the major centres." In *Offshore Finance Centers and Tax Havens: The Rise of Global Capital,* edited by M. P. Hampton and J. P. Abbott. West Lafayette: Purdue University Press, 43–79.

Leyshon, A. and Pollard, J. 2000. "Geographies of industrial convergence: The case of retail banking." *Transactions of the Institute of British Geographers* 25(2): 203–220.

Leyshon, A. and Thrift, N. 1995. "Geographies of financial exclusion: Financial abandonment in Britain and the United States." *Transactions of the Institute of British Geographers* 20: 312–341.

Leyshon, A. and Thrift N. 1997. *Money/space: Geographies of Monetary Transformation.* London: Routledge.

Leyshon, A. and Thrift N. 2007. "The capitalization of almost everything: The future of finance and capitalism." *Theory, Culture and Society* 24: 97–115.

Lim, K. F. 2010. "On China's growing geo-economic influence and the evolution of variegated capitalism." *Geoforum* 41(5): 677–688.

Lim, K. F. 2019. *On Shifting Foundations: State Rescaling, Policy Experimentation, and Economic Restructuring in Post-1949 China.* Oxford: Wiley.

Lin, L.-W. and Milhaupt, C. J. 2013. "We are the (national) champions: Understanding the mechanisms of state capitalism in China." *Stanford Law Review* 65: 697–760.

Link, S. 2013. "Politics or efficiency? Three questions on the Ford Motor Company and Alfred D. Chandler's managerial revolution." EUI Working Paper MWP 2013/31. https://cadmus.eui.eu/bitstream/handle/1814/28678/MWP_2013_31.pdf?sequence=1&isAllowed=y [accessed December 19, 2020].

Lips, W. 2018. "Great powers in global tax governance: A comparison of the US role in the CRS and BEPS." *Globalizations* 16(1): 104–119.

Lipsey, R. L. 1994. "US foreign trade and the balance of payments, 1800–1913." National Bureau of Economic Research Working Paper No. 4710.

Lipton, E. and Merced, M. J. 2009. "Wall St. firm draws scrutiny as US adviser." *New York Times* (May 18). https://www.nytimes.com/2009/05/19/business/19blackrock.html.

Lissakers, K. 1977. *International Debt, the Banks, and U.S. Foreign Policy: A Staff Report Prepared for the use of the Subcommittee on Foreign Economic Policy of the Committee on Foreign Relations of the United States Senate.* Washington, DC: US Government Printing Office.

Lively, R. A. 1955. "The American system: A review article." *Business History Review* 29(1): 81–96.

Lo, A. W. 2004. "The adaptive markets hypothesis." *Journal of Portfolio Management* 30(5): 15–29.

Lovelock, P. 1997. "The China Telecom (Hong Kong) IPO: Money for nothing?" Centre for Asian Business Cases, School of Business, University of Hong Kong Case Study 99/29C.

Lublin, J. S. and Grind, K. 2013. "For proxy advisors, influence wanes." *Wall Street Journal* (May 22). www.wsj.com/articles/SB10001424127887323336104578499554143793198.

Lucas, D., Goodman, L., and Fabozzi, F. 2006. *Collateralized Debt Obligations: Structures and Analysis*, 2nd edn. Hoboken, NJ: Wiley.

Lybecker, M. E. 1973. "Regulation of bank trust department activities." *Yale Law Journal* 82(5): 977–1002.

MacCallum, R. C., Widaman, K. F., Zhang, S., and Hong, S. 1999. "Sample size in factor analysis." *Psychological Methods* 4: 84–99.

McCauley, R. and McGuire, P. 2014. "Non-US banks' claims on the Federal Reserve." *BIS Quarterly Review* (March): 89–97.

McDowell, D. 2011. "The US as 'sovereign international last-resort lender': The Fed's currency swap programme during the great panic of 2007–09." *New Political Economy* 17: 157–178.

McDowell, L. 1997. *Capital Culture: Gender at Work in the City*. Oxford: Blackwell.

McGregor, R. 2010. *The Party: The Secret World of China's Communist Rulers*. London: Allen Lane.

McGuire, S. and Chan, M. 2000. "The NY–LON life." *Newsweek* (November 13), 40–47.

McLaughlin, T. 2016. "Fidelity gives BlackRock an early leg up in Robo advice brawl." *Reuters* (December 16). https://www.reuters.com/article/us-fidelity-blackrock-robo-idUSKBN1452BN

McNabb, W. 2015. "Letter sent by F. William McNabb III, Vanguard's Chairman and CEO, to the independent leaders of the boards of directors of the Vanguard funds' largest portfolio holdings of the boards of directors of the Vanguard funds' largest portfolio holdings." http://conferences.law.stanford.edu/directorscollege2015/wp-content/uploads/sites/35/2015/06/Breakout-Shareholder-Engagement.pdf.

Mahoney, J. F. 1966. "Backsliding convert: Woodrow Wilson and the 'Seven Sisters.'" *American Quarterly* 18(1): 71–80.

Maielli, G. and Haslam, C. 2016. "General Motors: A financialized account of corporate behaviour 1909–1940." *Accounting Forum* 40(4): 251–264.

Makortoff, K., Savage, M., and Butler, B. 2021. "Cameron 'lobbied senior Downing St aide and Matt Hancock' to help Greensill." *The Guardian* (April 10). https://www.theguardian.com/politics/2021/apr/10/revealed-david-cameron-stood-to-gain-from-218m-greensill-trust [accessed April 11, 2021].

Malkiel, B. G. 2003. "The efficient market hypothesis and its critics." *Journal of Economic Perspectives* 17: 59–82.

Malkiel, B. G. 2005. "Reflections on the efficient market hypothesis: 30 years later." *Financial Review* 40: 1–9.

Malkiel, B. G. 2013. "Asset management fees and the growth of finance." *Journal of Economic Perspectives* 27: 97–108.

Malkiel, B. G. 2019. *A Random Walk Down Wall Street: The Time-Tested Strategy for Successful Investing*. New York: Norton.

Maples and Calder. 2003. "Location is key for structured investment vehicles." International Law Office.

Marchant, C. 1999. "Financial regulation and supervision offshore: Guernsey, a case study." In *Offshore Finance Centers and Tax Havens: The Rise of Global Capital*, edited by M. P. Hampton and J. P. Abbott. West Lafayette: Purdue University Press, 43–79.

Marian, O. M. 2015. "Home-country effects of corporate inversions." *Washington Law Review 90*: 1–72.

Mariathasan, M. and Merrouche, O. 2012. "The manipulation of Basel Risk weights: Evidence from 2007–10." Oxford Department of Economics Discussion Paper Series No. 621. https://www.economics.ox.ac.uk/materials/papers/12210/paper621.pdf.

Markusen, A., Hall, P., Campbell, S., and Deitrick, S. 1991. *The Rise of the Gunbelt: The Military Remapping of Industrial America*. Oxford: Oxford University Press.

Marshall, J. N., Pike, A., Pollard, J. S. et al. 2012. "Placing the run on Northern Rock." *Journal of Economic Geography 12*: 157–181.

Martin, R. ed. 1999. *Money and the Space Economy*. Chichester, UK: Wiley.

Martin, R. 2002. *Financialization of Daily Life*. Philadelphia: Temple University Press.

Martin, R. 2011. "The local geographies of the financial crisis: From the housing bubble to economic recession and beyond." *Journal of Economic Geography 11*(4): 587–618.

Martin, R. and Pollard, J. 2017. *Handbook on the Geographies of Money and Finance*. Cheltenham, UK: Edward Elgar.

Mason, T. 2017. "U.S. digital adviser forecast: AUM to surpass $450B by 2021." *S&P Global Market Intelligence*. https://www.spglobal.com/our-insights/US-Digital-Adviser-Forecast-AUM-To-Surpass-450B-By-2021.html.

Massa, A. 2020. "Why BlackRock has a role in the Fed bond-buying spree." *Bloomberg* (May 21). https://www.bloomberg.com/news/articles/2020-03-25/why-blackrock-has-a-role-in-the-fed-bond-buying-spree-quicktake?sref=45uaXh1D [accessed December 27, 2020].

Massey, D. 1995. *Spatial Divisions of Labour: Social Structures and the Geography of Production*. New York: Routledge.

Maurer, B. 2008. "Re-regulating offshore finance?" *Geography Compass 2*(1): 155–175.

Maurer, B. and Martin, S. J. 2012. "Accidents of equity and the aesthetics of Chinese offshore incorporation." *American Ethnologist 39*(3): 527–544.

Mazzucato, M. 2013. *The Entrepreneurial State: Debunking Public vs. Private Sector Myths*. London: Anthem.

Mehran, H. and Stulz, R. M. 2007. "The economics of conflicts of interests in financial institutions." *Journal of Financial Economics 85*: 267–296.

Mendales, R. 2009. "Collateralized explosive devices: Why securities regulation failed to prevent the CDO meltdown, and how to fix it." *University of Illinois Law Review 5*: 1359.

Metcalf, T. 2021a. "New York pulls away from London as top finance hub, survey says." *Bloomberg* (February 16). https://www.bloomberg.com/news/articles/2021-02-16/new-york-pulls-away-from-london-as-top-finance-hub-survey-says?sref=45uaXh1D [accessed March 12, 2021].

Metcalf, T. 2021b. "Dublin is top Brexit relocation spot for finance firms, EY finds." *Bloomberg* (March 2). https://www.bloomberg.com/news/articles/2021-03-02/dublin-is-top-brexit-relocation-spot-for-finance-firms-ey-says?sref=45uaXh1D [accessed March 12, 2021].

Michaelides, A. 2014. "Cyprus: From boom to bail-in." *Economic Policy 29*: 639–689.

Michie, R. C. 1991. *The City of London: Continuity and Change 1850–1990*. London: Macmillan.

Michie, R. C. 2004. "The City of London and the British government: The changing relationship." In *The British Government and the City of London in the Twentieth Century*, edited by R. Michie and P. Williamson. Cambridge, UK: Cambridge University Press, 31–55.

Michie, R. C. 2006. *The Global Securities Market: A History*. Oxford: Oxford University Press.

Milberg, W. 2008. "Shifting sources and uses of profits: Sustaining US financialization with global value chains." *Economy and Society 37*: 420–51.

Milgrom, P. R., North, D. C., and Weingast, B. R. 1990. "The role of institutions in the revival of trade: The law merchant, private judges, and the Champagne fairs." *Economics & Politics 2*: 1–23.

Miller, H. 2018. "Swiss banking secrecy rule dealt setback in month to forget." *Bloomberg* (October 19). https://www.bloomberg.com/news/articles/2018-10-19/swiss-banking-secrecy-dealt-fresh-setback-in-a-month-to-forget?sref=45uaXh1D.

Milne, A. and Onorato, M. 2004. "An absence of regulatory design? Recent European directives and the market for corporate bonds." *City Research Series No. 4*.

Ministry of Commerce. 2010. "Statistical bulletin of China's outward foreign direct investment." http://images.mofcom.gov.cn/hzs/accessory/201109/1316069658609.pdf [accessed July 16, 2013].

Minsky, H. 1980. "Capitalist financial processes and the instability of capitalism." *Journal of Economic Issues 14*(2): 505.

Minsky, H. P. 1957. "Central banking and money market changes." *Quarterly Journal of Economics 71*(2): 171–187.

Minsky, H. P. 1986. *Stabilizing an Unstable Economy*. New Haven, CT: Yale University Press.

Minsky, H. P. 1992a. "The capital development of the economy and the structure of financial institutions." Levy Economics Institute Working Paper No. 72.

Minsky, H. P. 1992b. "The financial instability hypothesis." Levy Economics Institute Working Paper No. 74.

Minsky, H. P. 1992c. "Schumpeter and Finance." In *Market and Institutions in Economic Development: Essays in Honour of Paulo Sylos Labini*, edited by S. Biasco, A. Roncaglia and M. Salvati. London and New York: Macmillan, 103–115.

Mishkin, F. S. 2006. *The Economics of Money, Banking, and Financial Markets*. Boston: Pearson.

Miyazaki, H. 2003. "The temporalities of the market." *American Anthropologist 105*(2): 25–65.

Molho, A. 1995. "The state and finance: A hypothesis based on the history of late medieval Florence." *Journal of Modern History 67*: S97–S135.

Moon, A. 2003. "Cayman Islands securitization." *Mondaq*. https://www.mondaq.com/caymanislands/securitization-structured-finance/21207/cayman-islands-securitisation [accessed March 23, 2021].

Mooney. 2017. "BlackRock Bets on Aladdin as genie of growth." *Financial Times* (May 17). https://www.ft.com/content/eda44658-3592-11e7-99bd-13beb0903fa3.

Morck, R. 2005. "A history of corporate governance around the world." *Conference Report*. Washington, DC: National Bureau of Economic Research.

Morrison, A. and Wilhelm, W. 2007. *Investment Banking: Institutions, Politics, and Law*. Oxford: Oxford University Press.

Mueller, K., Bharwani, P., and Araya, R. 2006. "CDOs with short-term tranches: Moody's approach to rating prime-1 CDO." *Moody's Investors' Service Structured Finance Special Report*.

Mueller, R. C. 1997. *The Venetian Money Market: Banks, Panics, and the Public Debt, 1200–1500, Vol. II*. Baltimore: John Hopkins University Press.

Muellerleile, C. M. 2009. "Financialization takes off at Boeing." *Journal of Economic Geography* 9(5): 663–677.

Munro, J. H. 2001. "The 'New Institutional Economics' and the changing fortunes of fairs in medieval and early modern Europe." *VSWG: Wirtschaftsgeschichte* 88(1): 1–47.

Munro, J. H. 2003. "The medieval origins of the financial revolution: Usury, rentes, and negotiability." *International History Review* 25(3): 505–562.

Munro, J. H. 2014b. "The dual crises of the late-medieval Florentine cloth industry, 1320–1420." In *Textiles and the Medieval Economy: Production, Trade, and Consumption of Textiles, 8th–16th Centuries*, edited by A. L. Huang and C. Jahnke. Oxford: Oxbow Books, 113–148.

Munro, J. H. A. 2014a. "The technology and economics of coinage debasements in medieval and early modern Europe: With special reference to the Low Countries and England." In *Money in the Pre-Industrial World: Bullion, Debasements and Coin Substitutes*, edited by J. H. A. Munro. Cambridge, UK: Cambridge University Press.

Murphy, R., Seabrooke, L., and Stausholm, S. N. 2019. "A tax map of global professional service firms: Where expert services are located and why." Copenhagen Business School Working Paper. https://openaccess.city.ac.uk/id/eprint/21868/7/D4.6WorkingPaper.pdf [accessed December 19, 2020].

Nash, R. C. 1997. "The balance of payments and foreign capital flows in eighteenth-century England: A comment." *Economic History Review* 50(1): 110–128.

Natarajan, S. 2021. "Goldman CEO warns remote work is aberration, not the new normal." *Bloomberg* (February 24). https://www.bloomberg.com/news/articles/2021-02-24/goldman-ceo-warns-remote-work-is-aberration-not-the-new-normal?sref=45uaXh1D [accessed March 8, 2021].

National Commission on the Causes of the Financial and Economic Crisis in the United States 2011. *The Financial Crisis Inquiry Report*. Washington, DC: US Government Printing Office.

National Resources Committee. 1939. *The Structure of the American Economy: A Report Prepared by the Industrial Section under the Direction of Gardiner Means*. Washington, DC: United States Government Printing Office.

Naughton, B. 2006. *The Chinese Economy: Transitions and Growth*. Cambridge, MA: MIT Press.

Navin, T. R. and Sears, M. V. 1955. "The rise of a market for industrial securities, 1887–1902." *Business History Review* 29(2): 105–138.

Ndikumana, L. and Boyce, J. K. 2018. "Capital flight from Africa: Updated methodology and new estimates." *Political Economy Research Institute (PERI) Research Report*. https://www.peri.umass.edu/publication/item/1083-capital-flight-from-africa-updated-methodology-and-new-estimates [accessed December 18, 2020].

Neal, L. 1990. *The Rise of Financial Capitalism: International Capital Markets in the Age of Reason*. Cambridge, UK: Cambridge University Press.

Neal, L. 1992. "The disintegration and re-integration of capital markets in the 19th century." *Business and Economic History* 22: 84–96.

Neal, L. 2000. "How it all began: The monetary and financial architecture of Europe during the first global capital markets, 1648–1815." *Financial History Review* 7(2): 117–140.

Neal, L. 2011. "The evolution of self and state regulation of the New York Stock Exchange, 1688–1878." In *Law and Long-term Economic Change: A Eurasian Perspective*, edited by D. Ma, and J. L. Van Zanden. Stanford: Stanford University Press, 300–322.

Neal, L. and Quinn, S. 2001. "Networks of information, markets, and institutions in the rise of London as a financial centre, 1660–1720." *Financial History Review* 8(1): 7–26.

Neef, D. 2014. "Digital exhaust: What everyone should know about big data, digitization and digitally driven innovation." Upper Saddle River, NJ: Pearson FT Press.

New York Times. 1933. "New Detroit bank backed by R.F.C. joins General Motors in control, each subscribing half of $25000000 stock." *New York Times* (March 22).

Nirenberg, D. 2013. "US taxation of non-US investors in securitisation transactions." In *The International Comparative Legal Guide to Securitisation*, edited by M. Nicolaides. London: Global Legal Group, 12–22.

Nolan, P. 2001a. *China and the Global Business Revolution*. New York: Palgrave.

Nolan, P. 2001b. *China and the Global Economy*. New York: Palgrave.

Nolan, P. 2012. *Is China Buying the World*. Cambridge: Polity.

North, D. C. 1993. "The paradox of the West." Working Paper. http://dlc.dlib.indiana.edu/dlc/bitstream/handle/10535/4158/9309005.pdf [accessed January 21, 2020].

Nougayrède, D. 2013. "Outsourcing law in post-Soviet Russia." *Journal of Eurasian Law* 3(6): 383–449.

Nougayrède, D. 2019. "After the Panama Papers: A private law critique of shell companies." *International Lawyer* 327–367.

Nye, J. S. Jr. 2015. *Is the American Century Over?* Cambridge: Polity.

Jensen, K., and Harper, C. 2007. Obama top fundraiser on Wall Street. *Washington Post* (April 18).

Office of the New York State Comptroller. 2011. "DiNapoli: Wall Street bonuses declined in 2010." Press release. http://www.osc.state.ny.us/press/releases/feb11/022311a.htm

Ogilvie, S. 2014. "The economics of guilds." *Journal of Economic Perspectives* 28(4): 169–192.

O Riain, S. 2012. "The crisis of financialisation in Ireland." *Economic and Social Review* 43: 497–533.

Oxfam. 2000. "Tax havens: Releasing the hidden billions for development." Oxfam GB Policy Paper. http://policy-practice.oxfam.org.uk/publications/tax-havens-releasing-the-hidden-billions-for-poverty-eradication-114611.

Oxfam 2014. "Working for the few: Political capture and economic inequality." Briefing Paper 178. http://www.ipu.org/splz-e/unga14/oxfam.pdf

Ozawa, T. 2001. "The 'hidden' side of the 'flying-geese' catch-up model: Japan's dirigiste institutional setup and a deepening financial morass." *Journal of Asian Economics* 12: 471–491.

Palais, H. 1959. "England's first attempt to break the commercial monopoly of the Hanseatic league, 1377–1380." *American Historical Review* 64(4): 852–865.

Palan, R. 1999. "Offshore and the structural enablement of sovereignty." In *Offshore Finance Centers and Tax Havens: The Rise of Global Capital*, edited by M. P. Hampton and J. P. Abbott. West Lafayette: Purdue University Press, 18–42.

Palan, R., Murphy, R., and Chavagneux, C. 2010. *Tax Havens: How Globalization Really Works*. Ithaca, NY: Cornell University Press.

Palan, R. and Nesvetailova, A. 2013. "The governance of the black holes of the world economy: Shadow banking and offshore finance." City Political Economy Research Centre 2012–03.

Palley, T. I. 2002. "Endogenous money: What it is, and why it matters." *Metroeconomica* 53(2): 152–180.

Palpacuer, F. 2008. "Bringing the social context back in: Governance and wealth distribution in global commodity chains." *Economy and Society* 37: 393–419.

Pamlin, D. and Long, B. 2007. "Rethink China's outward investment flows: report to the Trade and Investment Policy Programme." Washington, D.C.: World Wildlife Fund.

Pan, F. and Brooker, D. 2014. "Going global? Examining the geography of Chinese firms' overseas listings on international stock exchanges." *Geoforum 51*: 1–11.

Papke, L. E. 2000. "One-way treaty with the world: The U.S. withholding tax and the Netherlands Antilles." *International Tax and Public Finance 7*: 295–313.

Parr, J. B. and Budd, L. 2000. "Financial services and the urban system: an exploration." *Urban Studies 37*(3): 593–610.

Pasiouras, F., Tanna, S., and Gaganis, C. 2011. "What drives acquisitions in the EU banking industry? The role of bank regulation and supervision framework, bank specific and market specific factors." *Financial Institutions & Market Instruments 20*: 29–77.

Patman, W. 1968. "Commercial banks and their trust activities: Emerging influence on the American economy." *Staff Report for the Subcommittee on Domestic Finance of the Committee on Banking and Currency of the U.S. House of Representatives*. Washington, DC: US Government Printing Office.

Peck, J. and Theodore, N. 2007. "Variegated capitalism." *Progress in Human Geography 31*: 731–772.

Peck, J., Theodore, N., and Brenner, N. 2012. "Neoliberalism resurgent? Market rule after the great recession." *South Atlantic Quarterly 111*: 265–288.

Peck, J. and Tickell, A. 2002. "Neoliberalizing space." *Antipode 34*: 380–404.

Pelfrey, W. 2006. *Billy, Alfred, and General Motors: The Story of Two Unique Men, a Legendary Company, and a Remarkable Time in American History*. New York: Amacom.

Peter, G. von 2007. "International banking centres: A network perspective." *BIS Quarterly Review* (December): 33–45.

Petry, J., Fichtner, J., and Heemskerk, E. 2021. "Steering capital: The growing private authority of index providers in the age of passive asset management." *Review of International Political Economy*, 28(1), 152–176.

Pezzolo, L. and Tattara, G. 2006. "Una fiera senza luogo. Was Bisenzone an offshore capital market in sixteenth-century Italy?" Working Paper, Department of Economics, Ca' Foscari University of Venice No. 25/WP/2006.

Phelps, N. 2007. "Gaining from globalization? State extra-territoriality and domestic impacts—The case of Singapore." *Economic Geography 83*(4): 371.

Philippon, T. and Reshef, A. 2009. "Wages and human capital in the U.S. financial industry: 1909–2006." Discussion Paper 7282. London: Centre for Economic Policy Research.

Philips, M. 2013. "How the robots lost: High frequency trading's rise and fall." *Bloomberg* (June 6). http://www.bloomberg.com/bw/articles/2013-06-06/how-the-robots-lost-high -frequency-tradings-rise-and-fall#p1.

Picciotto, S. 1992. *International Business Taxation: A Study in the Internationalization of Business Regulation*. London: Weidenfeld & Nicholson.

Picciotto, S. 1999. "Offshore: the state as legal fiction." In *Offshore Finance Centers and Tax Havens: The Rise of Global Capital*, edited by M. P. Hampton and J. P. Abbott. West Lafayette: Purdue University Press, 43–79.

Picciotto, S. 2016. "Taxing multinational enterprises as unitary firms." ICTD Working Paper 53. https://opendocs.ids.ac.uk/opendocs/bitstream/handle/20.500.12413/12773/ICTD_ WP53.pdf [accessed March 14, 2021].

Pike, A. and Pollard, J. 2010. "Economic geographies of financialization." *Economic Geography 86*: 29–51.

Piketty, T. 2014. *Capital in the 21st Century*. Cambridge, MA: Harvard University Press.

Piketty, T. and Saez, E. 2012. "Income inequality in the United States, 1913–1998." *Quarterly Journal of Economics 118*: 1–39.

Pirenne, H. 2014. *Medieval Cities: Their Origins and the Revival of Trade—Updated Edition.* Princeton, NJ: Princeton University Press.

Pisani, B. 2021. "The 'fear of missing out' fund shows there really is an ETF for everything." *CNBC* (March 15). https://www.cnbc.com/2021/03/15/the-fear-of-missing-out-fund-shows-there-really-is-an-etf-for-everything.html?__source=iosappshare%7Ccom. apple.UIKit.activity.PostToTwitter [accessed March 15, 2021].

Pistor, K. 2010. "Host's dilemma: Rethinking EU Banking regulation in the light of the global crisis." *Columbia Law and Economics 378.*

Pistor, K. 2013. "A legal theory of finance." *Journal of Comparative Economics 41*: 315–330.

Pistor, K. 2019. *The Code of Capital: How the Law Creates Wealth and Inequality.* Princeton, NJ: Princeton University Press.

Podkul, C. and Rivas, A. 2020. "How Coronavirus upended a trillion-dollar corporate borrowing binge and kicked off a wave of bankruptcies." *Wall Street Journal* (June 24). https://www.wsj.com/articles/how-coronavirus-upended-a-trillion-dollar-corporate-borrowing-binge-and-kicked-off-a-wave-of-bankruptcies-11592991001 [accessed February 27, 2021].

Polanyi, K. 2001. *The Great Transformation: The Political and Economic Origins of Our Time (2nd Edition).* Boston: Beacon Press.

Ponemon Institute. 2019. "2019 intangible assets financial statement impact comparison report." Aon sponsored report conducted independently by Ponemon Institute. https://www.aon.com/getmedia/60fbb49a-c7a5-4027-ba98-0553b29dc89f/Ponemon-Report-V24.aspx [accessed December 26, 2020].

Poon, J. P. H. 2003. "Hierarchical tendencies of capital markets among international financial centers." *Growth and Change 34*(2): 135–156.

Pozsar, Z. 2018. "Repatriation, the echo-taper and the €/$ basis." *Global Money Notes* #11. New York: Credit Suisse. https://research-doc.credit-suisse.com/docView?language=ENG&format=PDF&sourceid=emcsplus&document_id=1080159501&serialid=aTLhvGKTNzOcCGepV3GdfaqUCIwiKgNs7b1cnj30b%2B0%3D [accessed January 19, 2020].

Pozsar, Z. Adrian, T., Ashcroft, A., and Boesky, H. 2010. "Shadow banking." *Federal Reserve Bank of New York Staff Report No. 458.* https://www.newyorkfed.org/medialibrary/media/research/staff_reports/sr458.pd [accessed December 18, 2020].

Pryke, M. and Lee, R. 1995. "Place your bets: Towards an understanding of globalisation, socio-financial engineering and competition within a financial centre." *Urban Studies 32*(2): 329–344.

Pujo, A. 1913. *Report of the Committee Appointed Pursuant to House Resolutions 429 and 504 to Investigate the Concentration and Control of Money and Credit.* Washington, DC: US Government Printing Office.

Quah, D. 1996. "The invisible hand and the weightless economy." Centre for Economic Performance Occasional Paper No. 12. http://eprints.lse.ac.uk/2271/.

Quinn, S. 2008. "Securitization of sovereign debt: Corporations as a sovereign debt restructuring mechanism in Britain, 1694 to 1750." Working Paper. Available on SSRN.

Rajan, R. 2010. *Fault Lines: How Hidden Fractures Still Threaten the World Economy.* Princeton, NJ: Princeton University Press.

Rau, P. R. 2000. "Investment bank market share, contingent fee payments, and the performance of acquiring firms." *Journal of Financial Economics 56*: 293–324.

Rawlings, G. 2005. "Mobile people, mobile capital and tax neutrality: Sustaining a market for offshore finance centres." *Accounting Forum 29*: 289–310.

Rawlings, G. 2007. "Taxes and transnational treaties: Responsive regulation and the reassertion of offshore sovereignty." *Law & Policy 29*: 51–66.

Raza, H., Gudmundsson, B., Zoega, G., and Kinsella, S. 2016. "Two thorns of experience: Financialisation in Iceland and Ireland." *International Review of Applied Economics 30*: 771–789.

Reed, H. C. 1981. *The Pre-eminence of International Financial Centres*. New York: Praeger.

Reklaitis, V. 2015. "Here's the advice you get from vanguard's new robot-human hybrid." *MarketWatch* (May 18). https://www.marketwatch.com/story/heres-the-advice-you-get-from-vanguards-new-robot-human-hybrid-2015-05-18.

Ridley, K. 2020. "Ex-Barclays bankers cleared over 2008 Qatar fees in blow to UK fraud office." *Reuters* (February 28). https://www.reuters.com/article/us-britain-barclays-qatar-idUSKCN20M1IT [accessed April 3, 2020].

Robards, T. 1972. "President leaves Drexel Firestone." *New York Times* (May 9). https://www.nytimes.com/1972/05/09/archives/president-leaves-drexel-firestone-tire-maker-decides-to-play-more.html

Roberts, S. 1994. "Fictitious capital, fictitious spaces: The geography of offshore financial flows." In *Money, Power and Space*, edited by R. Martin R., N. Thrift, and S. Corbridge. Oxford: Blackwell, 91–115.

Rodrik, D. 2011. *The Globalization Paradox*. Oxford: Oxford University Press.

Roos, J. 2019. *Why Not Default? The Political Economy of Sovereign Debt*. Princeton, NJ: Princeton University Press.

Rosenbaum, E. 2018. "BlackRock, world's biggest investing company, is planning to nickel-and-dime you." *CNBC* (May 9). https://www.cnbc.com/2018/05/09/blackrock-is-developing-tools-to-spur-millennial-and-gen-z-investing.html.

Rosenberg, N. 1960. "Capital formation in developing countries." *American Economic Review 50*(4): 706–715.

Rouwenhorst, K. G. 2016. "Structured finance and the origins of mutual funds in 18th century Netherlands." In *Financial Market History: Reflections on the Past for Investors Today*, edited by D. Chambers and E. Dimson. CFA Institute Research Foundation, 207–226.

Roy, W. G. 1999. *Socializing Capital: The Rise of the Large Industrial Corporation in America*. Princeton, NJ: Princeton University Press.

Rutter, R. 1964. "DuPont to break final G.M. ties." *New York Times* (November 17).

S&P Global. 2017. *SPIVA US Scorecard, year-end 2016*. https://us.spindices.com/documents/spiva/spiva-us-year-end-2016.pdf.

Sampson, A. 1981. *The Money Lenders: Bankers in a Dangerous World*. London: Coronet Books.

Samuelson, P. A. 2009. "Advance of total factor productivity from entrepreneurial innovations." In *Entrepreneurship, Growth, and Public Policy*, edited by Z. Acs, D. Audretsch and R. Strom. Cambridge: Cambridge University Press, 71–78.

Sanchez-Sibony, O. 2014. "Capitalism's fellow traveler: The Soviet Union, Bretton Woods, and the Cold War, 1944–1958." *Comparative Studies in Society and History 56*(2): 290–319.

Sanders, D. 2020. "World's biggest banks 2020: Japan's biggest banks surge past others in balance sheet growth." *Global Finance* (November 12). https://www.gfmag.com/magazine/november-2020/worlds-biggest-banks-2020 [accessed December 30, 2020].

Sassen, S. 1991. *The Global City: New York, London, Tokyo*. Princeton, NJ: Princeton University Press.

Sassen, S. 1999. "Global financial centres." *Foreign Affairs 78*(1): 75–87.

Savage, M. and Williams, K. 2008. *Remembering Elites*. Chichester, UK: Wiley-Blackwell.

Sawyer, M. and Aquila, F. 2013. "ISS's declining influence in shareholder votes." NYSE Governance Series Corporate Board Member June Newsletter. https://www.sullcrom.com/ Publications-Sawyer-Aquila-Author-Article-ISS-Declining-Influence-Shareholder-Votes-NYSE-Governance-Series-Corporate-Board-Member-June-Newsletter-2013.

Schatzker, E. 2017. "Larry Fink Q&A." *Bloomberg* (April 18). https://www.bloomberg.com/ features/2017-blackrock-larry-fink-interview/.

Schliefer, A. and Vishny, R. W. 1997. "A survey of corporate governance." *Journal of Finance* 52: 737–783.

Schmidt, V. A. 2003. "French capitalism transformed, yet still a third variety of capitalism." *Economy and Society 32*: 526–554.

Schumpeter, J. A. 1934. "The theory of economic development: An inquiry into profits, capital, credit, interest, and the business cycle." *Harvard Economic Studies Vol. 46*.

Schumpeter, J. A. 1942. *Capitalism, Socialism, and Democracy*. New York: Harper.

Schwarcz, S., Markell, B., and Broome, L. 2004. *Securitization, Structured Finance, and Capital Markets*. Durham, North Carolina: Carolina Academic Press.

Seabrooke, L. and Wigan, D. 2014. "Global wealth chains in the international political economy." *Review of International Political Economy 21*: 257–63.

Seabrooke, L. and Wigan, D. 2018. *Global Wealth Chains: Managing Assets in the World Economy*. Oxford: Oxford University Press.

Seaward, L. 2017. "The small republic and the great power: Censorship between Geneva and France in the later eighteenth century." *Library (Land) 18*(2): 191–217.

SEC v. Tourre, 2013. No. 10 Civ. 3229 (KBF), BL 145,867 (SDNY June 4, 2013).

Segal, J. 2016. "BlackRock is making big data bigger." *Institutional Investor* (November 1). https://www.institutionalinvestor.com/article/b14z9p1z99mmlg/blackrock-is-making-big-data-bigger.

Sharman, J. 2012. "Chinese capital flows and offshore financial centers." *Pacific Review 25*(3): 317.

Sharman, J. C. 2005. "South Pacific tax havens: From leaders in the race to the bottom to laggards in the race to the top?" *Accounting Forum 29*(3): 311–323.

Sharman, J. C. 2006. *Havens in a Storm: The Struggle for Global Tax Regulation*. Ithaca, NY: Cornell University Press.

Sharman, J. C. 2009. "The bark is the bite: International organizations and blacklisting." *Review of International Political Economy 16*(4): 573–596.

Shaxson, N. 2011. *Treasure Islands: Tax Havens and the Men Who Stole the World*. London: Vintage.

Shaxson, N. and Christensen, J. 2013. "The finance curse: How oversized financial centres attack democracies and corrupt economies." *Tax Justice Network Report*. https://www. taxjustice.net/cms/upload/pdf/Finance_Curse_Final.pdf.

Sherman, M. 2009. "A short history of financial deregulation in the United States." Washington, DC: Centre for Economic and Policy Research. http://www.openthegovernment. org/otg/dereg-timeline-2009-07.pdf

Shiller, R. 2003. "From efficient markets theory to behavioral finance." *Journal of Economic Perspectives 17*(1): 83–104.

Shiller, R. 2008. *The Subprime Solution: How Today's Global Financial Crisis Happened, and What to Do About It*. Princeton, NJ: Princeton University Press.

Shinn, J. 2015. "Big asset shift of Japan's GPIF is secret weapon of Abenomics." *Institutional Investor* (April 22). http://www.institutionalinvestor.com/article/3447097/

investors-pensions/big-asset-shift-of-japans-gpif-is-secret-weapon-of-abenomics.html? ArticleId=3447097&p=1#.VdB63flViko

Shleifer, A. and Vishny, R. W. 1997. "A survey of corporate governance." *Journal of Finance* 52(2): 737–783.

Sikka, P. 2008. "Enterprise culture and accountancy firms: New masters of the universe." *Accounting, Auditing, & Accountability Journal 21*(2): 268–295.

Sikka, P. and Willmott, H. 2010. "The dark side of transfer pricing: Its role in tax avoidance and wealth retentiveness." *Critical Perspectives on Accounting 21*: 342–356.

Simmel, G. 1978. *The Philosophy of Money.* Abingdon: Routledge & Paul Kegan.

Simon, M. C. 1998. "The rise and fall of bank control in the United States: 1890–1939." *American Economic Review 88*(5): 1077–1093.

Singer, P. 2000. *Marx: A Very Short Introduction.* Oxford: Oxford University Press.

Skidelsky, R. 2010. *Keynes: A Very Short Introduction.* Oxford: Oxford University Press.

Sloan, A. P. 2015. *My Years with General Motors,* digital edn, edited by John McDonald. Lake Oswego: eNet Press.

Smith. 2017. "BlackRock pivots to US West Coast as part of tech push." *Financial Times* (November 5). https://www.ft.com/content/a1393e7c-c0ac-11e7-b8a3-38a6e068f464.

Smith, R. G. 2005. "Networking the City." *Geography 90*(2): 172–176.

Sorkin, A. R. 2009. *Too Big to Fail.* New York: Viking.

Spillane, C. 2012. "Chinese, Southeast Asians purchase half of new London homes." *Bloomberg News* (April 20). http://www.bloomberg.com/news/2012-04-19/chinese-southeast-asians-buy-half-of-new-central-london-homes.html.

Spiro, D. E. 1999. *The Hidden Hand of American Hegemony: Petrodollar Recycling and International Markets.* Ithaca, NY: Cornell University Press.

Stal, E. and Cuervo-Cazurra, A. 2011. "The investment development path and FDI from developing countries: The role of pro-market reforms and institutional voids." *Latin American Business Review 12*: 209–231.

Stevens, O. P. 1962. "A current appraisal of foreign base companies." *Taxes 40*(2): 117–120.

Stewart, H. and Makortoff, K. 2021. "Business card puts Greensill founder at the heart of Downing Street." *The Guardian* (March 30). https://www.theguardian.com/politics/2021/mar/30/business-card-puts-greensill-founder-at-the-heart-of-downing-street [accessed April 11, 2021].

Stewart, J. 2013. "Low tax financial centres and the financial crisis: The case of the Irish." IIS Discussion Paper 420.

Stewart, J., Bayer, K M., and Bräutigam, L. 2015. "Shadow banking and the offshore nexus— Some considerations on the systemic linkages of two important economic phenomena." CAE Working Paper.

Stiglitz, J. 2002. *Globalization and Its Discontents.* London: Penguin.

Stiglitz, J. 2010. *Freefall: Free Markets and the Sinking of the Global Economy.* London: Allen Lane.

Stocking, G. W. 1958. "The Du Pont-General Motors case and the Sherman Act." *Virginia Law Review 44*(1): 1–40.

Strange, S. 1981. "The world's money: expanding the agenda for research." *International Journal: Canada's Journal of Global Policy Analysis 36*(4): 691–712.

Strange, S. 1986. *Casino Capitalism.* Oxford: Blackwell.

Strange, S. 1994. "From Bretton Woods to the casino economy." In *Money, Power and Space,* edited by R. Martin, N. Thrift, and S. Corbridge. Oxford: Blackwell, 49–62.

Strange, S. 1997. *Casino Capitalism.* Manchester: Manchester University Press.

Strange, S. 1998 *Mad Money.* Manchester: Manchester University Press.

Streeck, W. 2010. *Re-forming Capitalism: Institutional Change in the German Political Economy.* Oxford: Oxford University Press.

Strine, L. E. 2005. "The Delaware way: How we do corporation law and some of the new challenges we (and Europe) face." *Delaware Journal of Corporation Law 30*(3): 673–696.

Stringham, E. 2002. "The emergence of the London Stock Exchange as a self-policing club." *Journal of Private Enterprise 17*(2): 1–19.

Stulz, R. M. 2005. "Presidential address: The limits of financial globalization." *Journal of Finance 60*: 1595–1639.

Summers, B. J. 1980. "Negotiable certificates of deposit." *Federal Reserve Bank of Richmond Economic Review* (July–August): 8–19.

Sushko, V. and Turner, G. 2018. "The implications of passive investing for securities markets." *BIS Quarterly Review* (March): 113–131.

Sutherland, D. and Matthews, B. 2009. "'Round tripping' or 'capital augmenting' OFDI? Chinese outward investment and the Caribbean tax havens." Leverhulme Centre for Research on Globalisation and Economic Policy (GEP), University of Nottingham.

Sutherland, D. and Ning, L. 2011. "Exploring 'onward-journey' ODI strategies in China's private sector businesses." *Journal of Chinese Economic and Business Studies 9*(1): 43–65.

Svirsky, G., Festa, D., Redwine, A., and Pickering, E. 2012. "Bankruptcy court overrides CDO indenture provision requiring noteholder consent to liquidation after accelerating default." *Pratt's Journal of Bankruptcy Law 8*(1): 3.

Swamynathan, Y. 2018. "Broadcom completes move to U.S. from Singapore." *Reuters* (April 4). https://www.reuters.com/article/us-broadcom-domicile/broadcom-complet es-move-to-u-s-from-singapore-idUSKCN1HB34G [accessed February 17, 2020].

Swan, M. 2015. *BlockChain: Blueprint for a New Economy.* Sebastopol, CA: O'Reilly Media.

SWIFT. 2020. *RMB Tracker: Monthly Reporting and Statistics on Renminbi (RMB) Progress towards Becoming an International Currency* (October). https://www.swift.com/our-solutions/compliance-and-shared-services/business-intelligence/renminbi/rmb-tracker [accessed February 27, 2021].

Sylla, R. 1982. "Monetary innovation in America." *Journal of Economic History 42*(1): 21–30.

Sylla, R. 1985. "Early American banking: The significance of the corporate form." *Business and Economic History 14*: 105–123.

Sylla, R. 1998. "U.S. securities markets and the banking system, 1790–1840." *Review, Federal Reserve Bank of St. Louis* (May/June): 83–98.

Sylla, R. 2002a. "Financial systems and economic modernization." *Journal of Economic History 62*(2): 277–292.

Sylla, R. 2002b. "A historical primer on the business of credit rating." In *Ratings, Ratings Agencies, and the Global Financial System*, edited by R. M. Levich, G. Majnoni, and C. M. Reinhart. Boston: Kluwer, 19–40.

Sylla, R., Wilson, J. W., and Wright, R. E. 2006. "Integration of trans-Atlantic capital markets, 1790–1845." *Review of Finance 10*(4): 613–644.

Tabarrok, A. 1998. "The separation of commercial and investment banking: The Morgans vs. the Rockefellers." *Quarterly Journal of Austrian Economics 1*(1): 1–18.

Taleb, N. 2008. *The Black Swan: The Impact of the Highly Improbable.* London: Penguin.

Taviani, C. 2015. "An ancient scheme: The Mississippi Company, Machiavelli, and the Casa di San Giorgio (1407–1720)." In *Chartering Capitalism: Organizing Markets, States, and Publics*, edited by E. Erikson. Bingley: Emerald.

Tax Justice Network (TJN). 2012. *2011 Financial Secrecy Index.* http://www.financial secrecyindex.com/2011results.html

Taylor, J. E. 2002. "The bund: Littoral space of empire in the treaty ports of East Asia." *Social History 27*(2): 125–142.

Taylor, P. J. 2000. "World cities and territorial states under conditions of contemporary globalization." *Political Geography 19*: 5–32.

Taylor, P. J. 2004. *World City Network: A Global Urban Analysis*. London: Routledge.

Taylor, P. J. 2011. "Competition and cooperation between cities in globalization. Research Bulletin No. 351." Globalization and World Cities Research Network, Loughborough University.

Taylor, P. J., Catalana, G., and Walker, D. 2004 "Multiple globalisations: Regional, hierarchical and sectoral articulations of global business services through world cities." *Service Industries Journal 24*: 63–81.

Taylor, P. J., Derudder, B., Faulconbridge, J., Hoyler, M., and Ni, P. 2014. "Advanced producer services firms as strategic networks, global cities as strategic places." *Economic Geography 90*(3): 267–291.

Taylor, P J., Ni, P., Derudder, B., Hoyler, M., Huang, J., and Witlox, F. 2011. *Global Urban Analysis: A Survey of Cities in Globalization*. Earthscan: London

Tedlow, R. S. 1988. "The struggle for dominance in the automobile market: The early years of Ford and General Motors." *Business and Economic History 17*: 49–62.

Tett, G. 2009. *Fool's Gold: How Unrestrained Greed Corrupted a Dream, Shattered Global Markets and Unleashed a Catastrophe*. London: Abacus.

Tett, G. 2018. "AllianceBernstein's Nashville move threatens New York and London. Digital disruption makes it easier for financial companies to relocate." *Financial Times* (May 3). https://www.ft.com/content/e483a6ea-4e23-11e8-9471-a083af05aea7.

TheCityUK, 2010. "Fund Management." www.thecityuk.com/assets/Uploads/Fund-management-2010.pdf.

Thiemann, M. 2014. "In the shadow of Basel: How competitive politics bred the crisis." *Review of International Political Economy 21*(6): 1203–1239

Thomas, D. 2021. "City of London bosses warn against post-Brexit deregulation." *Financial Times* (January 18). https://www.ft.com/content/1a2c7e3d-2bd9-4f9c-90c1-0732df98488e [accessed March 1, 2021].

Thomas, W. A. 1998. "An intra-empire capital transfer: The Shanghai rubber company boom, 1909–1912." *Modern Asian Studies 32*(3): 739–760.

Thrift, N. 1994. "On the social and cultural determinants of international financial centres: The case of the City of London." In *Money, Power and Space*, edited by R. Martin R., N. Thrift, and S. Corbridge. Oxford: Blackwell, 327–355.

Tilly, C. 1985. "War making and state making as organized crime." In *Bringing the State Back* edited by P. B. Evans, D. Rueschemeyer, and T. Skocpol. Cambridge, UK: Cambridge University Press, 169–191.

Tilly, C. 1989. "Cities and states in Europe, 1000–1800." *Theory and Society 18*(5): 563–584.

Ting, A. 2014. "iTax—Apple's international tax structure and the double non-taxation issue." *British Tax Review 1*: 40–71.

Tobin, J. 1978. "A proposal for International Monetary Reform." *Eastern Economic Journal 4*(3–4): 153.

Tobin, J. 1984. "On the efficiency of the financial system." *Lloyds Bank Review 153*: 1–15.

Tooze, A. 2018. *How a Decade of Financial Crises Changed the World*. London: Allen Lane.

Töpfer, L. M. 2018. "Inside the global financial network: The state, lead-firms, and the rise of fintech." *Dialogues in Human Geography 8*(3): 294–299.

Töpfer, L. M. and Hall, S. 2018. "London's rise as an offshore RMB financial centre: State–finance relations and selective institutional adaptation." *Regional Studies* 52(8): 1053–1064.

TowersWatson. 2011. "The world's largest asset managers." www.towerswatson.com/united-kingdom/research/2942

Tracy, R. and Krouse, S. 2016. "One firm getting what it wants in Washington: BlackRock." *Wall Street Journal* (April 20). https://www.wsj.com/articles/one-firm-getting-what-it-wants-in-washington-blackrock-1461162812.

Treanor, J. 2016. "Libyan investment authority loses $1.2 billion dispute with Goldman Sachs." *The Guardian* (October 14). https://www.theguardian.com/business/2016/oct/14/goldman-sachs-libyan-investment-authority-lawsuit [accessed February 27, 2021].

Tsang, S. 2007. *A Modern History of Hong Kong: 1841–1997*. London: I.B. Taurus.

Tschoegl, A. E. 2000. "International banking centres, geography, and foreign banks." *Financial Markets, Institutions & Instruments* 9(1): 1–32.

Tucker, P. 2018. *Unelected Power: The Quest for Legitimacy in Central Banking and the Regulatory State*. Princeton, NJ: Princeton University Press.

Ugolini, S. 2017. *The Evolution of Central Banking: Theory and History*. London: Palgrave Macmillan.

Ugolini, S. 2018. "The origins of Swiss wealth management? Genevan private banking, 1800–1840." *Financial History Review* 25(2): 161–182.

UNCTAD. 2015. *World Investment Report 2015: Reforming International Investment Governance*. Geneva: United Nations.

Urban, M. A. 2018. "Producing investment returns at the margin of finance: A frontier talent proposition." *Geoforum* 95: 102–111.

US–China Economic and Security Review Commission (USCC). 2020. *Chinese Companies Listed on Major U.S. Stock Exchanges*. https://www.uscc.gov/sites/default/files/2020-10/Chinese_Companies_on_US_Stock_Exchanges_10-2020.pdf [accessed December 30, 2020].

US Securities and Exchange Commission (SEC). 1971. *Institutional Investor Study Report*, House Document 92-64, referred to the House Committee on Interstate and Foreign Commerce, Washington, DC.

US Securities and Exchange Commission (SEC). 2020. *Office of the Investor Advocate: Report on Activities, Fiscal Year 2020*. https://www.sec.gov/files/sec-investor-advocate-report-on-activities-2020.pdf [accessed February 22, 2021].

US Treasury. 2012. "June 2012 Treasury Bulletin." Washington, DC: US Government Printing Office.

Usher, A. P. 1934. "The origins of banking: The primitive bank of deposit, 1200–1600." *Economic History Review* 4(4): 399–428.

Vaghela, V. 2021. "Amsterdam topples London as Europe's main share-trading hub." *Bloomberg* (February 11). https://www.bloomberg.com/news/articles/2021-02-10/amsterdam-topples-london-as-europe-s-main-share-trading-hub-ft?sref=45uaXh1D [accessed March 2, 2021].

Vaghela, V., Edwards, A., and Miller, M. 2021. "Brexit pushes most Europe share trading off top U.K. venues." *Bloomberg* (January 4). https://www.bloomberg.com/news/articles/2021-01-04/brexit-pushes-almost-100-of-europe-share-trading-off-u-k-venue?sref=45uaXh1D [accessed March 2, 2021].

Valkanov, E. Kleimeier, S. 2006. "The role of regulatory capital in international bank mergers and acquisitions." *Research in International Business and Finance 21*: 50–68.

Valmori, N. 2021. "Looking for new markets in a time of revolution: The U.S. securities market, 1789–1804." In *The Cultural Life of Risk and Innovation*, edited by C. Y. Hsu, T. M. Luckett, and E. Vause. New York: Routledge.

Veblen, T. 1923. *Absentee Ownership and Business Enterprise in Recent Times: The Case of America*. New York: B. W. Huebsch.

Ventura, J. and Voth H. J. 2015. "Debt into growth: How debt accelerated the first industrial revolution." NBER Working Paper 21, 280.

Venturi, F. 1991. *The End of the Old Regime in Europe, 1776–1789, Part I: The Great States of the West*. Princeton, NJ: Princeton University Press.

Vitali, S., Glattfelder, J. B., and Battison, S. 2011. "The network of global corporate control." *PLOS One* DOI: 10.1371/journal.pone.0025995.

Vlcek, W. 2007. "Why worry? The impact of the OECD harmful tax competition initiative on Caribbean offshore financial centres." *The Round Table: The Commonwealth Journal of International Affairs* 96(390): 331–346.

Vlcek, W. 2010. "Byways and highways of direct investment: China and the offshore world." *Journal of Current Chinese Affairs* 39: 111–142.

Vlcek, W. 2013. "From road town to Shanghai: Situating the Caribbean in global capital flows to China." *British Journal of Politics & International Relations* 16: 534–553.

Voon, T and Mitchell, A. 2010. "Open for business? China telecommunications service market and the WTO." *Journal of International Economic Law* 13: 321–378

Vyas, S. and Kumaranayake, L. 2006. "Constructing socio-economic status indices: How to use principal component analysis." *Health Policy Plan* 21: 459–468.

Wade, R. and Veneroso, F. 1998. "The Asian crisis: The high debt model versus the Wall Street–Treasury–IMF Complex." *New Left Review* 1(228): 3–22.

Wainwright, T. 2009. "Laying the foundations for a crisis: Mapping the historico-geographical construction of residential mortgage backed securitization in the UK." *International Journal of Urban and Regional Research* 33(2): 372–388.

Wainwright, T. 2011. "Tax doesn't have to be taxing: London's 'onshore' finance industry and the fiscal spaces of a global crisis." *Environment and Planning A* 43(6): 1287–1304.

Walker, P. 2021. "Rishi Sunak told David Cameron he had 'pushed the team' over Greensill." *The Guardian* (April 8). https://www.theguardian.com/politics/2021/apr/08/rishi-sunak-told-david-cameron-he-he-had-pushed-the-team-over-greensill [accessed April 11, 2021].

Wallerstein, I. 2004. *World Systems Analysis: An Introduction*. Durham, NC: Duke University Press.

Wallis, J. J. 2001. "What caused the crisis of 1839?" NBER Working Paper Series on Historical Factors in Long Run Growth. Historical Paper 133. Cambridge, MA: National Bureau of Economic Research.

Walter, A. 1991. *World Power and World Money: The Role of Hegemony and International Monetary Order*. New York: St Martin's Press.

Walter, C. E. and Howie, F. J. T. 2011. *Red Capitalism: The Fragile Financial Foundations of China's Extraordinary Rise*. Singapore: Wiley.

Ward, I. 1991. "Settlements, mortgages and aristocratic estates 1649–1660." *Journal of Legal History* 12(1): 20–35.

Wardwell, K. H. 1983. "The unsung death of state takeover statues: Edgar vs. MITE Corp." *Boston College Law Review* 4(4): 1017–1052.

Warf, B. 1995. "Telecommunications and the changing geographies of knowledge transmission in the late 20th century." *Urban Studies* 32(2): 361–378.

Warf, B. 2000. "New York: The Big Apple in the 1990s." *Geoforum* 31(4): 487–499.

Warf, B. 2002. "Tailored for Panama: Offshore banking at the crossroads of the Americas." *Geografiska Annaler 84*: 33–47.

Warf, B. 2004. "Financial services and inequality in New York." *Industrial Geographer 2*: 110–126.

Warf, B. 2006. "International competition between satellite and fiber optic carriers: A geographic perspective." *Professional Geographer 58*(1): 1–11.

Warner, M., Ng, S. H., and Xu, X. 2004. "'Late development' experience and the evolution of transnational firms in the People's Republic of China." *Asia Pacific Business Review 10*: 324–345.

Waxman, S., Froio, N., Feldman, E., and Antonacci, R. 2004. "Delaware: The jurisdiction of Choice for securitisation." Potter Anderson & Corroon LLP. http://corporate.findlaw.com/corporate-governance/delaware-the-jurisdiction-of-choice-in-securitisation.html [accessed June 24, 2017].

Wee, G. 2012. "Frankly Fink: How 'boring' built the world's largest asset manager." *Washington Post* (September 30).

Wei, Y. D., Li, W and Wang, C. 2007. "Restructuring industrial districts, scaling up regional development: a study of the Wenzhou model, China." *Economic Geography 83*: 421–444

Weichenrieder, A. J. and Mintz, J. 2006. "What determines the use of holding companies and ownership chains?" Oxford University Centre for Business Taxation Working Paper Series 803. http://www.sbs.ox.ac.uk/centres/tax/symposia/Documents/2007/A%20Weichenrieder%20Holding_companies_15March07.pdf.

Weidenbaum, M. L. and Hughes, S. 1996. *The Bamboo Network: How Expatriate Chinese Entrepreneurs Are Creating a New Economic Superpower in Asia*. New York: Simon & Schuster.

Weisenthal, J. 2021. "To understand Bitcoin just think of it as a faith-based asset." *Bloomberg* (January 21). https://www.bloomberg.com/news/articles/2021-01-21/bitcoin-is-a-faith-based-asset-joe-weisenthal?sref=45uaXh1D [accessed February 27, 2021].

Weiss, L. 1997. "Globalization and the myth of the powerless state." *New Left Review 225*: 3–27.

Weyzig, F. 2013. "Tax treaty shopping: Structural determinants of foreign direct investment routed through the Netherlands." *International Tax and Public Finance 20*: 910–37.

White, L. J. 2010. "Markets: The credit rating agencies." *Journal of Economic Perspectives 24*(2): 211–226.

Wilczynski, J. 1976. *Multinationals and East–West Relations: Towards Transideological Collaboration*. Boulder: Westview Press.

Wildau, G. 2017a. "China central bank declares initial coin offerings illegal." *Financial Times* (September 4). https://www.ft.com/content/3fa8f60a-9156-11e7-a9e6-11d2f0ebb7f0 [accessed December 18, 2020].

Wildau, G. 2017b. "China forex reserves break 8-month run of declines." *Financial Times* (March 7). https://www.ft.com/content/6d15d68c-0315-11e7-ace0-1ce02ef0def9 [accessed March 2, 2021].

Willmer, S. and Kumar, N. 2017. "Why Google and Amazon Keep Fidelity and BlackRock up at night." *Bloomberg* (December 13). https://www.bloomberg.com/news/features/2017-12-13/hey-google-am-i-diversified-why-fidelity-fears-silicon-valley.

Wilson, C. 1941. *Anglo-Dutch Commerce and Finance in the Eighteenth Century*. London: Cambridge University Press.

Wójcik, D. 2002. "Cross-border corporate ownership and capital market integration in Europe: Evidence from portfolio and industrial holdings." *Journal of Economic Geography* 2(4): 455–491.

Wójcik, D. 2011a. *The Global Stock Market: Issuers, Investors, and Intermediaries in an Uneven World.* Oxford: Oxford University Press.

Wójcik, D. 2011b. "Securitization and its footprint: The rise of the US securities industry centres 1998–2007." *Journal of Economic Geography* 11: 925–47.

Wójcik, D. 2012. "The end of investment bank capitalism: An economic geography of financial jobs and power." *Economic Geography* 88(4): 345–368.

Wójcik, D. 2013a. "The dark side of NY–LON: Financial centres and the global financial crisis." *Urban Studies* 50: 2736–2752.

Wójcik, D. 2013b. "Where governance fails: Advanced business services and the offshore world." *Progress in Human* Geography 37(3): 330–347.

Wójcik, D. 2018. "Rethinking global financial networks: China, politics, and complexity." *Dialogues in Human* Geography 8 (3): 272–275.

Wójcik, D and Burger, C. 2010. "Listing BRICs: Issuers from Brazil, Russia, India and China in New York, London and Luxembourg" *Economic Geography* 86: 275–296.

Wójcik, D. and Camilleri, J. 2015. "'Capitalist tools in socialist hands?' China Mobile in global financial networks." *Transactions of the Institute of British Geographers* 40(4): 464–478.

Wójcik, D. and Ioannou, S. 2020. "COVID19 and finance: Market developments so far and potential impacts on the financial sector and centres." *Tijdschrift voor Economische en Sociale Geografie* 111(3): 387–400.

Wójcik, D., MacDonald-Korth, D. and Zhao, S. X. (2017) "The political–economic geography of foreign exchange trading." *Journal of Economic Geography* 17(2): 267–286.

Wong, J. 2004. "The adaptive developmental state in East Asia." *Journal of East Asian Studies* 4: 345–362.

Wood, P. A. 1991. "Flexible accumulation and the rise of business services." *Transactions of the Institute of British Geographers* 16: 160–172.

Woods, N. 2006. *The Globalizers: The IMF, the World Bank and Their Borrowers.* Ithaca, NY: Cornell University Press.

World Bank. 2012. *World Governance Indicators.* http://info.worldbank.org/governance/wgi/index.asp.

World Bank. 2020. *World Development Indicators.* World Development Indicators.

World Federation of Exchanges (WFE). 2020. "Domestic market capitalization: Market statistics—November 2019." https://focus.world-exchanges.org/issue/november-2019/market-statistics [accessed December 30, 2020].

WPP. 2016. "BrandZ top 100 most valuable Chinese brands 2016." *WPP and Milward Brown   report.*   https://www.wcom/news/2016/03/brandz-top-100-most-valuable-chinese-brands-2016 [accessed March 7, 2021].

Wray, L. 2009. "The rise and fall of money manager capitalism: A Minskian approach." *Cambridge Journal of Economics* 33(4): 807–828.

Wray, L. R. 1992. "Commercial banks, the central bank, and endogenous money." *Journal of Post Keynesian Economics* 14(3): 297–310.

Wray, L. R. 2000. "The Neo-Chartalist approach to money." Working Paper. https://papers.ssrn.com/sol3/papers.cfm?abstract_id=1010334 [accessed December 26, 2020].

Wray, L. R. 2011. "Minsky's money manager capitalism and the global financial crisis." *International Journal of Political Economy* 40: 5–20.

Wright, J. F. 1997. "The contribution of overseas savings to the funded debt of Great Britain 1750–1815." *Economic History Review* 50(4): 657–674.

Wrigley, N., Currah, A., and Wood, S. 2003. "Investment bank analysts and knowledge in economic geography." *Environment and Planning A* 35: 381–387.

Xie, Y. X. and Bird, M. 2020. "The $52 trillion bubble: China grapples with epic property boom." *Wall Street Journal* (July 16). https://www.wsj.com/articles/china-property-real-estate-boom-covid-pandemic-bubble-11594908517 [accessed December 18, 2020].

Yablon, C. M. 2007. "The historical race: Competition for corporate charters and the rise and decline of New Jersey: 1880–1910." *Journal of Corporation Law* 32: 323–380.

Yang, X. and Stoltenberg, C. 2008. "Growth of made-in-China multinationals: An institutional and historical perspective." In *Globalizing Chinese Enterprises*, edited by I. Alon and J. R. McIntyre. Palgrave Macmillan: New York, 61–76.

Yergin, D. 1990. *The Prize: The Epic Quest for Oil, Money, and Power*. New York: Simon & Schuster.

Yeung, H. W., 2000. "Local politics and foreign ventures in China's transitional economy: The political economy of Singaporean investments in China." *Political Geography* 19: 809–840.

Yeung, H. W., 2009. "Regional development and the competitive dynamics of global production networks: An East Asian perspective." *Regional Studies* 43: 325–351.

Yeung, H. W. 2011. "From national development to economic diplomacy? Governing Singapore's sovereign wealth funds." *Pacific Review* 24: 625–652.

Yeung, H. W. and Liu, W. 2008. "Globalizing China: The rise of Mainland firms in the global economy." *Eurasian Geography and Economics* 49: 57–86

Yeung, H. W. C. 1999. "The internationalization of ethnic Chinese business firms from Southeast Asia: Strategies, processes, and competitive advantage." *International Journal of Urban and Regional Research* 23: 88–102.

Yu, L., Berg, S. and Guo, Q. 2004. "Market performance of Chinese telecommunications: New regulatory policies" *Telecommunications Policy* 28: 715–732.

Zakaim, E. and Deméocq, A. 2008. "International structured finance: Europe, Middle East, Africa: 2007 review & 2008 outlook." *Moody's Investor Service Special Report*.

Zaloom, C. 2005. "The discipline of speculators." In *Global Assemblages: Technology, Politics, and Ethics as Anthropological Problems*, edited by A. Ong and S. Collier. New York: Blackwell, 253–269.

Zey, M. 1993. *Banking on Fraud: Drexel, Junk Bonds and Buyouts*. New York: Walter de Gruyter.

Zhao, X. S., Zhang, L., and Wang, D. T. 2004. "Determining factors of the development of the national financial centre: The case of China." *Geoforum* 35: 577–595.

Zook, M. and Grote, M. 2017. "The microgeographies of global finance: High-frequency trading and the construction of information inequality." *Environment and Planning A* 49(1): 121–140.

Zorome, A. 2007. "Concept of offshore financial centers: In search of an operational definition." IMF Working Paper 07/08. Washington, DC: International Monetary Fund.

Zucman, G. 2015. *The Hidden Wealth of Nations: The Scourge of Tax Havens*. Chicago: University of Chicago Press.

Zysman, J. 1983. *Governments, Markets and Growth: Financial Systems and the Politics of Industrial Change*. Ithaca, NY: Cornell University Press.

Index